The American Police Novel

The American Police Novel

A History

LeRoy Lad Panek

McFarland & Company, Inc., Publishers

Jefferson, North Carolina, and London

LIBRARY OF CONGRESS CATALOGUING-IN-PUBLICATION DATA

Panek, LeRoy.
    The American police novel : a history / LeRoy Lad Panek.
      p.   cm.
    Includes bibliographical references and index.

    ISBN 0-7864-1688-2 (softcover : 50# alkaline paper) ∞

    1. Detective and mystery stories, American — History and criticism.
2. Police in literature.   I. Title.
PS374.P57P37   2003
813'.087209 — dc22   2003018518

British Library cataloguing data are available

On the cover: badge ©2003 Corbis Images; skyline ©2003 PhotoSpin

Manufactured in the United States of America

McFarland & Company, Inc., Publishers
  Box 611, Jefferson, North Carolina 28640
  www.mcfarlandpub.com

For Christine

Acknowledgments

My sincerest thanks go to all who helped make this book happen: to Martin Priestman for starting me on this slippery slope; to the librarians at McDaniel College's Hoover Library; to Elizabeth and James MacCornak for the gift of the extensive collection of American crime fiction to Hoover Library facilitated by Gail Shaivitz Oppel and Phil Uhrig; to Rex Burns, Mike Jahn, Dan Mahoney, Ed Dee, and Barbara D'Amato for answering my electronic queries; to Barbara D'Amato and Robin Burcell for providing photographs; and especially to Christine, who put aside higher pursuits to read what follows.

Contents

Preface

There's never one around when you need one. That's one of the problems with cop books. No canon. The available printed and web-based lists of what are called "police procedurals" are all incomplete. Even when cop writers themselves make allusions in their books to the canon they always skimp: they cite McBain and Wambaugh, and sometimes Daley, and leave it at that. George Dove, the only critic to write about the form extensively, not only missed or purposely omitted a number of early cop writers, he also had the misfortune to write *The Police Procedural* before the real deluge of cop books hit in the 1980s and 1990s. From the mid-twentieth century onward quite literally hundreds of writers have devoted themselves to writing fiction based on what cops do and what cops are. One of my purposes, therefore, is to provide readers with a fuller idea of who did what and when they did it in the world of fiction about cops.

Another problem is that the terminology is squishy. From the 1970s onward, books about cops have carried the label "police procedural." It's applied to all sorts of very different books with very different plots: thrillers, cozies, documentaries, psychological novels, and more — as well as to the small class of books modeled on Ed McBain's formula from which, I surmise, the term originated. Reviewers attach the term to writers as different as Nora Roberts and Joseph Wambaugh. Mostly it's meaningless. It's meaningless because what cop books have in common isn't plotting, as is the case in the detective story part of crime fiction. It's not even the attention that writers pay to describing the ways police officers and departments do what they do, the "procedural" material: this varies greatly, from writers who scarcely mention what goes on at the cop house to writers who are absorbed by the daily routines of police officers and police forces. What defines this class of books is character. Cop books are those that have a police officer or police officers as their central focus, and that use narration and action to display and examine the traditional as well as the changing internal and external, forces that make cops a unique class of individuals.

Those changing external forces are a problem, too. By their nature, cop books aren't just fiction about characters who are cops. In part they are about sociology and social history. Cop books wrestle with traditional issues tied to the police as an organization: sloth, corruption, mismanagement, brutality. And part of their attraction to writers and readers alike is that cop books recount and reflect upon current events. The changing nature of crime, court decisions, the findings of official commissions, and legislation all influence the ways in which real and imaginary police officers and police forces act. So cop books are about Ted Bundy and John Wayne Gacy; about the Lexow, Andrews, Wickersham, Knapp, Kerner and Christopher commissions; about Escobido, Miranda, and O. J. Simpson; and about Equal opportunity and affirmative action. All of these things have affected, and in some measure defined, the ways characters act and feel in cop books.

For most of the past century the role of police in fiction was also influenced by the ways in which the detective or mystery story developed in the United States. The vogue for Sherlock Holmes, the great detective, along with the bright and plucky amateur detective, dominates much detective fiction up until mid-century. At the same time, the hard-boiled hero and the hard-boiled outlook serve as an undercurrent. Both influence the ways in which writers draw their characters and, perhaps more importantly, dictate the way in which they articulate their plots. The progress of the police novel involves writers who tailor conventional detective story plotting to a new hero and new reality, writers who make their cops heroes of thrillers, and writers who seek new kinds of plots to tell police stories.

There are other, complicating external forces that affect cop books. Over the past century police heroes have played an increasingly significant role on the radio, in the cinema, and then on television in the United States. One can neither view the public image of the police officer nor understand the progress of cop books in this country without at least acknowledging radio programs like *Dragnet*; films like *Lethal Weapon* or *Speed*; or television programs from *Hill Street Blues* to *Miami Vice* to *Homicide, Life on the Streets* to *COPS*. Although in what follows I try to note the role played by radio, television, and the movies in forming the changing perceptions of the police over the years, my principal focus has been on what has happened in books.

There are a lot of different kinds of law enforcement agencies in the United States — FBI, DEA, Secret Service, district attorney's investigators, sheriffs and their deputies, fish and game wardens, and now airport security. The list, in fact, goes on and on, and one can find books about most of them. But not here. What follows concerns only books about police officers, both because books about cops by far outnumber books about other kinds of law enforcement personnel and because cops have their own set of issues not shared by other kinds of agents of the state. Also, American writers do not hold a monopoly on writing about cops. In Britain, for instance, the form is arguably as popular as in this country. This book, however, covers only American writers.

Even limiting the scope of this study to books about American police officers leaves almost more than anyone can handle. The subject is too new, too few people have thought about cop books, there are too many writers and too many books, and there is too much that could be — needs to be — said. What follows, then, is not a detailed and complete literary history of the American cop novel — would that it were. Neither is it a full examination of all of the important works and important writers — would that it were. Instead, it is an introduction in which I hope I have sketched the major developments of the cop book, outlined the most important issues, and touched on the works of most of the significant writers. Throughout I have tried, insofar as I could, to let the books speak for themselves.

In the way of all introductions, then, I hope that what follows will lead readers to develop a keener interest in and fuller understanding of an important, engaging and potentially fascinating new acquaintance.

-one-

The Road to the Police Novel

It is worth remembering that police have not been around all that long. Compared with other social institutions — churches, schools, governments, marketplaces, armies, etc. — in the last half of the twentieth century police forces were still in, if not their youth, then maybe their early adolescence. Like most adolescents, police forces were bound to face problems growing up. There have been, to be sure, multitudinous challenges associated with the increasingly complex job of law enforcement in the United States. Over the past century and a half, crime and crime rates have undergone graphic and horrific changes. Social attitudes have altered, and, indeed, the law itself has shifted in its emphases. Police officers and police departments have struggled to make and remake themselves in order to cope with these changes. Considering what police officers were and are supposed to stand for, they should have always been seen as heroes. But they were not.

Coincidentally, police departments and mass audience popular literature both entered crucial stages of their development at the same time — at the middle of the nineteenth century. At that time, family story papers and then dime novels in the United States were searching for new kinds of heroes to replace the old ones inherited and copied from imported British sources. A number of new character types presented themselves in the popular literature of the 1870s and 1880s — the frontiersman, the cowboy, and even the scientist. While the character of the private detective emerged from this sorting out of heroes, the character of the policeman did not. Indeed, it took

Police invade the regular detective story (Helen Reilly's Inspector McKee replaces the gifted amateur as hero). Popular Library, 1933.

over one hundred years for popular literature to begin looking at the cop as a potential hero. And thereby hangs a tale.

On the History of Police Forces

As we all ought to know, in the English-speaking world police forces began with Sir Robert Peele's creation of the Metropolitan Police of London in 1829, followed in 1842 by the addition of the plainclothes detective division eventually quartered at Scotland Yard. It took a bit longer for police forces to emerge in the United States. New York had its own police force in 1845 and both Philadelphia and Chicago began theirs in 1854. As in Britain, adding detectives to the force of patrolmen took a bit longer — New York added a detective division to its police force in 1857, Philadelphia in 1859, and Chicago in 1861. But these early departments were scarcely equipped to handle the problems of America's burgeoning cities. The original Chicago day shift consisted of nine men. Under New York's chief George Walling, the cops kept order in certain vital parts of the city only through the means of "strong arm squads," groups of officers who would simply drive criminals away from specific locations with their nightsticks.

In fact, in a number of cases having a police force was just as bad as not having one — sometimes worse. In 1857, finding them too corrupt to change, the New York state legislature fired all of New York City's policemen and appointed a new chief. The same thing happened in other jurisdictions too. Both Boston and Chicago temporarily disbanded their detective divisions in 1864 for inefficiency and corruption. Whether appointed by Albany or Annapolis or Harrisburg, the history of American police departments in the nineteenth century was a chronicle of corruption. The Lexow Commission of 1894 revealed a New York City police department where officers bought their jobs and recouped the expenses through extortion from legitimate and illegitimate businesses and where suspects were routinely brutalized. Although he may have referred to a policeman's nightstick in one of his most famous expressions, as one of the New York City's Police Commissioners Teddy Roosevelt tried but did little to change the wholesale corruption and ineptitude of the city's police. At the turn of the century the Andrews Committee found the same to be true about the Philadelphia department. Also at the turn of the century, one of Lincoln Steffens' exposés was the discovery of the "big mitt ledger" containing daily accounts of police graft in Minneapolis. And the corruption didn't stop at the turn of the century. In 1913 a New York City citizens' committee reported that among the city's police

The corruption is so ingrained that the man of ordinary decent character entering the force and not possessed of extraordinary moral fiber may easily suc-
cumb. About him are the evidences of graft and the enjoyment of irregular
incomes substantially increasing the patrolman's salary. Inadequate condem-
nation is shown by his associates in the force for such practices; on the con-
trary, there is much indirect pressure which induces him to break his oath of
office.... Such a system makes for too many of the police an organized school
of crime [Myers 358].

Smedley Butler, Philadelphia's Public Safety Director, estimated in 1923
that most of his city's police received from $150 to $200 a month in payoffs.
Mayor LaGuardia's police chief fired 300 New York cops, rebuked 3,000,
and fined 8,000 during his first six years in office. In 1931–32 the Wickersham Commission, the National Commission on Law Observance and
Enforcement, met.

The Wickersham Commission's most famous product was the Report on Lawlessness in Law Enforcement, a searing indictment of police misconduct. The
report concluded that the "third degree," the willful infliction of pain and
suffering on criminal suspects, was "widespread." The commission discovered
that "official lawlessness" by police, judges, [and] magistrates ... was widespread in many jurisdictions, including major cities. It investigated illegal
arrests, bribery, entrapment, coercion of witnesses, fabrication of evidence,
"third degree" practices, police brutality, and illegal wiretapping.... As the first
fully documented report on police misconduct, it galvanized public opinion
and mobilized reform efforts. At the municipal level, it strengthened the hand
of a new generation of reform-minded police chiefs. At the national level, it
helped to foster a new climate of opinion regarding the need for legal controls
over police misconduct. This was reflected in the first important Supreme Court
decisions imposing constitutional standards on local criminal justice officials,
beginning with Powell v. Alabama (the Scottsboro Boys case) in 1932, the year
after the commission delivered its report [www.lexisnexis.com/academic/2upa/
Aj/WickershamComm].

The commission made a number of far-reaching recommendations,
including repeal of Prohibition and putting police officers in the civil service system, exempt from the influence of politics and politicians. In the
1930s the new approaches to police work centered on moving from the spoils
system to making police forces into paramilitary organizations (advocated
by, among others, Washington, D.C., police chief Richard Sylvester) and
applying "scientific" principles to the prevention and detection of crime (a
movement led by August Volmer, the chief author of the Wickersham report).
When these innovations went into effect some things changed. Some did not.

That cops were not drawn as heroes in popular fiction in the nineteenth
century hardly evokes much surprise. Enough evidence existed in newspapers to paint all cops as members of a venal, lazy, brutal, and inept profes-

sion. On top of that, an overwhelming perception existed that nice people should have nothing to do with cops. Cops were supposed to keep the lower classes in line. And, recalling that Cesare Lombroso was the most eminent and accepted criminologist at the end of the nineteenth century, criminals and the lower classes in general were viewed as scarcely human — Lombroso held that they were examples of devolution. In point of fact, even reading about cops and crime had the potential to destabilize one's moral equilibrium. Anthony Comstock said so in his *Traps for the Young* (1883) and he even helped to convince the Massachusetts legislature to prohibit the sale to minors of books or magazines containing criminal news or police reports. Even in the first quarter of the twentieth century the notion persisted that stories about crime and the police were traps for the young or were at least objectionable to "the best kind of people." Article VII of the Code of Ethics adopted by the American Society of Newspaper Editors in 1923 reads:

> *Decency.* A newspaper cannot escape conviction of insincerity if while professing high moral purpose it supplies incentives to base conduct, such as are to be found in details of crime and vice, publication of which is not in the public good [Crawford 285].

William Randolph Hearst in instructions to his papers used good taste as the test for reporting on crime and the cops:

> Make a paper *for the best kind of people.* The masses of the reading public are better and more intelligent than newspapermen seem to think they are. Don't print a lot of stuff that nice people are supposed to like and do not, but omit things that will offend nice people.
>
> Avoid *coarseness* and *slang* and a *low tone.* The most sensational news can be told if it is written properly.
>
> Don't use words like "murder," "scandal," "divorce," "crime," and other rather offensive phrases when it is possible to tell the story without them [Crawford 231].

Indeed, few writers really knew much about policemen and police forces; remember that Philadelphia had no police force when Poe wrote "The Murders in the Rue Morgue" in that city in 1841.

Julian Hawthorne's Cop

The only real examples in the nineteenth century of fiction that portrayed the policeman as a hero came from Nathaniel Hawthorne's son, Julian, in his books about a real New York City police detective, Thomas Byrnes. These began with *The Great Bank Robbery from the Diary of Inspector Byrnes* (1887) and included *An American Pennman* (1887), *Another's Crime* (1888), *Section 558; or the Fatal Letter* (1888), and *A Tragic Mystery* (1888). If they were not such awful books, they could be considered the first police novels. Mixed in with loads of sentimental slop, Hawthorne brought in

1. an actual crime as the basis for his plots (*The Great Bank Robbery* recounts the actual robbery of the Manhattan Savings Institution);

2. police documents (in the same novel Hawthorne refers to *Professional Criminals of America*, an important "rogues gallery" used by police before Bertillion measurements or fingerprints);

3. a portrait of an heroic police officer (based on real NYPD detective Thomas Byrnes);

4. depiction of the complications for police work caused by the law (in *The Great Bank Robbery* Byrnes has to find a way to both observe *habeas corpus* strictures and keep a suspect under his control); and

5. description of police routine in examining crime scenes and shadowing suspects.

In *The Great Bank Robbery* Hawthorne takes pains to portray Byrnes as a great man, but he also wants his readers to know that Byrnes is thoroughly respectable:

> This was a tall and well built man of perhaps thirty five years of age, with a face expressive of quiet but penetrating intelligence, and a bearing that denoted power, self-confidence and reserve. He was neatly and unobtrusively dressed, and he looked like a prosperous man of business of the higher class [70].

Not looking like a copper was important — not looking, in other words, low class and threatening. Thus the same occurs with Mr. Gryce, the New York City detective in Anna Katharine Green's *The Leavenworth Case* (1878). He "was not the thin, wiry individual with the piercing eye you are doubtless expecting to see" (5). The best detectives portrayed in the popular fiction of the nineteenth century, however, weren't policemen. They were private eyes.

Private Eyes

Even while American cities established police departments, private detectives staked a claim on the marketplace for service and protection. Gil Hayes, perhaps the first American private eye, set up shop in New York in 1845, and by the early 1850s private detective agencies had opened in Chicago, Baltimore, Philadelphia, and St. Louis (Hartsfield 42). The most prominent of these, of course, was Allan Pinkerton's business in Chicago, founded in 1851. A lot of this had to do with money. First of all, the prevailing system of offering rewards for the return of stolen property instead of the capture of the thief gave rise to a system of fee-splitting between thief and thief-taker. Detectives, private and public, would make arrangements to return stolen property and then split the reward with the thieves. Secondly, private detective agencies said they could — and they probably could — do a better job than official police forces. Pinkerton, in fact, offered to take over policing Chicago for less than the city paid its police, but was turned down. The private agencies simply knew more about criminals and how to catch them. In 1897, the Pinkerton Agency's extensive accumulation of photographs of criminals became the basis of the National Bureau of Criminal Identification. More importantly, unlike the police, private detectives were not limited by civic jurisdictions and could, and did, chase crooks all over the country. For private individuals and for many businesses, one of the other significant advantages of private detectives was the avoidance of scandal and disgrace. Avoiding scandal and disgrace, as opposed to observance of the law, is one of the outstanding features of nineteenth-century crime fiction in both America and Britain. And by hiring one's own detective one could keep things out of the courts. Plainly enough, people with money or property preferred to procure the services of private rather than public police. The Jewelers Protective Union and Security Alliance signed up with Pinkerton in 1893, and the American Bankers Association signed up with the firm the following year. They all had Pinkerton signs in their windows.

Pinkerton

Part of the problem encountered in forming the image of policemen and police forces in the nineteenth and even the twentieth century lies in the dual function of their duties. The whole idea of policing began with the motive of preventing crime before it happened. The adoption of patrolmen's uniforms in Britain and later in the United States came from this notion. The earliest organizers of forces believed that the conspicuous presence of police officers would deter crime. Maybe it did and maybe it does. But not much. Additionally, not much excitement or glory attached or attaches to something that doesn't happen. The excitement, glory, and even heroism come from detective work — identifying and catching criminals after they have committed crimes. So right from the start the role of the detective had the potential for limelight. Municipalities were slow in creating detective bureaus in their police forces. Not only that, private detectives promoted their services better than government agencies could. Allan Pinkerton may have been a better detective than a lot of city cops, but he most certainly was a better promoter, and he came on the scene when advertising and brand names were beginning their march to saturate American culture. Pinkerton's

logo of the unblinking eye and motto "we never sleep" became the basis for
the popular term for private detective, "private eye." It was the Kleenex or
Coke of its day. Additionally, Pinkerton understood the power of popular
fiction to create an attractive image of the private detective and to drum up
business. Although they were no doubt ghost written, sixteen novels appeared
bearing Pinkerton's name as author beginning with *The Expressman and the
Detective* in 1874 and ending with *A Double Life and the Detectives* in 1884.
In reality they were more sales prospectuses than novels: their sole purpose
was to extol the skill of Pinkerton and his agents, and display the company's
efficient, tenacious, and polite service provided to its clients. Another
significant part of the Pinkerton sales strategy expressed in these novels
resided in portraying police officers as inept and corrupt. Thus the following passage from his *Claude Melnotte as a Detective and Other Stories* (1875):

> One reason why the professional detective is so often unsuccessful is that he is
> so well known.... All the bar keepers know him, and have an extra "smile" for
> him — gratis. In like manner he is "dead-headed" in hotels, theaters, restau-
> rants, and elsewhere, until he becomes, not only one of the best known men
> in town, but also one of the greatest "sponges" in the community. He dresses
> well, though a little loud perhaps, hob nobs with professional gamblers, and
> is often "hail fellow well met" with the thieves themselves. He is most likely
> their boon companion, and gets his regular percentage of the very "swag" which
> he is hired to discover. If the losers are willing to pay more than the thieves
> can sell their plunder for elsewhere, the detective receives the money and returns
> the goods. In any event he gets his share. The whole class of detectives are ready
> to sell out or are already sold [14–15].

Novels were so tied to the Pinkerton agency's business practices that
after Allan's death in 1884 his son, Frank, rolled out seven more Pinkerton
novels, beginning with *Dyke Darrell, the Railroad Detective, or the Crime of
the Midnight Express* in 1886. Even before the introduction of Sherlock
Holmes to the United States in *Harper's Weekly* in 1893 changed the way
every reader was to view "consulting detectives" and the police, private
detectives had a firm grasp on American popular literature. Partly this was
due to the hold of sensation novels like Collins' *Woman in White* and Mrs.
Henry Wood's *East Lynne* on middle-class literature, novels that emphasized
the satisfactions of fear, romantic moodiness, hysteria, and details of juicy
family scandals above the details of detection, apprehension, arrest, and conviction. This is the case with the first American novel with pretenses to being
a detective novel, *The Dead Letter* (1866) by Seeley Register (Metta V. Victor), in which the detective, Mr. Burton, a consultant to the police, has a
tragic past and the assistance of a clairvoyant. Partly the dominance of the
private detective came from the merging of stereotypes — detective, cowboy,
romantic hero — in the dime novel. Cap Collier, the first of the dime novel

detectives, combined a number of stereotypes just as he slipped into and out of his disguises. Partly, though, it had to do with the image created by the Pinkerton Agency. A bit of this can be seen by noting that Rodrigues Ottolengui in his *A Conflict of Evidence* (1893) identifies his detectives as agents of Boston's Pilkington's Detective Agency. Close enough.

Cops at the Turn of the Century

The image of the police at the turn of the twentieth century suffered the double whammy of competing with Doyle's Sherlock Holmes stories and the assaults of muckraking journalists and writers and the reform movements they inspired. The genius amateur or private detective crowded the pages of middlebrow magazine fiction in the first quarter of the twentieth century. Craig Kennedy, The Thinking Machine, Luther Trant, Scientific Sprague, Average Jones, Madelyn Mack — there were a bunch of them, and their discoveries and adventures required police only as an admiring audience or as servants to haul off the guilty at the close of the action. This, of course, followed literary fashion — Doyle's detective based on Poe's detective. The fashion was only enhanced by the fact that when the most famous private detective of the early twentieth century, William Burns (founder of the Burns Detective Agency), turned to fiction, his book, *The Crevice* (1915), depicted a detective modeled on Sherlock Holmes rather than on Burns' real experiences and successes. The police enter fiction more insightfully and perhaps more accurately in the reporting and the fiction of muckrakers. As noted above, Lincoln Steffens touched on police corruption in each city he wrote about for *McClure's Magazine* (and eventually in *The Shame of the Cities*). Thus

> Minneapolis was an example of police corruption; St. Louis of financial corruption. Pittsburgh is an example of both police and financial corruption [101].

Richard Harding Davis in his short story "The Frame-Up" (1915) included background of a case of police killing a witness to their illegal acts and then covering up the crime. The most violent portraits of police at the turn of the century appear in Josiah Flynt and Francis Walton's *The Powers That Prey* (1900). In the collected short stories police cooperate with and take bribes from crooks, frame innocent men, and rig elections. Flynt and Walton consistently describe cops as brutal:

> I ain't stuck on England or the coppers here, but the coppers can't cut up with a bloke here the way they do in the States. 'Course they hammer me every now an' then when they take me to the station house, but that's just a habit they've got into. You see people over here won't let 'em do any hammerin' in the streets, an' as they've got to get exercise somehow, they do the hammerin' at the sta-

tionhouse. They ain't so wise as our coppers, but they ain't so crooked either ["A Dead One" 256–257].

The muckrakers' vision of cops, crime, and society, however, was far from a negative one. They believed that the application of reason and science provided the most prudent means to deal with society's ills. Thus Ida Tarbell, in addition to going after the evils of Standard Oil, wrote a series of pieces for *McClure's* on the work of Alphonse Bertillion and his method of identifying individuals. Not coincidentally, *McClure's* also published Arthur B. Reeve's scientific detective tales. S.S. McClure, in fact, hired Harvard's Hugo Musterberg to write a series of pieces on the police, crime, and criminals in 1907 and 1908 ("The Third Degree," "Hypnotism and Crime," and "The Prevention of Crime"). Fat lot of good any of this did when Congress mandated prohibition and transferred graft from politicians to bootleggers and gangsters who paid better.

In the 1920s the detective short story that had largely ignored the police became the detective novel that largely ignored the police. Genteel "golden age" American writers, who mostly followed the fashion of British writers, ignored cops more than did those who invented the American hard-boiled story. And few wanted to use a cop as a hero or to organize a novel around what the police really do.

Cops in the Golden Age

In 1950, when Raymond Chandler wrote "The Simple Art of Murder," he used hypothetical cops to review the validity of the typical golden age novel — the kind S.S. Van Dine, Ellery Queen, and all the others wrote: "The boys with their feet on the desks know that the easiest case in the world to break is the one somebody tried to get very cute with; the one that really bothers them is the murder somebody thought of only two minutes before he pulled it off" (12–13). Twenty years earlier Ellery Queen, without very much success, tried to anticipate this kind of objection to his kind of detective novel in the forward to *The French Powder Mystery*. Here Inspector Queen says:

> Ordinary crime detection ... is almost wholly a mechanical matter. Most crimes are committed by "criminals" — that is to say, by individuals habituated by environment and repetitious conduct to the pursuit of lawlessness. Such persons in ninety-nine out of a hundred cases have police records.
>
> The detective in these ninety-nine hypothetical cases has much to go on. Bertillion measurements — fingerprint records, intimate photographs, a complete dossier [vi].

Queen, like most golden age writers, divides thinking into two parts — the mechanical part and the creative part. They assume that the first was easy and programmed while the second was hard and rare, the province of the genius. In detective fiction the emphasis on detection as a means of exploring the intellect began with Poe the romantic, matured with Gaboriau, and got passed on unconsciously by Arthur Conan Doyle. At the beginning, crime didn't necessarily attach to fiction making this point about amateur detectives. Heroes often solve problems, not crimes; Poe's "Gold Bug" and the Sherlock Holmes pieces like "The Adventure of the Dancing Men" concentrate on mechanical and creative thinking without any reference to crime or criminals. That crime became necessary to this sort of fiction was a phenomenon of the early twentieth century — and American writers, starting with S.S. Van Dine, emphatically make the point that if one wrote about detectives, one had to write about crime, serious crime. This has many advantages for the writer — particularly the addition of "high seriousness" to problem solving and the rush provided by the hunt. But it also means that one has to deal with cops. Indeed, S.S. Van Dine and Ellery Queen, two of the earliest American golden age writers, give cursory nods toward the police at the beginning of their early books. The dust jacket of S.S. Van Dine's *The Canary Murder Case* (1927), for instance, displays a facsimile of Sergeant Heath's case-file card on the murder of Margaret O'Dell. And both Van Dine and then Queen proclaim at the start that their narratives come from the files of the New York Police Department. Thus Van Dine:

> In the offices of the Homicide Bureau of the Detective Division of the New York Police Department, on the third floor of the Police Headquarters building in Center Street, there is a large steel filing cabinet; and within it, among thousands of others of its kind, there reposes a small green index card on which is stated: *ODELL, MARGARET. 184 West 71st Street. Sept. 10. Murder: Strangled about 11 p.m. Apartment ransacked. Jewelry stolen. Body found by Amy Gibson, maid* [*The Canary Murder Case* 1].

And then Queen:

> *The Roman Hat Mystery* is based on records actually to be found in the police archives of New York City [13].

But this is only a feint toward verisimilitude. For most golden age writers, dealing with cops meant dealing with them as little as possible.

S.S. Van Dine and Ellery Queen

The Van Dine books do not have a lot to do with cops, but he does regularly use Sergeant Heath as a means of inflating the reputation (and ego) of his amateur detective:

Sergeant Ernest Heath of the homicide bureau, who had been in charge of both the Benson and Canary cases; and although he had been openly antagonistic to Vance during the first of these investigations, a curious good-fellowship had later grown up between them. Vance admired the sergeant's dogged and straightforward qualities; and Heath had developed a keen respect — with certain reservations, however — for Vance's abilities [*The Greene Murder Case* 20].

The Ellery Queen novels, moreover, deal with cops a bit more. Cops, of course, have to be there in both Van Dine and Queen. Since in all of the books' solutions the amateur detective reevaluates evidence and arrives at novel and surprising conclusions, there has to be someone there to collect and evaluate it in the first place — the "mechanical matter" quoted above. That meant cops, medical examiners, and such forensic experts as were available at the time — typically fingerprint and ballistics technicians. And, to be sure, the cops need to be there to haul off the culprit, unless, of course, he or she has done "the honorable thing." Other than the inverted father-son relationship, wherein Ellery, the son, teaches his father, Inspector Richard Queen, how to go about his business, the police in the Ellery Queen novels do not receive much attention from the author. But they do get some.

Following up on the notion that "Ordinary crime detection ... is almost wholly a mechanical matter," the Ellery Queen novels show an organization — the New York City Police homicide squad — dedicated to that end, with Inspector Richard Queen at the controls. Thus, in *The American Gun Mystery* (1933),

Inspector Queen was that admirable executive, was surrounded by the grim halo of work.... It was the very nature of his job to find fault with small and insignificant details. He was the scientist of trifles, a passionate devotee of minutiae. And yet his old nose was never so closely pressed to the ground that he could not keep in perspective the broadest view of the terrain [50].

There is mechanical or military precision in the way he commands his squad — and they respond. Here's what happens at the murder scene in *The French Powder Mystery*:

Six detectives strolled into the room. Ritter, a burly man, closed the door behind him.
"Hagstrom, your book." The detective snapped out a small notebook and a pencil.
"Piggott, Hesse, Flint — the room".... The three detectives grinned and dispersed to different portions of the room. They began a slow, methodical search of furniture, floors, walls.
"Johnson — the bed!" One of the two remaining men went directly to the wall-bed and began to examine its contents.
"Ritter — stand by" [35].

Out of this corps of coppers supposedly there to get the facts and apply them to the crimes and then criminals, the Queen novels concentrate on Inspector Queen and Sergeant Velie. Most of the characterization of Inspector Queen comes from his peculiar relationship with his son, who repeatedly corrects his mistakes, real and potential. Living in luxury with a son who has a million-dollar vocabulary, the Inspector is "small, pert, like a white-thatched bird" (*French Powder* 33). He was, as noted above, an administrator — although one woefully ignorant of the real police world of the late 1920s and early 1930s. Thus in *The French Powder Mystery* he complains about a new police commissioner and his massive reorganization of the department:

> Number one — reorganized the Missing Persons Bureau. And poor Parsons got the gate I don't know... Number two — scrambled seven precinct-captains so thoroughly that they need road maps to get back to familiar territory. Why? You tell me... Number three — shifted the make-up of Traffic B, C, and D. Number four — reduced a square two dozen second-grade detectives to pounding beats. Any reason? Certainly! Somebody whose grand-uncle's niece knows the Governor's fourth secretary is out for blood.... Number five — raked over the Police School and changed the rules. And I know he has his eagle eye on my pet Homicide Squad...
>
> You haven't heard anything yet.... Every first-grade detective must now make out a daily report — in line of duty, mind you — a daily personal report to the Commissioner's office [17–18].

As anyone who read the newspapers in the 1930s knew, shakes-ups like this one were almost always the result of an exposure of massive and deep-rooted (and chronic) corruption in the police force. But not in the police world of Ellery Queen.

In addition to the Inspector, the Queen books repeatedly introduce Sergeant Velie, who is not management, but labor — powerful, efficient, lower-class labor. "Heading the procession was a gigantic individual in plainclothes, with a face that seemed composed of overlapping plates of steel, and a thunderous step. This Goliath was Sergeant Velie ... a man of few words and mighty, if uninspired, deeds" (*American Gun* 61). The faithful servant, Velie always materializes to organize things for Inspector Queen and do what is asked of him by his betters with an even temper. Queen used Velie's size as a contrast to his boss, the Inspector, and his cultural limitations as a contrast to Ellery's sophistication. Notably, like S.S. Van Dine's Sergeant Ernest Heath before him, Velie uses lower-class diction and incorrect grammar that is a world away from that of the Inspector, Ellery, and (one assumes) the readers.

Erle Stanley Gardner

Erle Stanley Gardner, another prolific golden age writer, straddled the hard-boiled pulp world and the more middle-class detective novel. His Perry Mason and other lawyer books in the 1930s fall into the latter category. Gardner's books ignore the police even more than the Van Dine and Queen books do. Since they deal with lawyer heroes and exonerating those falsely accused by the state, however, the Gardner novels cannot entirely ignore cops and what cops do. But most of what police do serves as background to what the lawyers have to do and consequently only needs to be reported, not described firsthand. Typically Paul Drake, Mason's private detective, summarizes what the police have been up to. Then, too, it was Perry Mason's (and Gardner's other fictional lawyers') business to keep his clients' business and his eventual court surprises from the police. On a few occasions Gardner actually brings cops on the scene — always briefly. He pretty consistently describes them as hulks or slobs. The cop in *The Case of the Sulky Girl* (1933) is "a burly man with square shoulders, thick neck and scowling forehead" (160); the cop in *Murder Up My Sleeve* (1937) moves "his ponderous bulk on tiptoe" (88); and in *The Case of the Lucky Legs* (1934) Mason warns a client to be on the lookout for cop cars and cops:

> Some time tonight you'll probably see a police car drive up here. You can prob-ably tell it by the license. If you can't, you can tell it by the kind of car it is. It'll either be a car from the homicide squad, and, in that event, three or four broad-shouldered men who look like cops in plain clothes will get out of it; or else it will be a radio car [82].

Mostly Gardner portrays cops as incompetent. Thus Mason in a run-in with the continuing character Sergeant Holcomb says in *The Case of the Howling Dog* (1934):

> The only reason I collect good money for what I do, is because I've demon-strated my ability to do it. If the taxpayers didn't give you your salary check every month until you'd delivered results, you might go hungry for a few months — unless you showed more intelligence than you're showing on this case [111].

And in return for his contempt, the police officers in the novels have to take it because they're dealing with lawyers. In fact, they sometimes even express admiration for Perry Mason. Sergeant Holcomb does in *The Case of the Baited Hook* (1940):

> All right Mason ... I don't like your methods. Some day I'm going to throw you in the can, but I do appreciate good detective work when I see it and I'm enough of a cop to pull for a guy who solves crimes, even if I don't like the way he goes about it [278].

Like Van Dine and Queen, Gardner avoids issues of corruption and overt brutality in connection with his police characters—although he does occasionally remind his clients, as in *The Case of the Substitute Face* (1938), that "police will push you around" (81). Unlike Queen, however, police in the Gardner novels of the thirties do not even perform as servants. They serve as nuisances.

Rex Stout

For Rex Stout they are still nuisances, but they have their uses—at least in creating his narratives about Nero Wolfe and Archie Godwin. Stout frequently introduces incidental police officers—Archie usually calls them dicks, or gumshoes. And Stout has a regular cast of these incidental cops—Lieutenant Rowcliff, Purley Stebbins, Sergeant Heath. Their minimal descriptions fasten on the usual one of size—most of them are big guys—and their lower-class natures. In *The Red Box* (1936) one of the incidental cops "was a wiry-looking man in his shirt sleeves with little fox ears and a Yonkers haircut" (229). When they have dialogue they "grunt." They always want to be tough guys; in *The Rubber Band* (1936) Sergeant Heath looked "down at me. He was an inch or two taller than me to begin with, and he was stretching it. He made his voice hard enough to scare a schoolgirl right out of her socks" (112). And, to be sure, they're not very smart: "The saps Cramer had left up at Milton's studio had to go into a huddle before they would even admit he wasn't there" (*Over My Dead Body* 107). The one surprise with respect to the police in Stout's books in the 1930s is the substantial description of the third degree session in *The Red Box*. Here Archie witnesses cops beating up a suspect in the basement of the police station: One cop "reached out and slapped him a good one on the left side of his neck, and then with his other hand on his right ear" (229). The other one "did show some variation; he was more of a pusher than a slapper. The gesture he worked most was to put his paw on Gebert's ear and administer a few short snappy shoves and then put his other paw on the other ear to even it up" (232). Hard-boiled as he is, Archie is more critical of their technique than its implications: he says "The cop was about on the mental level of a woodchuck; he had no variety, no change of pace, no nothing but a pair of palms and they must have been getting tender" (232); and "I felt sorry for the poor dumb cops, seeing that they didn't have brains enough to realize that they were just gradually putting him to sleep and that in another three or four hours he wouldn't be worth fooling with" (231).

But if regular police play only minimal roles in the Nero Wolfe novels, Stout uses Inspector Cramer as a major narrative functionary. True, Cramer has about him a few of the appendages of police work—he usually has lesser cops with him, he worries about the commissioner's temper, and Stout occasionally attaches him to police work not connected with Nero Wolfe:

> Cramer was in his office when I got there.... He was smoking a big cigar and looked contented. I sat down and listened to him discussing with a couple of dicks the best way to persuade some Harlem citizen to quit his anatomy experiments on the skulls of drugstore cashiers [*The League of Frightened Men* 245].

In this respect, much like Inspector Queen's classification of usual and unusual crime in *The French Powder Mystery*, Nero Wolfe admits in several novels that usually Cramer and his police do a competent job:

> For instance, Inspector Cramer. He is an excellent man. In nine murder cases out of ten his services would be much more valuable than mine; to mention a few points only, I need to keep regular hours, I could not function even passably where properly chilled beer was not continually available, and I cannot run fast.... But it is utterly futile, in this case or any other case in which we are interested, to give consideration to the contents of Mr. Cramer's bean [*The League of Frightened Men* 158].

But Cramer hardly functions in the novels as a police officer. Rather he serves as a second Watson character to Archie's first-string role in that stereotype. His presence and his limitations magnify the brilliance of Wolfe, the great detective. And it helps that Cramer's job depends on Wolfe's help, too: "Now that I've emptied my bag for you, how about you doing the same for me? Then you'll have your fee, which is what you want, and I'll have an excuse for keeping my job, which is what I need" (*The Red Box* 60). Then, too, Cramer fulfills the role of the reader in the reader-writer game employed by Stout and most other golden age detective story writers: he wants answers. Indeed, a substantial portion of each novel in which he appears consists of conversations between Cramer and Wolfe in which the police inspector asks, wheedles, cajoles, begs, and even threatens the person who has the answers but withholds them. It's all for fun. But real cops would have probably dragged the fat man before a judge and seen how long Nero Wolfe could hold out on jailhouse cooking. Probably not long.

Good Cops of the Golden Age

Among the regular, mainline, golden age writers, however, a few did choose police officers as their heroes. Indeed, there seems to have been a small spike of interest in cops as heroes of regular detective stories around 1930. Thus Rufus King, Anthony Abbott, and Helen Reilly all write about cops. They are firmly committed to the pattern of the great detective just as were Van Dine, Queen, Stout, and Gardner, but as ancillary material — the filler around the big brain's solving of the crime — they used policemen and police procedure.

Rufus King

In 1929 Rufus King abandoned his wealthy amateur detective, Reginald DePuyster, for a police hero in *Murder by the Clock*. King's hero is Lieutenant Valcour, a naturalized American of French Canadian descent who is a detective in the New York Police Department. That he is more the private detective comes up in the later novels where, even though it is by the police commissioner's direction, he handles a case in upstate New York (*Somewhere in This House* [1930]) and one involving the Lesser Antilles (*The Lesser Antilles Case* [1934]). In the first novel, however, King grounds Valcour more firmly in the NYPD. *Murder by the Clock* begins with what amounts to a review of contemporary attitudes toward the police. Thus, "Whenever she [Mrs. Endicott] thought about it at all she thought of the force as an efficient piece of machinery, the active parts of which one observed daily from one's motor as healthy and generally good-looking young men who controlled traffic" (*Clock* 1). Then her thoughts turn to cops portrayed in the theater: "Most of the characters had been brutal, in spite of a pleasant tender-heartedness reluctantly betrayed toward the final curtain" (*Clock* 2). And then the traditional fears about the police of society folks strike her: "The police had a habit of finding things out — unexpected things, irrelevant to any matter on hand.... She would have to be careful" (*Clock* 5). These fears disappear when Valcour enters, a detective with a "competent foundation in culture he had acquired at McGill University" (*Clock* 7). In addition to his detective, King presents uniformed officers as efficient and admirable: "They were intelligent-looking young men, well built, alert, and their uniforms were immaculate — five competent blue jays outlined sharply against the gray walls" (*Clock* 28). Even officer Cassidy, King's comic Irish cop, fits the pattern.

Valcour has his own views of police work and its defects. The cops, King would have it, are efficient. Thus at the initial murder scene

> The department's experts automatically began to function at once. A photographer was already arranging his apparatus to make pictures of the body.... A finger-print man went about his duties along the lines laid down by established routine [*Clock* 33].

A part of the "established routine" involves the third degree: "According to the temperament and station of the suspects, one of the various forms that go to make up the properly dreaded third degree would be employed and a confession obtained" (*Clock* 59). While Valcour acknowledges that routine works for most criminals and most mundane crime, it has its limitations:

He held a sincere respect for the Central Office men, but at the same time felt that their work was too methodically routine to permit their darting along interesting tangents or wasting time in strolls along bypaths that might lead to fertile fields. There was no criticism in his mind at all. He admired the system that had been established, and the expert functioning of its units and departments. He knew very well that its average of successes was greater than its average of failures. But it was deficient in that elusive, time-taking, and sometimes expensive thing known as the "personal equation." It reminded him at best of a machine [*Clock* 58].

King, then, has it both ways. He bolsters confidence in the personnel and methods of the police department at the same time that he describes an outre crime and a genius detective.

Anthony Abbott

Anthony Abbott (Charles F. Oursler) dedicated his first Thatcher Colt novel, *About the Murder of Geraldine Foster* (1930), "To the standing army of the City of New York — The Police Department." His hero, Thatcher Colt, was police commissioner of New York City:

Under the lamp-light the Commissioner was a striking figure, with his huge and powerful frame and a soldier's face. He was the best dressed man in public life, and regarded by the more frivolous newspapers as a flaneur or, at best, a dilettante in crime, yet not since the days of Theodore Roosevelt had the Department known a chief of such strength, courage and decision. His black hair was crisp and closely cut, his brown eyes sombre and resolved and in his firm features lived action and authority [*Geraldine Foster* 4].

He has gathered around him a crew of professionals, new professionals. Colt, like every other writer, brings in the lab people: "Fred Merkle, photographer, Williams, the finger-print wizard from the Bureau of Criminal Identification, and young Beetson, who would make plaster moulds in the window sill. Only Doctor Multooler was missing" (*About the Murder of the Circus Queen* 164). But more important are the cops. First there is Captain Laird:

A tall, slender, keen-eyed officer in middle years. Laird was one of the first University men to choose a career in the Police Department. At Dartmouth he had been a track star and now the thirty-four detective sergeants under his command were all athletes [*Geraldine Foster* 5].

It's not just that the commanders are educated; Abbott includes the police academy, or "Police College," across the street from headquarters where Colt lectures police recruits. Here Abbott reflects the progressive movement in police history, begun by August Vollmer, police chief of Berkeley, California and founder of university police studies at Berkeley and Chicago.

Indeed Thatcher Colt mentions Vollmer when he wheels out a lie detector in *Geraldine Foster*: "It is the invention of one of my old friends, Captain August Vollmer" (172). Education, scientific tools, and discipline (and removal from politics) were the bases of Vollmer's new approach to police work in the 1920s. Abbott includes education, and in addition to the lie detector, Thatcher Colt uses "scopalamin" (i.e. truth serum) in *Geraldine Foster*, too. In *About the Murder of a Man Afraid of Women*, Colt's friend and opponent, Dougherty, the D.A., says

> You put speed into the department; you gave it armor plate and modern weapons; you told politicians to go to hell ... and you brought science into the police work of this burg for the first time in a big way. You're the one that recognized that sociology has a part in police work; that psychiatry has too, and that key detectives, at least, need a foundation in law [6].

Notably, it's only key detectives who "need a foundation in law." It's because Abbott retains the traditional view that most cops are pretty thick. All they need, in fact, is intelligent and educated officers. Suiting the military references Abbott attaches to Colt, the commissioner has a disciplined army at his disposal to do mundane tasks:

> Thatcher Colt then told his thirty detectives what he wished them to do. He was talking to men distinguished not for their imagination, their education, or their intelligence. Instead, they were known, like bull-dogs, for getting their teeth into something and refusing to let go [*Geraldine Foster* 220].

And to make all of these points by contrast, Abbott invents characters like Inspector Flynn ("a police official of the old school — honest, fearless, capable, and unswervingly loyal, even when dubious as to the value of all the modern police methods in which Colt delighted" [*The Circus Queen* 79]). In addition to describing some of Vollmer's ideas and practices, Abbott provides explanations of other facets of police work. He explains how headquarters and men on patrol interact through call boxes, and gives a candid review of the third degree. In *Geraldine Foster* Colt sends two suspects "downstairs" to get the third degree:

> Nor by this do I mean to pretend that physical violence is no longer practiced. It is still practiced, although not so much as before. But such treatment is reserved for men who will respond to nothing else, who are themselves violent creatures intimidated by nothing except violent physical pain. Moreover, the results from such manhandling are no longer so effective in court. A prisoner roughly treated in the third degree can call his lawyer the next day, exhibit his bruises, have them photographed, and the pictures of the wounds will be shown at the trial to discredit his enforced revelations. The chief value lies in getting a confession that can be substantiated by confirming details subsequently checked up [*Geraldine Foster* 139–40].

In the preface to Abbott's first novel he goes to some lengths to criticize the crime story about the "brilliant amateur" and explains that the police

> solve their cases by knowing their business and attending to it — by vast and
> competent organization, patience and determined hard work, together with
> some ingenuity and an occasional streak of luck. We should not be deluded
> into believing that such men are incompetent or corrupt [*Geraldine Foster* x–xi].

Ignoring the fact that police commissioners do not investigate crimes, Abbott went on to write not only this novel but seven more about the great detective doing things the same way as Philo Vance or Ellery Queen.

Helen Reilly

At the same time Abbott wrote about Thatcher Colt, Helen Reilly began a series of books, starting with *The Diamond Feather* (1930), that feature another New York policeman, Inspector Christopher McKee. McKee fits the conventional mold of the great detective. He, like all of the rest of the big-brain detectives, possesses a vast store of obscure knowledge — in *McKee of Centre Street*, for instance, he discourses on camellias. Like the typical amateur hero, he is tall and lean, and he has focus: "He flung himself with renewed vigor at obstacles, sent men scurrying, emptied his mind of extraneous detail..." (*Centre Street* 35). Reilly, however, embellishes her books with details of police work and lards them with praise of the NYPD. Her view of the cops fastens on their efficiency. This is the point of her description of the department's radio room:

> The radio room was an inverted finger bowl of dull gold. Light flowed back
> from the rounded walls, stopped at a patch of sky dark above the ventilators.
> In the middle of the floor three big tables formed a hollow square at one end.
> The top of the tables was a map of the five boroughs divided by colored cords
> into little red sectors and bigger gray ones. Scattered over the red sectors were
> numbered brass disks representing the green scout cars carrying two uniformed
> men, one to each red division and, moving about the gray ones, the unrecognizable master cars loaded with detectives, machine guns, tear gas and smoke
> bombs. There was a microphone at the far end of the room; at right angles a
> short distance away, the sending apparatus [*Centre Street* 3].

When the news comes in about the murder at the speakeasy in *McKee of Centre Steet*,

> Six words alone were required for all concerned to report to the scene of the
> crime, medical examiner, district attorney on homicide duty, his stenographer,
> fingerprint men, photographer, district and borough commanders, the assistant chief, and the police commissioner himself, every one of them available
> at any hour of the day or night [5–6].

Reilly touches on mechanical and scientific aids to police work. Radio cars, she points out, make things easier: "The effortless functioning of a perfect police machine relieves wear and tear on the individual and permits each man to work at the highest degree of efficiency" (*Centre Street* 42). And she points out that the police photographer uses the same kind of unique wide-angle lens used by the Surete in Paris. Indeed, Reilly sometimes uses the machine metaphor to summarize police work, as in "The two men went back to the office. And once there the vast machinery for the tracking down of missing men was at once put into operation" (*Centre Street* 85).

Reilly adds dedicated, efficient, clean-cut men to the police machine; for instance, in the radio room passage cited above she adds "There were two operators inside the square, keen young men in blue broadcloth shirts, head sets on, watching the movement of patrols with intent eyes" (*Centre Street* 4). At the top of the department, Reilly describes the "slim, spare, steady-eyed" police commissioner:

> And as he strolled up the aisle, each officer in the room knew — and this knowledge was heartening — that Carey would follow and direct, if necessary, every resource known to the department, until, and in spite of New York's multitudinous affairs, this crime had been solved [*Centre Street* 25].

While he has men and resources like these, Reilly's hero really doesn't need them (except for maybe crowd control) because the solutions to the crimes in the books come from his own intellect and instincts.

George Bagby

With *Murder at the Piano* (1935), George Bagby (Aaron Marc Stein) introduced Inspector Schmidt (Schmidty) of the New York Police, a character who continued to appear in novels into the 1960s. The fictitious Bagby is the narrator and acts in that capacity because, reminiscent of Julian Hawthorne's connection to Inspector Byrnes, he is Schmidt's ghostwriter. He also serves in the capacity of the Watson character in the novels, as well as providing one side of the peppy repartee Stein included as one of the draws of his books. From the term "flatfoot" the author locates Schmidt's defining feature in his feet:

> You have to know about the Inspector's feet if you are to understand the man. He would be the first to acknowledge that for most of his success he is indebted to his feet. It has been his misfortune that he has never been able to recover from the pavement pounding apprenticeship he served in his earliest days on the force. Those long days and nights of pounding a beat had been a cruel strain on his feet, and the damage had been permanent [*Bird Walking Weather* 13].
>
> It is my guess that originally he was not the contemplative type, but all this sitting around waiting for his feet to cool off promoted contemplation, pro-

duced the leisure needed for the logical ordering of his mind [*Bird Walking Weather* 14].

In addition to the recurring motif of Schmidt's feet, the forthrightness and occasional vulgarity of his speech differ from the speech of the upper-class characters with whom his cases invariably bring him into contact. Thus this excerpt shows Schmidt at perhaps his worst:

> "Chinese doctor? Naw. There's no Chinks in this. Did I ever tell you about the Chink I caught putting rat poison in bird's nest soup?"
> "No, you didn't."
> "That was a tough case" the Inspector sighed. "The soup tasted funny but you couldn't tell anything from that. All that Chink food tastes funny" [*Ring Around a Murder* 12].

As the fictions would have it, Schmidt and Richard Queen hold the same rank in the same police department, but the proletarian features Stein adds to his hero make Schmidt an anomaly among the genteel high-rank-ing cops who appear in other golden age books. Even though Schmidt is nominally a police officer, the Bagby books have little to do with the police. Schmidt occasionally whisks in and out of headquarters at Center Street, but mostly spends his time calling on suspects with his civilian pal Bagby. Other cops come in only incidentally and are the big, basically dense guys one expects to find in books of the 1930s: "Schmidty looked our policeman over appraisingly. He was a big lad, an easy six foot two with plenty of heft to him and hands like sledge hammers" (*Bird Walking Weather* 11). Schmidt has access to police reports, which the author uses more as devices to sim-plify the narration than to reflect police procedure. In their plots the Bagby books follow the golden age patterns closely; that the great detective is a police officer comes from the writer's desire to introduce an eccentric hero rather than a real cop.

Doris Miles Disney

Beginning to write in the 1940s, Doris Miles Disney used a police hero in her first novel, *Compound for Death* (1943). Her entire approach, how-ever, looked back to attitudes toward the police held in nineteenth-century detective fiction. This shows most clearly at the beginning of the novel, when Tyler Burnell disappears and his family puts off calling the police for the same reason families don't call them in *The Moonstone* or Seeley Register's *Dead Letter*— the fear of scandal. The family also worries about the compe-tence of the police, and with good reason:

> The Parkerton Police Department was housed in an old wooden building with offices above it. While Him hesitated near the plate-glass window, debating

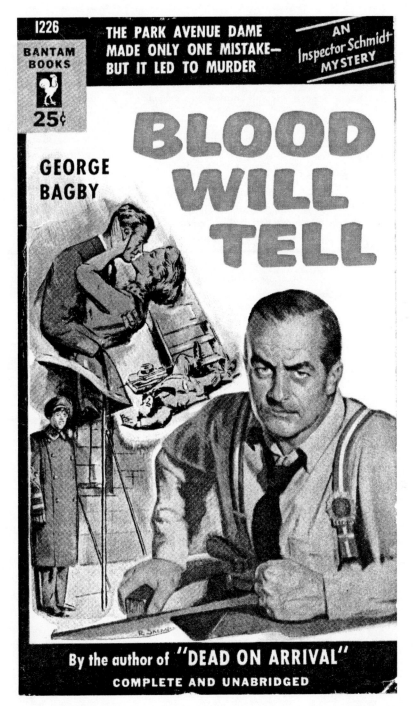

THE PARK AVENUE DAME
MADE ONLY ONE MISTAKE—
BUT IT LED TO MURDER

AN
Inspector Schmidt
MYSTERY

GEORGE
BAGBY

BLOOD WILL TELL

By the author of "DEAD ON ARRIVAL"

COMPLETE AND UNABRIDGED

Bantam moves the police officer, sex and violence to the cover of the paperback
of Bagby's *Blood Will Tell* (1954).

with himself whether or not it would be worth his time to go in and inquire for the chief of police — the Parkerton chief of police, according to Detective Steve Fisher, was so dumb that he was incapable of determining between one portion of his anatomy and another [*A Compound for Death* 28].

Fortunately the Burnells don't have to deal with the Parkerton cops. They have the services of Jim O'Neil, the county detective. Disney cuts O'Neil from the same cloth from which most golden age writers cut their amateur sleuths:

> He was a man in his late thirties with an easy, pleasant smile and an affable manner.... He was above medium height with an unremarkable set of features, a thick crown of black hair and brilliant hazel eyes.... He looked capable and intelligent ... a man who knew his business [*Compound for Death* 20].

O'Neil knows nuances and perceives the underlying truth when listening to witnesses and suspects. In short, he is the great detective. His assistants, though, are cops. There's Steve Fisher: "big, burly, and competent-looking" (*Compound for Death* 60). Disney also introduces Sergeant Wood:

> He came into the waiting room. He was a thickset man of medium height with a heavy, serious-looking face. No great intelligence and no humor at all lightened it; but he had the appearance of a most competent plodder [*Appointment at Nine* 19].

Golden Age Reprise

In the works of the golden age writers between the World Wars, then, the police do not matter much. The preoccupation of writers like Van Dine, Queen, Gardner, Stout, and the rest was on the big-brained civilian. Even when the genius detective is a cop, he looks, behaves, talks, acts, and thinks like the amateur detective who was the staple of golden age detective fiction. Insofar as they present police officers, these writers reinforce class distinctions, distinctions not just between the civilian genius and the cops but also between high-ranking police and low-ranking police, between big-city cops and cops in the boonies. Regular police officers are often shown as huge, often menacing, mentally limited, semi-literate, and often as more than inept. When they are not this kind of cop, they are clean-cut and efficient, obedient parts of a machine. On the plus side, the machine metaphor comes in most often when describing police departments, suggesting that they are social instruments in which disciplined policemen who know their jobs function as parts of the social mechanism that keeps people safe from mayhem and "routine" (i.e. lower-class) crime. These machines, moreover, are operated and controlled by an educated elite that knows how to manage and deploy its forces and which uses scientific innovations to enhance police work. This is especially the case when it comes to the somewhat reticent descriptions of the third degree, which is clearly restricted to lower-class individuals. No notice goes to the real problems of policing America's cities — recruitment, overwork, stress, training, corruption, sloth, brutality, and many other issues faced then and now by real police departments, police officers, and the public. But that's not what these writers tried to do, and cops to them were a bit of edging necessary to frame their fictional diversions based on bizarre, or at least difficult, circumstances, and suspects not from the "criminal" class.

Hard-Boiled Cops

Hard-boiled writers had few illusions about anything, and they had even fewer about the police. Readers of pulp magazines in the 1920s and 1930s got a weekly or monthly dose of police indifference, incompetence, corruption, and brutality. Even the mildest descriptions of cops in the pulps don't do much for their image. One of these, Frederick Nebel's description of the cop house in "Rough Justice" (1930), just makes cops seem repulsive:

> At police headquarters on Clark Avenue, Detective Hocheimer sat at a battered desk and gnawed at the stem of a corncob pipe. He sat in his shirt-sleeves, bald head splotched with red heat spots and high blood pressure, white hairs above the ears damp, thick jowls hanging over a soiled white collar [*Black Mask Boys* 162].

Other writers' descriptions get more basic. In Daly's "Three Gun Terry Mack" (1923) the hero tells the girl that "I knew the police, and I knew that they'd put me through the jumps before I ever got my lawyer" (*Black Mask Boys* 68). Paul Cain in "Parlor Trick" (1932) gives the double whammy of corruption ("Sure — why don't you call a cop? Frankie had everybody from the chief down on his payroll" [*Arbor House Treasury* 117]), and brutality ("You ought to of called the police. They'd be after giving Gus a break ... with a length of hose" [117]). This hint of police brutality and Archie Goodwin's depiction of the third degree in *The Red Box* are timid and tame when placed aside the third degree scene in Robert Leslie Bellem's *Blue Murder* (1938):

> "A lawyer, huh?" the second dick said. He walked up to me and doubled his right fist and bashed it square against my jaw. "There's your lawyer, you bastard."
> I swayed in the chair, but a lot of guys grabbed me and wouldn't let me fall. The beefy plainclothes dick hit me again, on the other side of my jaw. I felt something click and snap inside my mouth, and I felt around with my tongue and found where a molar had been knocked loose. I spat it out. It made a funny dead tunk! on the concrete floor when it hit. I tasted blood inside my mouth.

> Then they all started working me over. I was yanked to my feet, and some-
> body grabbed my shirt and ripped it off me. Then three of those bastards
> started hitting me with their locust clubs. They biffed me over the head and
> they smashed the clubs down on my shoulders and back [42].

And there is another even more graphic paragraph that follows this one.
Bellem, to be sure, represented the slimy bottom of the pulp world. But
most pulp writers in the 1920s and 1930s had little good to say about the
police — except for Hammett and Chandler. If theirs was not always a wholly
sympathetic view of the police, it was far more thoughtful.

Dashiell Hammett

Dashiell Hammett knew a lot about private detectives, having been a
Pinkerton agent. Small wonder, then, that all of his heroes — the Continental Op, Sam Spade, Nick Charles — were private eyes. His portrayal of
cops in his works, however, is not that simple. In his first novel-length
fiction, *Red Harvest* (1929) Hammett draws the police, all the police, of Per-
sonville as a sorry lot. They are rotten at the top with the wholly corrupt,
brutal and stupid Chief Noonan who was just the leader of another gang.
And Hammett shows them as slovenly at the bottom with the Op's arrival
in town:

> The first policeman I saw needed a shave. The second had a couple of buttons
> off his shabby uniform. The third stood in the center of the city's main inter-
> section — Broadway and Union Street — directing traffic, with a cigar in one
> corner of his mouth. After that I stopped checking them up [3].

These guys don't even match up with all of the machine and army
metaphors floating around in the genteel detective books of the 1920s and
1930s. The portrait of the police in *Red Harvest* is, in many ways, an aber-
ration. Hammett sort of liked cops. From his earliest Continental Op stories, the Op out of necessity often visits the police station, and frequently
teams up with a police officer. Indeed, one of the continuing characters in
the Continental Op stories is O'Gar. San Francisco Detective Sergeant O'Gar
appears in seven *Black Mask* stories: "Crooked Souls" (1923); "The Tenth
Clew" (1924); "Zigzags of Treachery" (1924); "Women, Politics, and Murder" (1924); "The Golden Horseshoe" (1924); "Creeping Siamese" (1926);
and "The Big Knockover" (1927). Hammett essentially makes O'Gar the
Op's colleague. The Op admires his brains, noting that O'Gar is "a squat
man of fifty who goes in for wide-brimmed hats of the movie-sheriff sort,
but whose little blue eyes and bullet head aren't handicapped by the trick
headgear" ("Women, Politics and Murder" 194). And he accepts that O'Gar
"is as good a man as the department has, and he and I have always been

lucky when we tied up together" ("The Golden Horseshoe" 238). In the *Black Mask* stories Hammett also introduces detective Pat Reddy. In "The Scorched Face" (1925): he notes that "Pat was the youngest member of the detective bureau — a big blond Irishman who went in for the spectacular in his lazy way" (365). And to enhance Reddy's character, Hammett then goes on to relate a story from Pat's days in uniform when he arrested a rich man's wife for a traffic violation and made it stick in spite of bullying and intimidation.

In the later novels Hammett sorts out working men from bosses. He makes his old cops more proletarian. Thus he points out that O'Gar and Reddy are big, somewhat slovenly guys: when he brings them back to play roles in *The Dain Curse*, O'Gar, is "a burly, solid man of fifty" (153) and Reddy is "a big, jovial youngster, with almost brains enough to make up for his lack of experience" (154). Moving to *The Maltese Falcon*, Detective Tom Polhaus is "a barrel bellied tall man with shrewd small eyes, a thick mouth, and carelessly shaven dark jowls" (201); and John Guild in *The Thin Man* is "a big sandy man of forty eight or fifty in a gray suit that did not fit him very well" (609). Readers see each of these characters doing police work in the novels — O'Gar and Reddy working a crime scene, Polhaus working another, and Guild arresting a criminal at Nick and Nora's apartment. Indeed, Guild tells Nick about remembering him when he was a patrolman and Nick was a private eye. Just as importantly, each also treats the hero with respect, as a colleague. Proletarians all, they care about their work and not about superficial things like appearance or speech. Looking at the dialogue, especially in the earlier *Black Mask* stories, cops like O'Gar speak tersely, ungrammatically, and use slang — some of the basic elements of hard-boiled style. Hammett presents the reverse of the proletarian cop with Lieutenant Dundy in the good cop versus bad cop scene in Spade's rooms in *The Maltese Falcon*. Dundy is "a compactly built man with a round head under short-cut grizzled hair and a square face behind a short-cut grizzled moustache. A five-dollar gold piece was pinned to his necktie and there was a small elaborate diamond-set secret-society-emblem on his lapel" (303). Hammett draws him as a pretentious bully who treats Spade as a suspect to be threatened and bullied. But Dundy is more boss than cop. Rather than simply being a private eye writer, like the more conventional contributors to *Black Mask*, Hammett moves beyond the stereotypes of the police officer and begins to acknowledge the cop as a competent, honest working man deserving of respect.

Raymond Chandler

The same thing happens in Chandler. In his stories written for *Black Mask* and other pulps Chandler introduces a number of policemen as subsidiary characters. Pete Anglich, the hero of "Pickup on Noon Street" (1936), for example, is a "narcotics squad undercover man." Chandler uses the good cop and bad cop team in "Smart Aleck Kill" (1934); "Trouble Is My Business" (1939); "Red Wind" (1938); and "The Guns at Cyrano's" (1936). He also uses the cops as angry straight men for Carmady's wisecracks in "The Guns at Cyrano's" and for Marlowe's witticisms in "Trouble Is My Business." He makes Detective Violets McGee a continuing character who refers cases to the hero in "Mandarin's Jade" (1937) and "Bay City Blues" (1938). He puts cops into most of his novels, some good and some bad. In *The Big Sleep* (1939) there's a bad one. Captain Conjager is "a cold eyed hatchet faced man, as lean as a rake and as hard as the manager of a loan office" (98). But Conjager's appearance is brief. Chandler comments more extensively about police and police work in *Farewell, My Lovely* (1940).

In *Farewell, My Lovely* Chandler gives his most comprehensive portrayal of police. In the novel Marlowe's most brief descriptions and encounters are with the neat and efficient Lieutenant Randall: "He was a thin quiet man of fifty with smooth creamy gray hair, cold eyes, a distant manner. He wore a dark red tie with black spots on it…. Behind him … two beefy men lounged like bodyguards" (64). Besides Randall, Chandler punctuates the book with the sloth and indifference Marlowe encounters in Lieutenant Nulty, beginning with

> A cop named Nulty got the case, a lean-jawed sourpuss with large yellow hands which he kept folded over his kneecaps most of the time he talked to me…. Dirty brown linoleum covered the floor and the smell of old cigar butts hung in the air. Nulty's shirt was frayed and his coat sleeves had been turned in at the cuffs. He looked poor enough to be honest, but didn't look like a man who could deal with Moose Molloy [12].

In the novel, Chandler acknowledges police routine, but also emphasizes the action hero's impatience with it:

> And the prowl car boys are not supposed to touch him [the corpse] until the K-car men come and they're not supposed to touch him until the coroner's examiner sees him and the photographers have photographed him and the fingerprint man has taken his prints. And you know how long all that is liable to take out here? A couple of hours [59].

More powerfully, however, he concentrates on the wholesale corruption of the Bay City police, from the history of Chief Riordan ("He was fired. It broke his heart" [75]), to the oily Chief Wax, to detectives Blaine and Galbraith, who mug and kidnap Marlowe. With Galbraith (whom Marlowe calls Hemingway) Chandler makes the same point as the muckrakers did — it's the system that corrupts cops:

"Cops don't go crooked for money. Not always, not even often. They get caught in the system.... And the guy who sits back there in the nice corner office ... he ain't giving the orders. You get me?"

"What kind of man is the mayor?"

"What kind of guy is a mayor anywhere? A politician. You think he gives the orders? Nuts. You know what's the matter with this country...?" ...

"A guy can't be honest if he wants to" [194].

After listening to this discussion, in fact, Chandler has Marlowe become briefly preoccupied with cops: "I thought of cops, tough cops who could be greased and yet were not all bad, like Hemingway. Fat prosperous cops with Chamber of Commerce voices, like Chief Wax. Slim, smart and deadly cops like Randall, who for all their smartness and deadliness were not free to do a clean job a clean way" (199). Then Marlowe meets Red, an ex-cop like himself, who helps him get to Burnette's gambling ship. In fact, Chandler made Red a commentator on contemporary cops. Thus he describes Olson of the pickpocket detail, who isn't above framing suspects, and he talks about Blaine and Galbraith:

Blaine's bad, the other guy is just a tough cop, neither bad nor good, neither crooked nor honest, full of guts and just dumb enough, like me, to think being on the cops is a sensible way to make a living [211].

Then there is his final comment:

The trouble with cops is not that they're dumb or crooked or tough, but that they think just being a cop gives them a little something they didn't have before. Maybe it did once, but not any more [212].

Cops, in short, are like everyone else. The significance of all of these comments about the police in *Farewell, My Lovely* lies in the fact that they were new. Chandler made most of his novels by rewriting short stories. *Farewell, My Lovely* was a rewrite of "The Man Who Liked Dogs" and "Try the Girl" published in *Black Mask* in 1936 and 1937 respectively. We need to note that none of the comments about the nature of the police appeared in the *Black Mask* works. Chandler added them when he made the short stories into the novel. The point, then, is that either he adapted his view of the cops to different audiences — the readers of pulp magazines and then the readers cultivated by Alfred Knopf, who published *Farewell, My Lovely*— or he had thought more seriously about cops' lives between 1936 and 1940. Or maybe both.

Radio Cop Shows

Between the wars, people spent more time listening to the radio than they did reading pulps or more genteel detective stories, and crime shows took up a great deal of broadcast time. Ken Crossen notes that by 1945 crime programs occupied an average of ninety minutes a day and that each show was heard by more than five million listeners (*Don't Touch That Dial* 155). Not many writers even today can aspire to numbers like these. Up until the advent of television in the 1950s, a lot of these crime programs converted print sources into radio dramas. Thus *The Adventures of Sam Spade* (1930–56) on NBC, Mutual, and then ABC; *The Adventures of Ellery Queen* (1939–48) on CBS, NBC, and then ABC; *The Adventures of Charlie Chan* (1932–48) on NBC and then Mutual; *The Adventures of the Thin Man* (1941–50) on NBC, CBS, and then Mutual; *Perry Mason* (1943–55) on CBS; *The Adventures of Nero Wolfe* (1943–51) on NBC and Mutual; *Philo Vance* (1945–50) on NBC; and *The Adventures of Philip Marlowe* (1947–51) on CBS. Then, too, series were created for radio, like *Mr. District Attorney* (1939 to 1954) on NBC and then ABC. Shows about cops appeared on the air, too.

While the thirties saw several police shows come and go, like *Calling All Cars* from 1933 to 1940, the real growth in cop shows on the radio came after the end of World War II: thus in 1949 listeners across the United States could tune in *True Detective Mysteries* (on the air since 1929); *Gang Busters* (on the air since 1936); *Under Arrest* (on the air since 1946); *Official Detective* (on the air since 1947); *Call the Police* (on the air since 1947); and the new shows for that year, *Dragnet* and *Broadway Is My Beat*. These bursts of fifteen to thirty minutes on the airwaves made the police into heroes — something fiction had declined to do up to that point. Emulating J. Edgar Hoover's use of the media to enhance the public image of the FBI, many of these shows served larger public relations purposes of police departments and had the express cooperation and even participation of high-ranking cops. Thus Los Angeles police files were opened as a source of information for *Calling All Cars*, and LAPD Chief James Davis introduced the shows. *Gangbusters* was first narrated by Col. Norman Schwartzkopf, a retired superintendent of the New Jersey State Police, then by Lewis Valentine, Mayor LaGuardia's commissioner of police. *Dragnet* acknowledged the assistance of Chief William Parker at the close of each episode. And there was *Policewoman*, about the career of Sgt. Mary Sullivan of the NYPD, ending with Sullivan herself commenting after each show (*Don't Touch* 168). On local radio *Homicide Squad*, broadcast by KEX Seattle, based its programs on exploits of the local police department (*Don't Touch* [166]); *State Police Dramas* from WHAM in Rochester covered New York State Police cases, and *Tales of the Oklahoma Highway Patrol* from WKY in Oklahoma City did the same thing. Conditioned by the pervasiveness of public spirit and public service during the war, the express purpose of all of these shows appeared in the opening for *Gangbusters*:

With the cooperation of the leading law enforcement officials of the United States, Gangbusters presents facts in the relentless war of the police on the underworld.... Authentic case histories that show the never-ending activity of the police in their work of protecting our citizens [*Radio's Golden Age* 131].

These shows made listeners aware of real, or more real, crime. The oldest of the cop shows, *True Detective Mysteries*, offered rewards for the capture of highlighted criminals, and *Wanted* "used the actual voices of the people involved in the crimes ... the criminals, the victims, arresting officers, etc." (*Radio's Golden Age* [374]). They also preached for public confidence in and support of the police, aired a bit of action, and held police officers up as heroes. But one cannot tell much about a hero in fifteen minutes, or even half an hour.

Lawrence Treat

Before 1945 Lawrence Arthur Goldstone, writing under the penname Lawrence Treat, had written five detective novels, beginning with *B as in Banshee* in 1940. He had no particular intention of doing anything especially new when he wrote his sixth novel, *V as in Victim*, in 1945. But he did. *V as in Victim* concerns investigations into a murder and a hit-and-run death, along with the coincidental connections between the two. Its cast of characters resembles the assembly of stereotypes common to the detective novels of the period: the nasty old man, the virginal and frightened girl, the fashionable art dealer, the drunken nymphomaniac, and the forthright aged spinster. The writing is neither better nor worse than that found in the average detective novel of the period. In most respects, *V as in Victim* belonged to the library of detective fiction that deserves to be forgotten. Granted, the book had a prominent detective theme—the role of the scientist and scientific evidence versus inept and old fashioned police methods—but that theme went back to the turn of the century with R. Austin Freeman's Thorndyke stories in Britain and Arthur B. Reeve's Craig Kennedy stories in America. Treat's innovation was in his heroes. They are cops.

Mitch Taylor enters the novel first. He's mostly a pathetic, lower-middle-class slob. In his introduction, Taylor could have been any of the inept and lousy cops from the fiction of the 1930s:

Mitch Taylor, detective third grade, sat hunched over a desk in the detective room of the Twenty-First Precinct and drew circles on a sheet of paper. He was a short, chesty man with dark dry hair brushed back over his forehead. His lips, overthick, were firmed up in an aggressive pout. There were no planes or angles to his features and no shading to his complexion [1].

His off-the-rack clothes don't fit him well. He has a wife he adores but doesn't understand. He had no particularly high purpose in becoming a cop:

Then he wondered why he'd joined the force.

  He'd never thought about it much, although for most of his boyhood he had
more or less assumed that eventually he'd be a cop. There were plenty of reasons for it. He had the tradition, he had stamina, he had sense. He liked people, and he disliked buying and selling. His uncle who was a cop used to say,
"Well, Mitch, some day you'll be wearing the uniform." Mitch had accepted
the fact much as another boy would have accepted the prospect of going into
his father's business [21].

Being a cop has, for Mitch, its advantages. "There was security and a
decent income. He'd be with people like himself, who thought his thoughts
and spoke his language. He'd belong" (21). But it has its drawbacks as well.

At the beginning of the novel being a cop for Mitch means too much
work. At the opening of the novel he doodles rather than writing reports
and complains about the job:

  Only a jackass ever got himself into the department. You worked every day in
  the week and you didn't get overtime and you never went anywhere except in
  bad weather and if anything happened you were supposed to take over, no matter what [2].

It also means being part of an organization with written and unwritten rules. One of them is that cops don't ever get anywhere without a "rabbi,"
an older, higher-ranking officer who would boost one's career. Hogan, related
to his mother, was Mitch's rabbi, but since Mitch barely hangs on to the
lowest detective rank, Hogan hasn't done much for him lately — or Mitch
hasn't done much for himself. He knows that advancement comes from breaking a big case and having a clean record. The latter consumes him. "He
learnt to fear above all else the crank civilian who wrote letters and got him
up on charges, for that marred his record" (22); "He learnt stoicism and morale
and the trick of passing the buck, so that there were as few marks on his record
as possible" (22). This, of course, makes him one pathetic policeman:

  He rarely entered anything as a crime, since it might remain unsolved. Instead
  he listed the bulk of his work as investigations, for an investigation didn't have
  to carry through to arrest [22].

So rather than working he creates fictions for victims of crime, like the
temporizing and excuses he makes up for the old woman who has been
robbed and the delicatessen owner whose till has been dipped into.

The character point Treat wanted to make in *V as in Victim* centered
on the conversion of Mitch Taylor from a slobbish do-nothing flatfoot into
an investigator enthusiastic, energetic, and successful in his work. This
comes, ironically, when his desire to shirk his duty brings him in contact
with the other main character, Jub Freeman. But that may not have been
the most important thing he did with the introduction of Mitch Taylor.

At the scene of a hit-and-run accident Taylor wants to shift the responsibility for the investigation to someone else and has the inspired idea of calling the police laboratory. In comes Jub Freeman, the lab man, who, more than Taylor, looks like a hero:

> He was a quiet, pleasant guy, not much taller than Mitch, with alert features and dreamy blue eyes. He was on the blond side and he had plenty of weight [11].

Jub, like Mitch, had drifted into police work: he "had looked around for a steady job with civil-service status. Clerk's work he abhorred. Somebody mentioned the police department and it struck Jub that it would be as good as anything else, and less boring" (52). At the accident scene Freeman collects paint scrapings and pieces of broken headlights for analysis at the lab, and when Taylor accidentally stumbles over a murder victim a short time later Jub vacuums up hair and fibers and collects a swab from the victim's wound at the crime scene. But Freeman is more than a collector of bits and pieces. Faced with a police establishment either ignorant of or suspicious of science and the uses of physical evidence, when he returns to the lab with his collection of bits and pieces he tells his colleague that "I want to show those bastards what the laboratory can do. I want the two of us to solve a homicide complete, here in this room" (47). At the lab they make a cast of dental impressions, look through microscopes, send a dead cat out for an autopsy, and subject paint scrapings to spectroscopic analysis. Indeed, Freeman waxes ecstatic about the spectroscope and what it can accomplish. Throughout the rest of the novel, moreover, Freeman's and Taylor's roles merge — Taylor enthusiastically collects evidence and dumps it at the lab and Freeman plays detective by going out to interview witnesses and suspects. He also falls in love with one of them.

Were it not for Taylor and Freeman, *V as in Victim* would be entirely forgettable as a detective novel. Likewise, were Taylor and Freeman not cops, they, too, would be entirely forgettable. But they are, and in their creation Treat, perhaps unwittingly, invented many of the conventions that would drive the police novel throughout the rest of the twentieth century. Here's what they are:

1. The Job: being police officers for both Freeman and Taylor is a job. In describing their decisions to become cops, Treat makes it clear that neither sought police work as a calling or vocation. They must deal with superiors, as well as with established rules and procedures. "There was only one trouble with a job like this. They figured you were on it every single minute, without a break. When was a guy supposed to eat? Or go to the bathroom? Huh?" (74). Jobs also mean bosses, and Treat includes this with "Mitch had

long ago decided that softening of the brain was an occupational disease that started when you got to be a lieutenant" (64); Treat's police heroes differ from amateur genius detectives in that they need to work to survive, and from hard-boiled private eyes driven by a quixotic sense of justice.

2. Copspeak: cops have their own particular jargon and slang. Treat does not do much with this, but he does include a bit when Mitch puts in a call to "the MVHS" and then explains that it means Motor Vehicle Homicide Squad. There is little real cop slang in *V as in Victim*. Publishers in the 1940s would not have printed it anyway. But Treat gives a small indication that he knows about police jargon.

3. Police in the Family: While Mitch had no ambition to become a police officer, "His uncle who was a cop used to say, 'Well, Mitch, some day you'll be wearing the uniform.' Mitch had accepted the fact much as another boy would have accepted the prospect of going into his father's business" (21). Sons following fathers and then daughters following their fathers would become a conspicuous facet of the cop novels of the next half-century.

4. The Family of Police: The bonding of police officers as both a virtue and a vice of the job would become one of the most important themes in cop books. Thus in *V as in Victim*: "He'd be with people like himself, who thought his thoughts and spoke his language. He'd belong" (21); "Among themselves, the police subscribed to a philosophy of live and let live. Like the inmates in a jail, they were banded together against the rest of the world" (130).

5. Cops versus Civilians: because Treat adheres to the conventions of the golden age novel he does not show a great deal of this. However, it appears when Mitch worries about "civilians" writing complaints that will besmirch his record.

6. Transmission of Cop Knowledge: throughout the book Mitch recalls the advice given to him as a rookie by the veteran Charlie Corrigan.

7. Partners: One of the principal points of the book is the development of Taylor and Freeman as partners, or at least potential partners.

8. Police Truisms: In *V as in Victim* they chiefly consist of Corrigan's advice to the young Taylor: "He was using common sense, which was fifty percent of police work" (23); "Keep your eyes open, and you get the breaks when you don't expect them" (121); "When you don't know what else to do, you look.... You never know what you're going to come across" (192). Later truisms will include clichés about crime — murders being solved in forty-eight hours, victims knowing one another, etc.

9. Cop Tales: Among themselves, cops are talkers. Reflecting this, Treat inserts Corrigan's story about cracking a case by helping a ten-year-old boy fish a nickel out of an iron grating (121) and Freeman's story about

his first scientific arrest and its failure (170). These inserted anecdotes do not advance the plot but rather reflect cop knowledge, the inclination of cops to tell stories, and a potential means of providing a fuller portrait of the police world than available in a simple narrative.

10. Politics and Politicians in the Department: Treat makes it clear that individual influence and politics play a major role in police officers' lives. Thus Mitch talks about rabbis twice: "There was no sense in being a cop unless you had a rabbi. A rabbi was a guy with influence, who took care of you" (21) and "You got promoted because you had a rabbi. That was what counted" (126). Treat also notes the place of influence versus effort in "You don't get to be an inspector because you work. Not in this world" (149).

11. Paperwork: Treat gives the nod to this aspect of police work in Mitch's initial observation that "I don't like paper work" (1). He also alludes to one of the NYPD's actual report forms: "They were the follow-up reports on the Jarvis case, the D.D. 5's on blue paper. The original report was on white" (62).

12. Temptations on the Job: At the opening of the novel Mitch takes it for granted that one of his fellow detectives is spending much of his shift in a bar. When he visits a deli he eats without paying. Alcoholism, "cooping" (hiding out rather than working during one's shift), and what the Knapp Commission would later term "grass eating" (accepting what amount to small gratuities) have long been problems associated with police work.

13. Old versus New Policing: Treat makes the tension between scientific and non-scientific investigation one of the major themes of *V as in Victim*. Indeed, one of the bosses says that "What you should have done is crack down right off and got a confession. Remember that, Freeman. The old way's always the best" (170).

14. The Shabby Police Station: The squalor of cops' working conditions would become a repeated issue in cop novels. Thus at the beginning of *V as in Victim* "Mitch stared at the ceiling and wondered whether the paint chips would start flaking off tonight or wait until next week. He tried to remember when the place had been painted, but his memory didn't go that far back. The point was that the building was falling apart. He remembered how some smart rookie with a law degree used to beef about the age of the precinct houses. He had some theory about their psychological effect. Nobody had liked the guy much and he'd gone into the army and Mitch had heard he'd got his in France. But now that he was dead, Mitch could admit that maybe he had something" (2).

15. Weather: Like letter carriers, police must always be on the job. One of the ways of emphasizing this is through having the weather become both a nuisance and an impediment to the cop's role. Thus in the middle of the

novel Treat introduces a whopping storm for Jub Freeman to slosh around in.

In *V as in Victim*, then, Treat mentions many of the points that will later drive the police novel. He had, in fact, taken some pains to achieve accuracy in these, having spent time with police officers and at police stations absorbing background. For the first time he presented readers with characters built on issues and attitudes of real police officers. However, all of these are conventions that affect character, not plot. In plotting Treat remained committed to the surprise ending of the traditional golden age detective story. And as Chandler emphasized in "The Simple Art of Murder," real police work has little resemblance to the contrived conventions of this kind of fiction. With all that Treat achieved with *V as in Victim*, the real development of the police novel would have to wait until the 1950s.

-two-

The 1950s and 1960s

The police novel emerged during the first two decades after World War II. Slowly. Whether or not this happened because of Lawrence Treat's example is problematic; cop writers cite Britain's John Creasy and France's Georges Simenon more often as providing inspiration than they give credit to Treat. In the 1950s and 1960s, moreover, radio and then television programs about police officers generated new and widespread interest in cops. Writers, in fact, credit *Dragnet* even more frequently than literary sources. From the purely literary point of view, however, the real birth of the cop novel depended on writers possessed of different motives: on a reporter turned cop turned novelist, on several paperback writers, and on writers tinkering with the conventional detective story. It is worth remembering that in the 1950s the character patterns of the great detective, the amateur, and the hard-boiled private eye were handed down from older generations of mystery writers and, in the way of popular fiction, needed to be updated or abandoned. It is sobering to recall that Mickey Spillane was the best-selling detective writer of the 1950s. The police hero offered one way in which to make the mystery story contemporary. The development of a new kind of hero, a hero working with a squad or the team, also helped the cop novel gather some of its speed. In the cop books of the 1950s and 1960s the emphasis shifted away from the cerebral properties showcased in the traditional detective story to routine, to the mechanical and human procedures that were increasingly important in professional police work in the twentieth century. During the

Kantor's *Signal 32* is the first realistic novel about police work written by a police officer. Random House, 1950.

period cop novels grew from nothing to become a small eddy in the stream of mystery fiction. But they wouldn't stay that way for long.

MacKinlay Kantor

The police novel began, but not quite in earnest, in the 1950s. MacKinlay Kantor walked a beat in New York City from 1948 to 1950; before that he reported for the *Cedar Rapids Republican* and *Des Moines Tribune*, wrote a number of juvenile books and novels for adults, and served as a war correspondent with both the Royal Air Force and the U.S. Air Force. In 1950 he quit the cops and wrote *Signal Thirty-Two*.

Signal Thirty-Two is not a detective or a mystery story. It is a police novel, or, given the perspective of more than fifty years, one kind of police novel. In *Signal Thirty-Two* Kantor uses a skeletal morality play to present moral and immoral individuals (the good Joe Shetland and the corrupt "Blondie" Dunbar) and their interaction with an innocent young man (Dan Mallow) as a framework for a documentary on the lives and duties of ordinary patrolmen. That Kantor focuses on patrolmen, as opposed to detectives, is one of the most significant aspects of the book. Before Kantor everyone wrote about detectives, and his look at regular cops was as revolutionary in the 1950s as Wambaugh's look at regular cops would be in the 1970s. In *Signal Thirty-Two* Kantor gives a thick slice-of-life of the daily activities of the men of the 23rd Precinct of the New York Police Department, to whom he dedicated the novel.

Kantor devotes the largest part of that slice to describing the miscellaneous chaos connected to the average patrolman's day. Kantor divides the book into three sections (Late Tour, Day Tour, Four-to-Twelve), and the largest part of each of these sections involves presenting the number and variety of incidents and crimes that cops face daily. He does this in several ways. The novel begins at the precinct before roll call, with Joe Shetland silently doing a semi–stream of consciousness on each of the men in the squad (an ethnic mix—Garney, Seton, Kilmurvey, Capek, Meath, Calkins, Callaway, Vose, Prinz, Doone, Berner, Underhill, Kummer, Colligan, McCabe, Parino, Swaney, Covington, McFarland, Pappas, O'Toole, McGarrt, Flower, Quimby, Aaronson) and the kinds of things they have or will encounter on their tours of duty:

> Climb, climb, climb patrolman Doone: it's always on the top floor. The neighbors have their heads sticking out of the doorway. They are saying "In there! Isn't that terrible? He's hitting her again and breaking things up. Oh, I wish somebody would do something!" and so go slow, Doone, because you've got twenty-six years in the department and you've been dodging another exami-

nation of that bum pump of yours, and you're not very big anyway, and this man who has been beating up his fourteen year old daughter is a big guy and he's pretty hysterical now [9].

Then Kantor presents a day of riding in a patrol car in Sector Two with Joe Shetland and rookie Dan Mallow. The tour can hardly be called uneventful: They deal with a distraught child, a too-loud party, a disoriented driver from another state, an uninvited guest, and capture two rapists. Later in the novel Kantor slides in summary patches of the daily life of a patrolman: Shetland and Mallow notify the the wife of an accident fatality, mediate a domestic budget dispute, put out a fire, investigate a robbery, question a woman who has been abducted and forced into prostitution, and break up a dog fight (246). Kantor, then, devotes a significant portion of *Signal Thirty-Two* to making the point that the average policeman's life is very, very hectic, and that domestic incidents largely involving poor people comprise the majority of the "crime" these policemen encounter.

In addition to depicting police routine, *Signal Thirty-Two* also literally documents police procedure. While not yet into the alphabet of acronyms that would overtake coptalk shortly, the novel's title introduces readers to the world of police jargon — signal thirty-two means an officer needs assistance. In several places Kantor introduces facsimiles of official paperwork, and he quotes several passages from the actual NYPD manual.

Along with this documentation of the actual working life of the average police officer, Kantor tries to show the impact of police life on the individual cop. Cops, he tells readers, are manifestly underpaid. Shetland advises young Mallow where to buy used uniform shirts, the cops have to buy their own pistols and ammunition, and in the days before they were standard equipment, Mallow and Shetland go in together to buy a heater for their radio car. Kantor also briefly touches on the irrational uses of authority cops sometimes face. To avenge a slight and to assert his authority, their sergeant puts Shetland back on foot patrol because he found a mess (left by the previous shift) in the trunk of their radio car. Kantor also portrays a system that can be abused. Chiefly Blondie Dunbar demonstrates this. Dunbar cheats on examinations at the academy, sleeps during his patrol shift, commits petty thefts, solicits sexual favors while on the job, bribes his sergeant for a cushy assignment, and is undeservedly promoted to detective. In the morality framework of the novel, however, he receives his just desserts when Mallow forces him to confess one of his more egregious misdeeds and resign from the force.

Kantor also shows that police work occasionally brings cops into contact with sordid and brutal facts of life. In his opening review of his colleagues and their jobs, Shetland includes the following:

> Not that the place didn't smell like a son-of-a-bitch when he was alive, because
> he was sick and couldn't walk downstairs, so he kept going to the bathroom
> over in the corner.... That was before he got real sick ... and then he went to
> the bathroom in bed. (But now he has passed such demands of hideous emis-
> sions of the flesh, and is contributing his own private pungent personal odor
> to the assorted stenches that gathered around him before he died so caked, so
> wasted; though after forty-eight hours or so of post-mortal July heat he seems
> to be putting on a lot of weight.) [5]

That's the sordid. Here's the brutal:

> Still the stupid going-home pants presser was hauled into a doorway and kicked
> in the testicles.... Still milk bottles crashed on car hoods, still the thin-breasted
> girl-children whimpered as orgasm was rammed against them in unventilated
> bedrooms, still the babies were deserted.... Still tigers walked lashing their tails
> along the upper sectors ... there were more tigers than the law allowed, and
> not enough zoo-keepers to hold them mute and unravening [139].

To this world, Kantor's cops react with as much profanity as publishing norms of the time would allow (which isn't much), with racism ("spik"
is a usual epithet, along with fake Spanish-English), with very occasional
brutality ("If you don't want to get cut, and don't want to shoot anybody,
you've got to beat the shit out of them. That's better than killing a guy, isn't
it?" [37]), and with frustration. The most pointed example of this comes
with the battered spouse who has her husband arrested, and then refuses to
charge him in court. For the first time, too, Kantor touches on the stresses
put on a marriage by police work. Mostly, however, *Signal Thirty-Two* dwells
on duty.

Throughout the novel, Kantor makes the good cop/bad cop distinction. However, he puts more emphasis on Shetland and Mallow, the good
cops. In Shetland Kantor draws the reverse of Dunbar, the bad cop: after a
tragedy connected with a youthful romantic mistake, Shetland devotes his
life to the police force. Indeed, after Shetland's internal monologue about
the other men in his squad, Kantor concludes with "They would not know
his concern for them, his brothers, or his addiction to the grotesque life they
led" (16). Shetland acts as a mentor to Mallow and in the end he is killed
while he serves and protects. Shetland teaches Mallow the ins and outs of
police procedure, and the necessity for common sense and humanity in the
execution of their duty as cops. Kantor made Dan Mallow the paragon of
virtue and duty. We can see this in one of the little talks Mallow gives to
himself while on duty, in which he recalls his encounter with cops before he
joined the force: "They did not abuse, they did not bully or threaten. They
were grave and purposeful, and their very self-contained gravity had an
effect" (143). That's the kind of cop Mallow becomes. He does his duty,

risks his life, and he ignores the petty quirks and injustices of the institution he serves. But he cannot and does not ignore crime; that's why he forces Dunbar to turn himself in and resign at the end of the novel.

Kantor did a number of remarkable things in *Signal Thirty-Two*. He abandoned detectives and focused on the lives of beat cops. He moved from the big case to a welter of smaller cases, many of them domestic. He provided a wealth of details of ordinary police work based on his own experience as a police officer. He touched on many of the same themes Treat brought to *V as in Victim*: the role of partners, the storytelling, the difference between police and civilians, the temptations of the job, the bother of bureaucracy, etc. He added an overtly moral tone to the story about police and what they do. Finally, as seen in the stream of consciousness passages and the complex organization of the narrative, he tried to lift a story about the police out of popular fiction and move it into literary realms. In that he failed.

Hillary Waugh

Hillary Waugh had been writing detective novels since 1947, stories he would later call "private-eye-cute-young-couple novels" ("The Police Procedural," in *The Mystery Story*, John Ball ed., 163). Then he became a police writer. By his own account, true crime brought him to the police novel:

> I chanced upon a slim paperback entitled, *They All Died Young*. It was a collection of ten true murder cases in which the victims were young women.
> I went through the stories one by one, and was never the same thereafter. They had a vividness, a chilling horror to them that no fiction I had ever read or written could approach....
> ...I thereupon determined to write a fictional murder mystery that would sound as if it had really happened. Since it is not private eye–cute young couples who work real homicides, but sheriffs, police chiefs, and police detectives, this meant a totally new approach — by me at least — to the art of mystery writing [*The Mystery Story* 163–4].

The result was *Last Seen Wearing* (1952), followed by eleven novels about Chief Fred Fellows beginning with *Sleep Long, My Love* (1959). Then there are the three post–McBain books about New York City Detective Frank Sessions beginning with *"30" Manhattan East* (1968).

When he began, Waugh moved somewhat gingerly away from the conventions of the detective story. Up until *"30" Manhattan East* he uses small towns as his settings, makes his principal investigator a police chief as opposed to a working detective, and retains some of the light tone of the traditional golden age detective story in the occasional banter of his characters and the semi-comic irascibility of the main character, whether it is Chief

Frank Ford in *Last Seen Wearing* or Fred Fellows in *Sleep Long My Love*. Even in Waugh's later books he never moves far from traditional detective-story plotting. The immediacy Waugh found in reading his true crime book comes across in his introduction of violent sex crimes in his novels. Both *Last Seen Wearing* and *Sleep Long, My Love* involve murders committed because of illicit affairs. Illicit affairs may have been the submerged cause for murder in many earlier detective novels, but Waugh brings them out in the open. Additionally, he often couples sex crimes with the mutilated bodies of the female victims — the bloated corpse in the river in *Last Seen Wearing*, the headless, limbless body in *Sleep Long, My Love*, the shattered corpse on Harlem pavement in *The Young Prey* (1969).

Waugh uses devices in the novels to bring them closer to police than to "private eye–cute young couples" books. Thus the title of his first police novel comes from the routine wording of police bulletins — "last seen wearing." Waugh also uses specific dates and times as chapter headings — *Sleep Long*, for instance, goes from February 26, 1959, to March 13, 4:15 P.M. He inserts facsimiles of telegrams to the Erie, Pennsylvania, police in *Sleep Long*, and one of a supplementary complaint form in *"30" Manhattan East*. In the latter novel Waugh refers repeatedly to detectives filling out DD5 forms and supervisors reading them. During the course of the novels the police contact and receive information from police departments of other jurisdictions — and the FBI. Waugh also presents a believable impression of a small-town police station:

> It was early afternoon when Fellows got back to Stockford. Detective Sergeant Wilks was eating lunch at the chief's desk in the little office behind the main room, munching a sandwich and washing it down with coffee from a thermos when the chief came in.
> "You get coffee on my papers," Fellows said, "and I'll skin you."
> "Papers? You mean the crossword puzzle and the movie schedule and the circulars?"
> "I've got your pay reports there too." Fellows went to the chest-high windows that looked out onto the green from the ground level of the basement. The room was small with a rolltop desk and swivel chair, a wooden table, three glass-faced cabinets, a straight chair crowded in its confines. The walls were a neutral tan and decorated with a large collection of nude calendar girls in color" [*Sleep Long* 61–2].

And in the Frank Sessions books he gives relatively sanitized descriptions of NYPD squad rooms. As in *V as in Victim*, Waugh's policemen tell coptales — from the anecdote illustrating the stupidity of criminals in *Sleep Well* to the one about the cop who solved his big case by copying down all of the license plate numbers in the block in *"30" Manhattan*. These serve to illustrate an immediate point (that criminals are dumb, etc.) and to suggest the experience and workload of policemen in books that concentrate on narrating one significant case. While Chief Fellows is the main character, Waugh surrounds him with detectives and patrolmen (chiefly Wilks) to whom he gives names and who undertake some of the routine work. Rather than character, Waugh's most prominent point about police work lies in his emphasis on routine and details.

From the beginning Waugh's emphasis on routine focuses on sifting through bales of information, a procedure that often turns out to be fruitless. Thus the point made by observers in *Last Seen Wearing* when Chief Ford and his crew muck about in a drained lake is

> The two men did not press the matter and conceded that Ford, in his meticulous way, was merely taking advantage of the dry lake bed to make sure, lest the question later arise, that there was nothing there [67].

The emphasis on "meticulous" detail becomes even more apparent in *Sleep Long* when the police not only question lots of people but also wade through vehicle registrations ("873,000 cars in a population of two million. Over two thousand of them match the one we're after" [97]), dentists' patient records, and employment records of a number of out-of-town companies. After many such searches Chief Fellows decides on one even bigger:

> This is going to be a rough assignment, Sid, but we're going to catalogue every single office and working man in the Stockford area. He's a white-collar man, judging from the reports. We believe he's a salesman, but he could be anything, a lawyer, store clerk, pharmacist, possibly even a theater usher. It doesn't matter what he is, we're going to cover them all. We're going to get a list of employees from everybody who hires people in that area and we're going to check on all of them [*Sleep Long* 159].

Indeed, the discovery of the criminal in *"30" Manhattan East* turns on details—an incomplete autopsy done by a country physician and a thorough one done by the professionals in New York City. But routine does require something else. In *Last Seen Wearing*, on the matter of routine Chief Ford finds patience as the main feature of police work: "We're going to sit tight and wait and pretty soon, something's going to happen and we'll have her. That's what police business is all about" (86).

Waugh presents his small-town characters, chiefs Ford and Fellows, as hard-working, moderately good-natured men who participate (albeit minimally) in domestic life—in *Sleep Long* readers learn about Fellow's churchgoing habits. Fellows describes his job in terms of its social utility:

> Sure seventy percent of the murders go unsolved, and that's why there's so much murder. Every time the police have to throw in the sponge on a killing, it means the temptation for another man to kill is just a little stronger. Every

time a slayer gets caught and punished, it makes the temptation for others just a little less. Someone's life might be saved by our catching this man [*Sleep Long* 156].

The New York novels about Frank Sessions present a different picture. First of all, there are a lot more cops in every scene. And some of their conversations reflect cops' professional concerns, from their fear of the department issuing non-lethal weapons discussed in *"30" Manhattan East*, to the discussion about the reaction against cops caused by the rioting at the Democratic Convention of 1968, and the overriding concerns about the Miranda warnings that drive *The Young Prey*. On top of that, Frank Sessions is a much darker character—more from the hard-boiled tradition than a middle-class guy doing a job. Waugh depicts him as a loner and a callous womanizer. While *"30" Manhattan East* introduces a cast of suspects that could have inhabited a golden age novel, Waugh brings shocking details into the novel. A policewoman does a body cavity search of the murder victim, and Waugh gives a semidetailed description of an autopsy, a feature that would soon become a convention of the police novel. Indeed, in the New York books, written well over a decade after Waugh started the police novel in small-town Connecticut, the barbarians and libertarians—as well as hippies and "fags"—have taken over. The title, characters, and plot of *The Young Prey* reinforce this view. And the cops in the New York books complain repeatedly about the lack of public support for "law and order." Countering this, Waugh's NYPD characters attain heroic stature more than in the earlier novels. Thus there are officers like Joseph Sullivan:

> Lt. Joseph Xavier Sullivan, commanding officer of the homicide squad, came in at half past seven. He was a tall, square-built man in his early forties who weighed a rock-ribbed two-twenty and looked as if he could still make the Fordham football team. His hair was graying, his clothes were as well cared for as Frank Sessions' own, and he had a wife and two young daughters in a home on Long Island. This was a man who moved carefully among the public as if aware that the image of the homicide squad and the police department were in his care [*"30" Manhattan* 111].

And there is the average copper:

> In the police business you had to arrest people—sometimes dangerous people. You had to take risks and go forward where the average man hung back. A policeman wouldn't watch out the window while Kitty Genovese was being stabbed to death. A policeman wouldn't turn away because he might otherwise get involved or might get hurt [*"30" Manhattan* 136].

After the Frank Sessions books Waugh returned to writing more mainstream detective stories. He earned the label of "father of the police procedural," but this was a role that he surrendered in the mid–1950s. What

Waugh did was emphasize the routine nature of some of the tasks that form the basis of police work. However, by limiting himself to small-town cops in the 1950s, Waugh did not investigate the characteristics of urban police work and the urban police officer that were to become the driving forces of the cop novel for the remainder of the century. A bit later Ed McBain did.

Jack Webb

The year that Waugh published *Last Seen Wearing* also saw the debut of the two Jack Webbs. The famous one brought his *Dragnet* show to television in 1952. The other Jack Webb wrote fifteen novels between 1952 and 1964. They all have suggestive titles — like *The Big Sin* (1952), *The Naked Angel* (1953), *The Bad Blonde* (1957) — and their paperback issues have semi-salacious cover art showing blondes exposing a bit of leg and a hint of cleavage. In this respect, the stories Webb tells don't deliver. They may contain leggy, even romantically aggressive blondes, but they never go into the bedroom. What they do deliver, over the space of a hundred pages or so, is a narrative that switches back and forth from bad guys doing various nefarious things (kidnapping, making dope, stealing diamonds, etc.) to some of the doings of the Los Angeles Police Department Homicide Squad, but especially to the action of Webb's two heroes.

Webb presents various kinds of cops in his novels. First come the conventional, older officers like the boss, Captain Cantrell:

> Captain William Averell Cantrell at fifty-one years of age had reached a point toward which he had been steadily slogging since the day thirty-three years ago when for the first time he had buttoned on a blue uniform, picked up a heavy oak night-stick, and set out to walk a beat [*Broken Doll* 34].

To a lesser extent there is Lieutenant Allison's type:

> Allison had been on the Vice Squad for fifteen years. A rock. A lot of interests had tried to get rid of him. Big money interests. Not even the Gough regime had been able to shake him loose though there had been some talk [*Broken Doll* 96].

And there is also Schwartz:

> Schwartz was a harness bull of the old school, the only man left on the force who had walked the South Central beat alone. There was talk of a confession he had got out of a naked stumblebum with a thick closed door between him and his wire coat hanger [*Deadly Sex* 71].

Then there are the younger cops upon whom Webb concentrates in his novels:

G2403
SIGNET 40¢ BOOKS

THE SIZZLING THRILLER BY JACK WEBB
THE BAD BLONDE

A SIGNET BOOK
Complete and Unabridged

Above and on following page: Jack Webb (John Farr) and Jonathan Craig provided police heroes for paperback readers of the 1950s and 1960s. Webb, Signet, 1956; Craig, Belmont, 1973.

BT
BELMONT
TOWER
BT50581
CDC
95¢

The Case of the Beautiful Body

Jonathan Craig

SHE WAS BEAUTIFUL
AND SHE WAS DEAD—
NOW DETECTIVE SELBY
HAD TO LEARN JUST HOW
BAD SHE HAD BEEN.

A Pete Selby
Stan Rayder
Detective Thriller

Lean, angular, redhead Dan Adams, and stocky, dark-haired Sammy Golden, two young men, working their way through the middle thirties, nice guys, the kind you'd like for a neighbor, whether like Adams you had a pretty wife, a couple of kids, and a veteran's loan on three bedrooms, one-and-one-quarter baths, and just enough lawn to keep you busy on your day off, or whether, like Golden, you walked alone, three flights up to a bachelor apartment. Two personable young men well on their way to becoming experts in violent death [*Broken Doll* 12].

Red Adams is a hard-working, intelligent police officer. Samuel Elijah Golden is the unconventional one. He is single, Jewish, and a loose cannon. Webb makes him something of the hard-boiled detective in policeman's clothing. Golden drives Captain Cantrell nuts because of his frequent expeditions into trouble, and Webb notes that Golden, dragging his partner down with him, frequently gets flopped back into uniform for infractions of departmental rules. Golden, in fact, has two partners — one on the force, and Father Shanley, a young Roman Catholic priest.

In all the novels coincidence brings the old friends, priest and cop, together. While the conjunction opens lots of possibilities for discussion of morality, of law, of crime, of vocation, and of human nature, Webb ignores them in the rush of his short books. The impact of the friendship of Golden and Shanley resides first in the thriller plotting advantage of having one save the other at the end of the action. The more prominent impact, though, is on characters on the periphery of crime. Webb presents characters who might become criminals, but because of the intervention of Shanley and Golden are able to step back into normal lives. This often happens because they ignore or circumvent normal police procedures. Instead of following the path that the infant form of the police novel was taking, Webb used the trappings of police work to decorate what are essentially hard-boiled stories, more concerned with the largest concerns of justice than the immediate concerns that preoccupy police officers and police departments.

Jonathan Craig

Jonathan Craig wrote ten novels about NYPD detectives Pete Selby and Stan Rayder from 1955 to 1966. Although the mildly prurient intent of the paperback covers suggests that the books are less than serious accounts of police officers and police work, Craig is very serious about cops and what they do. Stan Rayder, a less experienced homicide detective, acts as partner, assistant and gofer for Selby, the narrator of Craig's Sixth Precinct series. In *The Case of the Beautiful Body* (1957) one of the suspects tells Selby and Rayder that "New York cops are the best in the world" (114) and in *Dead Darling* we learn that the Missing Persons Bureau of the NYPD "sometimes performs feats that are little short of miraculous"(47). Like *Dragnet* on the radio and then on TV, Craig's books are police panegyrics, books that accept and document the dedication and efficiency of the police by presenting heroes who are paragons and depicting modern police procedure. And even though Craig's books are short paperback originals, he manages to pack a great deal of police procedure into them. The second paragraph of *The Case of the Beautiful Body*, for example, takes readers immediately into the cops' world:

> According to the UF61 form we'd picked up from the desk office on our way through the muster room, the squeal appeared to be an H&R, a homicide-and-rape [5].

Here Craig gets paperwork, the police station, coptalk, and cop classification into one sentence. Indeed, Craig's intent is to familiarize his readers with the workings of the New York City Police Department. He explains how cases are assigned:

> In New York City, despite the large number of specialized squads and bureaus — including several homicide squads — the sole responsibility for the investigation of whether a petit larceny or a homicide rests with the precinct detectives catching the squeal. Precinct detectives may call on any or all of the other units of the department for assistance, and they may ask for and receive the assignment of as many as two hundred other detectives to help them check out suspects and leads — but both the initial and ultimate responsibility for the case is theirs alone [*The Case of the Beautiful Body* 19].

Craig drops in material on crime statistics — "Rape is, after all, a very common crime, and the incidence is much greater than is generally supposed" (*The Case of the Beautiful Body* 27); on how the BCI, Bureau of Criminal Identification, works; on interrogation technique — "Evasions are sometimes necessary; otherwise the person being interrogated reacts emotionally to such a degree that questioning him effectively becomes almost impossible" (*The Case of the Beautiful Body* 41); and on the legal role of the medical examiner. Although his books use one-case plots, he does attempt to portray the press of work on the cops by inserting brief mention of past cases and by briefly showing other cops working on other cases.

Craig shows his heroes having a few light moments. Selby and Rayder occasionally engage in mock verbal sparring, and in *The Case of the Beautiful Body* the men in the squad room derive some dubious humor from the idea of vasectomies. In the main, however, Craig shows them as serious men. Thus when Selby interrogates a suspect who speaks like a beatnik, the detective reproves him for his speech and makes him respond in standard English. And Selby does not like to hear about cooping (sleeping on the job) even in jest. Selby alludes to the fact that even while in training he did extra reading on police science. Craig compounds all of this by having his detectives work on serious and shocking cases, usually involving at least the suspicion of rape attached to murder. He makes Sergeant Barney Fells the model that Selby and Rayder follow:

> He'd made his job not only his life work but his life itself. He'd worked long hours, and slept short ones and gone back to work again; and he had, even before he was forty, become something of a legend [*The Case of the Beautiful Body* 69].

But it is not simply Fells' hard work that makes him a detective, it is his passion for justice, especially for the dispossessed: "I used to do something about it. The ones nobody else cared about were the ones I cared about the most. I used to work on them on my own time, and I didn't give a good goddamn whether they were somebody else's squeal or not" (*The Case of the Beautiful Body* 70–71).

Ed McBain

One of Ed McBain's advantages is that when he turned to writing police stories he had not served an apprenticeship as a detective story writer, as had Treat and Waugh. Ed McBain's, or Evan Hunter's, first book was the best-selling *Blackboard Jungle* (1954), a novel drawn from his experiences as a high school teacher. He, therefore, had not practiced writing according to the prescriptions of the golden age novel popularized by Howard Haycraft and other critics of the 1940s and '50s or by Ellery Queen's various enterprises. Also, unlike Waugh, who denied having been influenced by Jack Webb's radio and television program *Dragnet*—in 1976 Waugh wrote that "no procedural writer I have talked to points to *Dragnet* as a source of inspiration" (*Mystery Story* 165), McBain hinted at *Dragnet*'s influence on his police books by peppering his early ones with references to Joe Friday and Frank Smith, the television program's detectives. Additionally, McBain, from 1956 to 1959, wrote for a different form and, presumably, different audience than did Treat and Waugh—before 1959, like Webb and Craig, McBain wrote paperbacks. And all of his early books are short. McBain's first police book is one hundred and fifty pages long and his early books rarely exceed one hundred and sixty pages. So, when McBain wrote *Cop Hater* (1956), he was able to do new things with the infant form of the police novel.

McBain is most famous for ensemble characterization. In Otto Penzler's *The Great Detectives*, in retrospect he describes his intent:

> The original concept ... was to use a squadroom full of detectives as a conglomerate hero. I would try to portray accurately the working day of a big-city cop, but I would do so in terms of a handful of men whose diverse personal-

The cover of Ed McBain's first book moves from sensationalism to echoes of *Dragnet*. Pinnacle, 1956.

ities and character traits, when combined, would form a single hero — the 87th Precinct. To my knowledge, this had never been done before, and I felt it was unique [90–91].

Part of McBain's aim may have been creating the collective hero, but part of it was also his desire to keep the thing going, to create a series of books; thus he continues the interview with Penzler by adding that "the concept would enable me to bring new men into the squadroom as needed, adding their particular qualities or defects to the already existing mix, while at the same time disposing of characters who no longer seemed essential." One can see this in *Cop Hater*, where McBain introduces Steve Carella, Bert Kling, and Lieutenant Byrnes early on, and then brings in and characterizes Hal Willis near the novel's conclusion. At any rate, during the 1950s McBain introduces and forms action for his major players — first Carella, Kling, Byrnes, and Willis, then Meyer Meyer, Arthur Brown, and finally Cotton Hawes. They are stereotypes. And as much as he would like readers or critics to believe that he wanted a collective hero for his books, Detective Steve Carella takes over the role of hero in almost all of the 87th Precinct books. McBain created Carella as the all-American hero — handsome, rugged, smart, honest, romantic. Here's his first appearance:

> He was a big man, but not a heavy one. He gave the impression of great power, but the power was not a meaty one. It was, instead, a fine-honed muscular power. He wore his brown hair short. His eyes were brown, with a peculiar downward slant that give him a clean-shaved Oriental appearance. He had wide shoulders and narrow hips, and he managed to look well dressed and elegant even when dressed in a leather jacket [*Cop Hater* 7].

In making his love interest, Teddy, a deaf mute, McBain emphasizes Carella's devotion to nurturing and protecting innocence. Indeed he becomes even more the all–American when he marries Teddy and they have twins. While Carella is the hero, Bert Kling is the novice — McBain introduces him as a patrolman in *Cop Hater* and later promotes him to detective. Cotton Hawes is the lover, Meyer Meyer is the borsht belt comedian, and Arthur Brown is the 1950s ideal African American.

While he deals in stereotypes, one of McBain's major achievements was in introducing not just a group but the first ethnically diverse group of cops — white, black, Jewish, Hispanic. Before Chester Himes' Grave Digger and Coffin Ed hit the streets of Harlem in 1957, McBain had created two black detectives — or the same black detective twice. David Foster in *Cop Hater* is the first draft for Arthur Brown:

> And packed into this rectangle — North and South from the river to the park, East and West for thirty-five blocks — was a population of 90,000 people.
> David Foster was one of those people.

David Foster was a Negro.

He had been born in the precinct territory, and he had grown up there, and when he'd turned 21, being of sound mind and body, being four inches over the minimum requirement of five feet eight inches, having 20/20 vision without glasses, and not having any criminal record, he had taken the competitive Civil Service examination and had been appointed as a patrolman.

The starting salary at the time had been $3,725 per annum, and Foster had earned his salary well. He had earned it so well that in the space of five years he had been appointed to the Detective Division. He was now a 3rd Grade Detective, and his salary was now $5,239 per annum, and he still earned it well [9–10].

Foster is one of the cops killed in *Cop Hater*, but McBain reincarnates him in Arthur Brown. McBain's concept of Brown comes out in *Fuzz* (1970):

Detective Arthur Brown did not like being called black.

This might have had something to do with his name, which was Brown. Or his color, which was also brown. Or it might have had something to do with the fact that when he was but a mere strip of a boy coming along in this fair city, the word "black" was linked alliteratively with the word "bastard." He was now thirty-four years old and somewhat old-fashioned, he supposed, but he still considered the word derogatory, no matter how many civil rights leaders endorsed it. Brown didn't need to seek identity in his color or his soul. He searched for it in himself as a man, and usually found it there with ease [153].

McBain doesn't just add an African American to the squad, he also brings in a Hispanic detective. In *The Heckler* (1960) he emphasizes Detective Frankie Hernandez's ethnicity as well as his struggle for acceptance as a person:

For the most part, Frankie Hernandez was a highly respected man. He came out of the streets in one of the city's hottest delinquency areas, carrying the albatross of "cultural conflict" about his youthful neck, breaking through the "language barrier" (only Spanish was spoken in his home when he was a child) and emerging from the squalor of the slums to become a Marine hero in the Second World War, and later a patrolman ironically assigned to the streets which had bred him. He was a Detective 3rd Grade. It had been a long hard pull, and the battle still hadn't been won — not for Frankie Hernandez, it hadn't. Frankie Hernandez, you see, was fighting for a cause. Frankie Hernandez was trying to prove to the world at large that the Puerto Rican guy could also be the good guy [39–40].

Meyer Meyer, as McBain's repeated descriptions assert, had fought the racial prejudice fight, growing up in a gentile neighborhood with a funny name to boot. McBain's point in all of these characters resides in his insistence that race or creed make no difference to these men. They are all man, and they are all cops. And as McBain increasingly illustrates in his books, their fundamental characteristics are those of middle-class working men.

Although he found it a hard go, in the first book Carella thinks about hav- ing read James Joyce's *Ulysses*. That kind of highbrow thing disappears from the books pretty quickly. By the time of *Ax* (1964) Hawes and Carella have a three-page discussion of the movie *The Locusts* that ends with:

> "And the hero?"
> "Oh, he's been around on television. I forgot his name, too." Hawes hesi- tated. "Actually the locusts were the stars of the picture."
> "Yeah," Carella said.
> "Yeah. They had one scene where there must have been eight million locusts hopping all over everybody. I wonder how they got that scene."
> "There probably was a locust trainer," Carella said.
> "Oh, sure.
> "I saw a picture called *The Ants* once," Carella said.
> "How was it?"
> "Pretty good. It sounds a little like *The Locusts*..." [35].

The Locusts is scarcely *Ulysses*. The cops of the 87th Precinct squad tell stu- pid jokes, complain about their salaries, and razz one another about girl- friends and wives. Most fundamentally, though, McBain shows their middle-class virtues in the idea of families. In the middle of *Killer's Choice* (1958), in fact, McBain shifts scenes from Meyer's family dinner, to Lt. Byrne's family dinner, to Bert Kling and Claire Townsend's after-dinner necking, and in each home Steve Carella's wounding is the topic of conver- sation. It's families talking about family.

That McBain's cops are hardworking goes without saying. They're always on the job — on the streets or, occasionally, pushing paper. The 3:00 A.M. call from the precinct is a commonplace in the novels. And they always have too much to do: "The precinct, in all truth, could have used a hun- dred and sixteen detectives and even then been understaffed" *Cop Hater* (9). This point is also one of the things McBain learned to convey through his plotting, indicating through several devices that police work consists of a barrage of cases all at the same time. McBain's cops are clean-cut and they are honest, scrupulously honest. He does occasionally acknowledge that police corruption exists:

> If you're a cop, you know all about graft.
> You know that if somebody is "taking," it is usually the senior man on the beat who later splits with the other men who share the beat on a rotating basis. You know this because you also know there is nothing that can screw things up like a plentitude of cops with outstretched hands. When too many hands are reaching, the sucker may suddenly decide that he is really being taken but good, and one fine day the desk sergeant will receive a call from someone [*Ax* 58].

Carella and his colleagues at the 87th, however, are models of rectitude. Repeatedly throughout the novels McBain presents examples of this:

> Carella didn't bother answering him [the bartender]. He finished his beer and was reaching into his pocket for his wallet when the bartender said, "It's on the house, officer."
> "I'd rather pay for it, thanks," Carella said [*Ax* 50].

Indeed, even with the issue of police brutality, McBain places the blame on the public rather than the individual or the system. Thus Detective Roger Haviland, killed in *Killer's Choice*, began as a kind individual ("a nice-type happy-guy smiling faced cop," *Killer's Choice* 47) until being beat up by a gang. After that, elliptically,

> As far as he was concerned, they could all go out and. Every last one of them could go and. Their mothers could go and. Their fathers could go and.... Everybody could go and. In Macy's window.
> It was unfortunate.
> A lot of people suffered because of what a half dozen kids did to Roger Haviland a long time ago [*Killer's Choice* 48].

Unlike Haviland — who comes to be disliked by all of the members of the squad — McBain's other characters don't rough up suspects or prisoners. In fact, in *Killer's Choice* Hawes says he has never seen a prisoner mistreated.

McBain shows his cops doing their job. Their job involves going from place to place — often unpleasant places:

> Cops, too, are cops. They are used to tenements. They are used to entering dimly lit hallways and seeing broken mailboxes. They are used to garbage cans stacked on the ground floor, and narrow steps leading to each landing of the multiple dwelling. They are used to the smells of the tenement and the sounds of the tenement [*Killer's Choice* 76].

They are used to unpleasant people, too. McBain's cops conduct short interviews with terse answers — the form most suited to the one hundred and sixty pages of McBain's books. It's hardly brain surgery and it's hardly the stuff that occupies the heroes of the mystery or detective story. McBain repeatedly makes this point. Meyer Meyer in *The Heckler* says "I don't read mysteries. They only make me feel stupid" (13) and in *Ax* Carella says "If there's one thing I can't stand, it's puzzles" (99). In the 1990s McBain's characters express the same view but in zestier language:

> "What the fuck's the Orient Express?" Parker asked.
> "You know, Agatha Christie."
> "Who the fuck's that, Agatha Christie?" [*Windows* 218].

McBain's cops are average men who do routine things. He makes Detective Bush the spokesman for this reality in the first novel:

All you need to be a detective is a strong pair of legs, and a stubborn streak. The legs take you around to various dumps you have to go to, and the stubborn streak keeps you from quitting. You follow each separate trail mechanically, and if you're lucky, one of the trails pays off. If you're not lucky, it doesn't. Period [*Cop Hater* 15].

If police work isn't pounding the pavement, it's shuffling paper. In *Killer's Payoff* Hawes thinks to himself that "Police work is simply getting everything in triplicate" (112). While McBain does not show his cops doing much paperwork in the 1950s and 1960s, he lets his readers see a whole lot of it. Even the smallest occasion prompts McBain to drop a facsimile into his novels. In *Cop Hater* there's a pistol license application, a ballistics report, an autopsy report, Carella's worksheet, a criminal record card (an item McBain would later label IB report); in *The Heckler* there's a room drawing, a lab report, an evidence tag (front and back), a case report, a complaint desk report, and a ferry schedule; in *Killer's Payoff* there's an identification bureau record, a central complaint desk report, a bank book page, a check, a gasoline charge receipt, and a map. Some of them sprawl across two pages. A lot of the time these bits of verisimilitude do not play much of a role in solving the cases. That's not their principal function. McBain includes the facsimiles as another means of creating the impression of detailed realism. For the same reason, at the opening of every book McBain tells his readers that "the police routine is based on established investigatory techniques."

On top of creating an ensemble of vivid middle-class characters for his police heroes, McBain did several other things upon which his success rested. Maybe the most important of these is his plotting. First of all, he did not write detective or mystery novels — his are not whodunits. He dispenses with most of the machinery of the detective story that depends on inserting clues about the villain's identity and often just brings the bad guy in at the end of the story — as the conclusion to the work that the cops had done. Just as importantly, McBain's books are hardly novels. They're long short stories — sometimes two short stories combined. This affects pace, but it also acknowledges that while police routine and details are important, they can also be pretty mundane. And so he found means of indicating these things in capsule form — the facsimiles, the beginning allusion to cases in progress, etc. Within the very short space of his novels McBain attempts to display the reality of police work in his plots by including or alluding to more than one action: sometimes he runs two cases throughout his books, and sometimes he has characters make capsule comments on their cases while the main case occupies the focus of the novel. In addition to plotting, McBain differs from earlier writers in his tone. In all the books he develops a rapport by speaking directly to the readers — with "you." Along with this there are passages of sarcastic wit — indeed, in *Cop Hater* we learn that "Sarcasm is the weapon of the intellectual" (56). With this weapon McBain encourages readers' sympathetic understanding of policemen and what policemen do.

McBain sets his books in a fictional locale; even though Isola bears many resemblances to New York City, McBain insists that it is not. It's a parallel universe, or perhaps a not-so- parallel universe, because in it, even though they mirror some of their qualities, McBain's policemen are ultimately exempt from some of the inevitabilities that affect the lives and the work of real cops.

Chester Himes

The next cops on the scene after McBain lived in a world far away from the 87th Precinct. Chester Himes' cops lived and worked in Harlem. Himes knew about cops from the other side. In 1928 he was arrested for armed robbery in Cleveland and sentenced to twenty-five years in the Ohio State Penitentiary. In stir, schooled by hard-boiled fiction, he made himself a writer.

> When I could see the end of my time inside I bought myself a typewriter and taught myself touch typing. I'd been reading stories by Dashiell Hammett in *Black Mask* and I thought I could do them just as well [Reilly 452].

Released in 1938, Himes became a part of the American literary scene when he went into voluntary exile in Paris in 1953. In Paris Marcel Duhamel, the translator of Himes' *If He Hollers Let Him Go*, suggested that he write a detective novel. This became *A Rage in Harlem* (1957) and introduced two New York police detectives — Grave Digger Jones and Coffin Ed Johnson. Living in Paris, Himes didn't have a lot of current knowledge about American police and police forces, but he did have his memories of being severely beaten by the cops in Cleveland and Cleveland Heights when he was arrested in 1928, and he had the models of the hard-boiled heroes he found in *Black Mask* — as well as the French enthusiasm for things noir.

Unlike white police writers, Himes writes about a community not just threatened by, but awash in crime. He shows some of this from the police perspective when Lieutenant Anderson reviews the day's homicide reports with Coffin Ed and Gravedigger in *Cotton Comes to Harlem* (ellipses Himes'):

> He leafed through the reports, reading charges: "Man kills his wife with an axe for burning his breakfast pork chop ... man shoots another man demonstrating a recent shooting he had witnessed ... man stabs another man for spilling beer on his new suit ... man kills self in a bar playing Russian roulette with a .32 revolver ... woman stabs man in stomach fourteen times, no reason given ... woman scalds neighboring woman with pot of boiling water for speaking to her husband ... man arrested for threatening to blow up subway train because he entered the wrong station and couldn't get his token back..." [14–15].

Ed and Digger know all about this. As black men and as policemen they understand the reality and hypocrisy of the system:

> We've got the highest crime rate on earth among the colored people in Harlem. And there ain't but three things to do about it: make the criminals pay for it — you don't want to do that; pay the people enough to live decently — you ain't going to do that; so all that's left is let 'em eat one another up [*Cotton* 14].

The only alternative open to the cops, then, is "make criminals pay for it." Here Himes' heroes face a predicament. The bureaucrats officially and publicly oppose what would come to be known as "excessive force": "The commissioner feels there must be some way to curtail crime besides brute force" (*Cotton* 14). As a consequence of this official stance, Ed and Digger receive repeated reprimands and suspensions for using excessive force from the big bosses — but notably not the precinct bosses. But in Himes brutality comes in different forms. There is good brutality and bad brutality. The bad kind comes from the white cops: "It's the white men on the force who commit the pointless brutality" (*Cotton* 14). The good kind comes from Detectives Jones and Johnson. Their brutality has a point.

From the first novel, Himes describes his detectives as big, country men — they look like "two hog farmers on a weekend in the Big Town" (*Cotton* 13). In Harlem they have a reputation as very, very dangerous men. Thus

> Coffin Ed had killed a man for breaking wind. Grave Digger had shot both eyes out of a man who was holding a loaded automatic. The story was in Harlem that these two black detectives would kill a man in his coffin if he so much as moved [*All Shot Up* 32].

Before it became current street language, Mammy Louise couples Ed and Digger's dangerousness with their roles as cops when, as they leave her place, she says "You can't stop dem from goin' nowhere. Them is de mens'" (*All Shot Up* 21). But Ed and Digger's meanness has more basis than just gossip and reputation. While Coffin Ed is the more violent of the two because of the injury he received in *A Rage in Harlem*, they both operate on the premise that "These colored hoodlums had no respect for colored cops unless you beat it into them or blew them away" (*Cotton* 31). And so they routinely beat up both witnesses and suspects. In *All Shot Up*, for example, after the white cops have failed to find out anything from the witnesses in the Paris Bar, Ed and Digger enter and systematically beat up the witnesses until they come up with useful information. Caught between the official censure of brutality as a police technique and the reality of policing the ghetto, Ed and Digger's boss, Lieutenant Anderson, insofar as he can, lets his two star detectives operate, essentially, as hard-boiled private eyes from the thirties and forties would. In fact, Himes shows Jones and Johnson acting like private eyes in the way he concludes the action and resolves the confusion in the plots. Unlike Jackson's notion in *A Rage in Harlem* that "As soon as colored folks got on the side of the law, they lost all Christian charity" (10), Ed and Digger effect private justice. Part of this Himes demonstrates in the way Digger and Ed approach traditional police corruption:

> They took their tribute, like all real cops, from the established underworld catering to the essential needs of the people — game-keepers, madams, street-walkers, numbers writers, numbers bankers. But they were rough on purse snatchers, muggers, burglars, con men, and all strangers working any racket [*A Rage* 49].

Himes' two detectives both pursue bad people and undertake superficially illegal acts that benefit the community. Thus at the end of *All Shot Up* Ed and Digger give the villain's ill-gotten money to charity, and at the end of *Cotton Comes to Harlem* Himes shows the old rag picker living in luxury in Africa.

Himes' books are not police books but rather books about Harlem, books told in the fashion of African American folk tales with clever exaggerations and chuckles at the absurdity of life. Thus in *Cotton Comes to Harlem* Himes narrates the church lady walking down the street with the back of her dress removed by a cutpurse, and in *All Shot Up* he puts in the tale of the tire escaping from the auto parts thief. Grave Digger and Coffin are part of all of this. Through them, nonetheless, Himes makes small but emphatic points about police, their corporate behavior, and their relationship with the African American community.

Elizabeth Linington

By the 1960s McBain's formula began to spread. Starting in the 1960s Elizabeth Linington began writing police novels under a variety of aliases. As Dell Shannon she wrote thirty-five between 1960 and 1984, as Lesley Egan she wrote twenty-four between 1961 and 1984, and as Anne Blaisdell she cranked out twelve more between 1962 and 1983. There are a lot of them. They all struggle to be pedestrian.

In her books Linington introduces a lot of cops. Many of them play subsidiary roles in the novels: helpers, functionaries, yes-men like Piggott, Palliser, Goldberg, Higgins, Dwyer, Galeano, Landers, and Hackett, and other detectives in the Dell Shannon books. Middle class men to a one, they work hard, and, the narrator tells us explicitly, do not even use foul language when put under stress. The women characters, like Philippa O'Neill, eagerly type out the men's reports and jump at the chance to get married and quit the force. Linington's cops are squeaky clean — they get search warrants before entering private property, and they never lift a finger against suspects or prisoners. There's no police brutality in Linington's L.A.— not even against the indigent or African Americans or Hispanics. "You've got some funny ideas about us, Lee. We don't beat up people these days. Not colored people or white people — or even Martians" (*Death* 461). In the Leslie Egan books, the two principal detectives, O'Connor and Varallo, are middle-class men like their subordinates who, when they are not preoccupied with their jobs, center their attention on their wives and families. Writing as Dell Shannon, however, Linington also adds an anachronistic figure in her main policeman, Lt. Luis Mendoza. He is the great detective from the golden age tradition. As Shannon tells it, after growing up in the L.A. barrio Mendoza inherited a fortune from his grandfather and lives in high style — fancy cars, fancy house, fancy everything. He also has a wife, children, and cats. Linington makes Mendoza into the master of police technique and routine and she also gifts him with piercing insight into what he calls the "nuances" of crimes and criminals. Thus the Shannon books combine two or more plots, one of which demonstrates the operations of routine police work, and the other spotlighting Mendoza's gifts.

Linington makes no secret that one of her roles is to promote the Los Angeles Police Department. Going off the air in 1959, the year before Linington entered the police novel business, Jack Webb's televised *Dragnet* served as an inspiration. LAPD badge 714 sits in the center of the cover of the Bantam paperback edition of Linington's *Streets of Death*. Badge 714 was Joe Friday's badge number. Indeed, Linington acknowledges this in *The Mark of Murder* where a Miss Webb tells Mendoza that "I used to be crazy about *Dragnet*. It surely made out you're a real crack police force" (424). And Linington more than agrees with *Dragnet*'s promotion of the LAPD. In the same book the narrator says

> The city [Los Angeles] had tripled in population in the last ten years; the chief was clamoring for more money to hire more cops. The city was policing a territory ten times the size of New York City with a quarter as many cops, and the city had the top police force in the world [*Mark* 387].

Like McBain, one of Linington's purposes is to show readers the torrent of cases the police must deal with every day. She not only uses the capsule summary — the paragraph that lists all of the crimes on the day's blotter — but, as mentioned above, also multiple plots. In a couple of cases, such as *Streets of Death* and *Scenes of Crime*, Linington wraps a number of brief accounts of crimes committed and solved within a framing account of a long and protracted case. She portrays really busy cops. They, likewise, make use of routine — boring, wearing, routine — to identify and track down the bad guys. In *The Root of All Evil*, for instance, one of the clues is that the rapist drove a particular kind of truck, so early in the book

> they were going through the list, gleaned from the D.M.V. records from Sacramento, of all such trucks registered in L.A. County. No guarantee that the right one was on the list, no guarantee that the right one was registered in L.A. County. But it was quite a list and was taking time and manpower to go through. If it didn't turn up anything interesting, then they'd ask Sacramento for wider coverage and start over again [*Root of All Evil* 6].

Periodically through the book Linington describes the detectives pouring over these and other lists in order to identify the rapist.

While earlier writers clearly viewed the police as the protectors of society, with Linington this view darkens and she sees perverse forces at work in America: "The weakened moral fiber, relaxation of standards, all the easy welfare, bread and circuses — and the pornography" (*Streets of Death* 173). She sees it as a recapitulation of the Cities of the Plain — the end of civilization. And she sees this as both abetted and accelerated by "do-gooders" as well as by "unrealistic judges, and all those silly people who want to set up a Police Board of civilians to watch over us" (*Death* 520).

Unheralded and unappreciated, the police officer stands against this chaos:

> The police were the barrier, he thought, between the honest citizens and the dirt. The incredible muck at the bottom of things. The average citizen saw the police in the person of the neat-uniformed traffic officer, white-gloved, his gun neatly sheathed at his hip. The average honest citizen hadn't any remote conception how very dirty the bottom of things was, that the police had to probe, getting down in the muck themselves to do so [*Root of All Evil* 46].

It was Linington's good fortune, then, that she could conceive of and create a world in which good, honest, hardworking policemen could keep the barbarians at the gates and go home at night to their wives and their neat suburban homes.

E.V. Cunningham

The seething tensions of the early 1960s between the U.S. and the Soviet Union caused best-selling writer Howard Fast to turn not to a secret agent, as had Ian Fleming a decade earlier, but to a cop. In 1962 Fast, writing as E.V. Cunningham, introduced one of the ubiquitous fictional cops named Clancy in *Phyllis*. *Phyllis* turns on a plot by anti-nuke scientists to force disarmament by threatening to detonate atomic devices in New York and Moscow. The assembled brain power of the New York cops and the Feds select homicide detective Tom Clancy to go undercover and find the missing rogue American scientist:

Fifteen days before I had been Detective Sergeant Thomas Clancy of the New York City Police, attached to homicide, with the reputation, beneficial and otherwise, of being an intelligent cop on his way up. Five feet, eleven inches, one hundred and seventy pounds, blue eyes, brown hair, and a college education, I was frequently reminded that I had a considerable future [27].

Clancy appreciates good police work, and Cunningham inserts brief mention of efficient shadowing and other aspects of the cop's job. Cunningham, however, endows Clancy with other traits, and in so doing takes him outside of the development of the cop novel. Thus, not only did he have a college education, but before he joined the force Clancy taught physics, and in *Phyllis* the bosses call on him to take on an undercover assignment teaching physics at a college in New York City. Because of his experiences in the war and the loss of his wife to leukemia, the hero is passionately opposed to nuclear weapons. With this educated, principled, and romantic hero, Cunningham introduces the clash-of-culture theme (a theme that would be fully developed in the 1970s and 1980s) when Clancy works with a Russian investigator in New York. Cunningham also leans heavily on the theme of thick-headed bureaucrats versus the intelligent and principled individual. Indeed, at the close of the novel the police commissioner perversely turns Clancy over to the rubber hose squad, which brutally debriefs him from his assignment. The hero's liberation in *Phyllis* comes both in the growth of his love for the title character and from his decision to quit the department.

Robert Fish

Robert L. Fish, writing as Robert L. Pike, created two American police heroes, Lieutenant Clancy (in three novels beginning with *Mute Witness* in 1963), and Lieutenant Jim Reardon (in four novels beginning with *Reardon* in 1970). They are largely throwbacks to the era of the great detective.

In Clancy Fish presents the great detective in cop's clothing. In the novels Clancy pulls all of the enigmatic pieces of the stories' puzzles together, sometimes, as in *Mute Witness*, refusing or neglecting to tell his superiors or his subordinates what he is doing and what he knows. While the novels may have an action close, Clancy does not usually carry a pistol and does not like them. As a crime solver he may be a whiz, but as a cop, Fish portrays Clancy as shopworn and frayed:

He was a slender man in his late forties, a bit above medium height, dressed in a drab blue suit, a cheap white shirt with blue striped tie inexpertly tied, and a dark blue hat that failed to conceal the streaks of gray that were beginning to mark his temple. The thin face beneath the shadow of the worn brim was drawn, lined with weariness; his dark eyes were expressionless [*Mute* 1].

Part of this Fish uses to distinguish the cop from "businessmen": "He shrugged; neatness was for businessmen" (*Mute* 22). His office in New York's 52nd Precinct is as shabby as Clancy's clothes:

> A small battered desk that served Clancy's predecessor as well as several before him, took the place of the broad mahogany desk that graced Mr. Chalmer's office. The tiny room had bare walls and hard wooden chairs; together with the scratched and battered filing cabinets they crowded the little office. And the view gave, not on the East River with its magnificent bridges and colorful, jaunty boats cutting white check-marks across the blue surface, but on a clothesline bent across a narrow air-shaft and sagging dispiritedly under a load of limp underwear and patched overalls [*Mute* 9].

In the manner of classic detective fiction, the clothesline outside of Clancy's office gives him the clue to unraveling the first mystery in *Mute Witness*. In terms of real police work, Fish seeds brief mentions of paperwork throughout the novels. And he emphasizes Clancy's exhaustion and reminds readers by citing date and time at the head of each chapter. Readers, however, see little of the inside of the 52nd Precinct house. They see more of Clancy's crew. Clancy's crew mostly consists of detectives Kaproski and Stanton. Fish draws them as big men, he makes them Clancy's gofers, and makes loyalty to Clancy their most outstanding characteristic. Fish, like most other writers, depends on the convention of the big cop; in one instance Fish writes that "Stanton bulked over the startled little man" (*Mute* 116). It is one of the reasons he depicts his hero as slender.

Indeed, Fish portrays the precinct more as a group of buddies than a collection of cops. Clancy's boss, Captain Wise, is Clancy's boyhood friend and protector and carries on that role in the department. And Mary Kelly, the precinct's policewoman, would like to be more than a pal to the lieutenant:

> Mary Kelly was a woman in her late thirties, with a rather plain but pleasant face, and a very decent figure. Her outstanding feature was her eyes, but she didn't know it. She also didn't know why nobody ever called her just plain "Mary" instead of her full name of "Mary Kelly," but they hadn't. Mary Kelly also thought that a nice man like Lieutenant Clancy shouldn't live without a wife to warm his bed [*Mute* 127].

It is Clancy's chums who help him solve mysteries, not the fact that he is a cop. Indeed, Fish uses the fact that Clancy is a cop as an impediment to his role as a detective. The district attorney has it in for Clancy and hounds him, the impossible hours grind Clancy down, and working within regulations would be an impediment — if he followed them. But for the greater good Clancy ignores regulations like reporting murders and turning homicide cases over to the Homicide Bureau. And he is able to accomplish the greater good because he solves cases and because he has so many good friends who cover for him.

In *Reardon* the plotting is the same but the hero is different. Unlike Clancy, he possesses what passed for manly attributes in the popular literature of the 1950s and 1960s. "He was a stocky man in his early thirties; he had a rugged yet remarkably sensitive face with sharp, intelligent gray eyes" (6). Reardon swills martinis and has an eye for the ladies — both his woman friend, Jan, and the victim-villain in the novel. Pike tries to create an air of insouciance around his hero by making him superficially casual about police work and humdrum routine, while at the same time showing him dedicated and detail-oriented. Unlike Clancy, Reardon spends a fair amount of time at San Francisco police headquarters and has to interact with his bosses (who are entirely tolerant of Reardon's occasional whim or instinct-driven behavior), and Pike provides a few glances at routine — *Reardon* features an automobile accident report that figures heavily in the plot. In addition to this bit of cop novel convention, Pike touches on the domestic difficulties the job causes in Jan's arguments with Reardon about him neglecting her and their relationship — an argument resolved in Reardon's favor. While they may not quite be the group of pals that surround the hero in the Clancy books, Reardon, nonetheless, has his buddies. In addition to a number of subsidiary cop characters Pike makes the eager, younger, naïve Detective Dondero Reardon's sidekick partly so he can write repartee for them, and partly so that he can have his hero outdistance him in the brain department.

Joseph Harrington

Joseph Harrington's *The Last Known Address* (1965), *Blind Spot* (1966), and *The Last Doorbell* (1969), insofar as it's possible, are genteel police books. Harrington's speakers usually use words like "darned" for emphasis, and when they are moved to stronger language it is never recorded. The hero, Detective Lieutenant Francis X. Kerrigan, fits the cop profile: "One glance at the hard face, the thick shoulders under conventional blue serge, and people knew that Kerrigan was a policeman — a cop to put it bluntly" (*Last* 51). And Harrington has it several ways with Kerrigan's toughness. His toughness is wholly justified, it serves as a counter to the growing judicial sympathy for criminals, but it's also a thing of the past:

> There was too much violence in his record, too many punks shot and sent to the hospital. No matter that practically all of those incidents had occurred in the years when he patrolled tough beats, and he had citations for them. This was the day and age when policemen were supposed to treat even overt lawbreakers with "dignity"— with restraint and even courtesy. A policeman with violence in is record had three strikes against him [*Last* 31–2].

In contrast to this, Harrington makes Kerrigan kind, thoughtful, and polite. He serves as a mentor to Detective Jane Boardman — a female NYPD officer who makes detective (and detective first grade at that) several years before Lillian O'Donnell's Norah Mulcahaney achieves the same imaginary feat. Unlike other writers, who emphasize public indifference, Harrington presents an optimistic view of the relationship between the police and the public:

> On the latter count, Kerrigan didn't share some recent journalistic disgust with citizens who avoided being involved in cases. He had seen hundreds of them, well-meaning, honest people, called back to court ten, fifteen, or twenty times, and losing ten, fifteen, or twenty days' pay, waiting to be called, and more often than not they were never called at all [*Last* 118].

Finally, in the plots, Harrington treats horrific subjects in a genteel manner — as in *The Last Doorbell* where the crime, a pustule of kidnapping, child sex abuse, and murder, is sparingly mentioned.

Unlike the trend among later writers to emphasize instinct and imagination as the special and unique abilities possessed by police heroes, Harrington stresses determination and hard work:

> He was so darned hardheaded and unfeeling. No, that wasn't the word. He had feeling all right. Frank did, but he never let it show. He simply hated theories. He simply punched doorbells by the dozens, by the hundreds, the thousands, and asked his flat, unimaginative questions. Stubborn, endless questions. He had a remarkable record; he had worked out a lot of successful endings, but none of them could be attributed to brilliant deductions. Just to the patient, dull, plodding business of following leads, asking those endless questions [*Last* 54].

As proof, in *The Last Doorbell* Kerrigan waits for people in order to find the minutest scraps of information, rings tons of doorbells, and sits in an office for two days, watching the routines of a secretary. Kerrigan views police work as a job — "Look, Jane, this business is a trade, just like any other trade" (*Last* 103). And the honest, dedicated worker will learn it fast and well.

While Harrington fastens on Kerrigan and Boardman as possessing ideal police qualities, the books acknowledge that cops come in many varieties:

> New York policemen were as different as any individuals could be. There was Wilson, lazy, telling people to come in to report a felony several days after it happened. Lou Silverman, a nice enough chap, who would run a mile away from the scene if he saw a fight between a white and a Negro. Alfredo, who watched himself carefully and always jumped on the right side of every fence and would go places. And there were the Detweilers, earnest, stubborn people who were dedicated cops, and who would laugh in your face if you told them so. The Kerrigans, who said it was a pleasure to get away from crime and didn't

meant it at all.... There were policemen who wanted to get their twenty years in, to retire immediately thereafter on a pension; there were Detweilers and Kerrigans who retired only when the mandatory age limit forced them to retire—and lived unhappily ever after [*Last* 35–6].

Lazy and upwardly mobile cops come in for Harrington's scorn. In the books they receive their due—Alfredo, in *The Last Doorbell*, is flopped back into uniform and transferred when the brass discover his duplicity in trying to take the credit for Jane and Kerrigan's work. The bigger problem, however, resides with the courts, and Harrington's belief that sympathy has shifted from the victim to the criminal. Rather than whining about it, however, Harrington's heroes just keep on working.

John Ball

John Ball's *In the Heat of the Night* (1966) became one of the best-known police novels of the era. Two films, one of which won an Academy Award, and a 140-episode television series added to its celebrity. Almost all of this grew from the racial theme upon which Ball based the novel—the degrading effects of racism and its defeat through the growth of understanding. Ball chose to discuss these issues using the context of police officers and a police department.

In the Heat of the Night presents a number of the dilemmas of small-town police departments. The town of Wells has scarce resources to spend on its police force. Its new police chief's credentials include no law enforcement experience beyond being a corrections officer in Texas. In the novel Ball emphasizes the tension between the mayor and town council and the police department. Chief Bill Gillespie gets calls from the mayor and other town potentates giving him advice about how to do his job. Indeed, the introduction of Virgil Tibbs into the murder investigation is a crafty political stratagem suggested by a councilman—if the police fail to solve the murder they can blame the failure on Tibbs, and if Tibbs succeeds the police can take the credit. At the start of the novel the town's police try to handle the case using only the most rudimentary police routine—photographs are taken at the crime scene, and a physician pronounces the victim dead. After that, the police routine in Wells boils down to rounding up "suspicious" persons (thus the dragnet that brings Tibbs to the police station to begin with) or finding suspects in their files (hence Gillespie's hasty assumptions about Harvey Oberst at the beginning of the novel).

The most prominent point of *In the Heat of the Night* resides in the racial theme. But in his articulation of that theme Ball used a number of police motifs. The most obvious of these is the contrast between Tibbs' training and experience and the archaic and slipshod practices of the officers of the Wells police force. Thus Patrolman Sam Wood

> had not had any special course training for his job; he had simply been put on the payroll, had been briefed for a day on his new duties, and then had gone to work [8].

Tibbs, on the other hand, has been to college, has worked his way up through the ranks from patrolman to detective ("Some of the best training in the world and ten years experience. Everybody who joins the Pasadena force starts out by going to school. It's amazing how much they teach you in a comparatively short time" [94]), and he demonstrates his training by his meticulous attention to detail. Ball repeats these points with his second series character, Jack Tallon, chief of the Whitewater, Washington force. In *Police Chief* (1977) Tallon works to turn his small force into professional police by instituting training and emphasizing integrity. Perhaps notably, Ball, East Coast born, could have made Virgil Tibbs and Jack Tallon cops from New York or Philadelphia or Boston, but made one of his heroes a member of the Pasadena, California police force and the other a former LAPD detective — a testament, perhaps, to the publicity apparatus of Chief Parker and the LAPD, and to Jack Webb's *Dragnet*.

Along with this Ball takes some pains to show police officers as fundamentally upstanding, hardworking men. He makes a point, albeit a small one, of letting readers know that Wells is not the cliché southern town that derives its income from a speed trap on the main North/South highway. Ball's cops fit in with tradition in that they are all very big men. Gillespie is six-four, Sam Wood and all the other cops at the Wells station are big and burly, and Jack Tallon is no shrimp. He does this both because that was the way cops were supposed to be, and because in the Virgil Tibbs books their size presents a contrast with the smaller (but wiry) hero. While they may be racists at the beginning of *In the Heat of the Night*, Ball presents his cops as conscientious men. With Patrolman Sam Wood, Ball uses the term "duty" repeatedly and early on tells readers that Sam tries to make up for his lack of training by reading books about police work and the law. Unlike cops habituated to casual corruption, Sam Wood pays for his meals at the lunch counter where he stops for his breaks, and drives his patrol route alert and conscientious. Ball makes him a fundamentally moral man in many ways. Indeed, Sam feels shame and regret after he suggests that Tibbs may have used some of his spare time "to find some nice black girl to shack up with" (81). Ball rewards Sam Wood's dedication to duty by showing the raising of his consciousness in racial matters, and by having Virgil Tibbs recommend that he be promoted to sergeant. The same elevation of consciousness happens to Chief Gillespie.

Ball, being basically a traditional detective story writer, could have used the genius detective versus the dumb cop plot, or, updating it, he could have contrasted the genius detective with dumb, redneck cops. He surely uses the genius part, in that Virgil Tibbs is smarter than anybody else in the vicinity. But the cops of Wells are neither dumb nor essentially rednecks. They are working men, and they recognize Tibbs' dignity and humanity because he both works better than they do and teaches them how to do their job more efficiently. Published two years after the Civil Rights Act of 1964 guaranteed equal rights in employment to all races, *In the Heat of the Night* showed how working together could result in racial understanding among a group of "normal" lower-middle-class men who were unremittingly conscientious, honest, brave, and chaste.

Dorothy Uhnak

At the beginning of the twentieth century Mrs. Lola Baldwin of Portland, Oregon, became the first woman to be a regular member of a police force in America. For more than half a century, however, female police were rare. Granted, Mary Sullivan of the NYPD had her own radio program, *Policewoman*, in the 1930s, but the role of the woman on any police force was circumscribed and minimal. It was that way when Dorothy Uhnak joined the New York Transit Police in 1953. For Uhnak it pretty much remained that way: she, for instance, was demoted from detective for taking maternity leave. She wrote about her experiences in her autobiography *Policewoman: A Young Woman's Initiation into the Realities of Justice* (1964). Uhnak also used them in her novels, three of which feature Detective Christie Opara.

In *Policewoman* Uhnak recounts the training and experiences of a woman police officer in the 1950s. At the police academy Uhnak was one of three women in a class of one hundred and four; they were excused from physical training and from learning how to search individuals. As a sworn police officer her duties began with assisting with female corpses, acting as jailer for women prisoners, and typing for the guys in the detective squad. Later on Unhak was allowed to work as a partner with male detectives in cases involving women and children. Two things stand out in Unhak's recounting of her experiences as a policewoman. The first is the solidarity of police officers. Thus she quotes much of the speech given at her graduation from the police academy:

> You are going to find out that the only brother you have in the world is your brother police officer; he is the only man in the world you can talk to who will understand you. Not your blood brother who you were raised with.... If he isn't a cop too, you and he will be speaking about the same things to each other in different languages. You will have more in common with a village consta-

ble in a town of four hundred people than you will with your own brother because that village constable lives in the same world as the first-grade detective in any city in the world; he has seen people with the same eyes, the cop's eyes. Most people are aware of the insularity of a police group; they give various interpretations to this insularity, mostly of a derogatory nature. But you will find, as you become police officers, that this is not only a natural development, but an essential one, because only a policeman ... can understand the policeman's language and the policeman's world and the policeman's life. It is foreign and incomprehensible to everyone else and it cannot be communicated to them [*Policewoman* 12].

The second is the need for police officers to develop a shell, the need to protect one's emotions from the horror and squalor police officers often encounter. Thus an older policewoman counsels Uhnak:

"You see, I've learned a trick. Be my guest, benefit from my vast and superior experience. A very simple trick. Just this — you never look at their eyes. You never look at their faces." She looked down at her hands, straightened the fingers out, then looked back at me. "You see, in that way, they can't haunt you. You can't remember what they look like, and so you forget them. Just like that!" She snapped her fingers almost in my face. "Voices are very easy to forget, and words — they don't mean a goddamn thing. Don't look at their eyes and you're home safe" [*Policewoman* 44].

In the Christie Opara books — *The Bait* (1968), *The Witness* (1969), and *The Ledger* (1970) — Uhnak took some pains to portray her police hero as an average, all-American woman. Thus in *The Ledger* the witness Opara is guarding makes this assessment of her:

Elena took careful, interested measure of the girl before her. About her own age, maybe a little younger, slim in a wiry way that approached thinness. Her body was hidden under a heavy blue turtleneck sweater but it was apparent that she was small-breasted and narrow-hipped. The plaid skirt was short enough to reveal long, slender legs which were covered by blue tights and fur-lined boots to the knees. Elena studied the wide-open, all-American girl face [20].

But Opara isn't just any all–American girl. She is also a cop and Uhnak concentrates on those things that make her different from male cops. Some of this has to do with family. Unhak makes her hero a widow — a widow of a policeman killed in the line of duty — who lives with her son and her mother-in-law. Thus throughout the books, when she is on the job Opara occasionally feels guilt for not being at home with her boy ("'Gee Mickey, I wish I could have been there.' It broke the lightening effect of her son's words: the old guilt surged through her. She was away from home too much, away from her son too much" [*The Ledger* 35]). And even at home, consistent with the point Uhnak made in *Policewoman*, she struggles to leave her job behind: "She took it home with her. As hard as she tried to leave it behind, the voices, the sickened faces, the screams and cries came home with her" (*The Ledger* 9). Not only at home, but on the job as well, Uhnak shows her hero as someone who feels — indeed, Unhak very often uses the phrase "to feel" in connection with her hero. Opara has to confront the emotional traumas connected with her private life, and she has issues on the job. As the only woman in the office, Opara also needs to struggle to be recognized for her accomplishments (as a first grade detective she is at the top of the ranks) and her competence instead of her typing skills. Opara claims no special privilege in the workplace. Uhnak, however, acknowledges that a special role is accorded her. Appropriate to the times, Opara deals largely with women and children — in fact, she feels unsure of herself when confronting male criminals in *The Ledger*. More importantly, the men in the office treat her differently. Thus her boss, Casey Reardon muses that

> She reminded him of someone a very long time ago: the neighborhood tomboy of his youth who played every game with the boys, matching them point for point, demanding that they give her no special leeway. Yet, they had all been careful not to hurt her and doubly careful not to let her know of their caution [*The Ledger* 27].

As much as they are about crime and police work, Uhnak's early books have more than a casual connection to romances. Thus the interplay between Opara and her boss, caring then distant, intimate then aloof, mirror the heroine/hero pattern of the love romance. Indeed, at the conclusion of *The Ledger*, Uhnak resolves the personal and professional tension between Opara and Reardon by pointing them toward Reardon's bedroom.

After her books about Christie Opara, Uhnak moved away from the female police hero. While she is connected to the police world, the hero of *False Witness* (1981) is an ambitious assistant district attorney. *Law and Order* (1973) and *The Investigation* (1977) both feature male police officers. Indeed, Uhnak's later novels take a broader look at police issues, like the corruption that is central to *Law and Order*, than her Christie Opara books encompass. But then again, by the time she wrote them a lot of other writers were doing the same thing.

Collin Wilcox

Collin Wilcox followed the old pattern. He wrote several regular detective novels — books about a newspaper reporter named Stephen Drake — and then switched to a police hero. Thus in the late 1960s Wilcox looked around for a new hero:

I knew that police procedural books usually did well. Ed McBain in America, John Creasy in England, and Georges Simenon in France, to name only a few, were all solid successes (and still are) [*The Writer* 21].

So Wilcox introduced his Frank Hastings of the San Francisco Police Department in *The Lonely Hunter* in 1969. In "Writing and Selling the Police Procedural Novel" Wilcox recounts the extent to which he immersed himself in real police work:

And, yes, I've spent a little time at the San Francisco Homicide Bureau — two hours, I think. For the rest of it, I occasionally watch *Kojak, Dragnet, Adam-12, Police Story,* and in past years, *Lineup* (the best of the television lot, I think) [*The Writer* 20].

Consequently the Frank Hastings books present police procedure in only occasional bits of background.

Wilcox cuts his hero out of the same cloth as most other police writers. Hastings is a big, hard guy — he played football for Stanford and then for the Detroit Lions. As with all of the cops of the 1950s and 1960s, Hastings is a moral exemplar. Thus Wilcox presents avowals like this one made in response to Ann Haywood's ex-husband's taunts:

"I've always heard that policemen can get the law at a wholesale price, so to speak — just like car salesmen can get cars at cost. Cut-rate cars or cut-rate laws. What's the difference? Everyone's looking for a deal."

"Not everyone. Not me" [*Long Way Down* 81].

But then comes the difference, in the personal background recited in every novel. After a brief pro football career, Hastings married money, worked for his wife's father as a gofer, and became a drunk. Leaving his philandering wife and their two children, given the opportunity by an old friend, Hastings joins the San Francisco police department, becoming "the oldest rookie" in his class. Hastings is still a drunk; his old friend gives him an ultimatum, and he dries himself out. In all of this Wilcox did something new. He drew a police officer beset with problems — alcoholism and divorce. Wilcox makes Hastings' background and experiences somewhat more arresting than those of fictional cops before him because the Frank Hastings books are, uniquely, first person narratives. Wilcox's partial sketch of the cop as a flawed individual, then, looks forward to the next generation's unyielding frankness when it comes to exploring the frailties of police officers.

While his books center on Frank Hastings, like other police writers Wilcox provides ancillary characters to create the illusion of real police work. Wilcox's homicide squad has a WASP, a Jew, an Italian, and an Irishman. Friedman stays in the office, makes things happen from his end, and kvetches. Canelli is "an Italian schlemiel" who accompanies Hastings and luckily helps out. They are all stereotypes. Hastings even sees them that way: "If Friedman was the garrulous one, Canelli was the innocent and Markham the heavy, then Culligan was the silent one" (*Long Way Down* 56).

Wilcox also followed the conventional method of the police writer by pointing to the chaos of police work through plot. Some of the novels cover more than one case; *The Long Way Down* begins with Hastings capturing a sniper and then launches into the main case, and *The Disappearance* has two ancillary cases around the main one. In the Hastings books Wilcox also occasionally slips in passages of complaints (typically from Friedman) about city and department politics adding complexity to the police officer's role. In the end, however, police work is peripheral. This is due partly to the first person narration of a detective trying to solve a problem, partly to Wilcox's reliance on the interview with suspects, and partly this is due to Wilcox's leanings toward Ross MacDonald. Like MacDonald's books, many of the Hastings books explore familial relationships — even the hero's own with his children. Partly the light serving of police reality comes from the fact that Wilcox was a commercial writer who perceived that "the real-life homicide detective's work is essentially dull" (*The Writer* 20), but did not realize that the real-life detective's character and life were far from dull.

Cops in the 1950s and 1960s

Compared with later decades, police shows on American television were relatively rare in the 1950s and 1960s. As noted already, the 1950s began with Jack Webb's *Dragnet*, which aired until 1959. The California Highway Patrol was featured in the series *Highway Patrol* which ran from 1955 to 1959. At the end of the fifties *Naked City*, airing from 1958 until 1963, dramatized cops working in the 65th Precinct of New York City. In the 1960s Jack Webb brought *Dragnet* back to television in 1967 for a three-year run. Webb followed *Dragnet* with his series about patrol cops, *Adam 12*, on television from 1967 until 1975. In 1968 two more exotic cop shows made their debut: *Hawaii Five-O* (1968 to 1980), and *Mod Squad* (1968 to 1973). Films about cops during the two decades were infrequent and largely undistinguished. They included *Detective Story*, *On Dangerous Ground*, and *The Prowler* in 1951; *The Narrow Margin* in 1952; *The Big Heat* in 1953; *The Human Jungle* and *Rogue Cop* in 1954; and then, skipping to the late 1960s, *Madigan* in 1967; and *Bullit* (roughly based on Robert Pike's book *Mute Witness*) in 1968.

Just as service in World War I contributed to the way American hardboiled writers viewed theme and character, World War II had something to do with the development of the police novel. Most of the writers of the generation that invented the police novel had served in the armed forces during the war. And they wrote the kind of fiction one would expect from men who had served in World War II: fiction that developed around a group of men; fiction that highlighted the special bond of men under stress; fiction that contrasted distant authority with practical action; fiction that valued training; fiction that alternately praised and whined about the dreariness of routine; fiction that yearned for the peace and comfort of middle-class life; fiction that portrayed the struggle of good versus evil. Not coincidentally, too, cop fiction, especially in the early 1950s, emphasizes upright behavior and morality. Thus cops' personal dedication not just to police work but to justice in books by Kantor, Webb, Craig, and others rests upon a fundamental belief in right and wrong and the obligation of the strong to protect the weak.

The police writers of the 1950s and 1960s came upon the scene when the detective story was running out of steam. Products of the 1920s, both the golden age story and the hard-boiled story had reached their zenith in the 1930s. The morally ambiguous private detective did not well suit the middle class mores of post-war America, and the amateur dilettante had been growing more and more irrelevant even in the 1930s. Other than Ross Mac-Donald, the only major hard-boiled writer to emerge in the 1950s was Mickey Spillane. That tells a lot. The moral, hardworking, middle-class man held more attraction for the audiences of the period. Likewise the body of men who protected society provided more reassurance than the exploits of one hero, whether he was the great detective or the hard-boiled private eye. By a second coincidence, the police officer and police department as hero had become one of the most popular subjects of the new medium of television. In spite of Hillary Waugh's denial, most of the writers who began their work in the 1950s and 1960s make references to Jack Webb's television show *Dragnet*, with its morally upright hero upholstered with details of police work.

Beginning with Emile Gaboriau in the nineteenth century, one of the functions of the detective story has been to depict police techniques. Thus, over the years the descriptions of dusting for fingerprints, of making plaster casts, of doing chemical analyses, and other forensic techniques became accepted and expected parts of detective stories. In spite of Lawrence Treat's Jub Freeman's infatuation with his spectrometer, however, most of the twentieth century's advances in forensic science (computerized data bases, super glue fuming for fingerprints, DNA analysis, etc.) occurred well after the first wave of police writing. Writers of the fifties and sixties, then, had little to depend on other than examining records — records, and record keeping, that seemingly multiplied during the era. Recall, too, that these were paper records. Much of the police routine in the books of the period centers on the search for the right record that will focus the investigation of the crime. Driver's licenses, vehicle registration, rap sheets, employment records, receipts for purchases — they all play roles in the books of the period, and inserted facsimiles become standard features in them. Writers set all of this in a frenetic context — the ceaseless and overwhelming work of a police force with new crimes committed hourly. They developed new means of showing this, from the multiple plot story, to the frame story, to the summary paragraph about the cops' case load. However, as they continued into the 1960s and 1970s, the original group of writers discovered that centering books on routine and multiple action has a short shelf life. The points about the burden and chaos of police life once made do not need to be focused upon again and again. And so the police book based largely on routine and the police book depending on simulating the frenzied workload of the police are largely limited to the 1950s and 1960s.

One of the other apparent changes that shows up in the cop book of the 1950s was in the nature of the crimes in the books. By their very construction the cop books of the fifties announce that the cops are fighting what appears to be a huge and new crime wave. Not only that, the crimes have changed. In both asides and in main plots cop writers bring in murder for trivial reasons — arguments over spilling beer on a new suit lead to killing in Himes' Harlem. Scarcely a subject in earlier fiction, sex crimes, particularly rape, become a subject for a significant number of books. Waugh, Craig, and even Linington all have their cops chase and catch rapists, serial rapists. And juvenile delinquency, that term coined in the fifties, comes in occasionally — McBain's first book, after all, was *Blackboard Jungle*.

Well aware of the traditional association of police with corruption and brutality, writers of the fifties and sixties largely present squeaky-clean heroes, heroes who won't accept even a free cup of coffee and aver that only old-fashioned cops would ever rough anyone up. However, they are not so punctilious about constitutional guarantees. A number of writers mention their characters conducting what even they term "illegal wire-taps"; in *Killer's Payoff* Carella and Hawes "illegally opened ... [a suspect's] mail." McBain, in fact, makes a point of discussing individuals' ignorance of their rights in *Cop Killer*:

> Actually, they had said a hell of a lot more than they should have. They'd have been within their rights if they'd insisted on not saying a word at the lineup. Not knowing this, not even knowing that their position was fortified because they'd made no statement when they'd been collared, they had answered the Chief of Detectives with remarkable naivete [86].

And Kantor's cop notes that

> When these wise little commie punks, male and female, start quoting the Bill
> of Rights for their own purposes, chase them faster. You don't always need to
> meet them with a blackjack and a string of nippers, but you don't have to offer
> them a fudge sundae either [*Signal Thirty-Two* 7].

Indeed, occasionally the writers present situations in which the police con-
sciously manipulate justice for their own convenience:

> "He was probably framed on that rape charge," Friedman said airily. "You
> know how it is. Pretty soon guys like Clark become a departmental embar-
> rassment. Also, the judge gets tired of seeing them around, cluttering up his
> calendar. So we frame them, and the judge puts them away, and the indeter-
> minate-sentence racket takes care of the rest" [*Long Way Down* 135].

Throughout the period, then, writers casually mention police actions that
violate the rights of individuals. They accept that these are routine parts of
police work and are justified because their heroes are moral men and that
the protection of society is the greatest good.

Writers of the fifties and sixties largely ground their heroes in middle-
class values. They are rarely the great detective of the past, and writers make
this point partly through the emphasis on heroes following routine rather
than possessing encyclopedic knowledge or higher intellectual powers. Cases
are solved by routine, or by accident, or by the sheer stupidity of criminals.
The comfortable home, attractive, understanding wife, and wholesome children are in the background of most of the policemen's lives in the books of
the period. While most cop heroes continue to be big men, the writers of
the 1950s and 1960s humanize their heroes and make them appealing, even
handsome individuals. Part of the attraction of entering police work for them
lies in the security the job provides. The job, however, has been elevated.
Rather than cops being portrayed as the unskilled labor, the wheels and belts
of the social machine as they were in the 1930s and 1940s, the books of the
1950s and 1960s focus on police work as at least a semiskilled occupation
requiring intelligence and individual dedication and initiative.

Nonetheless, the model of the hard-boiled hero has a seductive pull on
some writers. Chester Himes' Gravedigger and Coffin Ed come rather directly
from the *Black Mask* tradition, and the unmarried, damaged, principled,
introspective hero who finds fulfillment in police work first makes his appearance with Wilcox's Frank Hastings. And this kind of hero, with the addition of the 1960s rebellion against authority, will appear more frequently in
the police books of the 1980s and 1990s. The world of the '50s and '60s cop
book is also demonstrably one for men. Indeed, the covers of Jack Webb's
and Jonathan Craig's paperback originals hint at (but do not deliver) soft-
core pornography. Even the egregious discrimination apparent to contemporary readers in Uhnak's *Policewoman* does not give rise in the narrative to

much outrage or demand for full participation in police work, and the romance underpinnings of the early Christie Opara books show that she remains very much a woman of the 1950s. Also, while a number of writers introduce minority cops, their emphasis, seen best in McBain's Arthur Brown, is not upon discrimination, but on African Americans and Hispanics having become just like the other middle-class characters in the stories.

At the beginning of the period MacKinlay Kantor took a relatively traditional view of the larger role of the police:

> They [criminals] could not be trusted in a world populated by weaker, less predatory and less assertive people. They were panthers or hyenas of the wilderness a-prowling; they had to be battled into subjugation and restrained by mesh and steel [*Signal Thirty-Two* 97].

Cops, then, protect decent people from the inevitable predators from the fringes of society. Approaching the 1960s, however, writers' visions become darker. They begin to see a wholesale breakdown of society. Thus a nun in *The Ledger* asks

> Do you know the backgrounds of the children who are in my care? They are the remnants of a society that hasn't worked. They are the products of rape, ignorance, lust, violence, atrocities, almost beyond belief [85–86].

Elizabeth Linington in *Streets of Death* applies an analogy from history

> Just like ancient Rome, E.M. The weakened moral fiber, relaxation of standards, all the easy welfare, bread and circuses — and the pornography — and you get all the senseless violence, the killings done for peanuts, the killers given a slap on the wrist and let go to do it again. Makes you wonder where it'll all end, doesn't it? [173].

The writers of the period show the police as society's bulwark against increasing chaos, and this without crack cocaine, drive-by shootings, the Son of Sam, John Wayne Gacy, the Knapp Commission, urban rage, Danny Miranda, Rodney King, and much, much more yet to come. The writers of the period overlook facts that suggested that some things about the police had hardly changed since the nineteenth century. The Gross Scandal of 1950 revealed that a Brooklyn bookmaker had paid a million dollars annually to the cops for protection (Maas 138). In 1960 Chicago replaced its police chief in response to a scandal "sordid even by Chicago standards" (Friedman 360). A 1966 study by Albert Reiss conducted in Boston, Washington, D.C., and Chicago showed that one out of every five policemen studied "was observed in a criminal violation" (Maas 138). Instead of confronting the real problems of police and policing (corruption on one hand and social ills on the other) the cop writers of the 1950s and 1960s depict policemen and police departments as beleaguered, but peopled by honest, hardworking, moral men. Robin Moore's *The French Connection* (1969) recounts the lengthy and painstaking investigation of drug dealers by Popeye Egan and Sonny Grosso that resulted in "the biggest narcotics bust in police history" in 1962. Cops like Egan and Grosso were the centurions who defended society against the barbarians who threatened the peace and serenity of the middle-class world.

Emblematic, perhaps, of the real world of the 1950s and 1960s, and presaging the world yet to come, in 1978 in *The Prince of the City* Robert Daley describes the indictment and conviction for corruption of some of the same police officers who worked with Popeye Egan and Sonny Grosso in the "French Connection" bust.

-three-

The 1970s

Until the 1970s the police novel existed as a minor subcategory of mystery fiction. Granted, in the 1950s and 1960s McBain, Linington, and a few others wrote books with a new way of telling cop tales and a new emphasis on the social and personal factors that affect cops' lives. And granted, too, that with Dorothy Uhnak, a police officer had already joined the small group of writers that chose to write about cops. But the seventies were different, and this was due to the new writers. Dallas Barnes adopted the McBain formula of multiple cases and brought to it his credentials as a Los Angeles police officer. More importantly, Joseph Wambaugh, another LAPD cop, sought new ways to tell his version of cop tales, accounts of how profane, vulgar, frightened, and flawed men cope with crimes and criminals more violent, shocking, and disturbing than those dealt with in previous mystery or cop fiction. And treating the bureaucracy coiled inside and outside of police departments, Robert Daley wrote about the NYPD, where he had served as one of its bureaucrats. Perhaps most powerfully of all, books featuring cop heroes made the best-sellers' lists with Lawrence Sanders' thrillers about serial killers. Finally, female heroes began to emerge in cop books, reflecting the passage of equal rights legislation, and writers like Hillerman showed a way to vary the hero pattern by looking at the way police serve in cultures different from those of the white citizens of America's large cities.

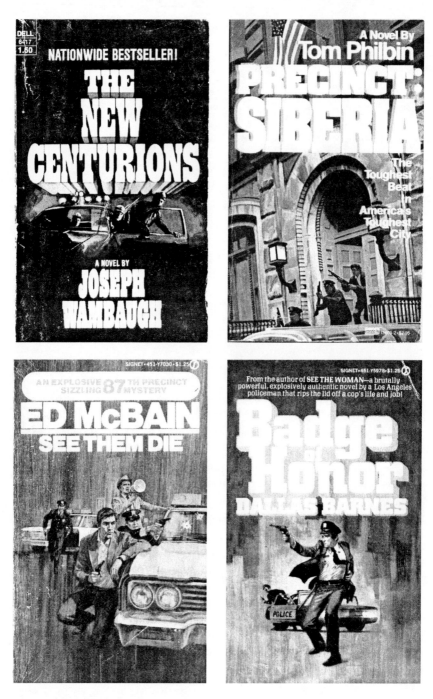

The police in action became one of the conventional motifs for the covers of police novels. *Top left:* Dell, 1972; *top right:* Fawcett, 1985; *bottom left:* Signet, 1976; *bottom right:* Signet, 1974.

Tony Hillerman

In the United States there are:

50 federal police agencies
49 state police departments (all except Hawaii)
1,316 special police agencies (transit systems, parks, etc.)
3,088 sheriffs' departments
13,578 municipal police departments [Cole 83].

There are also one hundred and thirty-five Native American tribal police agencies. That's a lot to choose from. Tony Hillerman chose the Navajo tribal police. And part of what his policemen confront is the chaos of jurisdiction:

> At the moment six law-enforcement agencies were interested in the affair at Zuni (if one counted the Bureau of Indian Affairs Law and Order Division, which was watching passively). Each would function as its interests dictated it must. Leaphorn himself, without conscious thought, would influence his actions to the benefit of the Dinee if Navajo interests were at stake. Orange Naranjo, he knew, would do his work honestly and faithfully with full awareness that his good friend and employer, the Sheriff of McKinley County, was seeking reelection. Pasquaanti was responsible for laws centuries older than the white man's written codes. Highsmith, whose real job was traffic safety, would do as little as possible. And O'Malley would make his decisions with the ingrained FBI awareness that the rewards lay in good publicity [*Dance Hall* 108].

The other thing Hillerman's policemen confront is that their principal job boils down to stolid routine. They drive hundreds of miles to solve petty crimes and track down petty criminals. As Jim Chee says in *Skinwalkers*: "The kind of people I arrest are mostly too drunk to remember who arrested 'em. Or care" (36). Indeed, the jurisdictional confusion, especially that of the FBI over murder committed on reservations, often leads to departmental indifference. Thus Chee's supervisor tells him that

> I think we ought to leave those cases to the FBI. The FBI's not going to break them, and neither are we, but the FBI's getting paid for it, and nobody's going to do any good on them until we have some luck — and taking you off your regular work isn't going to make us lucky, is it? [*Skinwalkers* 69].

Hillerman, of course, does not draw his cops, Leaphorn and Chee, as indolent time-servers. He makes both conscientious officers. Rather than use modern forensics — which, actually, would not be practical given the landscape — Leaphorn and Chee possess skills older than James Fenimore

Cooper, which they apply to detection. Every novel shows them to be expert trackers, reading and interpreting the significance of signs left in nature. In *Skinwalkers*, Hillerman even makes reference to Jim Chee's "efficient nose." Likewise they patiently and silently watch people and their surroundings before they make any move. Chee and Leaphorn also conduct interviews, and in them, as Navajos, they understand the necessity for patience and they understand the less-than-direct method of relating events on the part of Native American witnesses. Hillerman shows Leaphorn's efficiency as an administrator in *The Blessing Way* by depicting a large-scale map of his jurisdictions, which Leaphorn has marked with annotations both about the countryside and about the history of crimes.

When he began to write Hillerman recognized that the venue in the detective story is sometimes almost as important as the plot. Indeed, he saw that the framework of the detective story was a means of writing about things most important to him:

> Novels of mystery and suspense seem to be an ideal way to engage readers in a subject of life-long interest to me — the religions, cultures, and value systems of the Navajo and Pueblo Indians [Reilly 449].

And, of course, Hillerman went on to do just that; he engages readers with the cultures of the Navajo and other Native American peoples. In doing this he depicts the contrast of cultures — Anglo and Native, Navajo and Zuni, etc. — and the clash of those cultures as one of his principal means of investigation and exposition. Since law and the ways in which it is observed and enforced form the most basic of social institutions, Hillerman places police officers and what they do in his novels. From the very first novel, Hillerman points out the differences and difficulties police officers straddling two cultures face when dealing with the law: "The laws he enforced had been taken by the Tribal Council from the white man's laws and the white man did not recognize witchcraft as an offense" (*Blessing* 77). It's not just that the laws of the two cultures differ; Hillerman makes it clear that the cultures have very different attitudes toward crime ("Why did Navajos kill? Not as lightly as white men, because the Navajo Way made life the ultimate value and death unrelieved terror" [*Blessing* 156]), and, more importantly, toward evil. He places two relatively average men — Leaphorn a family man and Chee a bachelor — in the center of these complexities. Of the two, Leaphorn — perhaps because he is an administrator — holds less sympathy with traditional beliefs that cause harm to individuals, such as the belief in witches. Jim Chee, trained in the Navajo tradition as a singer, tries to reconcile old ways with the white culture's methods of detection, arrest, and punishment. Both of them lean toward the Navajo way when cultures and laws conflict.

While they do deal with police officers, Hillerman's novels stand outside of the mainstream of cop books because of their strengths. While he inserts bits of police conventions — the mass of paperwork, the multiple case load, the miscellany of trivial and serious crimes — they do not center on defining characters as police officers but as men evaluating and reevaluating a culture that existed before police were ever needed. Hillerman's significance in the history of the cop novel lies more in his influence on others who depict minority police officers (for example James Doss and Robert Walker, who depict Native American policemen in the 1990s) as well as on those who use the clash of cultures to define not the culture, as Hillerman did, but to define the police officer.

Lillian O'Donnell

Lillian O'Donnell began writing about the police in 1968 with *The Face of Crime*. Her approach to the form changed in 1972 with her first Norah Mulcahaney book, *The Phone Calls*, which she based on a series of obscene phone calls her mother had received and a ride-along she took with two New York City policewomen. The Mulcahaney books cover a variety of crimes, from rape, to black market adoption, to abuse of the elderly, to teenage crime. In chronicling Norah's rise from recruit to detective to sergeant to lieutenant, O'Donnell's books engage women's issues more fully and powerfully than earlier writers did, and they ground these issues in the political realities of a changing society and police department.

O'Donnell's hero partakes of two conventions — the romance and the police story. In the tradition of the romance, Norah Mulcahaney is a slightly flawed beauty:

> She was tall, slim enough, but too sturdy to be whistled at, often anyway. She had the fine Irish coloring: pale skin, dark, nearly black hair, and blue gray eyes with naturally thick lashes. Unfortunately these good points were marred by a square, much too prominent jaw which she was in the habit of thrusting out in moments of stress [*Leisure* 10].

Norah, moreover, is a motivated, dedicated, and increasingly skilled police officer. O'Donnell makes Norah's success in the police department a combination of opportunity, training, and passion for the job:

> He had given Norah Mulcahaney guidance and the chance to show what she could do. The fact that she had proved equal to the opportunity and had made detective wasn't the point. Making detective was still a hit-or-miss business; some officers waited for years for a chance to show their mettle, others never got the chance at all. Then and now, being a detective meant everything to Norah [*Leisure* 10].

She is a natural, and is recognized as such by the more perceptive men in the department.

> Quinn would have spotted her as a pro ... but the main thing was that she looked as though she belonged. It was in her coolness as she surveyed the scene [*No Business* 8].

While O'Donnell does not include any of the nastier forms of discrimination against women — PMS jokes, sexual aggression, etc. — Norah does face hostility from some of the men in her department, hostility that she usually chooses to ignore rather than confront. Instead she proves herself by what she does:

> She had never been an active women's libber. Norah believed in individual initiative; she thought that those women who had ability and diligence would achieve whatever they were after.... She had joined the force at the time of transition, while the women still worked out of a "pool" and were called upon to perform the routine, innocuous chores of matrons and clerks rather than police officers. Some of them were still in that rut. Nevertheless, she had thought that women in the police department had definitely come a long way [*No Business* 71].

The difference O'Donnell shows in Norah as a cop resides in a combination of her competence, self-discipline, the fact that she operates in a squad that allows and encourages initiative, and the fact that she takes charge. Thus, for instance, in the first crime scene in *Leisure Dying* Norah knows exactly what to do and does it without relying on the assistance of others. The books mention repeatedly that one of Norah's most important achievements had been controlling her energy and impetuosity. And O'Donnell even modifies the conventional connection between women and compassion to fit her hero's role as a police officer: "You couldn't bleed for every victim ... or you'd bleed dry in a week" (*Leisure* 108).

While the demonstration of Norah's ability and dedication to police work forms a significant part of her character, O'Donnell also fills out her hero's character with motifs from the romance novel. Thus O'Donnell's development of Norah's relationship with her future husband, Joe Capretto, recapitulates the conventions of blossoming love between mentor and student, the lothario tamed, the hostility of families, the temptation to infidelity, and the resolution of misunderstanding between strong-willed, independent people. The difference in her handling of these motifs lies first in the fact that O'Donnell sets them within the context of police work. Norah comes in contact with Joe because he helps her learn how to be a good police officer. The misunderstanding and resolution between strong-willed, independent people occurs in *Leisure Dying* because of police work. Indeed, police work binds Norah and Joe together:

> In fact, Norah and Joe Capretto had a great deal more in common than most
> married couples — they had their work.... The work, woven into their lives,
> was exciting, demanding of their full capacities. Joe often thought that he and
> Norah had the same kind of all-consuming passion for police work that an act-
> ing couple has for the theater [*Leisure* 20].

Thus the purposed end of the love romance motifs in O'Donnell is police
work rather than domesticity.

With police work, and women police officers, larger issues surface in
O'Donnell's books than individual ability and dedication. Throughout she
shows the corrosive influence of economics on both the police force and on
women police officers. O'Donnell's New York City cannot afford the police
force it needs. In her books O'Donnell often mentions deep cuts in police
personnel occasioned by the city's teetering financial condition:

> The city had been in crisis for a long time. Wave after wave of firings had
> shaken the department. With men uncertain about whether they would have
> a job, and the city uncertain about whether it could pay those who had...
> [*Leisure* 142].

Obliquely O'Donnell also alludes to the job cuts occasioned by the firings
that resulted from the findings of the Knapp Commission, a subject that
would become a central concern of writers of the eighties. As she makes clear
in *No Business Being a Cop*, women bear the burden of all financial crises —
they are the last hired and first fired.

Perhaps more disturbing than O'Donnell's view that New York cannot
afford a proper police force is her picture of the generational shift in the police
force. O'Donnell brings in a few older, wiser police officers like Joe Capretto,
the paternal Jim Felix, and Louis Deland:

> Louis Deland was a cop's cop — tall, cadaverous, with dark, crepey bags under
> his eyes. He looked as though he never sat down to a proper meal or got his
> full quota of sleep. Both were true. He had the typical cop reservation about
> women on the force: They should be matrons, do clerical work, handle juve-
> niles. Louis Deland, however, was a pragmatist. The current of the times was
> for equality for women, and you either went with the current or you got sucked
> under. Also, the chief was a fair man, and he had to admit that so far women
> had acquitted themselves well. He knew about Sergeant Mulcahaney; she was
> okay; she possessed a lot of natural instinct for the work [*Leisure* 35].

But O'Donnell also shows that young cops are very different. Thus in
No Business Being a Cop, O'Donnell has her hero assess the state of the department:

> The Janseen business depressed her because it was an indication of the degen-
> eration of the department. When she first joined the force, only seven years
> before, spirit had been high. In Norah's eyes every man had been a hero,

defender and avenger of the poor and helpless, and most policemen had at least tried to live up to that image. Bad cops had been one in a thousand. The ratio had shifted considerably in recent years [94].

It's not just that there are more bad cops, the whole structure of the police department is falling apart:

> officers no longer accepted the quasi-military structure and discipline of the department. They more than rebelled — going out on job actions, demonstrating, protesting hours and wages as they were doing then [*No Business* 2].

The onus for this falls upon male officers and commanders too timid to impose discipline. The only bright spot that O'Donnell shows is the infusion of new kinds of cops into a crumbling institution. And these include minorities, like Ferdie Arenas, a newly arrived Puerto Rican, and, of course, women. While some of them are as uncommitted as many male officers, O'Donnell focuses on Norah and other female cops, like Betty Taggert, who tells Norah that

> I've wanted to be a policewoman for as long as I can remember. I took the exam in '69 and had to wait nearly four years for an appointment. Meantime, I worked for the telephone company. It was a good job with good money, plenty of security, regular increases, all kinds of benefits, but when I got the appointment, I quit without a minute's regret ... I guess police work is in my blood [*No Business* 75].

Insofar as there is hope, it lies in police officers like her. As we shall see later, it's too bad that Frank Serpico didn't run across some of them.

Joseph Wambaugh

Joseph Wambaugh was a member of the Los Angeles Police Department for eleven years before he published his first novel. His LAPD is emphatically not the one portrayed by either of the Jack Webbs or by Elizabeth Linington, or even by Chiefs Parker and Davis in their public pronouncements. Wambaugh wrote about things that no earlier writer dared to touch, he broke the connection of the cop story with the mystery novel, and focused on issues that would drive the police novel for the remainder of the century. It is difficult to overestimate the importance of Wambaugh's novels about beat cops — *The New Centurions* (1971), *The Blue Knight* (1972), and *The Choirboys* (1973) — or his later narrative non-fiction — *The Onion Field* (1974), *Lines and Shadows* (1983), and *The Blooding* (1989) — or his fiction featuring detectives.

In his first books Wambaugh accomplishes two things. First he shifts focus from the detective to the beat cop, a part of police work largely ignored by earlier writers (except the other beat cop, MacKinlay Kantor). More importantly, Wambaugh redefines the meaning of middle class. For the last generation of writers middle class had meant possessing a home in the suburbs, a loving family, and conducting oneself in an upright manner. Gus, Serge, and Roy in *The New Centurions* and Roscoe Rules, Dean Pratt, Spencer Van Moot, Willie Wright, Calvin Potts, Francis Tanaguchi, Baxter Slate, Sam Niles, Harold Bloomguard, and "Spermwhale" Whalen in *The Choirboys* are essentially middle-class men as well. But they are middle-class men who have been indelibly marked by their jobs. First of all, Wambaugh shows them partaking in the traditional police vices, cooping and freebies. To this he adds sexual temptation and includes scenes of prostitutes performing fellatio in patrol cars. And he shows, especially in *The Choirboys*, cops pulling puerile pranks. In some ways most of Wambaugh's patrolmen are not very much different in age or inclination from middle-class fraternity boys. They are different, however, because they have an impossible job. Thus, Serge in *The New Centurions* comments on the difference between plainclothes and uniformed assignments:

> But at least they were inconspicuous enough to avoid being troubled by the endless numbers of people who need a policeman to solve an endless number of problems that a policeman is not qualified to solve, but must make an attempt to solve, because he is an easily accessible member of the establishment and traditionally vulnerable to criticism [*New Centurions* 205].

But it is more than this kind of job frustration that changes Wambaugh's cops. The critical fact for Wambaugh is that the system keeps cops from doing their job—from helping those who most need it. He takes aim at bureaucracy in *The Choirboys*, but Wambaugh also places a great deal of emphasis on what the law has done to cops. In their police academy classes cops are told that

> You're going to become very interested in the decisions handed down by the courts in the area of search and seizure. You're going to be upset, confused, and generally pissed off most of the time, and you're going to hear locker room bitching about the fact that most landmark decisions are five to four, and how can a working cop be expected to make a sudden decision in the heat of combat and then be second guessed by the Vestal Virgins of the Potomac, and all that other crap [New Centurions 20].

The most acute form of this is the Supreme Court's *Escobido* and *Miranda* decisions, and in response to them Wambaugh wrote the seminal *Miranda* book, *The Onion Field*. For the dilemmas cops face with the law, however, there exists for Wambaugh's cops a remedy. Even though in *The Blue Knight* Bumper Morgan gets caught lying, Wambaugh tells readers that it is an institutionalized practice among cops:

It was absurdly easy for any high school graduate with a year's police experience to skirt the most sophisticated and intricate edict arrived at by nine aging men who could never guard against the fact that restrictive rules of law simply produced facile liars among policemen. There wasn't a choirboy who had not lied in probable cause situations to ensure a prosecution of a guilty defendant [*Choirboys* 155].

Dealing with people, however, is a different matter. Wambaugh's cops see the worst things people do to one another. Thus as he follows each pair of partners in *The Choirboys* Wambaugh brings them into contact with horrors — suicide, rape and murder, child abuse and murder. As Galloway tells Serge in *The New Centurions*:

You're going to find out before too long that we're the only ones that see the victims.... The judges and probation officers and social workers and everybody else thinks mainly about the suspect and how they can help him stop whatever he specializes in doing to his victims, but you and me are the only ones who see what he does to his victims — right after it's done [51].

This knowledge makes suicide an occupational disease among Wambaugh's cops in both *The New Centurions* and *The Choirboys*. It leads to the hyper masculine "John Wayne syndrome" in some and makes other cops brutal and sadistic, like Roscoe Rules in *The Choirboys*. It turns them against everybody:

Nineteen plus years workin these streets has taught me that people are shit. They're scum. Only reason I don't treat em like Roscoe Rules or some a those black glove hotdogs is what's that do for you? Gets you fired for brutality or an ulcer or somethin. For what? The human race is no fuckin good but workin with these rotten bastards is all we got, right? It's the only game in town so you gotta play like you're still in the game. If you don't, if you drop out, you take your fuckin six inch Colt and see can you pull the trigger twice while you're eatin it. I just don't wanna off myself like so many cops do. So once in a while I do somethin that might look to you like I give a fuck about some a these scumbags. But there's nothin more rotten than people are [*Choirboys* 123].

This despair seeps into all aspects of Wambaugh's characters' lives. It causes alcoholism, divorce, and suicide. It is an occupational hazard that comes into police literature before Wambaugh — in Dorothy Uhnak's *Policewoman*, for instance. Because of their work police officers become cut off from the rest of society. The only refuge is brotherhood:

But they did have a secret which seemed to unite them more closely than normal friendship, and that was the knowledge that they knew things, basic things about strength and weakness, courage and fear, good and evil, especially good and evil [*New Centurions* 215].

Unlike most earlier writers, Wambaugh knew firsthand about the "blue brotherhood," and he uses this knowledge in a new way. First of all, he breaks with the tradition of writing about cops through the form and conventions of the detective story — inserted clues, crime and solution. *The New Centurions*, *The Blue Knight*, and *The Choirboys* come closer to fictionalized biography, focusing on lives and defining events in the lives of individuals. Indeed, *The Onion Field*, *Lines and Shadows*, and *The Blooding* are novelizations in the same vein as Truman Capote's *In Cold Blood*. On top of that, he patterns *The Choirboys* on Joseph Heller's *Catch 22*, in an effort to find yet another way of conveying the reality of police life. What Wambaugh does, in fact, with his early books is to move the police novel away from the detective story and to establish fiction about police officers as minority literature. He did this at a time when there was new interest in literature recognizing and portraying the uniqueness of other minority groups — women, African Americans, Hispanics, gays, etc. Indeed, Wambaugh specifically defines cops as a minority group when the narrator speaks about officers of a special squad in *Lines and Shadows*:

> They all started to have that feeling. "I don't give a damn. Who cares? What's any of it worth?" They all began feeling like a minority within a minority [248].

While portraying real police officers occupies the central position in Wambaugh's early books, they also present a wide variety of contemporary police issues. Chief, perhaps, among these is Wambaugh's portrait of police bureaucracy as, at best, inefficient and remote and, at worst, as buffoonish in its attempts to plan crime prevention. Efficiency, dedication, and common sense rarely rise above the rank of sergeant. In *The Choirboys* Wambaugh also presents the ineffectuality of police unions — "I'm sick of payin dues to the Protective League. I get more protection from a two year old box of rubbers" (*Choirboys* 165). Although not a major theme, Wambaugh does touch on racial prejudice in police departments — especially anti–Hispanic bias in *Lines and Shadows*. In all of his books Wambaugh takes notice of women police officers on the job with men. In *The New Centurions* he depicts the pull and dangers of chivalry:

> She sat relaxed much like a male partner and smoked and watched the street as Gus cruised, much like a male partner would, but it was nothing like working with a male partner. With some of the other policewomen there was no difference, except you had to be more careful and not get involved in things where there was the slightest element of danger. Not if you could help it, because a policewoman was still a woman, nothing more, and you were responsible for her safety, being the male half of the team [*New Centurions* 270].

By the time of *Finnegan's Week* (1993) Wambaugh moves on to the dangers of overcompensating:

A fleeting memory occurred to Bobbie. The director of security had once warned her that women in police work frequently take great risks because they don't want to call for backup from the men until they're sure they need it. But by then, it's often too late. He'd warned that many female cops has been needlessly injured and even killed, for fear of seeming to be the damsel in distress [311].

While his early focus on patrol officers provides little opportunity to bring in descriptions of forensics, Wambaugh went on to write *The Blooding*, a narrative account of the first use of DNA in a criminal investigation.

Serpico

In sum, Wambaugh changed the police novel in many ways. Perhaps one of the more telling tributes to his influence came when writer Peter Maas scoped out the contents of an apartment in Greenwich Village:

> More shelves between the windows overflow with books, among them Thoreau's *Walden*, the collected poems of Yeats, Baudelaire's *Les Fleurs du mal*, *Steppenwolf*, Dalton Trumbo's *Johnny Got His Gun*, and a best-selling novel about cops by a Los Angeles police sergeant, *The New Centurions* [9].

The apartment was Frank Serpico's.

In the early 1970s NYPD Officer Frank Serpico hit the headlines. He testified in court. He got the Knapp Commission really rolling. Peter Maas compiled his biography, *Serpico,* in 1973, and a film about his police career appeared in the same year.

As Maas tells it, all Frank Serpico ever wanted to be was a good cop. And he knew what went into making a good cop:

> This as much as anything was what had attracted him to police work in the first place, the authority and power that automatically went with it, and the ability to help and protect people [18].
>
> Serpico deeply believed in his concept of the cop as the community's friend and protector [194].

Maas' biography depicts Officer Serpico doing those things traditionally associated with good police officers. He delivers a baby, he saves people from a burning building, he arrests rapists, burglars, and robbers. Additionally, as shown in an incident where a detective brutalizes a suspect and Serpico later elicits a confession without the use of force, he knows that psychology works better than brute force. Maas shows Serpico as a principled, efficient police officer. The majority of Maas' narrative, however, brings Serpico into contact with the traditional problems of police forces — sloth and corruption. Early on in his career Serpico comes in contact with cooping, the practice of police officers sleeping rather than patrolling their beats. In one incident he finds not one cop snoozing, but a crowd of cops who have taken over the boiler room of a school and stocked it with cots and blankets for their on-duty naps. What shocks Serpico, however, is that this happens with the connivance of sergeants responsible for making sure their men are on duty. Perhaps more insidious than cooping, is cops on the "pad." Serpico finds that in his department graft has gone wild. At almost every turn cops don't just receive free meals and "police discounts," civilians and his fellow officers shove money at him in loose bills and in bulging envelopes. Most disturbing to Serpico is that corruption has disabled a system that could work:

> What Serpico found so ironic was that Stanard, Zumatto, and the other plain-clothesmen he met were really professional in the sense that they were first-class investigators, and they brought to their craft all the requisites this entailed — instinct, patience, technique, determination, and accurate intelligence provided by a carefully nurtured network of informers. If they wanted to, they could have wiped out a major portion of their number-one target — illegal gambling — almost overnight [167].

Indignant, from early in his career Serpico repeatedly tries to report the illegal acts he has witnessed. He, however, finds a bureaucracy and political apparatus unwilling to listen — a system that has covered up graft and corruption for so long that they are accepted as unfortunate but inevitable parts of police work. For his efforts to report corruption, Serpico's fellow officers ostracize him, the bosses transfer him and circulate rumors that he is "psycho," gay, or both. Late in the biography Maas even relates an incident in which an irate detective attacks Serpico with a knife in the squad room. In the end he is heard, by the grand jury and the courts, by the *New York Times*, by the mayor's office, and by the Knapp Commission.

The main thrust of Maas' biography emphasizes the heroism of his subject in his encounters with individual and corporate corruption. Underneath this, however, Maas articulates through Serpico an ideal view of police work and police officers, one that has failed to develop in the modern city. He understands that the source of the problem lies in the fact that the police have become isolated:

> Cops didn't think of themselves as part of the community. Too many of them, Serpico thought, had isolated themselves not only professionally but socially. They believed they were misunderstood by the "Outside world," that there was a general public antagonism toward them ... they tended to withdraw more and more into themselves and became contemptuous of the public. Cops, after all, saw the seamy side of life every day; they knew what the public was capable of. It colored their whole outlook [91].

Maas, through Serpico, is an advocate for the nationwide drive for community policing begun in the 1970s. Also through Serpico Maas sees the underlying problem in the lack of vocation among police officers. Thus, in Serpico's class of recruits in the police academy:

> Except for a recruit who had been a detective in a department store, nobody seemed interested in being a police officer in terms of what he could do, what he could accomplish [49].

The tragedy of modern policing for Maas and Serpico, then, is that it has become a job. And to the dedicated officer, knowing this compounds the tragedy.

Dallas Barnes

It is hard to believe that they describe the same organization, but Joseph Wambaugh and Dallas Barnes were both cops, and they both wrote about cops in Los Angeles. Beginning with *"See the Woman"* (1973) Barnes portrays what amounts to a pre–Wambaugh department, a *Dragnet* department. *"See the Woman," Yesterday Is Dead* (1976), and *Deadly Justice* (1987), all begin with dedications to members of the LAPD. Barnes follows the McBain tradition of including facsimiles of police documents as a means of building background. Since his books take place in Los Angeles, where so much police work has to be done by car, Barnes punctuates his narrative with radio calls. Here's a sample from *"See the Woman"*:

> "3A9, roger," said the link. "Units in the vicinity, OFFICER NEEDS HELP, a major 415 with shots fired, at Slauson and Overhill. Any units available to handle, identify."
> "3T34, rolling to Slauson and Overhill."
> "Roger, 3Tom34, your call is Code Two," the link answered.
> "12A43, responding to Slauson and Overhill."
> The link responded, "12A43, roger, back up 3Tom34 at Slauson and Overhill, Code Two" [29].

Barnes follows McBain by including a number of crimes in each book, and acknowledges coptalk by providing a glossary of "Police Terms and Abbreviations" at the front of *Badge of Honor* (1974). He also makes a special point to highlight the Herculean task that confronts the Los Angeles Police Department. In the prologue to *"See the Woman"* he counts off the personnel of the Department's Southwest Division — "After spreading the two hundred and seventy-five men over four different shifts; after manning the jail, the desk, the vice squad, station security; and after counting men on vacation, men with injuries or regular days off, there was one man for every 7,400 citizens" — and then he cites a sliver of a morning's crimes:

> The morning watch, working between midnight and eight A.M., had been on duty now for fifty-five minutes. They had handled three armed robbery calls,

two assaults with a deadly weapon, seven family disputes, two lost children, three abandoned children, one drowned child, one rape, two burglaries, and one murder, the result of an argument over a television show [ii].

Even though confronted by an increasingly difficult task, for Barnes the LAPD does its job and does it professionally. Barnes particularly depicts police commanders as efficient and professional. Thus, for instance, when Captain Gunning quickly and efficiently quells a mini riot in Watts at the beginning of *"See the Woman"* he first speaks to his men:

> "I want each of you to keep in mind that we're not going to act as individuals. We're going to work as a team. I don't want any overreaction. I know you're angry. We've taken a couple of hard punches this morning, but goddammit"—his voice was beginning to show the anger he felt—"we're professionals, and we're going to act like it" [37].

Indeed, in *Badge of Honor* Barnes stresses this aspect of the LAPD when a visitor goes to police headquarters:

> He was surprised at the lack of uniformed personnel in the chief's office. For some reason he had expected it to look like a commanding general's office. Instead it had the atmosphere and appearance of a well-organized and efficient corporate headquarters. One thing that he recognized was proper organization and efficiency [103].

Barnes' LAPD, moreover, is a compassionate one. He shows commanders' concern for the families of officers killed in the line of duty as well as their understanding of the stress of their men. For instance, when Sergeant Stryker's anger gets the best of him in *"See the Woman"* his commander puts his remarks in perspective rather than relieving him of duty. In his early books Barnes uses domestic metaphors for what the department means:

> Stryker welcomed the familiar sounds and smells of the station as he unlocked the door into the rear hallway. It was comforting to be back. Here, somehow, he felt strangely secure [*Badge of Honor* 72].
>
> Here inside the station he was secure. It was his home.... This station, this job, was his woman, he guessed [*Badge of Honor* 98–99].

Barnes takes pains to show that his police department is under siege. In his first two books the press and politicians and even the community attack the cops and the way they do their jobs. In *Badge of Honor* a senator demands a top-to-bottom investigation of the department, and in *"See the Woman"* the press and black radicals accuse the department of racism. Both books, however, show the department's antagonists discovering the error of their ways and recognizing the professionalism of the LAPD.

In addition to the police as organization, Barnes focuses on integration. A number of African American officers appear in the books. In *"See the*

Woman," for example, Barnes shows a black cop rocking the infant of a rape victim at the crime scene and frames the novel with an African American officer dying in his attempt to avenge the death of his white partner. Barnes' principal police partners — at first Stryker and West in *"See the Woman"* and *Badge of Honor*, and then Hollister and Fox in *Yesterday Is Dead* (1976) — bring together white cops (Stryker and Hollister) and African American cops (West and Fox). The African American members of the teams have earned the respect of their white colleagues:

> Hollister treated his black partner as less than an equal for their first few weeks. It was during the second month of their partnership that Fox proved his stomach was superior to Hollister's. Hollister had grimaced and covered his mouth as Fox helped a deputy coroner pull a two-foot broom handle out of a dead fruit's ass after he had succumbed to a drug overdose in the middle of his masochistic act. From that day on, Hollister figured Fox had earned his way into the fraternal order of homicide detectives [*Yesterday Is Dead* 15].

Barnes also shows his African American detectives earning their partners' respect by engaging in jejune interracial banter — about watermelons and white bread, for example. He does, however, reinforce the friendship between white and Black officers by showing their care and concern for one another when they come under fire.

After his first two books, Barnes becomes less sanguine about the dedication of individual police officers, seeing devotion to duty as a disappearing virtue. And he also comes to believe that he was witnessing the decline of the Los Angeles Police Department:

> The Los Angeles Police Department, long the proud progressive role model for police departments throughout the world, was suffering the same fate as its sister forces in Chicago, Philadelphia and New York. It was becoming political. Thus power and command, once entrusted to only those with experience and proven ability, were now, more and more, being bestowed on those who knew someone, had the right contacts.... Purlington could remember its beginnings. It started in the mid-seventies when the press began to pay attention to the opinions of then Chief of Police Edward M. Davis. Davis bathed in the limelight of television and used it as a springboard into the California State Assembly.... Finally a crack had appeared in the blue dynasty and politics swept in, making the fabled LAPD just another political department [*Deadly Justice* 200].

Barnes, however, did believe that there were a few heroes left.

Lawrence Sanders

In 1976 Collin Wilcox wrote out seven rules in his piece "Writing and Selling the Police Procedural," published in *The Writer*. His first rule was

Length should be 55,000 to 65,000 words, so that the price can be competitive. All of my Dodd, Mead and Random House books were 60,000 words. A few began longer, but were edited down to that length [20].

Here Wilcox describes most of the police books of the 1950s and 1960s — they were short novels. Lawrence Sanders changed that. His books about Chief (or ex–Chief) Edward X. "Iron Balls" Delaney are hefty volumes — the Berkley paperback of *The First Deadly Sin* extends to six hundred and thirty pages, big enough to fit three or four of McBain's or Linington's works inside. In the three Delaney novels (*The First Deadly Sin* [1973]; *The Second Deadly Sin* [1977]; and *The Third Deadly Sin* [1981]), Sanders moves the police novel away from the confines of the classical detective story and (in the first and last books in the series, at least) places his police hero into books structured and plotted like thrillers. *The First* and *Third Deadly Sin* both give equal coverage to cop and criminal: they focus not only on the detective and his assistants but also on the actions of the murderer. This, of course, was nothing new — double-focus plots do pop up in the police books of earlier writers. And earlier writers also wrote about deranged individuals who committed multiple murders. The times, however, were different when Sanders introduced Delaney in 1973; beginning with the Boston Strangler in 1962, and then on to Richard Speck and Charles Whitman, the 1960s was a decade of multiple and serial killers. Sanders, in fact, is so early in the game that he does not use the term "serial murders" but has Delaney classify them as "multicides." Indeed, Sanders capitalizes on serial killers. In both *The First* and *Third Deadly Sin* he recites the names of serial killers almost as a mantra: "Whitman, Speck, Unruh, the Boston Strangler, Panzram, Manson" (177). In *The Third Deadly Sin* he adds the latest serial killer and labels the villain in the novel "the Daughter of Sam." Just as nonfiction writer Ann Rule did in 1980 with her book on Ted Bundy (*The Stranger Beside Me*), Sanders aims at the public's fascination with serial killers — why they do what they do and how the police catch them. He also realizes the advantage that this double interest in abnormal psychology and police work offers the writer. Thus, while hardly subtle, *The First Deadly Sin* anatomizes the actions of a killer with the same motives as Leopold and Loeb, and *The Third Deadly Sin* offers an inside look at a killer controlled by a hormonal imbalance and raging premenstrual syndrome. Perhaps just as importantly, the string of connected murders offers Sanders the opportunity not just to show the police at work, but to demonstrate them working in a variety of ways in an atmosphere charged with stress and public hysteria.

Sanders' Edward X. "Iron Balls" Delaney technically is not a police officer except at the very beginning of *The First Deadly Sin*; he is retired.

Nonetheless Sanders makes police work so much a part of his character (he, for example, cannot stop thinking and seeing "like a cop") that he may as well still be on the force. Delaney is an old-fashioned cop. In fact in the first of the series Sanders connects him with Teddy Roosevelt's days as New York Police Commissioner, when Delaney takes a parallel nighttime, doorknob-rattling tour of his precinct with a newspaper reporter. Sanders portrays Delaney as a powerful man even in middle age:

> He had the solid, rounded shoulders of a machine-gunner, a torso that still showed old muscle under new fat. His large, yellowed teeth, the weathered face, the body bearing scars of old wounds — all gave the impression of a beast no longer with the swiftness of youth, but with the cunning of years, and vigor enough to kill [*The Third* 62].

He favors sturdy shoes and thick socks, he prohibits long sideburns on his men, and the innovation of women on the job makes him uncomfortable:

> The Desk Sergeant was a policewoman, the second of her rank in New York to be assigned to such duty.... She was a tall, powerfully built woman with what he termed to himself, without knowing why, a thunderous body. In truth, he was intimidated by her; but he could not deny her efficiency. The book was in order; nothing was neglected that could have been done.... But the moon was full, and Delaney knew what that meant [*The First* 151].

In spite of this limitation, Sanders makes Delaney into at least something of a scholar — he has written pieces on "Common sense and the New Detective" and "Hunch, Instinct, and the New Detective" (*The First* 406). And he also adds a bit of the intellectual to the mix: especially in *The First Deadly Sin* Delaney muses on his calling and the connections between order, logic, beauty, and truth.

With most of the rest of Sanders' policemen in the novels he uses research as a gauge of their competence. There is Detective Sergeant Thomas MacDonald, "Pops," who "was Delaney's choice to head up the research squad, and MacDonald was happy. He got as much pleasure from an afternoon of sifting through dusty documents as another man might get in an Eighth Avenue massage parlor" (*The First* 499–500). Then there is Inspector Benjamin Johnson:

> Inspector Benjamin Johnson was on the Commissioner's staff, in charge of statistics and production analysis. He was an enormous man, a former All-American guard from Rutgers. He had gone to fat, but the result wasn't unpleasant; he still carried himself well, and his bulk gave him added dignity. His smile was appealing, almost childlike — a perfect disguise for what Delaney knew was a hard, complex, perceptive intelligence. A black couldn't attain Johnson's rank and reputation by virtue of a hearty laugh and a mouthful of splendid teeth [*The First* 133].

Failures are men like Martin Slavin: "Lieutenant Martin Slavin looked like a bookkeeper who had flunked the CPA exam" (*The Third* 141). And somewhere in the middle, saved by his humanity, is Marty Dorfman: "He's a good administrator, keeps up on his paperwork. He's one of the best lawyers in the department. But he's not a good cop. He's a reasonable facsimile. He goes through all the motions, but he lacks the instinct" (*The First* 73). The ideal cop, then, is one who masters routine and detail and also possesses the imagination to look in new places and to draw conclusions from the accumulated data. Thus the novels recount both serial murders and serial areas of research. In *The Third Deadly Sin*, the task force examines the subscribers' list of a magazine and retailers of Swiss Army knives, as well as canvassing those licensed to possess Mace and sources of medic-alert bracelets. The crux of all of this, of course, is not just the mind-numbing research but the imagination required to know what to research.

In the novels Sanders touches on a number of other police matters. With Abner Boone in *The Second Deadly Sin* he presents a cop with a serious drinking problem, one that discipline and the love of a good woman ultimately help cure. He makes a very brief swipe at corruption by introducing a cameo of an ex-narcotics cop who had been on the take. Sanders also inserts pockets of comment on the impossibility of civilians understanding cops, and the unique characteristics of one who becomes a police officer:

> Too bad there wasn't a word for it: coppishness, copicity, copanity — something like that. "Soldiership" came close, but didn't tell the whole story. What was needed was a special word for the special quality of being a cop [*The First* 566].

In addition to this major police theme of the seventies, Sanders hangs *The First* and *The Third Deadly Sin* on political intrigue among the higher-ups in the department. In both books higher-ups call on Delaney to work for them in secret in order to thwart the efforts of rivals and to further their own political careers in the department.

Rex Burns

Rex Burns (Raoul Stephen Sehler) introduced detective Gabriel Wager in *The Alvarez Journal* (1975). In the Wager books Burns accomplishes a number of things. Hitherto mainly focused on police in New York or Los Angeles, Burns moves the police book to Denver: "In later Wager yarns, my attempt is to record a 'special history' of Denver and Colorado, the kind of emotional nuances that fiction can achieve but are generally frowned on by historians" (email 2/26/02). While writers had introduced African American cops — always in subsidiary roles — Burns created the first Chicano (or half–Chicano) police hero in Gabe Wager. Wager's racial background and racial prejudice play a role especially in the earlier novels. While Burns recalls reading Georges Simenon's police books before *The Alvarez Journal*, television and the cinema served as inspiration, rather than the American police writers of the 1950s and 1960s. It was his intent to bring what he saw as the essence of the procedural back to the police novel. He began writing police books

> as a reaction to what I term "the romance of violence" that was popular on TV and in movies in the 70's — the exaggerated villain, depiction of cops as straight-arrows defending us against dope fiends, reds, and Mafiosi dons. *The Alvarez Journal* was an attempt to portray real police work. This type of realism wasn't a new direction…. But it did seem that Hollywood and television were emphasizing frenetic action to carry their stories rather than the often banal … aspects of crime. So — there's not one shot fired in *The Alvarez Journal*, and our "hero" spends most of his time drinking coffee from styrofoam cups and sitting in a surveillance vehicle [email 2/26/02].

Reinforcing this drive toward portraying real police work, Burns attaches a list of police abbreviations and their meanings to the front of *The Alvarez Journal*, and in the series of articles on the police procedural run by *The Writer* in the 1970s Burns (as an English professor should) directs budding police writers to court records — "Affidavits, depositions, and transcripts" (*The Writer* 14).

Putting a new twist to the omnipresent complaints about the effect of bureaucrats on police work, Burns points not to people but to "modern police management" as the bane of effective police work:

> Modern police management worshiped quantification and statistics were forever being updated and refined and compared. If homicides declined a percentage point or two, crime was being beaten. If they went up, the bad guys were winning. There were figures on the ratio between solved and unsolved cases in every category, and a red pencil marked a quantifiable line between acceptable and unacceptable. There was even an annual time study of the number of crime reports divided into the total man-hours available for each division and section. The result indicated the average amount of time that could be allotted to each crime. In Homicide, it was sixteen hours" [*Strip* 89].

Burns juxtaposes police management with individual effort, intelligence, and dedication. Rather than serving as an aid in detection as it had in the novels of the 1950s and 1960s, paperwork by the seventies had become an impediment to police work: "Wager turned to work on routine papers: sheaves of forms that seemed to peak in quarterly, semiannual, and annual waves, always the same in content and result. Someone, somewhere must have one hell of a big pile of worthless paper, because none of it ever changed anything" (*Alvarez* 14). In a number of books Wager spends considerable time investigating by himself, following through on time union rules prohibit him from spending on official business, a particularly evident theme in *Strip Search* (1984). Burns also summons up the common cop theme of past versus present in this connection. With Wager the past was better:

> "He only works a forty-hour week?" ...
> "His wife wants to go see a movie."
> "Jesus H. Christ — it ain't the old cops!" [*Alvarez* 117].

Burns draws Wager as a dedicated police officer. Like so many other cops from the 1970s onward, he is divorced, but has managed to overcome it. He has a demanding job, but has managed to overcome it: "Still, no regrets; he had lousy pay, an insecure job, and hours longer than a whore" (*Alvarez* 21). He confronts the punctiliousness of the law but accepts it as much a part of his working conditions as a bureaucracy immune to common sense and ignorant about the way people behave. He has a Hispanic background, but identifies more with the new minority of which he has become a member:

> "Did you ever notice," Wager asked Jo, "how friendly civilians are after you tell them you're a cop? It's almost as warm and cozy as saying you have herpes" [*Ground Cover* 42].

Robert Daley

Robert Daley had more reason to know about the political intrigue inside the New York Police Department than most. He was Deputy Police Commissioner of New York from 1971 to 1972, the same time the Knapp Commission and the media exposed the breadth and depth of corruption in the department. After leaving the department Daley, too, participated in the exposé with his non-fiction book *Prince of the City*, an account of the federal investigation of widespread corruption in New York spurred by the revelations of officer Bob Leuci — featuring a cameo appearance by young federal prosecutor Rudy Giuliani. Daley, moreover, also turned his experience with the department into a number of novels, beginning with *To Kill a Cop* (1976).

Just as Wambaugh gives the police novel back to the patrol officer in his three early books, Daley shifts the focus from the conventional hero of the detective sergeant to upper-level police officers. *To Kill a Cop* features Chief of Detectives Earl Eischied, *The Year of the Dragon* (1981) has Captain Art Powers, *Hands of a Stranger* (1985) uses Inspector Joe Hearn, *Wall of Brass* (1994) features Chief of Detectives Bert Faber, and *A Faint Cold Fear* (1990) features Deputy Chief Ray Douglas. They are all officials in a huge organization: "Eishied liked to think of himself as an executive whose budget ran to $74 million a year, and who had three thousand employees" (*To Kill a Cop* 199). As an organization, however, Daley's department is subject to external political whims:

> The Mayor had sent them in with the usual mayoral mandate — increase efficiency; stamp out corruption. So far all they had done was force a good many older commanders to retire, replacing them with their own men, leaving most of the survivors jittery [*To Kill a Cop* 67].

And inside the department favoritism rules:

> The existing rating system was as big a failure as all the others which had gone before it, and this year's detectives were as cynical as the ones a generation ago. To detectives it wasn't what you did that counted, but who you knew. And they were right. How well connected was your rabbi? [*To Kill a Cop* 105–6].

Daley, then, depicts heroes whose careers can evaporate in a moment — who can lose their positions through transfers to backwater precincts, as happens to Ray Douglas in *A Faint Cold Fear*. *Wall of Brass*, in fact, centers on a system charged with politics, the jockeying for power in the department, the dirty tricks top police officials pull to make others look bad, and the mayor's cat and mouse game with the same officials. "The brass's sole function as he saw it was to exalt themselves by screwing cops" (*Tainted Evidence* 136).

Daley bases his choice of command-level police officials on the assumption that these jobs require particular and special talent not possessed by the average police officer:

> He cursed a system which sucked rough, ill-educated young men in at the bottom, which exalted and promoted them for physical bravery, but then informed them as they approached middle age that entirely different qualities were necessary [*To Kill a Cop* 75].

While Daley's heroes possess a full measure of physical bravery, he also shows them as deeply engrossed in thinking about how police work can be done more effectively — how real ability can be assessed, how divisions can be organized more effectively, etc. And, of course, how to survive the political games played by those who seek only power.

To hold up the need for this kind of hero, Daley presents a depressing picture of the lack of effectiveness of the police department. He matter-of-factly cites shocking statistics:

> Dixon's murder was like 65 percent of the homicides in this city.... The victim and the killer knew each other. That's the kind of homicides we solve. Most of the time the killer and the victim are still in the same room. The other 35 percent are the homicides we don't solve" [*To Kill* 55–6].

> They did not inform her ... that the arrest rate for burglary was only 18 per-

cent, and that the percentage of goods recovered was lower than that [*To Kill a Cop* 157].

Daley also finds part of the reason for losing the fight against crime in numbers and the attitude spawned by doing an impossible job:

> Would the detectives ever learn the answer? Probably not. They were too busy to ask why Rodriguez had shot his wife and then himself—they didn't have the time, and ultimately they didn't care what the answer might be. Having too many similar cases, they were no longer that curious [*Wall of Brass* 183].

In several books he uses a baseball metaphor to express his view of police attitudes:

> Most cops were defeatist.... It grew out of their vast cynicism. They were like players on a last-place team. They expected to lose. The world was a malignant place. Justice rarely triumphed [*Year of the Dragon* 185].

Nonetheless, Daley draws dedicated and effective cops who succeed, in spite of this pervasive insecurity and its resultant incompetence, in doing what the police department is supposed to do—fight crime. Eishied both worries about how to make promotions for people in his department fair and tracks down and shoots an urban guerilla, and Art Powers in *Year of the Dragon* finds a way to stymie the efforts of a Chinese drug lord.

Like Wambaugh, Daley makes the point that cops lie:

> But to deceive another human being was evil, and law enforcement personnel, he already realized, did as much lying—and maybe more—as the criminals they arrested.... They made promises to witnesses, to informants, that they knew they couldn't keep, and in the interest of taking felons off the street they swore out false search warrants and arrest warrants. If necessary to secure a conviction they often enough gave perjured testimony on the witness stand. All of this was unfortunate. To combat fraud, they multiplied fraud ... cops murdered truth every day. They destroyed trust. They were guilty of one of the worst crimes of all, the proliferation of the lie [*Year of the Dragon* 197–98].

Daley, however, goes one step further by indicating that the efficient cause of police mendacity should be traced to an inefficient and corrupt court system: Thus the complaint about the ubiquitous plea bargain in *Tainted Evidence*:

> They all knew what this meant. There were too many murders for too few prosecutors, too few judges, and too few courtrooms. However horrible these crimes, many would have to be plea-bargained away [31].

On top of this, Daley's cops view the judicial system itself as misguided, giving more power to criminals than to the police—in Daley, complaints about the Rosario Rule (that the prosecution must make all of its evidence

available to the defense) outweigh complaints about Miranda-Escobido —
and as a system that is as corrupt and corrupted as the police force: "Judges
… were motivated not by notions of justice, but by the fear of being reversed
on appeal" (*Tainted Evidence* 277). The courts, therefore, present yet another
obstacle to effective policing, an obstacle that Daley's heroes overcome, occasionally using extra-legal or even illegal means.

To explain cops, Daley often fastens onto church metaphors. He applies
them to the police hierarchy in *Hands of a Stranger*: "The Police Department in its outlook and rigidity often seemed to her a mirror image of the
Catholic Church, which in turn suggested that the rigidity of the clerical
mind and the rigidity of the police mind were the same" (23). And he uses
a different denomination to explain the minority status that had become a
fixture in police books of the 1970s:

> Possibly because cops constituted the most despised minority on earth, they
> not only clung together fiercely, they also tended, like the Protestant churches,
> to be ecumenical about it. The brotherhood was both vast and generous. Most
> times it admitted not only all cops, but also all law enforcement agents of what-
> ever kind worldwide. As with any religion, there were bound to be sects that
> had fallen away. Rites differed with the jurisdiction, dogma differed, but not
> much. In general all held the same faith. Their priests were all sworn, all
> ordained. All believed in the same true god [*Year of the Dragon* 272].

Daley notes that cops hear confessions, and by deciding whom to arrest and
whom not to arrest, they give absolution:

> A cop is a kind of priest, isn't he? Cops believe in absolutes, just like priests.
> Good and Evil. The law. Cops decide what's sinful and what's not, just like
> priests. And they can lay on hands just like a bishop. They can change a per-
> son's condition just by saying so: You're under arrest [*Year of the Dragon* 122].

But it's with the absolutes that Daley's heroes have trouble. Having
witnessed a callous, self-seeking hierarchy in their department and a Byzan-
tine and inept judicial system, Daley points to cynicism as the police officer's
usual defense. However, he specifically notes that the fundamental virtue of
his heroes is their romanticism — their ability to believe in something that
demonstrably does not exist, and their willingness to engage in battles that
usually can only be lost.

Jon A. Jackson

Jon A. Jackson's first police novel (*The Diehard* in 1977), like Rex Burns'
novels, moves away from New York and L.A. His books take place in the
9th Precinct of Detroit. Part of Jackson's intention lies in depicting a number of the precinct's personnel. Beginning at the top, he follows the antiau-

thority trend with Precinct Inspector Buchanan: "This was Precinct Inspector Buchanan of the Ninth, a small and handsome man who did not look like a policeman. He looked like an undersecretary of a foreign legation" (*Diehard* 21). Buchanan is the typical bureaucrat, hidebound by rules and at the same time confused by them. This shows best with the issue of police brutality, an issue that attracts much of Jackson's attention. In his attitude toward brutality Buchanan presents a capsule comment on the mores of police bureaucrats:

> Buchanan had an absolute horror of brutality charges. The whole department was very sensitive on the issue, but Buchanan was nearly pathological about it. Especially disquieting to the officers of the 9th was the realization that Buchanan was not against brutality *per se*, he was against brutality charges [*Blind Pig* 19].

Buchanan has his office toady in Lieutenant Johns:

> Lt. Darrow Johns was a portly man with dark-rimmed glasses. He was amiable and not stupid, but he looked like anything but a detective. He had a great virtue of absolute loyalty toward his superiors, a valuable factor when the superior had to choose between promoting two otherwise equally qualified candidates [*Blind Pig* 20].

Of note here is that neither Buchanan nor Johns looks like a cop. Jackson notes that Buchanan is unusually short and, in *The Blind Pig*, Mulheisen says he looks like "a seal" and Johns "looked like anything but a policeman." Jackson briefly mentions two efficient higher-ups: Mulheisen's friend Homicide Inspector Laddy McClain — whose most prominent cop detail is his big feet — and, in *The Blind Pig*, Inspector "Ike" Weinberg, "a calm, middle-aged man" (*Blind Pig* 121).

The precinct's detectives represent a mixed bag of humanity, albeit a resurrected mixed bag. There is Sergeant Maki, a reformed police officer:

> Sergeant Maki of the Ninth Precinct was known on the street as the Pivot. He looked like a forty-year old high-school basketball star, but that wasn't why they called him the Pivot. He used to have a habit of wheeling on a tough suspect and belting him. This would happen in the early hours of interrogation. It never happened anymore, but the name was still there [*Diehard* 139–40].

By *The Blind Pig* Jackson depicts Maki as utterly absorbed in police work, so much so that his third divorce is irrelevant to him. The same kind of conversion from bad cop to good cop happens with Detectives Jensen and Field. In *The Diehard* Mulheisen calls Jensen "a meanie," but in the next novel Jackson has Jensen partnered with Bud Field: "Bud Field, was a reticent but imaginative man. Together they [Field and Jensen] made one quite good detective" (*Blind Pig* 30). Other than his hero, "Fang" Mulheisen, Jackson pays most attention to Dennis Noell and the Big Four:

tionment

> Dennis Noell was the honcho of the crew. He was six-five, two hundred and forty pounds and had a nose like the prow of a ship. The whole squad was large and intimidating and they carried an armament of axe handles, tommy guns, a Stoner rifle, sawed-off shotguns, and .44 Magnums on their hips [*Diehard* 47].

Indeed by the second novel Jackson makes Noell even bigger; he's six-seven *in The Blind Pig*. The Big Four, an officially sanctioned strong-arm squad, roams Detroit with their automatic weapons prominently displayed in their big Chrysler sedan. In response to Mulheisen's disapproval of their methods, Noell tells him that "It ain't like that, Mul. It's war out there. You gotta whack 'em" (*Blind Pig* 23). In *The Blind Pig*, in spite of their inclination to violence, Noell and his beef trust prove to be effective police officers during the crisis of a wrecked train. There are several other detectives in Jackson's first two books, perhaps most notably Patrolman Marshall in *The Blind Pig*, whose eagerness and intelligence convince Mulheisen to become his departmental rabbi. But there are no women:

> "I mean, we have women detectives, but they aren't really detectives, somehow. They work on muggers and rapists, that sort of thing, and they help question female suspects, do personal searches, and so forth."
> "You mean they do specialized kinds of work," Lou said. "They're categorized. You don't see them pulling a routine shift like any other detective. A social worker might be a man or a woman, it doesn't make any difference. But a detective is a man, and then there are *women* detectives who do special things" [*Diehard* 200].

Jackson's books focus on detective Sergeant "Fang" Mulheisen. Jackson shrinks from attaching any special significance to detectives in general, or to Mulheisen in particular. This comes out in the following snatch of conversation in *The Diehard*:

> "I've heard the role of detective described as a peculiarly interesting and relevant one in terms of modern mythology," she said.
> "Who says?"
> "Usually it's a tall boy with narrow shoulders and wide hips," she said, "and he teaches at the New School" [*Diehard* 43–4].

As Jackson would have it, Mulheisen defies most stereotypes. He is middle aged and, although sexually active, lives with his mother outside of the city (and pays for a mail drop in Detroit to skirt departmental residence requirements). He is somewhat of a slob — his first appearance shows him at breakfast drinking beer and eating cold macaroni and cheese with his fingers. Mulheisen has an avuncular air about him, and frequently hands out cigars to people he meets. In Jackson's novels he largely acts independently, something that Jackson makes credible in a police officer by creating a past for his hero — Mulheisen's father had held political office and some, like Inspector Buchanan, believe that the son possesses his father's extensive political connections and wealth, neither of which is true. This illusion of wealth and power exempts Mulheisen from petty rules and politicians. Mulheisen connects back, although not uncritically, to the last generation of policemen. His friendship with a retired cop drives the action in *Grootka*, and in *The Blind Pig* he contrasts the effectiveness of old-fashioned methods with the heavy weapons tactics of the Big Four:

> What happened to the old nightstick routine? You bat the guy on the arm and he drops his gun. If he keeps up the funny business you spike him in the gut with the stick, or raise a knot on his head [22].

Jackson attaches the word "stupid" to Mulheisen several times. Mulheisen's introduction in the first novel reads: "Mulheisen stood in his undershorts staring at the note stupidly" (*Diehard* 9). That he is occasionally stupid, however, is only of part of Mulheisen's complicated self-awareness. Thus his musings when he sets off for an evening with a woman friend:

> He would tell her that he was contrary, that he sometimes appalled himself with his compliant nature, that he often thought he was full of crap and then the next day knew he was dead right about everything. It was a burden to be so indeterminate, so changeable, inconstant even [*Diehard* 178].

He, additionally, is the precinct's star detective. Jackson's novels take place in Detroit, where organized crime forms part of the historical picture. It plays a part in the first two books, and, to complicate matters, in Mulheisen's world –especially in *Grootka*— facts are sometimes not easy to find or simple to understand. Jackson does not endow his hero with any special attributes other than intelligence, a healthy work ethic, and, for lack of a better term, a bountiful capacity for enjoying what he does:

> Tired as he was — it was now after eleven — Mulheisen didn't feel like going home. Too much was happening. It would be unthinkable to head for bed, comparable to leaving a party just when they'd sent out for more beer [*Blind Pig* 126].

Mike Jahn

In 1977 Mike Jahn published his first police book, *Killer on the Heights*; five years later he published his second (*Night Rituals*), this time as Michael Jahn. They are different kinds of books. Like Rex Burns, Jahn reacted against a number of the conventions that had been established in the police book during the previous two decades. Indeed, *Killer on the Heights* may as well be a primer on police in the movies and on the tube in the 1970s — the nar-

rator of the book watches both *Dirty Harry* and *The French Connection* on
television, as well as broadcasts of *Kojak*, When he contemplates writing a
book his friend says "The book? You mean we can do our own Joseph
Wambaugh? I thought you said you didn't have a good cop story" (223).

Killer on the Heights includes a couple of miscellaneous observations
about police. The narrator emphasizes the stress experienced by New York
City police officers:

> Half the cops I know are crazy too. The uniformed guys about to go on shifts
> in Harlem sit in their cars, parked on the sidewalk in front of the 26th, star-
> ing straight ahead, chewing gum. Never say a word unless they're spoken to.
> Worst are the undercover narcotics men. They look and act like scroungy hip-
> pies. Long, dirty hair. Sweat-smelly armpits. They never shave, bathe infre-
> quently, and do nothing but sit around talking about dope.... The undercover
> guys have gotten so deeply into what they do, they've become the people they're
> supposed to arrest. Mad as hatters [118].

He also casually mentions police brutality:

> Having been steamed up by seeing the body in the park, Bacelli decided to
> break the rules and interrogate Browning in the back of the squad car while
> en route to the 26th. The fact that the route included St. Louis was never
> included in the official report. When Browning was lifted from the squad car
> in front of the 26th Precinct, he had confessed twice over to the murder [85].

Lieutenant Dan McAnn, a second-generation cop, narrates *Killer on
the Heights* and with him Jahn enters new (or old) territory. McAnn openly
uses offensive racial epithets. In the following, for example, he talks about
his partner:

> Vega, I learned today, objects to being called a nigger. He is, he says, a Puerto
> Rican or, if I must, a spic. But not a nigger. I told him, "The mere fact you
> get so testy about it makes you a nigger" [18].

In the book McAnn and Vega investigate a series of murders of African Americans and Hispanics in Morningside Heights. As *Killer on the Heights* proceeds Jahn seeks to mitigate McAnn's racism and show him conscientiously
investigating the crimes against minorities. At the end of the novel, however, readers discover that instead of a conventional police story Jahn has
written the cop version of *The Murder of Roger Ackroyd* but with yet another
twist — Vega, McAnn's loyal partner, is killed for having discovered the truth
about the murders, and the narrator has moved out of the city. But in the
very last line, in the fashion of too many policemen, he puts his gun to his
head.

In *Night Rituals* Jahn tells a more conventional police story. This book
recounts Lieutenant Donovan's efforts to solve what appears to be a string

of serial killings. Jahn makes the point that Donovan is not the usual cop —
he's neither brutal nor caught up in regulations, routine, and machismo:

> "You have a funny way about you for a cop, I mean you don't seem coplike.
> Does that make sense?"
>
> "Sure it does. My captain tells me the same thing. It may mean that I've
> never beaten up a suspect. I don't like coplike cops. After a while, they end up
> 'ten-fouring' everyone and can't seem to get a sentence out without telling
> everyone how tough they are" [47].

In many ways Jahn makes his hero the great detective:

> Donovan was thirty-eight and handsome, with a commanding look and the
> ability to speak to both Nobel laureates and numbers runners. He was so much
> respected on the street that his eccentricities were, in the main, forgiven [11].

In the later novels, in fact, Jahn makes Donovan into something of a polymath with encyclopedic knowledge of almost everything. In the first Donovan book the hero's eccentricities consist of spending a lot of his working
hours in bars, and his comic irascibility. Both of Jahn's early books contain
a great deal of black humor, abetted by the headings of his chapters. Jahn
also connects his hero with the last generation of cops, both in making him
the son of a cop and in his pronounced compassion: "Drunkenness is the
second refuge of the cop who is too easily upset. The twentieth century
teaches us not to care about our fellow man. Some old-timers like Donovan don't learn too good" (7). Donovan and McAnn, moreover, demonstrate
the opposite sides of the vigilante coin. The latter twists the law and his position in order to enact private revenge, while the former uses his position to
accomplish the revenge unavailable to private citizens — he assures victims
that he will both find and kill the murderer of innocents.

Almost as compensation for *Killer on the Heights*, the Donovan books
introduce Sergeant Thomas Lincoln Jefferson, the hero's African American
aide. Jahn holds that Jefferson, unafflicted by Donovan's eccentricities, will
go far in the police department, and is destined to be the city's first African
American police commissioner. And it is appropriate that Jefferson is Donovan's buddy, for Jahn portrays the current commissioner as Donovan's buddy
too. In fact, in the few instances that he portrays corporate police activities — like the careful costuming for press conferences at different stages of
investigations — Jahn describes them as smart and benign.

Cops in the 1970s

Television influenced the way people perceived police officers more than
books, and television programming in the 1970s was a great deal different
from that of the previous decades. During the 1970s and early 1980s Amer-

ican network television made the police drama one of the foundations of evening programming. In 1971 four police shows began (*Cade's County, Columbo, Dan August,* and *McMillan and Wife*); in 1972 five new shows appeared (*Hec Ramsey, Jigsaw, Madigan, The Rookies,* and *The Streets of San Francisco*); and in 1975 seven new cop shows debuted (*Baretta, Barney Miller, The Blue Knight, Bronk, Caribe, The Cop and the Kid,* and *Joe Forrester*). The turning point in terms of the presentation of realistic police officers occurred in 1973 with the premieres of *Kojak* and *Police Story.* For the latter Joseph Wambaugh served as creator and story consultant, and in 1975 he filled the same roles for *The Blue Knight* series. Dorothy Uhnak's policewoman appeared on television the year after *Police Story,* with an altered name, in the series *Get Christie Love.* In 1976 the networks televised a series on hero-cop Frank Serpico, aptly titled *Serpico.* Robert Daley's hero from *To Kill a Cop* gave his name to the 1979 series *Eishied.* In all, television of the 1970s accepted the police officer as a popular hero, and as a hero different from the stone-faced, squeaky-clean Sergeant Joe Friday of *Dragnet.* While it employed the names and some of the talents of writers of the period, American television in the 1970s could not present or convey some of the most serious themes developed in cop novels.

The writers of the period also made their way into the cinema in the 1970s. McBain's *Fuzz* became a film in 1972. Wambaugh's novels *The New Centurions* and *The Choirboys,* as well as his nonfiction piece, *The Onion Field,* appeared as films, respectively, in 1972, 1977, and 1979. Lawrence Sanders' *The First Deadly Sin* was filmed in 1980; Daley's nonfiction piece on Bob Leuci, *The Prince of the City,* became a movie in 1981; and James Mills' title *Report to the Commissioner* was attached to a film in 1974. None of these was remarkable for its success. The real impact of cops on film in the 1970s came from *The French Connection* (1971) and Clint Eastwood's *Dirty Harry* (1972). Fiction, however, was significantly different from the cinema, and the attitude and violence of Eastwood's Harry Callahan bear little resemblance to cops in cop novels.

The cinema, and to an even lesser extent television, gave few clues about what was really going on in the police world of the 1960s and 1970s. Those two decades were arguably the most tumultuous in the history of law enforcement in the United States. Beginning in the 1960s new and shocking crimes and criminals held the public's attention. Serial killings made the news first with the Boston Strangler in 1962, then the still unsolved Zodiac Killings of 1968, and ending the 1970s with the Son of Sam in 1977 and Ted Bundy in 1978. Richard Speck's murder of nurses in Chicago in 1966, Charles Whitman shooting from the tower at the University of Texas in 1966, and the Manson Family's murder of Sharon Tate in 1968 brought ghastly crimes and police work into full public view. Even more shocking to the national psyche were the assassinations of John and Robert Kennedy and Dr. Martin Luther King, Jr. Prefigured by the Watts Riots of 1965, National Guard troops across the country needed to reestablish order when urban police forces could not during the riots that followed King's murder. In most major cities, too, police were called upon to control sometimes unruly protesters and deal with acts of civil disobedience connected with the Vietnam War. For the first time in decades, however, new forensic weapons in the fight against crime began to appear: In 1972 the FBI organized its Behavioral Sciences Unit, followed in 1977 by AFIS, the FBI's automated fingerprint database. And in 1977 the first advance in fingerprinting in a century appeared with the discovery of super glue fuming.

The repercussions of these things only slowly began to be felt in the police books of the 1970s. The popularity of the serial killer book had to wait until the 1980s and 1990s and a new crop of serial killers — Wayne Williams, John Wayne Gacy, the Green River Killer, and Jeffrey Dahmer. Wambaugh and Barnes both include race riots in their books — the Watts Riot in Wambaugh's *The New Centurions* and a minor racial skirmish in Barnes' *"See the Woman."* Additionally, police action against black militant groups and individuals rarely becomes the subject of cop books, with Daley's *Cop Killer* (1978) standing as one of the very few to focus on the activities of black militants. A brief episode in Wambaugh's *The Blue Knight* (1973) is a rare example of a cop book acknowledging the problem of antiwar protesters. Some writers like Barnes, however, make the integrated force one of their main themes and black and Hispanic police occasionally come into the novels of the 1970s — Hispanic police with Rex Burns' books and later in Tom Lewis' *Rooftops*. More attention was given to minority cops in the novels of the 1980s, but it took until the 1990s before African American and other minority cops became featured as protagonists in cop novels. On the forensic front, although Lawrence Sanders' hero seeks the counsel of a psychiatrist to "profile" the serial killer in *The First Deadly Sin*, profiling belongs to writers of the next decade — as does the method of raising latent fingerprints using super glue. It took a decade longer for the real world of forensic science to penetrate fiction.

At the same time that crime and detection came into the public spotlight, police came under new and intense public scrutiny. There was the "police riot" at the Democratic National Convention in Chicago as detailed in the Walker Report (*Rights in Conflict: the violent confrontation of demonstrators and police in the parks and streets of Chicago during the 1968 Democratic National Convention of 1968. A report submitted by Daniel Walker, director of the Chicago study team, to the National Commission on the Causes and Prevention of Violence. December 1, 1968*). Cops hauled antiwar protesters from campuses from Columbia to Berkeley. The televised hearings of New York City's Knapp Commission (written up in *Report of the Commission to Investigate Allegations of Police Corruption and the City's Anti-Corruption Procedures. December 26, 1972*) revealed widespread corruption ranging from minor "grass eating" to flagrant "meat eating" crimes in that city's police force.

On top of these challenges and problems, in 1964 the U.S. Supreme Court decided in favor of the defendant in *Escobido v. Illinois*, and then in the better known of the twin cases decided for Danny Miranda in 1966, thereby changing forever the way police would do their jobs. The very makeup of the country's police forces was changed by the Civil Rights Act of 1964, ensuring that women and minorities would be guaranteed equal rights to serve as police officers. And the organization of police forces became subject to new methods of deployment and behavior, as seen especially in the creation of citizens' review boards and the movement toward community policing. Writers of the 1970s show the slow and grudging acceptance of women cops, but the books of the period show almost universal contempt for both courts' rulings on civil rights and the civilian interference threatened by review boards and community policing.

Although the full impact of changes in law and public policy would not be felt until the 1980s, insofar as police books of the 1960s and 1970s were concerned, they were against them. Most of the literal references to the Knapp Commission occur in the police novels of the 1980s. James Mills' *Report to the Commissioner* (1972) uniquely presents details of an internal affairs investigation of police corruption. In general the books of the 1970s accept meals on the arm and other examples of minor graft as time-honored and largely acceptable police practices. There is more than tacit agreement from most writers that a bit of brutality is okay — if it doesn't go too far. Both of the LAPD cops, Wambaugh and Barnes, make casual references to police use of the now illegal chokehold. Bumper Morgan's advice in Wambaugh's *The Blue Knight* can stand for the view of most writers during the 1970s:

> That was one of the first things we learned in the old days from the beat cops who broke us in. When a man takes a swing at you or actually hits you, you have the right to kick ass, that goes without saying. It doesn't have to be tit for tat, and if the asshole gives you tit, you tat his goddamn teeth down his throat. That way you'll save some other cop from being slugged by the same puke pot if he learns his lesson from you [146].

Writers do present extremes. Thus, much like Jon Jackson's strong arm squad, the Big Four, James Mills' *Report to the Commissioner* recounts the actions of the Black Knights:

And they used to go out, maybe three or four at a time, in one of their own cars, and when they saw black men on the street who looked wrong, or who they knew were dealing, or roughing people off, or something like that, they'd jump them. They never made any arrests, they just pounded people into the pavement. All very personal and unofficial, but everyone knew who they were and everyone knew they were cops ... they were really, really feared, because if they knew you were doing something wrong, they didn't bother to snowflake you or anything that sophisticated, they just "Hey you," slam, slam, slam, and that was it. Case closed [59].

Like Jackson, however, Mills' novel based on "documents" shows the ultimate uselessness of this kind of brutality in encouraging respect for the police and the law. While O'Donnell demonstrates how well a woman hero can function in a world of fictional police, women cops are largely ignored or scorned. Daley's Agnes Cusack in *To Kill a Cop* presents a picture of many police writers' views on the female police officers:

In addition she saw herself as a symbol for women everywhere trying to find and hold a place in a man's world, and all this responsibility seemed to come crashing down on her, so that, suddenly, it seemed to her that she wasn't tough enough, wasn't woman enough to handle it all at once. The police officer sat on the toilet lid sobbing into her hands [229–30].

There would be more on this subject, much, much more, in the next decade. There was no lack of coverage of the way police departments were led and organized. Even in books featuring upper-level cops, writers portray departments mired by politicians both within and without. In Wambaugh no one above the rank of sergeant can be trusted either professionally or personally. Tom Lewis gives a snapshot of the NYPD in *Rooftops* (1982):

Rodriguez looked around the squad room. He saw a bunch of generally decent, competent men; mostly Irish, some Jews, a few blacks. But they were all lifers in a nineteenth-century bureaucracy that had been outrun by the city's criminals [59].

Insofar as the new strictures put on police with respect to interrogations and search and seizure, writers show almost universal contempt and confusion among cops about *Escobido, Miranda*, and *Mapp v. Ohio* (one of the most significant probable cause cases). Liberal columnist Nat Hentoff stands almost alone in his outspoken support of the changes in law and implicit changes in police work in *Blues for Charlie Darwin* (1982) when a police sergeant says

I am not one of those law enforcement people who keeps complaining that the Supreme Court keeps putting handcuffs on the peace forces and takes them off the criminal forces. Every night I pray for the health of the Supreme Court because with such things as they gave us like Miranda, my boys had to stop fucking around. They had to produce solid cases [162].

Lawyer William Coughlin's hero in *The Stalking Man* (1979) expresses the most common view of the courts and society: "I'm a detective. Jesus! We proved every fact that existed, no more, no less.... We did our job. Society blew theirs" (36). Doing one's job, however, often means finding devious means around the law. Jon Jackson introduces the "Tennessee search warrant" in *The Blind Pig*, a warrantless search procedure whereby one police officer knocks on a door and an unseen officer yells "come in." Daley and Wambaugh both make it clear that cops lie to make their cases. Mostly, moreover, writers motivate their heroes by a higher — or at least what they perceive to be a more realistic — law than the interpretations of the Supreme Court. Dallas Barnes' hero in *Badge of Honor* sums up a great deal of cop novel sentiment when he says

> Those simpleminded ivory-tower imbeciles called judges do all their great work in defense of the constitution. Who in hell are we ... the fucking enemy [119].

Thus the view of the police has changed from that of an army managed and led by educated and intelligent men, held by writers before World War II, to that of middle-class men solving crimes with the aid of routines, held by writers in the 1950s, to that of a beleaguered minority upholding justice in the face of inept and corrupt bureaucrats and politicians, a court system divorced from reality, and a hostile public, held by writers of the 1970s.

Writers of the 1970s portray a wider variety of police officers than did earlier writers. The most obvious case, to be sure, is the portrayal of a few women and minority cops. Their new police characters, however, differ in a number of ways. First the cops of the 1970s are not thoroughly disciplined and devoted middle-class men, as were the heroes of the previous decades. Gone are the wife and kids at home in the suburbs. While the family tradition holds with characters who become cops because their fathers were cops, in the seventies social class seems to matter less than it did before and a number of characters have college educations. Divorce becomes frequent and alcoholism more common. Notions about the decay and end of civilization come in somewhat more often than in the previous decades, as does the feeling of being under siege, not merely by criminals, bosses, politicians, courts, and the media, but also by the public at large. The response to this is a new emphasis on police as separate from everyone else. Wambaugh labels cops a minority; Sanders in *The First Deadly Sin* uses the term fraternity. It becomes a major theme.

However, it takes more than feelings of ostracism to make a minority.

Thus the minority theme attaches to the examination of police language, which in the seventies broadens out from the explanation of technical terms and the few bits of police slang used in the last decades. Earlier novels make terms like "squeal" for complaint, "catching" for being on duty, and "grounder" for an easily solved complaint familiar expressions to readers. In addition to explaining acronyms and office slang (as do Mills in *Report to the Commissioner* and Barnes in *Badge of Honor,* by providing a glossary of police terms), writers in the seventies bring in slang that reflects cops' black humor — Daley's characters, for instance, replace the cliché DOA (dead on arrival) with DRT (dead right there), and Wambaugh's cops use the acronym NHI (no humans involved) to report the death of a prostitute. The list of slang terms for criminals begins to increase in the seventies (mutts, alligators, scumbags, turdbirds, snakes, skels) as does the list of terms applied to minorities (Jackson, for instance, refers to "Americanus Alabamus" in *The Diehard*). Perhaps the most telling recitation of cop slang occurs in *The Choirboys* in the collective search for an appropriate term for non-cops:

> If there was one thing Roscoe Rules wished, after seeing all of the world he cared to see, it was that there was a word as dirty as "nigger" to apply to all mankind. Since he had little imagination he had to settle for "asshole." But he realized that all Los Angeles policemen and most American policemen used that as the best of all possible words....
>
> Everyone went through the ordinary police repertoire for Roscoe Rules.
> "How about fartsuckers?'
> "Not rotten enough."
> "Slimeballs?"
> "That's getting old."
> "Scumbags?"
> "Naw"
> "Cumbuckets?"
> "Too long"
> "Hemorrhoids?"
> "Everybody uses that."
> "Scrotums?"
> "Not bad, but too long."
> "Scrotes, then"...
> "That's it!" Roscoe Rules shouted "Scrotes! That's what all people are: ignorant filthy disgusting ugly worthless scrotes!" [22-3].

For most writers shared danger and exposure to all of the frailties of mortality — as well as the grimmest facts of mortality (facts that writers of the next decade would make far more graphic) — coupled with the burdens of prejudice provide sufficient foundation for the increasingly prevalent notion of police as a minority. A few writers, however, begin to define cops, good ones at least, as possessing special characteristics. Thus Daley in his 1990s novel *Wall of Brass* describes

> the notion that a cop could be great at his job the way a musician could be great or a painter. That cop could be an artist of a kind. Art was the expression of insights and understanding that more ordinary people simply did not have, and would never have, was it not? [38].

Increasingly in the 1980s and 1990s writers would include special attributes possessed by police officers — intuition, cop eyes, etc.— as essential parts of their characters.

In many ways the police novel came of age in the 1970s. Wilcox, Burns, and O'Donnell all advised writers about how to write the police procedural in separate issues of *The Writer* (January 1976; May 1977; and February 1978 respectively), and John Ball featured police stories in the Mystery Writers of America's 1978 anthology *Cop Cade*. The ways writers presented police officers and police departments changed. Few writers depended on the routine of shuffling through documents (and displaying facsimile documents), an antique process in a decade when information was increasingly accessible by computer. More began to look at the characters of police officers and the personal and professional complexities occasioned by their jobs. In his first three novels, Wambaugh broke the police novel's inevitable connection with the mystery story, and the conventions of that form had increasingly less to do with the way writers constructed their storytelling. The "how-catchem" and the thriller increasingly supplanted the whodunit as a means of structuring novels. Indeed, in Jerome Charyn's books the police officer became the central figure in experimental fiction. The police novel of the seventies moved a bit out of New York and L.A. In a few cases, like K.C. Constantine's books, it went back to the small-town roots of Waugh's early novels. It moved to a few of America's other large cities (Denver and Detroit) and, most notably, it moved to Hillerman's Southwest and emphasized the clash of cultures as a significant theme of the police novel, the same theme that made Martin Cruz Smith's *Gorky Park* (1981) a bestseller.

In the late 1970s George Dove wrote an insightful series of articles for *The Armchair Detective* in which he outlined a number of significant themes of the police book — the overworked force, the hostile public, etc. In 1982 he published *The Police Procedural*, in which he sought to define the form and examine the works of significant writers. In his study, however, Dove chose to define the form in terms its adherence to the conventions of the mystery story, thereby excluding Kantor and Wambaugh from consideration. He leaves most paperback writers out entirely. Not only did Dove omit mention of a number of police writers — Craig, Daley, Harrington, Barnes, Jackson, and others, he also wrote his study at almost exactly the wrong time. In 1982 he undertook to study a form and a corps of writers that would undergo immense and unprecedented changes in the decades to come.

-four-

The 1980s

Cops in novels began to hit their stride in the 1980s. Not only did the writers of previous decades continue to produce cop novels — McBain, for instance, continued to turn out novels into the twenty-first century — but more writers turned to cop books than ever before. They designed their books to meet the differing tastes of mystery and thriller readers. Thus the cop cozy, the cop thriller, and the insider cop story, all implicit in the previous decades, continue to take shape during the 1980s. Female cops appear in increasing numbers, preparing the way for the wider variety of female heroes that appears in books of the 1990s. Significantly, more ex-police officers turn to fiction than ever before, bringing with them both the authority of their experience and a wider spectrum of police issues than found in earlier professional cop writing. In the eighties, too, serial killers attracted more and more attention from writers, and almost every writer of the decade felt the need to write at least one serial killer book. Along with this, cop books of the 1980s began to add new perspectives on police routines and procedure, perspectives gained from societal changes, from advances in forensic science, and from the kind of more thorough examination made possible by the increasing number of writers who paid attention to cops.

Female Writers and Female Cops

Given that the Civil Rights Act and affirmative action were enacted in the mid–1960s, ideally it would have taken until the mid–1970s before

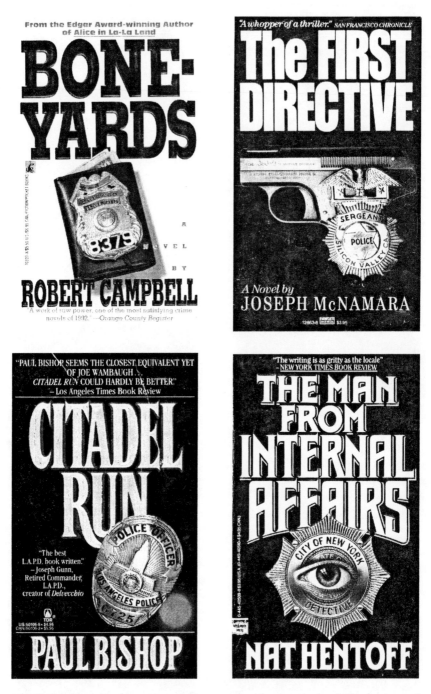

The badge became the most popular icon in the cover art of the 1980s and 1990s. *Top left:* Pocket, 1993; *top right:* Fawcett, 1984; *bottom left:* TOR, 1987; *bottom right:* Mysterious Press, 1985.

women on police forces attained the experience and time in rank to become detectives, the principal focus of the cop novel. But the ideal world and the real world aren't the same, and many American police departments resisted and dragged their feet when it came to moving women from their traditional roles as matrons and secretaries to that of full-fledged police officers. It's hardly coincidence, then, that writers of the 1980s make frequent references to affirmative action and tokenism in connection with developing their female heroes. During the course of the decade female cops move from being that Holy Grail of mystery writers, the innovation introduced into an old and fixed form, to being a routine part of the cast of characters found in every police station. While in the eighties male writers like Warren Adler and Paul Bishop create female heroes who engage both physically and intellectually in the action of thriller plots, the female cop writers of the period tend to locate their female heroes in cozy plots in which understanding and sympathy provide the key ingredients to successful police work. Interestingly, a number of the contemporary fictional women private eyes are ex-cops—from Nicole Sweet in Fran Huston's *The Rich Get It All* (1973), to Madge Hatchett in Lee McGraw's *Hatchett* (1976), to Anna Jugedinski in Phyllis Swan's *Find Sherri!* (1979), to Kinsey Milhone introduced in Sue Grafton's *A Is for Alibi* (1984). Except for Grafton's hero, critic Kathleen Gregory Klein finds them contemptible examples of detectives and of women. Women, it seems, mostly did better as cops than as PI's.

Susan Dunlap

Susan Dunlap's detective books began with *Karma* in 1981. *Karma* was initially published by PaperJacks, a subsidiary of Harlequin books, in an ultimately failed effort to establish a line of mystery stories marketed the same way Harlequin marketed romances. That *Karma* uses the cozy pattern of plotting and features a woman as the hero and a less than forceful rendering of women's issues, then, comes as no real surprise. One thing that *Karma* and Dunlap's other Jill Smith books demonstrate is the broadening appeal of police heroes to different kinds of readers.

Dunlap locates her hero, Jill Smith, in the place where modern policing began, Berkeley, California. While she briefly mentions Berkeley's People's Park and street vendors, her main focus does not lie in describing the place or in probing deeply into the mores of Berkeley's denizens. Instead they decorate the game board upon which Dunlap articulates her cozy plots. Her hero, Jill Smith, is a police officer rather than an amateur sleuth or a member of the new breed of women private eyes. However, she is a cop by accident. Thus in *Karma* Smith, the narrator, explains that

Some of the male officers had dreamed of being cops for years, but not me. I had gone to college, bummed around Europe and met Nat. By the time Nat and I had married, he'd been accepted in graduate school at Berkeley, and I had started looking for the perfect job.

The search had dragged on. My family offered money. Nat's family wrote about his working part-time. Nat began to suggest I was too particular, and I started to wonder if I was capable of finding any job. At that juncture, the patrol officer's exam was announced — women and minorities encouraged. I took it without hope. When I passed, it surprised me. It surprised everyone. And when I started the job, kept it and actually found I did well, the surprise took on a warm glow [33–34].

As is usually the case, Smith's dedication to police work erodes her marriage, which ends in divorce before the beginning of the first book. As the books proceed, Dunlap moves her hero from patrol officer to a coveted position on Berkeley's newly formed homicide squad. After the allusion to affirmative action in the first book, Dunlap continues in succeeding books to make occasional references to the difficulties of police work particular to women. Thus in *Diamond in the Buff* (1990) Detective Smith tells readers that

After the last ceremony when new officers were sworn, I had taken a couple of the women aside and said, "Berkeley's a small town. There are going to be times when you roll out and find the corpse of a friend's mother, or child, or the friend himself. You're going to feel like shit. But no matter how bad you feel, how justified that is, remember this: Women cops don't cry. A guy cries, people think that's a sign he's human, but a tear rolls down a woman officer's cheek, she loses credibility forever" [78].

Officers Connie Pereira and Seth Howard are among the few developed police officers in Dunlap's early books. In Seth Howard, Smith's rival and friend, Dunlap portrays the traditional cop: "A six-foot-six redhead, he looked like the archetypal Irish cop, right down to the grin. For any other cop, that quasi-humorous expression would have caused problems. But no one pushed Howard too far" (*Karma* 37–38). With Pereira, Dunlap notes that her life has been much more difficult than Smith's and, early on, gives more of her background:

Connie Pereira, with her suburban-housewife look, had caught a number of suspects off guard. In fact, Connie had rarely even visited the suburbs. She had grown up in Oakland, the oldest child of an alcoholic father. Her mother had been in and out of institutions that offered the only respite for the poor [*Karma* 110].

Dunlap's books use traditional mystery story plotting, with repeated interviews, steady accretion of facts, conflicting suspects, and surprise endings. Her hero is a cop because making her a cop provides a credible reason for her to be involved with solving crimes—a more credible reason in the 1980s than could be attached to an amateur or even a private detective. Absorption in problem solving also becomes devotion to duty. This, in turn, justifies Smith's minimalist style of living. Her sparse apartment and sleeping bag versus bed become demonstrations of the unrelenting life of the dedicated police officer rather than eccentricity. Dunlap gives readers only scant details about real police work. Jill Smith's periodic visits to the precinct and brief encounters with her African American lieutenant serve primarily as transitions between interviews and only incidentally give readers snippets of police routines—often Lieutenant Davis' absorption with budget problems and irritation with Smith for missing meetings. For the most part Dunlap's hero goes where and when she pleases, sometimes even ignoring the legal restrictions on police behavior. In *As a Favor* (1984), for example, Smith shuffles through confidential client records in a welfare office out of curiosity and without regard for proper police routine. While Seth Howard is a cop, he serves more as Smith's buddy and sounding board than as a fellow officer. Dunlap's novels, then, only incidentally deal with the hero as police officer but instead concentrate on the hero as the bright and inquisitive woman who solves puzzles just as amateur detectives did a generation ago.

Margaret Maron

Margaret Maron wrote eight books about Sigrid Harald of the NYPD. Maron's hero is lukewarm about affirmative action: "Sigrid Harald was not a particularly fervent proponent of the Equal Rights Amendment. She waved no banners, marched in no demonstrations, signed no petitions for the advancement of women. She was aware of how much she owed to the feminist movement, but she also knew the worth of her own brains and stamina" (*One Coffee With* 25). Harald, who has followed her hero father onto the force, occupies a particular position in the department. While not quite as restricted as the matron duty of the last generation's women cops, she is protected by her boss:

> McKinnon checked the work sheets and was glad to see that Lieutenant Harald's was the lightest case load at the moment. The young woman had shown herself capable of handling violence, but (although he would have denied it) Mac always breathed easier when he could legitimately give Anne Harald's daughter what he privately tagged "amateur" murders: the single eruption of violence between friends or relatives that usually left a remorseful killer confessing at the crime scene [*One Coffee With* 26].

This paternalistic attitude, to be sure, allows Maron to use a woman as the hero of cozy detective stories that depend on the hero's attempts to fathom relationships as opposed to finding and chasing bad guys.

Paternalism aside, in the first novel, *One Coffee With* (1982), Harald faces little prejudice from other cops in the department. Detective Tilden, "Tillie the Toiler," is obsequious toward Harald. Late in *One Coffee With* Maron notes that "Lower-ranking detectives stepped aside and melted back to their desks upon becoming aware of her [Harald's] presence" (171). Even when offered the chance to unload female cops' woes on an interviewing journalist, Maron has her hero fob the reporter off with pamphlets and phone numbers, irritated that such trivia interferes with her thinking about who poisoned whom.

Lee Martin

Lee Martin (Anne and Thomas Wingate) began writing about Fort Worth detective Deb Ralston in 1984 with *Too Sane a Murder*. Incidentally, Ann Wingate worked for the Fort Worth police and also writes mystery novels under her own name. In a number of ways the Deb Ralston books differ from all earlier books about women as cops. Martin makes occasional mention of the fact that there are few female cops, but usually without the rancor and outrage apparent in other writers' presentation of female heroes:

> I'd asked to be on the homicide squad, not the major case squad, but a token woman is likely to be out wherever she is most noticeable. The fact that I had turned out to be somewhat more than a token was now immaterial [*Death Warmed Over* 94].

The Deb Ralston books contain little evidence of overt and blatant antifeminism in the force and the bosses tend to treat Deb with respect and understanding. Indeed, in *Death Warmed Over*, Martin brings in an aggressively feminist cop from Dallas who tones herself down once Deb confronts her with her lack of propriety and manners. In addition to the pastel feminism of the books, Martin treats Fort Worth as a small town — in *Death Warmed Over* (1988), for example, the detective has known a number of the witnesses- suspects since her school days and has easy access to some information because she has been a lifelong member of the community. But that doesn't make Martin's books that different. What makes them different is their portrayal of the police detective as a real middle-class woman with children, husband, and dog. Martin laces in details about cooking and shopping: in *Murder at the Blue Owl* (1988) the hero worries about buying toilet paper and in *Death Warmed Over* she thinks about the price of boned chicken breasts. Martin mentions morning sickness and maternity clothes when at forty-two, the hero becomes pregnant. These details become more apparent because Martin chooses to narrate the books in the first person. Indeed, books by women about female cops tend to be written in the first person statistically more frequently than books about male cops — Lillian O'Donnell, Susan Dunlap and J.A. Jance in the eighties choose first person narration and in the next decade Noreen Ayres, Sherri Board, Patricia Cornwell, Barbara D'Amato, Kim Wozencraft, Robin Burcell, and Paula Woods all use the first person voices of their protagonists.

The Lee Martin books give only a bare nod to police work. *Murder at the Blue Owl*, for instance, focuses on a murder at a gathering of friends for a birthday party that the detective attends as a guest. To make it a cop book, throughout the narrative Martin has her detective seed in aphorisms about police work: thus, "for every legitimate call any police department gets ... there are probably ten false alarms" (49); "A book I read once said that the biggest difference between cops and ordinary people is that ordinary people run away from trouble, but cops run toward it" (120); and "This is called a fishing trip. Detectives go on a lot of fishing trips" (162). While Deb Ralston goes to the station, receives assignments from her captain, writes reports, and works long and exhausting hours, mostly she works by herself, sharing, occasionally, her ideas with her husband, who is only modestly interested in them. The issues in the books tend to center on domestic relationships. *Hacker* (1992) uses as background a wife who smashes a computer because her husband has been spending too much time with it instead of her; a history of sexual jealousy comes into play in *Death Warmed Over*. The substance of the books, in addition to the domestic details of the hero's life, follows the pattern of the traditional "cozy" mystery story.

Barbara Paul

Barbara Paul came to the police novel gradually. A writer of science fiction and standard mysteries, in *The Renewable Virgin* (1985) she introduced NYPD Detective Mirian Larch as one of the multiple narrators of the mystery. Paul describes Larch this way:

> No, no archetype for Mirian. More of an anti-archetype, in fact: I wanted a plain woman, a pragmatically competent woman, not a beautiful superwoman who can do all sorts of marvelous (and unrealistic) things. And I wanted an ethical heroine who would never use her looks to get what she wanted even if she could [www.sinc-ic.org].

One might add that in the first novel Mirian's role as a police officer — as opposed to an amateur or private detective — has only minimal effect on her character because it's not fully developed. Paul, as noted before, above all wants her innovation to be making Larch a "plain woman," and the first narrator in *Renewable Virgin* makes this clear:

> The policewoman was Detective Second Grade M. Larch, her I.D. had said;
> she had a gray potato face and was tired and fed-up looking. Either a long day
> or a frustrating one, probably both [7].

And so does the second narrator:

> The policewoman who'd taken Kelly Ingram into the Captain's office came
> back out, a doughfaced woman in her thirties who looked as if she knew her
> way around [21].

Both of these women, however, remark on Larch's sensitivity and compassion in her treatment of them.

In *Renewable Virgin* there are few named police characters; the most prominent is Larch's irascible boss, Captain Michaels. Actress Kelly Ingram and Fiona Benedict, two of the three narrators, both describe him as unappealing and offensive: "Michaels was sitting behind what looked like a brand new desk. He was an overweight, fiftyish man who looked first at my breasts and then at my face" (15). Half a page later Ingram remarks "I couldn't believe this guy. His body posture, his tone of voice — he was behaving as if he thought that was the way tough guys were supposed to act. Jimmy Cagney Nasty" (15). On top of this, Ingram says he has bad breath. Indeed, other than with the introduction of Mirian Larch and a bit of forensic science related to means of detecting gunshot residue, *Renewable Virgin* hardly qualifies as a police novel.

After *Renewable Virgin*, Paul used Mirian Larch "to do the investigating" (www.sinc-ic.org) in *He Huffed and He Puffed* (1989) and *Good King Sauerkraut* (1989). But it was not until *You Have the Right to Remain Silent* (1992) that Larch becomes the hero of a full-blown police novel. In that novel Paul focuses the plot on police work — murder, conspiracy, and terrorism — and uses her hero to focus police themes. One of them is the theme of partners, but here Paul avoids the conventional pattern of loyalty and mutual support by pairing Larch with two undesirable partners, one of whom is incompetent while the other is allied to the bad guys in the book. *Right to Remain Silent* joins a thriller plot about high-tech weapons with what turns out to be a domestic one — Mirian uncovers a mother who has contracted for the killing of one of her children because she cannot afford to raise them all. The title, then, refers both to the standard procedural warning to suspects as well as the effect of silence in the face of pathos and degradation on the police officer:

> Not for the first time she wondered why she had chosen a profession in which
> success inevitably meant a debilitating bout of depression. This always happened to her, this feeling of disappointment in the human race whenever she
> had to point a finger and name someone a killer [*You Have the Right to Remain
> Silent* 26].

Men Who Write About Women

Warren Adler

The same year Susan Dunlap began publishing her Jill Smith books, Warren Adler introduced Detective Fiona Fitzgerald of the Washington, D.C., police. From his first Fitzgerald book, *The American Quartet* (1981), Adler finds the means to magnify both the issue of women as police officers and the impact of politics on police departments' functions and priorities. To be sure, Adler gives Fiona a background familiar to fictional female cops:

> It was not, of course, a woman's place, and her father ranted and raved over such effrontery to the male imperative — until the day he saw her in her uniform, and then he collapsed in tears of pride. Her two older sisters had, in their way, followed the family's wishes. They had married cops and were busily producing future members of the "farces," as if new techniques of birth control had never existed.
>
> Once she had gained family approval, she took a further step, a master's in criminology at American University. This turned out to be a brutal attack on the maleness of her brothers-in-law, who had only their high school diplomas, creating family tensions.
>
> "Goddamned niggers, spics and broads are invading the forces" [*American Quartet* 20].

"Farces" reproduces Fiona's father's Irish brogue. In the first book Adler's hero is descended from two generations of New York cops, thereby moving the cops in the family motif to the distaff side.

Later Adler invents yet another background and another inherited motive for becoming a cop for his hero — by the time of *Senator Love* (1991) Fiona's father is a U.S. senator who lost his bid for reelection because of his stand on principles. Adler includes all of the usual prejudices policewomen face, including the jealous suspicions of her partner's wife — "She thinks that women get into police work so they can get laid a lot" (*American* 23). His hero, moreover, also faces prejudice because of her education: in *Senator Love* Adler reinforces this theme with Fiona's partner who, knowing about the prejudice against education held by many cops, never mentions his degree from Florida State. Once she has a senator father, Fitzgerald faces reverse snobbery from the working-class police establishment: "Was she really the alien she imagined, the daughter of power and privilege slumming in a blue-collar menage?" (*Senator Love* 12). Adler's unique point about the minority status encountered by his hero resides in the nature of Washington, D.C., and its police. By the 1980s African Americans comprised the majority of the District's population as well as its police force. Working in such a department Fiona experiences the racial tension felt by fellow officers and superiors. Thus in *American Quartet* Fiona's black partner says

"What's with you? Leave it alone. They're just itching to make us look like dummies. Like we can't run things. They think only white men..." He emphasized men "...can run things right." (119)

Complicating the racial theme, Adler takes advantage of the anomaly of D.C. government to magnify the theme of politics and the police. The anomaly is that the elected officials in D.C. must keep a wary eye on both the electorate and on the U.S. Congress, which votes on a significant portion of the city's budget. Thus officials like Fiona's boss, "the eggplant," need to keep a wary eye on both the sensitivities of mayor and the Congress.

> You can cut the heart out of a smacked-up nigger on the strip. You can rape some honkie teenage floozie in some back alley. You can waste some hood in front of the White House. That's okay for open cases. But if we can't close a killing in a public building, a fucking public building filled with tourists, then we all belong in the shithouse [*American* 66].

The other advantage D.C. provides for Adler lies in the fact that the city acts as a magnet for characters with unique, bizarre, and twisted motivations — politicians. Thus *American Quartet* interweaves the main plot, peopled with Washington power brokers, with the reelection bid of Fiona's congressman lover, and *Senator Love* focuses on both a senator and his flunkie and Fiona's affair with a political rainmaker.

In addition to displaying the obstacles confronted by a female police officer, Adler both demonstrates in the Fiona Fitzgerald books that women can do the job as well as men and that they bring special attributes to police work. For Adler this boils down to two things, Fitzgerald's ability to question female witnesses and her compassion. Thus, for instance, in *Senator Love* Fiona's feeling for the original victim stands out from official indifference to a ten-year-old crime:

> As a woman, Fiona had been especially appalled by these statistics. Also, she had never become completely inured to the horrible sight of these young female corpses, their features etched forever in the death mask of horror, their unseeing eyes offering compelling evidence of their violation. Just to see them was all the motivation that Fiona ever needed to pursue their murderers with all the single-minded purpose she could muster [*Senator Love* 31–32].

Women Who Write About Men

J.A. Jance

A lot of J.A. Jance's novels have legal-sounding titles — *Until Proven Guilty* (1985), *Injustice for All* (1986), *Trial by Fury* (1987), *Taking the Fifth* (1988), *Dismissed with Prejudice* (1989), etc. Unlike some writers who cement the action of their books on actual points of law, Jance's books use the law allusions to act as underlying referents. *Until Proven Guilty*, for example, concerns the murder of accused child abusers and molesters who have never been arrested or tried. Indeed, looking at the first novel alone it would have been hard to forecast the shape of Jance's later cop books. *Until Proven Guilty* is a hybrid book, bringing together elements of the police novel and the romance. In it the hero is swept off his feet by a beautiful and mysterious woman, and the book details the characters' respective secrets, the impediments to their union, their marriage, and agonizing choices the hero must make when his roles as husband and police officer conflict.

Nonetheless, Jance does use cop material in *Until Proven Guilty* and as her novels proceed she moves into the mainstream of cop writers — even though her detective hero, Jonas Piedmont Beaumont, inherits vast wealth and drives a Porsche 928. "Beau" serves as the first person narrator and hero of Jance's books. In *Until Proven Guilty* she introduces him as tall, divorced, and experienced, and dedicated (but not devoted) to his job:

> I feel the same way about the fifth floor of the Seattle Police Department. That's the homicide squad. I've worked homicide for almost fifteen years. I came to the fifth floor with all my illusions intact. I was convinced that murderers were the worst of the bad guys and that capturing killers was the highest calling a police officer could have. It took me a long time to lose that illusion, to figure out that murder isn't the worst crime one human can inflict on another. Maybe part of my disillusionment was just getting older and wiser. I don't know when I stopped viewing it as a sacred charge and started seeing it as a job [26].

In matters of characterization Jance tends towards brevity. She draws Ron Peters in *Until Proven* this way:

> Peters sometimes reminds me of an Irish Setter — tall, reddish hair, good-looking, loose-jointed, not too bright at times [9].

The same thing happens in *Dismissed with Prejudice* (1989) with the snap portrait of Detective Halvorsen:

> Halvorsen was my kind of cop — action first, bullshit and paperwork later. We had lost one round fair and square, and he was ready to get up and get back in the game [122].

She also tends toward brevity in her inserted comments on police work:

> Computers are good for lots of things, but not in the world of homicide investigations. For detectives, nothing beats a notebook and pencil [*Breach of Duty* 26].

Characterized by the use of his voice as narrator, Beaumont, like most cops, says he is concerned with the discovery of evidence, but Jance makes him more connected to trying to understand people: "Thinking about people involved, assessing them, trying to sort out the relationship — that's how I get on track with a case" (*Until* 25). And although he is aware of legal structures and strictures, Beaumont uses an illegal listening device in *Until Proven* and in *Breach of Duty* plays a bit fast and loose with the Miranda warning: "Those preliminary surprise visits with possible suspects — ones with no Miranda warning anywhere within hearing distance — may not hold up in court, but that doesn't mean they're not useful" (55). While his role in solving cases provides the focus for Jance's novels, she makes Beaumont's drinking and his alcoholism a minor and continuing theme. Begun after and because of the events in *Until Proven Guilty*, Beaumont's drinking gets to the point in *Dismissed with Prejudice* that he has blackouts and an enlarged liver. After that he joins AA and attends meetings to help him reclaim his life.

Jance provides a number of partners in her books. Beaumont's first is Ron Peters, whose penchant for healthy eating drives Beaumont up the wall — the same motif she brings in with partner Big Al Lindstrom, but his issue is quantity, not quality. A handicapped cop fills in for Big Al in *Without Due Process* (1992), and Detective Sue Donaldson makes her appearance as Beaumont's partner in *Breach of Duty*. In each case Jance develops bonds between the partners, with Beaumont eventually taking over support of Peters' children when he is wounded. For Jance, like most other police writers, it is the cops who fight crime while the bosses are intent only on their own self-aggrandizement. She also, moreover, makes points about the role of budget on police efficiency — in *Breach of Duty* characters hesitate to ask for DNA tests because of their expense and are too often foiled by the department's low-bid Local Area Network.

Faye Kellerman

In *Ritual Bath* (1986), *Sacred and Profane* (1987), and other books that chronicle the relationship between Detective Peter Decker and Rina Lazarus, Faye Kellerman developed a hybrid form that combines the clash-of-cultures police story with the romance. In the Decker/Lazarus books, both rest on the contrast between secular law and practice and Torah-based law observed by Orthodox Jews. The differences between the two not only make police investigations in the books more difficult, they also stand as an impediment to the developing love between Decker and Lazarus. While this is the principal focus of *Ritual Bath* and *Sacred and Profane*, Kellerman does include other police themes. In *Sacred and Profane* she brings in forensic dentistry, and in *Ritual Bath* Decker makes some brief comments about his experience and disillusionment with juvenile crime and policing. Decker, Kellerman's police hero, "was a good cop, smart and dedicated. But it worked against him. The brass constantly saddled him with all the rotten cases" (*Ritual Bath* 12). Like most police heroes of the time, he is divorced and police work fills the void in his life:

> He knew some women, and that helped, but the relief was short-lived. More and more he found himself coming back to the station after the sun went down [30].

Decker solves the case of a serial rapist in the first novel and a murder in the second. His principal focus, however, is Rina Lazarus, the threats to her safety along with the frustrations of his developing love for her. The surprise that Kellerman reveals in *Ritual Bath* is that, while adopted and raised by a Baptist family, Decker's birth mother was Jewish. And, even though he is a cop, he has also been to law school and practiced the profession until he found it unrewarding.

While Kellerman introduces other cops in the novels, they are not only subordinate to Decker, they are also flawed in one way or another. Perhaps the most appealing of Kellerman's subordinate cops is Detective Marge Dunn, Decker's partner.

> Her big-boned frame made people think she was a lot older than her twenty-seven years, but that was okay with her. She liked the respect her height and weight brought her. Her face, in contrast, was soft — large bovine eyes and silky wisps of blond hair. She was an enviable combination of toughness and femininity [*Ritual Bath* 11].

From there, the other cops go downhill. The other member of Decker's team is Michael Hollander, who "was fiftyish, bald, florid, and the proper weight for a man six inches taller" (*Ritual* 65). Decker describes Fordebrand, the homicide detective in *Ritual Bath*, this way:

> He's shorter than I am by a couple of inches, but he must outweigh me by at least sixty pounds of pure muscle. Naturally, his wife is this tiny little bird. Fordebrand also has phenomenally bad breath [140].

Kellerman does not describe any of Decker's colleagues as particularly attractive. Thus in *Ritual Bath* the commander of Decker's precinct, Captain David Morrison "was in his early fifties, built wiry, with thin gray hair and flaccid cheeks" (301). And Kellerman goes from first describing the appearance of the beat cops who repeatedly appear in *Ritual Bath* in terms of stereotypes — one pair is "two linebackers" (36), and the other is "the Latino and the muscleman" (185) — to describing the role they play as stereotypical: "The policeman-robot with whom she was talking was young" (130).

It is not the case that Kellerman's cops are corrupt or brutal or incompetent, they are just not very attractive — or they are the way they are in order to make Decker both more attractive and more intelligent.

Sons of Ed

More than two decades after McBain wrote *Cop Hater*, his influence continued to be felt. Broadly, those few writers who take the time to reflect on the history of the cop book always start by citing McBain as the pioneer and originator of the form. More specifically, some cop writers adopted his storytelling formula — using a continuing cast of characters who investigate multiple cases in each succeeding book. By the 1980s, however, most cop writers chose other plot and character patterns. But a few remained loyal to the McBain formula — Christopher Newman, Tom Philbin, and cop Bill Kelly and his collaborator Dolph Lemoult.

Christopher Newman

Christopher Newman has some of the best cop connections: he acknowledges William Caunitz for his help and was chosen to finish *Chains of Command* after Caunitz's death. Newman began writing his series about Joe Dante in 1986 with *Midtown South*, followed by *The Sixth Precinct* (1987), *Knock-Off* (1989), *Midtown North* (1992), *Dead End Game* (1994), *Killer* (1997), and *Hit and Run* (1997). In them Newman follows the long-established conventions of the police book by including a cast of supporting and lead characters. For the basis for his plots, however, he moves around a bit. *Killer* is a hunt-and-chase thriller, *Precinct Command* is a whodunit, and *Sixth Precinct* combines a police investigation of a murder and the planning of an unrelated murder.

All of Newman's books center on NYPD detective Joe Dante, maverick cop. He is another one of the paragons. As his boss tells him in *Sixth Precinct* "You're a street cop, Joey.... You'll always be a street cop. You're maybe the best this city has to offer at this moment" (22). And what makes him so good? First, he represents the best traditions of working-class New Yorkers:

> Beneath his clean-cut Manhattanized exterior, Joe Dante was still the kid from Canarsie. As long and hard as he may have chipped at them, a number of the rough edges remained. Ingrained were a traditional northern Italian Catholic upbringing, a strong work ethic, and a third-generation American's civic pride and sense of accomplishment. The cop son of a cop father [*Sixth Precinct* 9].

On top of this, Newman adds cop qualities:

His hunches were often uncanny, and he worked leads with the tenacity of a pit bull. Partners who had toured with him would go through the gates of hell with Joe Dante as backup [*Sixth Precinct* 33–34].

Here the work ethic comes in and so does loyalty, but Newman, along with other writers of the period, emphasizes on cop instinct. Indeed, *Sixth Precinct* opens with a vignette about Dante frustrating the robbery of a mom-and-pop grocery store because his instincts tell him the loiterers in the street were about to try to pull a heist. Along with hard work and instinct, Dante has a healthy contempt for the brass and bends rules to achieve success. This gets him in trouble, gets him suspended, gets him transferred around the city.

Of course it helps if one has powerful and influential friends, and Dante does: his patron, his rabbi, is Gus Lieberman:

Inspector Lieberman was a big, overweight bear of a man. An ex–Fordham Ram linebacker from the glory days, he'd gone to seed behind a gray metal desk. In his day he'd been as tough a street cop as they came. Tough and smart enough to avoid the promotional pitfalls of petty jealousies, arrogance, back-stabbing and other assorted enemy-making in the upper echelons of the job [*Sixth Precinct* 20].

Lieberman, of course, does eventually become the chief of detectives, and through his force of will and his wife's social prominence, continues to protect Dante from Dante's nemesis, the less-than-competent police commissioner.

Newman is one of the few writers to touch upon the complex role ethnic background and tension plays in the NYPD:

On the job, racial subgroups tended to gravitate together, a phenomenon reinforced by various heritage organizations, the most famous of which is probably the Irish Emerald Society. The Italian Confederation was also one of the job's strongest [*Sixth Precinct* 57].

The racial grouping, however, has little effect on Dante. His rabbi is Jewish, and Newman portrays African American cops as both Dante's direct supervisors and, in Jumbo Richardson, his partner, for whom Newman creates a detailed background with a mother-in-law and Richardson's off-duty role as coach of a Pop Warner football team.

With Dante's love life, Newman offers a variant to the cop as family man or the miscellaneous versions of divorced cop. Dante's lover is Rosa Losada. Bennington-educated Losada

was as stubborn in her single-mindedness and intense in her focus as Joe was. She'd proven that she was a cop's cop on the street. Now she was intent on getting as far up the job's brass ladder as a bright, beautiful, college-educated woman could…. She wanted to become the first woman chief of detectives [*Sixth Precinct* 9].

Dante wants her to quit, get married, have kids, and settle down. She does not, and as the books proceed she moves up in the police hierarchy — in *Precinct Command* she even contemplates running for Congress. The tempests in their relationship arise and then subside because they love one another and mutually accept Rosa's attachment to police administration and Joe's attachment to work on the street.

Tom Philbin

Tom Philbin, the son and grandson of police officers, also demonstrates in his Precinct Siberia novels the persistence of Ed McBain's pattern thirty years after he invented it. Like McBain, Philbin focuses on a particular precinct and develops a cast of continuing characters whose lives and careers are shaped by the precinct and the portion of New York City within the precinct's boundaries. Unlike McBain, however, Philbin stayed away from an average or representative police precinct and instead fastened on one that served as a dumping ground for the department's losers and misfits:

> It was places, precincts like the Five Three, that cops dreaded being sent to. Actually, you weren't sent; you were sentenced, and at any given time there was always a Fort Siberia. In the fifties and sixties there was Fort Apache. Before that there was Staten Island; there was a precinct in Harlem, one in Bed Stuy. It was punishment duty, except for cops who had the misfortune to be assigned there after the Academy. It was for misfits.
>
> Alcoholics who couldn't be helped, homos, psychotics, grass-eaters, drug users. Malcontents, thieves who couldn't be nailed, wheeler-dealers, cops who messed with the wrong people, and old cops who should retire but who wouldn't and, like old Indians, were put out on the plain to die [*Precinct Siberia* 5–6]

In *Cop Killer* (1986) Philbin uses Krupsek as a worst-case example of the kind of cop sent to the Five Three. Using the Knapp Commission terminology for the most corrupt kind of cop, Philbin tells readers that "IAD had unsuccessfully tried to prosecute him for meat-eating" (9), and he goes on to demonstrate that Krupsek is still "on the pad" — "He was on a regular pad with two other cops who patrolled the post — plus a piece for the sergeant — and was putting away four hundred a month to look the other way on numbers games and other activities" (9). And as a representative of traditional police corruption, Philbin describes Krupsek's cooping: "Krupsek never worked more than a few hours a tour, unless Bledsoe, the CO, or the lieutenant had the rag on on a particular day. He had a couple of apartments where he could coop" (9).

The point Philbin makes, however, does not concentrate on the corruption in the precinct, but on the way in which leadership and an awakened sense of duty transform losers into cops. His creates a cast of misfits and losers: Grady is a burned-out drunk, Getz is a pea-brained muscleman, Piccolo is a violent hothead, and Edmunton "had been assigned there for grass-eating — petty thievery that couldn't be proved" (*Undercover* 37). Not a loser or a misfit, but the victim of departmental injustice, there is also detective Barbara Babalino. All of them profit, grow, and mature because of the leadership of Detective First Grade Joe Lawless. About Lawless Philbin does not mince words: "Of all the human beings who had crossed his path in forty-two years of living, Joe Lawless was probably the best. The stuff, really, of which heroes are made" (*Cop Killer* 34). "Joe Lawless ... had been through many situations that not one in a thousand people could have withstood" (*Undercover* 17). Lawless

> didn't seem to be afraid of anything, though he never went around trying to show how tough he was. You just knew it. He reminded Grady of the late actor Steve McQueen. Looked a little like him too, with short blond hair, very blue eyes, and kind of battered features. Lawless just seemed to be able to eat anything, and he had this sort of inner tension, like a coiled spring [*Precinct Siberia* 13].

On top of his appearance and aura, Lawless' heroic qualities stem, according to Philbin, from his adherence to disciplined behavior, old values, loyalty and helpfulness to other cops. Indeed in the books Philbin emphasizes the role of partners in renovating the lives of his characters:

> The job was all Frank had. Like himself, Frank was divorced, had no kids. Just the job.
> And each other. They had been partners for two years now, and Frank really helped Edmunton through a tough period of his life. He had been going through a divorce, and they had shipped him to Siberia for grass-eating — taking small bribes. Frank had been a real friend [*Jamaica Kill* 5].

In his novelization of the film *The Rookie* (1991), Philbin reiterates the connection between police tradition and police virtue: "Pulovski was from the old school, a warrior, a cop's cop that nothing in life could take down" (114–15). In the Precinct Siberia books, in addition to Lawless, Philbin locates police tradition and wisdom in the one-shot scene with Sergeant Sam Turner, the roll call sergeant. Turner both serves as a disciplinarian for the beat cops of the Five Three and provides daily "survival tips" gleaned from police officers around the country; one of these tips saves Barbara Babalino's life in *Precinct Siberia*.

More than simply following the McBain tradition of using multiple

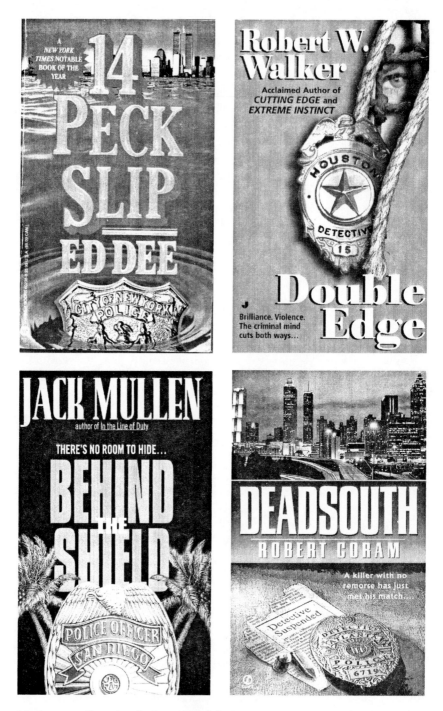

More covers featuring badges. *Top left:* Warner, 1995; *top right:* Jove, 1998; *bottom left:* Avon, 1996; *bottom right:* Signet, 1999.

plots to illustrate the complexity and chaos of police work, Philbin's multiple plots make points about the success and maturation of his characters and the broad meaning of police work. The plots include threads that solve serious and brutal crimes like murder and rape. Other threads involve protection of the aged and dispossessed from predators. Finally the threads involving Arnold Gertz revolve around seemingly trivial crimes—like the missing goats in *Precinct Siberia*—that nonetheless are important both to the citizens and to the detective.

Real Cops

Of course there was Wambaugh. He provided the model of a cop who made his experiences and views about police officers into fiction, best-selling fiction. Then, too, education may have had something to do with the increasing number of cops and ex-cops who took to writing—during the last decades of the century more and more departments sought out college graduates as recruits as well as encouraging cops to go to school. McNamara with his Ph.D. perhaps presents the best demonstration of this trend. Add to that the fact that cops like to tell stories, many of them in cop bars. Dan Mahoney's experience serves as an example:

> I already had an agent before I wrote the first word. He was present in a bar while I was pontificating and telling police stories, and he bought me a drink and said I should certainly write a book [email 5/15/02].

Then, too, there was the need for cops to work out in fiction the meaning and the impact of current crises confronting police departments, as well as the pressures, old and new, that assault individual police officers.

Bob Leuci

One of Michael Grant's characters in *Line of Duty* (1991) makes the following pronouncement:

> To a policeman, the lowest scum of the earth is a cop who gives evidence against brother officers. Names like Phillips, Leuci, and Winter were all spoken with bitterness in station-house locker rooms [191].

Twelve years after the Knapp Commission met and six years after Robert Daley portrayed his personal role and suffering in uncovering police corruption in New York in *The Prince of the City*, Bob Leuci began to write police novels. *Double Edge* (1991) and *Sweet Baby James* (1991) take place in Washington, D.C. Leuci's best-known novels, however, are about the NYPD. All of them reflect on the ways in which individuals make painful moral decisions and deal with corrupt institutions. *Doyle's Disciples* (1984) treats the conflict of an idealistic young cop who uncovers a history of corruption centered upon a chief inspector who is also his lover's father; *Odessa Beach* (1985) propounds as its thesis the misuse of well-intentioned informants and the decision not to work undercover for anyone; *Captain Butterfly* (1989) shows the victory of a virtuous female cop over a violent and corrupt precinct commander; and *The Snitch* (1998) reflects on an ambitious district attorney's attempt to seduce a cop to become an informant on police corruption. *Double Edge*, although set in D.C., also touches on corruption by noting the pernicious use of social influence on police matters.

Leuci's plots reflect his view of what happened to the New York Police Department and what happened to him in helping to bring its wholesale corruption to light. Understandably, inspecting his own experience forms the background of all the novels. In *The Prince of the City* Daley frequently notes Leuci's frustration and disillusionment with an investigation that should have revealed and eradicated corruption across the entire criminal justice system — not just the police department. Thus in *Doyle's Disciples* the narrator ironically reflects on the disproportionate impact of the thinly disguised Knapp hearings taking place in the novel:

> The [Roxbury] hearings, televised locally, were a midday event. Local newspapers ran outrageous stories of policemen shaking down everyone from tow truck operators to major drug dealers. The investigation and the hearings lasted eighteen months. The impact on the police department in New York was staggering: wholesale firings, forced retirements, in some cases prison terms. Toward the end of the eighteenth month, Roxbury asked his old roommate if his powers could be expanded to include members of the judiciary, the Bar, and in some areas, politicians. The mayor fired him. This was a police investigation [22–23].

In *Doyle's Disciples*, moreover, Bobby Porterfield discovers that Roxbury himself has an entrenched prejudice against cops. While Leuci's books focus on the heroes' struggles with police malfeasance, they also seek to gain therapeutic perspective of it as well. In *Doyle's Disciples* an honest New Jersey cop tells the hero that police have become corrupted through constant contact with multitudinous crime and with depraved criminals:

> You guys in New York adopt the street's morality.... The street's language, its values, become part of you.... After a while you're no longer law enforcement people. You become indistinguishable from the sewer rats that climb out of their holes at night to play in that sporting life you all talk about [155].

Leuci's heroes, however, escape the disease spread by crime, money, and corruption. While he makes a point of telling readers about his heroes' education (Porterfield is doing graduate study in social work and Alex Simon in

Odessa Beach has a masters degree) they are not paragons, brownnosers, or tattletales. Broken relationships and divorce plague the heroes. Minor malfeasance occurs and a character in *Doyle's Disciples* puts it into the context that "Cops that do things that maybe they shouldn't are, most times, the best street cops around" (192). Like other writers, Leuci couches cops' experiences in terms of warfare — the war metaphor occurs most often in *Double Edge* and he is one of the first police writers to introduce NYPD cop slang referring to police stations as "forts" — he mentions Fort Apache in *Doyle's Disciples*. But Leuci does not portray his heroes as centurions. Police work is exciting, thus throughout the books narrators glance over its service to society and emphasize the emotional rush heroes receive from doing real police work:

> He drove from the garage feeling an excitement rising in his stomach. Then that familiar, complicated emotion, the joy of the game and the dread of losing. To Delaney and Alex, it was a sport, even to himself he'd never been able to explain this rush [*Odessa Beach* 147].
>
> It occurred to Nick that being a New York cop can bring you the kind of exhilaration that the visitor with a return ticket gets when he travels to a war zone [*The Snitch* 70].

The dilemmas Leuci's characters face, moreover, do not come from police work. The stress they encounter comes from having to make decisions about the nature of the fallible institution of which they are part and whether to side with it or to abandon it and join those who would cripple it for their own ends. That is the case with Bobby Porterfield in *Doyle's Disciples* and Nick Manaris in *The Snitch*. And in both cases the heroes choose cops over lawyers and politicians. The rationale for choosing not to side with those who would destroy the institution to save it from its faults comes in Leuci's placing much of the blame for police corruption on the past. Past corruption, for instance, motivates the action in *Doyle's Disciples*, and in *Double Edge* the hero has to come to terms with his father, who was a brutal and corrupt Baltimore police officer. The hope, then, in Leuci, as in Lillian O'Donnell's books, lies in new kinds of leaders and new kinds of leadership. Fantasy or not, in *Captain Butterfly* Leuci shows a woman cop, Captain Marjorie Butera, winning the contest with brutality, corruption, and the old-boy network, and at the end of the novel the mayor appoints an African American police commissioner who makes Butera his First Deputy.

William J. Caunitz

William J. Caunitz did much to remake the cop book with his seven novels: *One Police Plaza* (1984), *Suspects* (1986), *Black Sand* (1990), *Excep-*

tional Clearance (1991), *Cleopatra Gold* (1994), *Pigtown* (1996), and (with Christopher Newman) his posthumous *Chains of Command* (1999). To begin with, he is one of the first police writers to make the profession of police work into a proper noun: in Caunitz's books, it's not "the job," it's "the Job," an activity that goes beyond employment and assumes a gargantuan role in individuals' lives. Along with this, his books typically stretch over the whole of the police department from commissioner, inspectors, lieutenants and detectives, to lab personnel, clerical workers and patrol officers. His books, of course, focus on individual heroes in the field, but Caunitz also goes to some pains to characterize, at least briefly, all of the members of the squads, giving brush strokes to their appearance and their personalities.

In spite of all of the dysfunction surfacing in the NYPD of the 1970s, the police force in Caunitz retains the traditional metaphor of family, brotherhood, and of the separation of cops from civilians. Along the same lines he describes the pressure police work puts on relationships; indeed, in *Suspects* Caunitz even includes the difficulties imposed on the relationship of a lesbian detective and her lover. Like earlier writers Caunitz explains cop talk — actually using that term in *Suspects*. And he goes on to give glances of insight into characters' lives and motivations as cops. Like the models of the last decades, Caunitz describes procedures. He gives readers the ideal and shows the reality of crime scene investigations, and he details the office procedures required by bureaucracy. Recent events and issues in the police world — the Knapp Commission, Community Review Boards, brutality, and high-profile crimes like the Green River murders mentioned in *Exceptional Clearance*— likewise enter Caunitz's books. The way cops deal with the law, a constant in cop novels since the early 1970s, comes in repeatedly — *Suspects* mentions the limitations of police work posed by the *People v. Skinner* as well as *People v. Rogers* and the "Plain View Doctrine"; in *Black Sand* cops circumvent search and seizure laws by calling in false reports about wanted persons being located in the places they want to search. And Caunitz repeats the same gloomy statistics of all cop books:

> Burglary complaints usually got a phone call, a fast PR job, and sympathy. Robbery complaints got to look at mug shots. If they were unable to pick out the perp, the case would be marked active for a few months, a few fives would be added to the case folder for color, and then the case would be marked: CLOSED, NO RESULTS [*Black Sand* 62].

The fact that Caunitz was a NYPD lieutenant, of course, adds weight to all of these conventional elements of the police novel.

Just as Wambaugh had done twelve years earlier, Caunitz brings greater frankness to the police novel. Especially in his earlier books Caunitz's cop houses bear similarities to the fraternity house in the film *Animal House*. In

One Police Plaza the station's dormitory is particularly reminiscent of a run-down frat house:

> Four bunk beds were flush against the wall. Large slivers of peeling paint drooped down from the walls and ceilings. Glossy posters of nude women covered the wall next to the beds. Heinemann lay on the bottom bunk, his right leg hanging over the edge. The men snored and the ripe smell of their farts hung in the air [66].

In *Suspects*, the precinct has a different situation but the same kinds of cops:

> The Nine-three was considered one of the best houses in the city to work in. There were few crimes, plenty of available women, and many good restaurants where the man on the post was always welcome [9].

A bit later readers see that "A lone policeman manned the telephone switchboard, whiling away his tour by flipping through worn copies of *Screw* and *Hustler* magazines" (139). Promiscuity is rampant. It even has the sanction of its own file:

> Forty years ago, when I come on the Job, this was called the "vulva file." Then in the middle seventies, when women started to come into the Job, the name changed to the "significant other file." Now it's the "B" list [*Pigtown* 33].

In *One Police Plaza* beer cans and empty pizza boxes litter the squad room and the lieutenant keeps a bottle of bourbon in his desk. Then there are also the matters of sexism and racism:

> Just take a look at what's happening in the Job today. We have cops with yellow sheets. Cops who cannot communicate in the English language. We're forced to hire females. Some of them don't weigh a hundred pounds soaking wet; they can't reach the accelerators of radio cars; don't have the physical strength to pull the trigger of their service revolvers. We were forced to lower the height requirement to accommodate women and Hispanics. We're becoming a department of goddamn dwarfs [*One Police Plaza* 263–64].

There is also the far more serious issue of brutality. In *One Police Plaza*, Malone recalls an episode that presents a dire forecast of the Abner Luioma case of the 1990s:

> "Lock the door and get his clothes off," the squad commander said, staring at the frightened man as Malone pushed him into the squad room. Giordano was handcuffed spread-eagled to the detention cage, Michelangelo's anatomical drawing of a man. The lieutenant handed Malone a Zippo lighter. "Burn the truth out of the fuck," the lieutenant ordered. Malone's hand shook as he approached him. One pass of the lighter under Giordano's balls was enough. "Esposito and Conti," he screamed. Known punks from Navy Street.
> "Take him down," the squad commander ordered. Malone released him.
> "Get over here, scumbag," the lieutenant barked.

Giordano approached hesitatingly, his hands covering his genitals.

"Bend over and spread your cheeks," the squad commander snapped. Giordano hesitated. The lieutenant slapped his back, forcing the torso down. "Spread 'em!"

Giordano reached back and spread the cheeks of his ass. The barrel of the squad commander's revolver was rammed into Giordano's anus. "This ain't no prick you feel in your ass, Guinea. It's my fuckin' gun. You're going to testify in court against your two friends.... 'Cause if you don't, one dark night I'm going to meet you in an alley and empty this gun into your asshole" [166–67].

The way in which Caunitz includes this and other very serious issues in his novels is to treat them as recollections, as part of the storytelling that is an integral part of cop fiction.

He also uses them as part of the theme of past versus present, a theme with an implicit message about the renewal of the police department and the police character. In this respect, none of Caunitz's heroes are young men: Malone (*One Police Plaza*), Scanlon (*Suspects*), Lucas (*Black Sand*), Stuart (*Pigtown* and *Chains of Command*), and Vinda (*Exceptional Clearance*) are all in their forties. Indeed, many of the members of the books' detective squads are in their forties — in *Pigtown* both Detectives Jerry Jordan and Hector Colon are in their forties. They are old enough to remember bad things and young enough to want police work to be law abiding and efficient. Additionally, his heroes are all lieutenants, and the rank of lieutenant cannot be achieved by younger men and women. On top of this, Caunitz wants to portray heroes who have suffered losses — Caunitz, for example, describes the erosion and ending of Malone's marriage in *One Police Plaza*, the loss of Scanlon's leg in *Suspects*, the death of Stuart's son in *Pigtown*. For them, then, the role of police work is not to serve society or the victims of crime — although neither is disregarded in the novels — but to fill a void in their lives, a void, in many cases, that police work helped to create in the first place. And it also corresponds to something in their characters. In *One Police Plaza* it's pride in one's skills: "But I still like being a cop. It's what I do best. Most of the homicides I catch are grounders; the rest are either drug related or mob hits and who gives a fuck anyway. But every now and then one comes along that cries to be solved" (92); in *Suspects* it's awakening and using the hero's "predatory instincts" (41).

In addition to bringing the familiar conventions of background and of character up to date, Caunitz broke both the connection of the police novel to the mystery story and its adherence to the McBain model. In general his books can be classed as thrillers — *One Police Plaza*, for instance, concerns international terrorism, *Black Sand* is a clash-of-culture treasure hunt story, and *Exceptional Clearance* is a serial killer book. They are thrillers rooted in police culture, featuring police themes, and focusing on the particular characters of police officers.

Joseph McNamara

In *Black Sand* Caunitz mentions a bit of incidental reading by Edgeworth, the chief of detectives:

> While he waited, with mounting impatience, he read a long and thoroughly puzzling article in the *Journal of the National Association of Chiefs of Police* written by a chief from a small western city, a prodigy who had a Harvard Ph.D. The article discussed ways of building departmental morale; Edgeworth found it as exotic and as irrelevant as a book by Margaret Mead on courtship in Samoa that he had read, under duress, while an undergraduate at Hofstra [175].

In 1984, Joseph McNamara, Harvard Ph.D. and chief of police in San Jose, California, published his first novel, *The First Directive*. That novel, narrated by the hero, centered on the incidental incompetence of the Silicon Valley Police Department. McNamara used the same characters in his next two books, *Fatal Command* (1987) and *Blue Mirage* (1990). In the later books the hero, Fraleigh, becomes chief of the Silicon Valley department. In *Code 211* McNamara moves the locale to San Francisco and introduces a new hero, Kevin McKay. All of the books deal with the impact of bureaucracy and politics on police work. In *The First Directive* administrative indifference and incompetence cause the existence of a serial rapist in the community to be overlooked. *Fatal Command* relates how a politically ambitious mayor uses a competent but naïve token African American police chief to further his career. In *Fatal Command* McNamara shows the tug-of-war in a town council over control of the police department, and examines the double standard of public officials and cops' morals and the different standards to which they are held. *Code 211* shows the police hierarchy punishing an innocent cop in order to cover up the criminal actions of another officer. From the beginning, consequently, McNamara's heroes, intent on doing their jobs well, supporting justice, and striking blows for suffering innocents, are mad as hell. In the first book Fraleigh has to be restrained from attacking his lieutenant and commits petty acts of insubordination as a demonstration of his contempt for a bad cop in a bad system. But McNamara would have it that there are a lot of bad systems. Fraleigh realizes on a trip to the East Coast in *The Blue Mirage* that things may be bad in Silicon Valley, but they are even worse in New York.

The main thrust of McNamara's books is to demonstrate the systemic troubles of police departments. To show this he makes his heroes outsiders who joust against the various forces that prevent the police from protecting and serving. McNamara leavens this serious theme in the first three books with the comic interplay between Fraleigh and his two partners, the Block and English. The Block is a simian hulk who communicates in monosyllables and English is a Stanford classics major given to rambling dissertations and name-dropping allusions to philosophers. On top of the semicomic frustrations his team supplies, the Block, English, and Fraleigh provide the support and sustenance for one another that the police department should but does not. McNamara also briefly explains the basic psychological attraction of police work, thus in *Code 211*: "The feeling something was about to happen, mingled with challenge and the slightest tinge of danger. People intrigues. Adventure. Usually it was boring crap, gritty sludge, or pure gore, but, she conceded, coping with the unknown lures us to police work and keeps us hooked" (88).

In addition to the points about institutions and character, part of McNamara's purpose is to give readers perspectives on current police topics and concerns. He includes references to real, high-profile crimes—he mentions poisoned Tylenol capsules in *Fatal Command*, the assassination of the mayor of San Francisco in *Code 211*, and the Atlanta child murders in *The First Directive*. Just as Caunitz refers to the new super glue fuming method of lifting fingerprints in *Pigtown*, McNamara takes pains to explain the application of advances in forensic science. Thus he explains the forensic background of fiber evidence used in the 1981 trial of Wayne Williams:

> Before the Second World War, clothing tended to be all cotton or wool material, mass produced. It was virtually impossible to differentiate one thread or fiber from another. But with our electron scanning microscope, we can isolate synthetic fibers now used by their shape, cross-sectional characteristics, and chemical constituents. It was the testimony on fiber evidence that convicted the killer in the Atlanta child murders [*The First Directive* 37].

Indeed, in *Fatal Command* McNamara includes one of the most pointed perspectives of the decade on the Supreme Court case most commented on by cop writers:

> "Back in 1966 a guy named Danny Miranda was arrested in Arizona on a rape charge. The cops questioned him in the station house and he confessed to the crime. The U.S. Supreme Court overturned the conviction because the cops hadn't told him he had the right to a lawyer and the right to remain silent. They made it a national rule. That's why we carry those little cards to read to suspects."
> "But was he guilty?"
> "Oh, yeah. But that wasn't relevant, as they say."
> "Did they, you know, beat a confession out of him? Or scare him into confession?"
> "No."

"And the confession, I mean, was it correct, truthful?"

"True as true can be."

"I wonder if the woman who was the victim felt as vulnerable as I do" [132].

As an actual police administrator, McNamara occasionally gives the nod to administrative problems. He includes random complaints about budget limitations and, perhaps uniquely, depicts the problems with organizing a modern police department. He describes the multiplying of necessary and desirable services in the following two passages from *Fatal Command*:

> The top priority was, as Louis kept reminding me, to provide an emergency response to 911 calls in less than five minutes. This sounded easy until we realized how many cops it took to guarantee that response twenty-four hours a day, seven days a week, fifty-two weeks a year. Cops are the only ones still making house calls twenty-four hours a day. At the same time we still had to have a training unit, a SWAT unit, a traffic enforcement unit, a crime prevention unit, school crossing guard units, detective units, internal affairs units, and so on. Most important was a payroll unit [45].
>
> Cops all wanted their area of expertise to be recognized. My head was spinning from suggestions that we form credit card fraud units, sting units, accident investigation units, white-collar crime units, computer crime units, career criminal units, juvenile-career criminal units, organized crime units, and even a residential graffiti investigation unit [57].

There is so much that can be and needs to be done, but, as McNamara would have it in his novels, so little one can do with a system mired in politics, indifference, and corruption. As English points out in *Fatal Command*, not a lot has changed since 1904: "The difference, so vividly pointed out by Lincoln Steffens in 1904 in his book, was that corrupt municipal political machines controlled our cities" (108).

Paul Bishop

English-born LAPD detective Paul Bishop started by writing a western, *Shroud of Vengeance* (1985), but then switched to writing cop novels with his second book, *Citadel Run* (1988). In his books Bishop introduced two separate groups of cops. One is a group of dedicated but fun-loving buddies including Calico Jack Walker, Wild John Elliot, and Tina Tamiko, introduced in *Citadel Run* and featured in *Sand Against the Tide* (1990). The second group centers on detective Fey Croaker and her team, Monk Lawson, Brindle Jones, A.B. "Alphabet" Cohen, Arch "Hammer" Hammersmith, and Rhonda "Nails" Lawless, featured in *Kill Me Again* (1994), *Twice Dead* (1996), *Tequila Mockingbird* (1997), and *Chalk Whispers* (2000).

Bishop's first group of characters grew from the offbeat plot of his first cop book, which centers on cops conducting an on-duty cop car race from

Los Angeles to Las Vegas and which itself is predicated on a view of police character:

> Doing a good job as a cop is like pissing in a dark suit — it feels good, but nobody notices. It's a no-win situation which drives us to look for stunts like this run to Vegas so we can make like a bunch of Girl Scouts — posturing and mouthing off for our peers, looking to show how crazy and tough we are. Policemen are no different than any of the warrior classes throughout history. The crazier you are, the more you show you don't give a damn, the more they respect you. Respect. We all want it. And the only way to get it is by being larger than life. Doing things everyone else is afraid to do. And if the public doesn't like it, then fuck 'em if they can't take a joke [*Citadel Run* 218].

Bishop modifies the bravado expressed above by noting that his heroes are throwbacks "to the days when policemen could still have fun on this job" (*Citadel* 131) and by combining the personal allure of police work ("Police work infected him, and working the street became as much an addiction as the rodeo" [*Citadel* 5]) with a grimmer realization of its futility:

> Sure, I like the feeling when we take an asshole off the street.... And there is a certain satisfaction, not only in helping an individual in a crisis, but in being the person where the buck stops. But you've taught me, and a year on the streets has shown me, there is no helping mankind [*Citadel* 242].

Bishop's first set of police heroes has more in common with the heroes of traditional adventure stories than with actual police officers. The leader of the buddies, Calico Jack Walker, an ex-rodeo rider, retires at the end of *Citadel Run*, but continues to lead the gang in *Sand Against the Tide*, a book that includes a Robin Hood plot, pirates, an evil master criminal, and an ex-cop with a vintage fighter aircraft who joins the buddies as they fight evil.

In the Fey Croaker novels Bishop continues to use the buddy pattern, but pulls his heroes a bit further away from adventure novel–types and moves them closer to the police world. Fey Croaker is a female police officer:

> At forty-something, creeping ever closer to fiftyish, Fey had been the homicide unit supervisor at the LAPD's West Los Angeles area for almost four years. She wasn't the department's only female homicide detective, but she was the only female supervising a major divisional homicide unit. On several occasions she'd paid the price for being a woman in the position, but there was no way in hell she was ever going to give it up without a fight. She'd come too far, both professionally and personally, to roll over and play dead when things got a little rough.
>
> Some of her co-workers believed she'd only been given the position due to the department's affirmative action movement. Fey, however, didn't much care if that was true or not. The fact was that she was in the position and she was damn good at it. She'd made her bones several times over, and she'd match her

unit's clearance rates against any other division in the city in a heartbeat [*Twice Dead* 5].

Croaker's team is made up of near paragons. Monk Lawson "was still young for a homicide detective, but he was very anal retentive and took pride in what he did. He was intuitive, methodical, and rarely made mistakes. He was also happily married, which made him a rarity" (*Twice Dead* 37). Hammer and Nails "were considered legendary when it came to burning bad cops" (*Twice Dead* 70). Even the least committed of the team, Brindle Jones, undergoes a transformation when she joins Croaker's team.

As Bishop's books proceed he takes on a more serious view of police officers and police work. In *Citadel Run* Bishop's hero states that "I became a policeman so I wouldn't have to grow up" (11). In the Fey Croaker books Bishop not only concentrates more on the professional attributes of cops, he also acknowledges the darker side of the LAPD that came to light in the 1990s. In *Sand Against the Tide* Bishop alludes to some of the department's scandals:

> There are bad apples in every bunch. You know as well as anybody that being a cop is like working in a human sewer — you can't walk through it without getting shit on your shoes.... Every once in a while, we end up with cops running murder-for-hire schemes, or burglary rings, like the one in the Hollywood Division a few years ago.... Internal Affairs has their work cut out for them [175].

And in 1997 he refers twice to the Christopher Commission and notes that "The department still had not recovered from the bloodletting and scandals that came to a head with the Rodney King case and the Days of Rage riots in 1992" (*Tequila Mockingbird* 62). Nonetheless, Bishop upholds the honor of police officers and police forces by reiterating the traditional argument of the police as an isolated minority. He also makes the distinction that cops possess and stand for morality. Thus in *Chalk Whispers* we get the following comment on rules and laws:

> Bend them? Hell, we break them every chance we get. But the difference is, we have a moral compass [312].

While Bishop consistently leans toward thriller plots with conspiracies within and without the department in order to demonstrate his characters' heroic qualities, in his later books he begins to focus on more human problems. *Chalk Whispers*, for instance, includes both the issue of the underground railway for abused women and children and details about Fey Croaker's own past as an abused child.

Bill Kelly and Dolph LeMoult

In 1987 NYPD cop Bill Kelly teamed up with writer Dolph LeMoult and, with *Street Dance*, began a series of books centered upon NYPD detective Vince Crowley. Throughout the series of Crowley books the writers revisit McBain in a number of ways. There is a continuing cast of characters around Crowley — mostly Walt Cuzak, Tommy Ippollito, and their pipsqueak boss, Lieutenant Gleason. There are multiple plots: *Street Dance*, for instance, has a murderer who castrates and disembowels transsexuals, and the murder of two old people accompanied by the rage of the New York Hassidic community. There are facsimiles — in *Dream Street* the writers include two UF61 INITIAL REPORT OF CRIME forms, an autopsy report, and a whole series of DD5 COMPLAINT FOLLOW-UP forms. There is also the continuing story of Crowley's love life, from the breakup of his marriage to the daughter of a wealthy family to his developing relationship with a reporter. It's a lot of material and it's a lot like McBain.

Kelly and LeMoult concentrate on using Crowley and his buddies to sing the praises of seasoned street cops, and they go to some pains to define the qualities possessed by all good cops:

> Vince had been on the force long enough to know that there were two kinds of men who made good cops. There were the guys who considered the job a noble, almost patriotic calling. For them police work was a moral duty, a social imperative for separating the criminals from the solid citizenry, the city's last thin line of defense against anarchy and total chaos.... They accepted as an article of faith that they were needed by a vulnerable and unwary public who were incapable of understanding or appreciating their mission.
>
> Then there were the guys who were simply fascinated by police work, procedures, and criminality. Their passion was the job itself, the intrigue and excitement of investigation.... They were good cops because their instincts rather than their consciences led them there. They were good cops because they had a knack for it, not a vocation [*Street Dance* 13].

For the writers, however, many things stand in the way of being a "good cop." The law, perhaps most prominently, acts as one of these impediments:

> Most of them believed that being a cop meant walking a tightrope between what was technically legal and illegal. They believed that while criminals were free to operate outside of society's rules and regulations, policemen were bound by a mystifying set of prohibitions that were designed by politicians for political reasons. It was understood that any cop who adhered strictly to these senseless prohibitions was a bad cop. To do the job the way it was supposed to be done, the rules had to be skirted, reinterpreted, forgotten, and sometimes disregarded in order to bring criminals to justice [*Street Dance* 13–14].

Kelly and LeMoult focus the conventional cops vs. law theme on the issue of instinct, that trained police officers gain or possess special senses that enable them to sort out the innocent from the guilty:

> good cops have an instinctive ability to tell the guilty from the innocent. Perps looked guilty, acted guilty, smelled guilty. Every pore of their bodies gave off an aura, a kind of musk that made them sitting ducks for any trained investigator worth his salt.... The suspects he collared were guilty and, for the most part, they were slime. The cops Vince knew thought they should be shot, then read their rights [*Street Dance*, 14–15].

The law, moreover, is not the only obstacle good cops face.

Kelly and LeMoult show a department reeling from the aftermath of the Knapp Commission investigations, a department where the mechanisms put in place to discover corruption undermine the entire institution. Thus *Death Spiral* (1989), published seventeen years after the Knapp Commission, articulates a theme common to New York cop books of the 1970s and 1980s: that the policies instituted to deter and discover corruption weaken the whole police fabric as much as corruption did.

> Less reassuring was his awareness that the police department had become a honeycombed network of spies and informers. Self-seeking little men with no scruples and great ambitions were exploiting the bond of brotherhood that had once been every cop's solemn watchword. Open communication between policemen had become a matter of who could be trusted [*Death Spiral* 61].

But for Kelly and LeMoult it is not just the Knapp stuff—field agents secretly placed throughout the department to spot and report corruption — but the department's new view of what constitutes professionalism:

> That was the main problem with the department today.... More and more, things were being run by inexperienced kids who were great at taking tests but didn't know the first thing about what was happening on the streets [*Dream Street* 11].

Amidst all of this Vince Crowley and his buddies feel "like survivors on a life raft," but it is not just the book cops that get them down, it is also a new generation "of kid cops with pimply faces and punk attitudes — women cops, gay cops, ethnic minority cops, cops with earrings and gold chains, cops with leather pants, with purple hair" (*Dream Street* 11). Kelly and LeMoult are most outspoken about women police officers. The cops in *Street Dance* treat affirmative action as a bad joke:

> "And now we got women cops..." He shrugged. "You and me know what that's all about. It's a fucking joke, that's what it's about. What we oughta do is tell the bad guys 'Look, we gotta have women on our side, so you guys should have women criminals just to make it fair.'"

He laughed. "I'll have to tell the Spring Man about that one. From now on, the Mafia's got to have fifteen percent women or we call off the game" [170–1].

While Kelly and LeMoult center all of their plots on murder and the depiction of NYPD police issues (including job actions) they also use compassion to define the nature and role of the "street cop." It's why in *Death Spiral* the writers have Crowley befriend and protect a homeless man from a cynical justice system.

John Westermann

In 1988 Long Island cop John Westermann published his first novel, *High Crimes*. It chronicles the actions of detectives Tree Nelson and Jimmy Tibaldi. Early on Westermann gives background on how the two became cops:

> Tree and Jimmy had gone to college together in that revolutionary time when schoolwork was optional. Their grade-point average combined was less than 4.0. They succumbed to the police recruiter on campus when it looked like the only offer of gainful employment they were likely to receive. Since then their degrees worked against them [16].

This passage, with its inferential irony about hard work and its reflection on the prejudice of police departments against higher education, sets out some of the premises of *High Crimes*. In Westermann's second book he includes a passage on the mentoring of novice officer Orin Boyd by his first partner:

> "You know what he did when he broke me in? Drove me into the woods in the middle of the afternoon and told me to listen to the radio calls, that he was gonna take a nap. We sat there for a couple of hours doing shit. At sundown we went hunting rabbits with our pistols."
> "Not much help, huh?" Jack said.
> "Actually he got his message across. Taught me to do as little as possible" [63].

Witnessing police in action only adds to Tree and Jimmy's confusion. In *High Crimes* they watch as their supervisor tries to get a suspect to move away from the edge of a roof from which he has been threatening to jump:

> "Check it out, kid... You get your black ass over here right now before someone hurts you bad... Someone like me."
> This is hardly, Tree thinks, the recommended procedure for talking down barricaded suspects or jumpers — not that kissing their butts and bringing them pizza works all the time either [67].

Unmotivated and poorly lead, Tree admits to himself that as detectives "We couldn't catch a cold.... The truth was, they had no idea what to do" (*High Crimes* 23). The focus, or lack of it, of their lives rests elsewhere:

After dinner Tree and Jimmy drove to Jimmy's apartment ... Tree watches Wheel of Fortune while Jimmy showers ... Vanna looks hot tonight, and Tree wonders if Pat Sajak is getting some of the good thing from her. He smiles grimly. Sex and death are all he thinks of. Sex and death. And golf, thank God [*High Crimes* 38].

The metaphor for police work Westermann's cops use at the beginning of *High Crimes* is "Me and Tree don't think of this as a career.... This is like driving a garbage truck, a garbage truck without a floor. You toss in the garbage ... you drive away. And voila!" (14). And so Tree and Jimmy screw around, leave work early, smoke dope, drink, womanize (or Jimmy does), and even do a small bit of intelligent, albeit unappreciated, police work. All of this changes when Jimmy is killed in the line of duty. After the death of Jimmy Tibaldi, Westermann complicates Tree's need to avenge his partner's death by presenting two threats to his hero—the bad guys and internal affairs. Dodging both inquisitor cops and criminals in order to do the right thing brings out Tree's heroic qualities, qualities not nurtured by his job as a cop but by his resources as an individual.

It's not that Westermann doesn't accept the reality of the Blue Brotherhood. He just modifies it around the edges. Thus in *Exit Wounds* Westermann includes this passage on police as minority:

"I've noticed that a great many cops feel persecuted—like a minority group member might."

"I suppose many of us do. We're certainly identifiable. The wonderful management we work for has something to do with it, too. Plus the fact that we aren't permitted to work in bars, run for political office, wear our hair long, grow beards, et cetera. They get an awful lot of control over our lives."

"Does it make you feel ... powerless?"

"Sort of. You show up a rookie, all enthusiastic, scared at first, then awed by what you see. No one tells you. You come to work in a place like the Thirteenth and it swallows you, takes you over almost completely. You are the job" [148].

In *High Crimes* Westermann cites a cynical but more powerful aspect of the cop-as-minority ethos—"a good cop is never hungry, horny, cold or wet. And that no one prays for peace like the beat police. And the priorities: your partner, your self, the union, the public, then the care and feeding of the dumbass bosses. But first, your partner" (93).

In all of his books Westermann focuses on cops' occupational diseases. In *Exit Wounds* the hero, Orin Boyd, begins the novel having been assigned to the morgue wagon for his screwups, and then the bosses give him a chance to redeem himself by being an undercover agent at Camp Cope, the department's drug, stress, and alcohol rehabilitation facility for wayward cops. In

Honor Farm Westermann cranks up the issues by placing Boyd, again as an undercover agent, at the country club prison where cops convicted of corruption serve their time. Westermann's heroes could care less about traditional police peccadilloes: "Don't expect to hear about cooping or whoring. My brothers on the bottom of the municipal barrel don't need more abuse" (*Exit Wounds* 5). Neither does he find that legal police procedures work to solve the problems that confront them, problems rooted in the venality, corruption, and evil of cops and of criminals. And so Westermann's heroes become thriller heroes, in effect vigilantes whose actions solve, and whose individual virtue justifies the solution to, the problems in the novels.

Robert Sims Reid

Robert Sims Reid, a member of the Missoula Montana police force, wrote five novels — two about Ray Bartell (*Big Sky Blues* [1988] and *Wild Animals* [1996]) and three about Leo Banks (*Cupid* [1990], *Benediction* [1992], and *Red Corvette* [1992]). Both of them are cops on the Rozette, Montana, police force. Rozette, as Reid describes it, is a town of some 70,000 souls, where indigents and domestic disputes are the usual problems faced by patrol officers and where the detective force of ten officers has neither the case load or the variety of serious crimes confronted by big-city forces.

In *Big Sky Blues* Reid focuses on patrol officers. In it he brings in the familiar themes. There's the law theme: "Bartell started to feel silly, worrying about the rights of a scrounge like that, who knew plain and simple that there are legal rules and street rules" (24). There's the cops-versus-citizens theme: "They're all assholes.... And I'm the rotten prick who'll arrest every one of them. I've arrested preachers on Easter, mothers on Mother's Day. Orphans. Retards. Babes in arms. Screw 'em" (25). There's the cops versus bosses: "Bartell was far enough down that he decided to take Haller on faith, though God knew that faith in any of the big shots around the Rozette P.D. was a pretty delicate item" (85). There's the brutality theme: "It always bothered Bartell to realize that once in a while hurting people made him feel better" (36). There's the past-versus-present theme:

> In the old days ... we'd have kicked in the door and mashed the prick and thrown his ass in jail and that would've been the end of it. If he was still alive. Now we're *responsible*.... We're even responsible to the jackass criminal himself for what we might do hurting him on account of the shit he started [222].

And on and on. Reid has the conventions of the patrol cop novel down pat in *Big Sky Blues*.

In his subsequent books Reid shows off the conventions of the detective cop novel. In *Cupid* he introduces Rozette P.D. Detective Leo Banks.

Banks works in cramped basement office and through him Reid recounts the routines of a small- town department called upon to solve few difficult crimes and many domestic ones. He includes the routine comic episodes: in *Cupid*, for example, a citizen reports cops as potential child molesters. He also gives patches of office humor. The Rozette detectives include one woman:

> Linda [Westhammer] is a small, tightly wound woman with blond hair she wears in a frizz. She's one of half a dozen women on the Department, all of whom regularly get more or less clubbed by innuendo [*Cupid* 34].

With Banks Reid provides background on how and why his hero became a cop in the first place. Riding a freight train, after leaving the navy, Banks winds up in Rozette, where he applies to be a cop:

> Seven of us applied for two jobs. We get hundreds of applications now, but in those days, when hair was something God gave people so they'd have a place to put flowers, becoming a cop wasn't much of an attraction [*Cupid* 7].

For Banks inexperience is a virtue:

> I'd spent my last year and a half doing petty investigations [in the Navy] at Bemmerton, a job that was mostly paper. I'd never been a civilian cop, so I didn't bring any bad habits to a profession fearful of habits that cannot be described as wholesome [*Cupid* 6].

Finally, Reid centers *Cupid* on a crime requiring forensic expertise — in this case forensic archeology.

Entwined through the conventions of the cop book, whether it's about patrol officers or detectives, Reid develops disturbing strands of loneliness, uncertainty, and despair in the lives of his police heroes. With partners, a bulwark theme of the cop book, Reid shows fragile connections between officers who cannot communicate essentials about their lives and experience with one another. Indeed, Reid builds *Big Sky Blues* on this theme. The connection between partners Bartell and Culp gradually seeps away, as does Bartell's relationship with his wife. Nothing dramatic, nothing spectacular, no defining moment. It just happens.

Reid emphasizes confusion with Bartell, but with Paul Culp in *Big Sky Blues* and then in the Leo Banks books he stresses aloneness. Both men live spartan lives. They have lost wives and children because of their jobs and are left very often with only stoicism as a thin protection against the weariness and confusion they find in their work. They, however, do have the wild and majestic nature of Montana. City cops don't.

Serialists of the 1980s

The rolling snowball of serial killer books can be attributed to a lot of things that happened within and without the world of the cop novel. It didn't hurt that Lawrence Sanders' books in the 1970s sold lots of copies. Then there was the contemporary interest — the trials of Bundy, Gacy, and Wayne Williams, as well as ongoing investigations into other serial killings — and the emerging popularity of the true crime book. Additionally, as the Soviet Union withered away, thriller writers needed a gigantic, implacable evil for their heroes to confront, and humanity has not spawned more evil than the darkness that lived in the tortured souls of John Wayne Gacy and Jeffrey Dahmer.

William Heffernan

Detective Paul Devlin of the NYPD appears in William Heffernan's *Ritual* (1988), *Blood Rose* (1991), *Scarred* (1993), *Tarnished Blue* (1995), and *Winter's Gold* (1997). Heffernan's pattern is to pair up his hero with an older detective, who offers experience and character contrast to the stereotypical Devlin, who has it all:

> Despite his rugged good looks, Devlin seemed almost boyish when he smiled.... He was tall and solid, with wavy black hair and dark blue eyes that could be surprisingly gentle or fierce. And there was a two inch scar on his left cheek — the gift of an earlier case — that turned almost white when he was pushed too far. Grogan had seen enough of Devlin's temper to know it was something best avoided. But he had seen another side of the man — his gentleness and patience. [*Tarnished Blue* 25].

In the first book, *Ritual*, a serial killer book plotted as a least-likely-suspect whodunit, Heffernan introduces Devlin, an already experienced homicide detective, but before describing the hero Heffernan brings in his much older partner, Stanislaus Rolk:

> Rolk was as rumpled as ever. His topcoat looked as though he had slept in it. His hair, streaked with gray, always seemed groomed with fingers instead of a comb. Rolk had a sharp, softly lined face. Not a cop's face, but the face of a bachelor uncle who appears for dinner every other Thanksgiving and Christmas, then fades from memory for the next year or so [*Ritual* 20].

After developing the bond between the partners, Heffernan reveals that Rolk is crazy as a bedbug and at the close of the novel he forces Devlin to shoot him, sending the hero into a cycle of depression and despair. Thus, on leave at the beginning of *Scarred*, in response to the comment about his track record with serial killers that "maybe you're just nuts enough to think like these guys" Devlin muses:

Yeah, and with the mental scars to prove it, Devlin thought. Two men dead. Two friends. First the Ritual case. Then the other one.... He didn't need another one, Devlin told himself. No one in his right mind needed even one [49].

But, of course, that doesn't keep him away from the job too long.

After Rolk, Heffernan does it straight when he introduces older partner number two, Grogan, whose hair at least sounds a lot like Rolk's:

> The man came across like an aging, overweight rummy in his baggy brown suit and rumpled shirt and tie. His face looked as though someone had stepped on it, and his unruly gray hair gave the appearance of having been combed with a rake [*Scarred* 14].

Grogan is profane, as opposed to Devlin's primmer speech ("Unlike most cops, profanity wasn't a normal part of Devlin's speech. It only appeared when he was really hot" *Tarnished Blue* 20). And with the contrast of Grogan and Devlin, Heffernan brings in the conventional cop novel theme of past and present. Grogan, of course, represents the past. He has no patience with the fashion for fancy forensics and the vogue for calling in the FBI to develop psychological profiles, and he repeatedly rails against them in *Scarred*:

> "You guys work the crime scene. You gather it all up and run it through your voodoo science shit. And when you hit a brick wall, you wait for another stiff so you can start again. Keep adding it all to your 'profiles.'" Grogan spoke the word with contempt.
>
> "Then when you've just about got it together, some rookie cop in East Jesus makes a traffic stop and accidentally nails your guy for you" [17].

And he voices racist and homophobic disgust with the new personnel policies of the NYPD:

> Used to be the Irish and the Italians and the Jews had their official organizations to push their people along. Then the fucking niggers and spics had to have one, and everybody had to live with that. Now the fruits got one. Shit, ten years ago, we found a cop was taking it up the Hershey highway, we dumped his fucking ass. Or at least put him in a job so miserable that he'd quit. Today we're supposed to celebrate the fact we got faggots on the force [*Tarnished Blue* 95].

In spite of the bigotry and mule-headedness, Heffernan makes Grogan a good cop, knowledgeable, dedicated, passionate; he adds pathos with his death in *Tarnished Blue*, and by emphasizing his biases Heffernan uses Grogan to make new cops like Devlin look even better. Heffernan counters the above two instances of Grogan's biases by having Devlin pay attention to scientific evidence and profiles even though he realizes that neither may pan out. And in *Tarnished Blue*, to demonstrate the hero's and the department's acceptance of diversity he adds Sharon Levy, a lesbian detective to Devlin's team and shows her saving his life at the close of the novel.

The other common cop motif that Heffernan uses is impatience with rules and bureaucracy. When Devlin goes to headquarters at One Police Plaza, Heffernan informs readers that "Street cops referred to the place as the Puzzle Palace, and the top three floors as the Emerald City—where all the phony wizards worked" (*Scarred* 65). Bureaucracy and structure get in the way in the kind of books Heffernan writes, books that pit a hero against a brilliant, hidden antagonist. He gets around this, by the time of *Tarnished Blue*, by inventing a special squad for Devlin and his team, one that reports directly to the mayor. By this device Heffernan both makes Devlin exempt from department bureaucracy and politics and enables him to take pot shots at the politicians and bureaucrats when he comes in contact with them.

William Bayer

While William Bayer covers the requisite police themes, his novels are darker and more inward than those of many other police writers. His first, *Switch* (1984), turns on a villain who switches the heads of victims; *Wallflower* (1991) follows a serial killer who glues the genitals of victims to their bodies; and *Mirror Maze* (1994) deals with muggings, industrial espionage, and murder. As Bayer's epigraph from Ross MacDonald at the start of *Mirror Maze* suggests, Bayer is concerned with abnormal psychology, with Freudian explanations for aberrant behavior, and with the detective as, in part, analyst. The opening scene of *Switch* at a cop's funeral sets the tone and perspective for all of Bayer's books:

> A melodrama, Janek thought, a drab, lousy middle-class melodrama. Not even a tragedy, because a cop's guilt is too petty and his honor too ambiguous and his flaws too minor to give him tragic stature. His torment comes from little things, not grandiose schemes to place himself above the gods. And so his self-inflicted death is a whimpering little end, just another hot-August-Sunday-morning-old-cop suicide [11].

In his books Bayer introduces a limited cast of police characters. In *Switch*, there is Chief Hart, for whom "it was a major effort ... to pretend to be a human being" (15). *Wallflower* brings in Chief of Detectives Kit Kopta, who, like Marjorie Buttera in Leuci's *Captain Butterfly* and the Ice Maiden in Caunitz's *Suspects*, is "the highest ranking woman in the history of the NYPD." Miscellaneous detectives, like Boyce in *Wallflower*, appear who lack what it takes to really do the job:

> He had a beer belly and not much hair. He'd combed a few thin brown wisps back carefully across his skull as if he thought they might cover his baldness and make him more attractive—but they didn't. The base of his face had a kind of squared off look that reminded Janek of the bottom of a paper bag.

But though his manner didn't proclaim great brilliance, Janek recognized a predatory look.... This was a mediocre detective inflamed by a stroke of luck [*Wallflower* 43].

Lieutenant Janek's team is different. There's Marchetti ("He had worked narcotics for three years and had acquired the habits of a narc — toughness, compassion, quick reflexes, and stubbornness" [*Switch* 26]), and Aaron Greenberg ("Aaron was a superb detective, a fine tracker, excellent at interrogation and brilliant on the phone" [*Switch* 46]).

Bayer lays out the ideal detective's qualities in *Wallflower* and in doing so he defines his hero, Frank Janek:

> The young ones here, all they talk about is DNA fingerprinting.... They don't understand that the greatest cases, the only ones that can justify living the best part of your life in the gutter, are crimes of the wounded spirit. And the detectives who solves [*sic*] crimes like that are men like us, men who have wounds of our own [*Wallflower* 9];
>
> Basically there're two kinds.... Scientists and artists. The scientists are puzzle solvers. They pore over evidence, figure out what's absent, then go after the missing piece. I'm probably more the artist type. I try to feel the case, identify with the perp, then generate the insight that will bring it all together. For me, the best cases are the psychological ones, where to solve them you have to go inside a mind and touch the madness [*Wallflower* 23].

Having become a star in the department, Janek gets singled out for all of the weird cases. Consequently he has to deal with brilliant but damaged and dangerous criminals. Indeed, in *Wallflower* the villain is a rogue psychiatrist. All of the criminals' bizarre and evil acts stem from childhood trauma. By splitting the narrative between cop and criminal, much in the manner of Lawrence Sanders' *The First Deadly Sin*, Bayer reveals both characters to the reader. Bayer extends the connection between police work and religion by emphasizing Janek's role as confessor. At the same time he also makes his hero a penitent, trying to atone for the deficiencies in his own relationships. In this regard, too, the useful part of police work lies in keeping the hero's mind off of his own inadequacies and failures: "Without cases to perplex him, taunt him in the night, he would begin to think about himself" (*Wallflower* 5).

Ridley Pearson

Ridley Pearson knows the field, does the work, and has the knack for writing popular cop novels. He was also in the right place at the right time. Given the increasing vogue in cop novels for serial killer plots, the right place was Seattle, the setting for all of Pearson's Lou Boldt books. Seattle

means serial killers — maybe it's the rain, but the region witnessed the atrocities, among others, of Ted Bundy and the Green River Killer. The right time
was the late 1980s — Pearson's *Undercurrents* was published in 1988. By that
time most of the advances in forensic science had had time to begin to attract
public notice and interest. Pearson sees science as the wave of the present:

> Educated as scientists, they didn't think like other cops. They worked as a
> team, speaking in half sentences, using techie jargon unintelligible to the lay-
> man. With their own nerd pack and a language all their own, these men and
> women remained on the social fringe of the police fraternity but played an
> increasingly important role in any investigation. The star witnesses in an inves-
> tigation were no longer the boyfriend or the observant neighbor but these ID
> Unit technicians. Convictions relied on a foundation of incriminating scientific
> evidence. A jury, even a judge, preferred to believe a computer-generated
> enlargement of work from an electron microscope rather than a woman like
> Agnes who had heard voices through a wall [*Angel Maker* 151].

In his books Pearson brings in profiling and the FBI's Behavioral Science Unit, his crime lab people use super glue fuming and lasers to find
fingerprints, computer morphing and cranial imaging replace the police artist,
and ground penetrating radar finds buried bodies. In addition to police psychologist Daphne Matthews, and Doc Dixon and Bernie Lofgrin, Pearson's
main scientists, he introduces a variety of forensic experts — *Chain of Evidence* (1995) has a forensic botanist, *Probable Cause* (1990) has a forensic psychiatrist, and *Angel Maker* (1993) has both a forensic anthropologist and a
forensic archeologist. Indeed, all kinds of technologies fascinate Pearson, and
in part he contrives his plots so as to explore them. In *No Witness* (1994),
for example, the villain's extortion by ATM gives Pearson the opportunity
to explain how cash machines work. Pearson's combination of serial killers
and the panoply of forensic science brings in new procedures for the police
procedural in that the multiplication of crime scenes creates the opportunity to apply a different and often novel investigatory technique each time.
To do this Pearson does his homework: in *Undercurrents*, for example, he
acknowledges the help of eight individuals (among them two M.D.'s, an FBI
Agent, a Seattle cop, a medical examiner, and a prosecutor) and credits four
people for "Research Assistance." For balance and for character development, however, Pearson acknowledges that science alone can't do the trick:

> Too often, that reliance [on lab work] translated into a dependence on the
> lab — a belief that the lab had all the answers. In the process, old-fashioned
> police work suffered [*The Pied Piper* 282].

And so in his Lou Boldt novels Pearson also portrays "old-fashioned"
police work. He draws a team of cops — John LaMoia, the lothario, and
Bobbie Gaynes, the requisite woman cop — led by Sergeant, then Lieuten-

ant Lou Boldt, and pays tribute to what the team means in police work: "It was at time like this, when everyone reached deep and suddenly rallied around each other in the crunch, that Boldt remembered what it was like to be a team, what he missed about the job" (*Angel Maker* 277). And in *Probable Cause* Pearson also makes clear the hero's role on the team:

> The thing about a homicide investigation, she realized, was that a dozen or so people contributed equally, most of them in a thankless fashion and unseen. The exciting element of any investigation was the teamwork. They were a small chamber orchestra — the medical examiner, the forensic investigator, the lab technicians, the latent-fingerprint experts, the various cops and patrolmen — autonomous, anonymous, and yet under the confident direction of the investigator who served as conductor [101].

While his earlier books introduce one-shot heroes (James DeWitt of the Seaside, California department in *Probable Cause* and Joe Dartelli of the Hartford, Connecticut PD in *Chain of Evidence*), Pearson's later books feature Lou Boldt of Seattle, introduced for the first time in *Undercurrents*:

> In the men's room he caught sight of himself in the mirror and realized that he looked older than his thirty-nine years.... His whole act needed a shine, not just his shoes. The age of his suit reflected a detective's salary; he had spilled coffee onto his new tie — when and where, he had no idea, he had missed a spot shaving ... his face was pale and gaunt... [2].

Boldt is a cop, and Pearson uses him to bring in or comment on a variety of police issues: corruption, job actions ("blue flu"), sexism, etc. Literate in the uses of science, Pearson also supplies Boldt with an emotional side. Repeatedly he notes the hero's sympathy for and with victims. Beyond sympathy, in *Beyond Recognition* (1997) Pearson even gives Boldt occasions of second sight:

> On rare occasions, his imagination overpowered him, ran away from him, leaving him a spectator as the crime played out before him. That night in early October was just such an occurrence [100–101].

Pearson gives Boldt an artistic side — he plays the piano — and threads domestic issues throughout the books: his wife's career, her affair, her cancer, her religious conversion, as well as Boldt's affair with the other main character in the books, Daphne Matthews. With Matthews, Pearson also deals with the ambivalence of psychology and police work. She is the department's psychologist and counsels cops as well as drawing profiles of criminals, positing the origins of their behavior and predicting their acts. In *Undercurrents*, when Matthews is confronted by the villain, whom she has sought to sympathetically understand as a portion of suffering humanity, she concludes that he is "an animal" and applauds Boldt's killing of him.

John Sandford

John Sandford (John Camp), along with William Bayer, William Heffernan, and Ridley Pearson, likes serial killers. Serial killers, of course, give the
cop writer plenty of advantages — they do things more than once and that
helps out with the plot; they potentially leave more evidence and that helps
out with getting in details; they terrorize communities and that helps out
with atmosphere; and they're nuts and that helps out with characterizing both
the villain and the hero. They also give the advantage of a connection with
real serial killers. From his first book, *Rules of Prey* (1989), Sandford fastened
on the predator metaphor and all of his subsequent books have the word
"prey" in their titles: *Shadow Prey* (1990), *Eyes of Prey* (1991), *Silent Prey*
(1992), *Winter Prey* (1993), etc.

Sandford's hero, Lucas Davenport, doesn't have a lot in his character
from cop conventions. Davenport is independently wealthy, having made and
making a bundle from developing games, another metaphor Sandford wants
to develop (the killer in *Rules of Prey* is a master gamer). Unlike J.A. Jance's
hero, another rich guy who drives a Porche, Davenport comes out of the
romantic tradition:

> He was slender and dark-complexioned, with straight black hair going gray at
> the temples and a long nose over a crooked smile. One of his central upper
> incisors had been chipped and he never had it capped. He might have been an
> Indian except for his blue eyes.
>   His eyes were warm and forgiving. The warmth was somehow emphasized
> by the vertical white scar that started at his hairline, ran down to his right eye
> socket, jumped over the eye, and continued down his cheek to the corner of
> his mouth. The scar gave him a raffish air, but left behind a touch of inno-
> cence, like Errol Flynn in *Captain Blood* [*Rules of Prey* 16–17].

Sandford gives readers the Native American business for the hunting
and tracking in the books, and the Errol Flynn business for Davenport's
swashbuckling. Women, Sandford shows, go for these sorts of things — in
Rules of Prey, for example, Davenport romances two women who eventually
meet and decide which of them he should be with, and in *Shadow Prey* there
is NYPD's Lily Rothenburg. Although on paper Davenport works for the
Minneapolis police department — starting as a lieutenant in *Rules* and rising
to deputy chief later on — he seems to do little or no paperwork, and he wan-
ders into the chief's office and tells the chief what to do. Sandford, however,
does provide some small doses of a few larger institutional issues — in *Night
Prey* (1994), for example, Sandford introduces a lesbian detective, and the
woman police chief (this, after all, is Minneapolis) needs to confront unrest
in her constituency because of a rapist's rampage. But Sandford also shows
his hero repeatedly breaking the law. He casually portrays Davenport beat-

ing suspects and prisoners, and in *Rules of Prey* the hero breaks into and searches two residences without warrants. Some of the departmental brass are suspicious of Davenport's methods and in *Rules of Prey* two particularly inept internal affairs cops try to dog his every move. Sanford lets us know that in this case clothes make the men:

> The senior cop was fat. His partner was thin. Other than that, they looked much alike, with brush-cut hair, pink faces, yellow short-sleeved shirts, and double-knit trousers from J.C. Penney [17].

The hero, however, is light years smarter than they are. Finally, more than just breaking a few rules, in *Rules* Davenport becomes a vigilante—at the end of the novel, because of the prospect of an insanity plea, he carefully arranges the scene and shoots the killer in cold blood after he tells him: "I thought of that. It would be like losing, seeing you get away alive. I couldn't stand that" (347–148).

While Sanford frequently mentions forensic details, like the references to DNA, hair and fiber, and tool marks in *Night Prey* (1994), they seem *pro forma*. He also bows to fashion and brings in a psychiatric profiler, a child-hood friend of Davenport who has become a Catholic nun. This enables Sandford to bring in analysis of the killer whose behavior readers have wit-nessed, thereby giving two perspectives on the aberrant criminal personal-ity. Sandford also adds to this the idea of the really smart (albeit insane) criminal, the criminal who knows police procedures and how to avoid and use them. In *Rules* the killer even goes to the library to read up on crime and criminals. In *Shadow* Sanford uses another serial killer pattern, that of the peripatetic criminal who is hard to catch because of the disparate locations of the crimes. Ultimately, therefore, to catch people like this, Davenport's talents need to go beyond reason, science, and even analysis, all of which the criminal has purposefully or accidentally thwarted. In *Night Prey*, Dav-enport gets a "feeling" about the crimes from reading autopsy reports. Sand-ford comments on this in pillow talk in later in the novel:

> But what you do ... somebody might die because you can't solve a problem that's solvable. Or like last winter, you seemed to reach out and solve a prob-lem that was unsolvable, and so people who probably would have died, lived.
> ...This isn't criticism. Just observation. What you do is really bizarre.... It's more like magic, or palm reading than science. I do science [she's a physician]. Everybody I work with does science. That's routine. What you do ... it's fas-cinating" [304–5].

The Chroniclers

Historical reconstructions have been part of mystery fiction for a long time, and a number of writers in the late eighties and early nineties use historical events as the basis for cop novels. There exists, moreover, a small group of writers intent not only on re-creating a real crime or police action from the past but also on presenting a grander, or at least larger, picture. These writers want to show the development of characters over a span of years and intend to present a broader portrait of a police department than is possible in one novel. Therefore their work spreads over several books that chronicle the rise and fall of individuals and the successes and failures of their departments (and by extension the cities) whose principles their lives help to define.

W.E.B. Griffin

W.E.B. Griffin (William Butterworth) likes the military. In 1982 he began the Men at War series with *The Lieutenants*, followed by another series about marines beginning with *Semper Fi* (1986). In 1988, under yet another pseudonym, John Kevin Dugan, Griffin, or Butterworth, began a series of novels about cops — his Badge of Honor series — with *Men in Blue*. As of this writing the series extends to seven novels. Epic, saga, soap opera, pick the term — Griffin uses a large canvas to portray the Philadelphia Police Department, its history, its organization, its regulations, its personnel, and its equipment. Here, for instance, is part of Griffin's description of cops' weapons:

> Senior officers, officers on plainclothes duty, and off-duty policemen were permitted to carry whatever pistol they wished, either their issue weapon, or one they had purchased with their own money, provided it was chambered for the .38 Special cartridge. Those who purchased their own weapons usually bought the Colt "Detective Special" or the Smith & Wesson Model 36 "Chief's Special," a five-shot, two-inch-barrel revolver, or the Smith & Wesson Model 37, which was an aluminum-framed version of the Chief's Special. There were some Model 38s around, "the Bodyguard," a variation of the Chief's Special which encloses the hammer in a shroud [*Men in Blue* 43].)

Communications particularly fascinate Griffin and he includes plentiful details about radio protocols and procedures. There are also facsimiles — in *Special Operations* (1989), for example, Griffin tosses in copies of orders sent to precincts and newspaper articles — but rather than emphasizing police procedures as they do in McBain and his followers, their purpose is to help create the illusion of historical accuracy in the books.

As the substance of his novels, Griffin brings in a large cast of characters, many of them continuing: cops, politicians, media folks, lawyers, and their assorted loves and relatives. Everyone has something to do with the Philadelphia PD. Mayor Carlucci is a former cop, and in his continuing hero, Peter Wohl, Griffin embodies the convention of police in the family with a vengeance:

> In 1854, following the Act of Consolidation, which saw the area of Philadelphia grow from 360 acres to 83,000 by the consolidation of all the tiny political entities in the area into a city, Karl-Heinz Wohl, Friederich Wohl's youngest grandson, managed to have himself appointed to the new police department.
>
> There had been at least one Wohl on the rolls of the Philadelphia Police Department ever since [*Men in Blue* 25].

Here Griffin not only employs a familiar cop theme, he also connects with his other series and the tradition of military service in families.

While they may have peccadilloes, Griffin's large cast of cop characters is almost uniformly heroic. Of course Peter Wohl is:

> Wohl did not look much the popular image of a cop. People would guess that he was a stockbroker, or maybe an engineer or lawyer. A professional, in other words. But he was a cop. He'd done his time walking a beat, he'd even been a corporal in the Highway Patrol. But when he'd made sergeant ... they'd assigned him to the Civil Disobedience Squad, in plain clothes, and he'd been in plain clothes ever since.
>
> It was said that Peter Wohl would certainly make it up toward the top, maybe all the way. He had the smarts and he worked hard, and he seldom made mistakes [*Men in Blue* 24].

Mat Payne, who enters the series as a recruit in *Special Operations* and eventually takes over the spotlight from Wohl, is a cum laude graduate of the University of Pennsylvania, a crack shot, and also related to the Griffin's extended family of cops. Taddeus Czernick is "a handsome, healthy, imposing man" (*Special Operations* 68), and so are all the rest of the major players from the top down to the beat cops—competent and dedicated. They solve many complicated and sensitive cases with acumen, courage, and impartiality; they neither ask for nor receive the credit they deserve. In *Special Operations* Griffin makes clear the high purpose of the Philly police department:

> Alone of America's major city police forces, Philadelphia police respond to any call for help, not just to reports of crime. It is deeply imbedded in the subconscious minds of Philadelphia's 2.1 million citizens (there are more than five million people in the Philadelphia metropolitan area) that what you do when Uncle Charley breaks a leg or the kid falls off his bike and is bleeding pretty bad at the mouth or when you see a naked woman just walking along Fairmont Park is "call the cops" [*Special Operations* 2].

While Griffin acknowledges that the elite branch of the Philly police force, the Highway Patrol, has some image problems with their leather jackets and swagger, his novels portray the department and its officers, as the series title suggests, with honor. Begun not quite a decade after the end of Frank Rizzo's last term as mayor of Philadelphia, however, the books largely overlook the impact on the city's police force and the city itself of the leather-jacketed, ex-cop mayor with a continuing reputation for brutality and racism, and who is reported to have said in the 1975 mayoral election that "I'm gonna make Attila the Hun look like a faggot after the election's over." But Griffin's cops exist in a quite different world and he portrays them in a quite different manner, a manner that has more similarities to the popular prime-time television soap operas like *Dallas* (1978–1991) *Knot's Landing* (1979–1993), or *Dynasty* (1981–1989) than to the cop novel of the eighties.

James Ellroy

James Ellroy's cops are not nice. But, for that matter, nobody in Ellroy is. The politicians certainly are not. Written in a jazzed-up, breakneck style, Ellroy takes on Los Angeles in the 1950's as a tabloid writer would. Indeed in *L.A. Confidential* (1990) he includes lengthy quotes from a scandal sheet as well as headlines and clips from newspapers. Mostly what Ellroy's fiction exposes is the wholesale corruption of the LAPD. From Chief Parker down, Ellroy's LAPD has little concern with serving and protecting anything other than itself. The only method the police employ is violence, and the sinister Lieutenant Dudley Smith, who appears in *Big Nowhere* (1988), *L.A. Confidential*, and *White Jazz* (1992), institutionalizes violence in the department's policies of "containment" (i.e. keeping the minority population and drugs confined to the ghetto) and intimidation against organized crime — beating up gangsters and sending them out of town. There is not a lot of difference between the cops and the crooks — or in their methods at least. And there is not a lot of difference in the politicians who use cops as bagmen and as muscle to keep themselves in office. Twisted though they may be, however, some of Ellroy's cops have a vision of and even an obsession with justice, but they are mortally wounded souls and the justice they seek is a justice that cannot be achieved in Ellroy's L.A.

Early in *L.A. Confidential* Ellroy presents what amounts to a catechism on getting ahead in the LAPD:

> One, would you be willing to plant corroborative evidence on a suspect you knew to be guilty in order to ensure an indictment?...
>
> Would you be willing to shoot hardened armed robbers in the back to offset the chance that they might utilize flaws in the legal system and go free?...

Would you be willing to beat confessions out of suspects you knew to be guilty?...

Would you be willing to rig crime scene evidence to support a prosecuting attorney's working hypothesis? [20].

In Ellroy's cop books not only are illegal practices the norm for the cops, violence also attends most of them. In *White Jazz*, one of the first scenes shows Lieutenant Dave Klein throwing a man he is supposed to be guarding out of a hotel window. Bud White in *L.A. Confidential* stuffs a man's hand into a garbage disposal during an interrogation:

Bud hooked him in the gut. Gilette rolled with it, grabbed a knife, swung. Bud sidestepped, kicked at his balls. Gilette doubled up; Bud hit the garbage switch. The motor scree'd; Bud jammed the queer's knife hand down the chute [194].

All of Ellory's cops shoot first, and the throw-down gun is almost a regulation part of their uniforms. A lot of the violence serves the ends of politicians or perverse departmental policy. Some of it, however, serves the ends of the characters' own demons. Ellroy, for example, shows this in *L.A. Confidential* with Bud White, whose own private mission is to impose justice on wife beaters, about whom he keeps meticulous records and visits upon them the punishment the courts and the system do not. However, there is no redemption. The manipulations of Dudley Smith frustrate White's attempts to remake himself in the second half of the novel, keeping him in the role of the department's licensed strong-arm man. And then there is the irony Ellroy attaches to Ed Exley, the well-born cop whose rise through the department Ellroy chronicles in *L.A. Confidential*. Beginning the novel naïve about real cops and goaded with reminders of his hero father and brother, Exley first compensates for his secret cowardice during World War II by shotgunning unarmed (and innocent) black men. He learns how to navigate the political shoals of the department. And finally he is forced to use two men he despises — Bud White and "Trashcan" Jack Vincennes — to solve the murders at the diner that serve as the central crime focus of *L.A. Confidential*. In the end of the book Exley achieves a kind of closure and a sort of justice. He winds up as a deputy chief and chief of detectives, but the final comment made to him in the book is "my God I don't envy you the blood on your conscience" (496).

Journalists and Other Professional Writers

The growing popularity of the cop novel shows both in the number of books and the number of writers who take up the form in the 1980s. Thus journalists like Adcock, Oster, and Pedneau turn to writing about cops; a Hollywood writer, Ed Naha takes up real cops and not Robocop, and Archer Mayor begins as a mystery writer and chooses to make his hero a cop.

Thomas Adcock

In 1984 reporter Thomas Adcock chronicled a year spent with the cops of New York's poshest precinct in *Precinct Nineteen*. He witnessed the police dealing with various felons — muggers, smash-and-grab artists, burglars, etc. — and wrote of the police officers as humane, dedicated, and efficient individuals. He also wrote about the precinct's cops as vulnerable and sometimes flawed people. One of Adcock's cops has to deal with the psychological aftershock of shooting a youth, another has to face the consequences of his adultery, and another has to confront the department's puritanical double standards. After *Precinct Nineteen* Adcock presented a darker view of the cops in his novels *Sea of Green* (1989), *Dark Maze* (1991), *Drown All Dogs* (1994), *Devil's Heaven* (1995), *Thrown Away Child* (1996), and *Grief Street* (1997). Here he has the same concern for human weaknesses exacerbated by police work. Detective Neil Hockaday, the hero of the novels, is a drunk by the time of *Devil's Heaven* and is eventually placed in the department's program that deals with the epidemic of alcoholism among its cops. That's one sign of the new police novel. Another is Adcock's brutal realism. Here is one of the grislier crime scenes from *Devil's Heaven*:

> The buck naked, masked dead guy was spread-eagled on his back in the middle of the kitchen floor. Blood was streaked everywhere across the checkerboard of the otherwise tidy blue and yellow tiles. Most of it had gone tacky, but here and there were puddles that remained brightly wet. The body was nearly empty of fluids and white as Elmer's glue. But still, tiny streams of blood dribbled from spike wounds in hands and feet. The guy had been nailed down to the floor. There was also a little blood still spurting out from below his deflated hips. I could see the curved handle of a crowbar between his upper thighs. From the looks of things, someone had rammed the steel rod up the poor bastard's backside [*Devil's Heaven* 68].

In *Devil's Heaven* Adcock also partially deconstructs his earlier generalizations about cops. In the novel the cops are sloppy:

> Civilians are under the false impression that cops are meticulous about little things like crime scenes. But cops are as sloppy as everybody else in America. Which is a big part of the reason so many bad guys are running around loose in the country [69].

Cops are homophobic:

> The cops have a way of not taking these cases seriously. Their attitude is, murdering queers can be ignored, beating queers can be ignored [116].

Cops like King Kong Kowalski, who uses his sap on suspects' genitals as part of processing them at the station, take brutality to a new level. And the new generation of police is disconnected, indifferent and yuppiefied:

> They had smirks on their faces, the kind worn by an unfortunate new generation of cop: New York's suburban occupation force.... They consider their union dues well spent on an army of lobbyists that keeps the legislators in Albany from including them in a law that says if you draw your paycheck in the City of New York you ought to live there. The president of this union lives so far out on Long Island he should be a lighthouse keeper [78].

For Adcock in *Devil's Heaven*, then, police work has lost its mission and indifference rules both the department and individual officers. However, there remain a few cops, like Hockaday and the gay cop who helps him during the novel, who preserve the higher goals of police work. And in Adcock these have to do with compassion for the dispossessed and attachment to the city they protect. Thus the hero's statement that "I try to be patient with the despised. By which I mean the winos and howlers and dopers — the lost souls, the skels, the seekers of refuge who somehow find their way to my city" (*Devil's* 193). At the same time, however, Adcock makes it clear that police work requires individuals to abandon normal human behavior. Like many other writers he describes the routine psychological adjustment to witnessing the effects of violent crime:

> Maybe I have come across grislier scenes in my career, but probably not many. On this occasion, as on all others, I was saved from going squirrelley by the general irreverence all cops who are mentally sound will exhibit when confronted by what is darkly known as permanent violence.... Also cops can become as chatty as a Dixie senator, as if filibustering against the kind of sudden death they know is the occupational hazard we share with the bad guys [*Devil's* 68–69].

Unlike many other writers, however, Adcock not only touches on the stresses cops face on the job and voices compassion for the dispossessed, he also makes his hero largely exempt from supervision and departmental procedures and shows him acting more like a compassionate and introspective private eye than a cop.

Jerry Oster

In the early 1980s Jerry Oster left his day job as a reporter and turned to novels. In *Sweet Justice* (1985) he introduced Jake Neuman, a cop character he carried over in *Club Dead* (1985) and *Nowhere Man* (1987). Indeed, Neuman makes cameo appearances even in the novels in which Oster uses his other main characters, like Joe Cullen. While some of the early books, such as *Sweet Justice*, focus on the street cop, Oster increasingly includes problems involving the police hierarchy; thus the murder of one police commissioner in *Internal Affairs* (1990) and allegations of sexual harassment against another in *Fixin' to Die* (1992). Both center on Detective Joe Cullen.

Oster makes a lot out of the contrast between real police work and that portrayed in the movies and on TV. In *Sweet Justice* Neuman has the first of his reveries about the differences:

> Maybe ... it was simply that Bobby had come to the realization that police work was ninety-nine percent shitwork and that the other one percent wasn't all that much more exciting.... He would have thought it would take Redfield a little longer to come to that realization, if only because there were far more police shows on television than there had been in the old days, and they held out, if nothing else, the prospect that police work was exciting — driving fast in unmarked cars with the siren stuck on the roof, kicking down doors and shouting at suspects to get their hands up, tackling purse snatchers and slamming them in the face with a handy garbage can, blowing hold up men through plate-glass windows, slipping into bed during your lunch hour with a slinky public defender. In Neuman's nonage, the only TV show had been *Dragnet*, which, in its way, had been true to the shitwork, although it had been guilty of an overdose of luck [116–17].

Following this, in *Nowhere Man* (1987) Neuman for the first time watches an episode of *Miami Vice* and muses on its mendacious images of police work throughout the novel. Oster uses the fantasies of police life portrayed in the movies as a springboard to a series of maxims about police work as Neuman experiences it:

> That was what it was like, police work: slumping on the sprung seats of a worn-out car with grimy windows, a grimy dash, no door on the glove compartment, one sun visor, ripped floor mats, a handle to roll the window or one to open the door but never both, halves of sets of seat belts, the stink of blood and vomit and pizza and sweat; squashing old coffee containers with your feet every time you changed the way you were slumping... [201].
>
> But Neuman was sitting in a grimy, smelly car with a guy on sick leave with something wrong with his gut, a suspect in a murder case who kept his popcorn in the freezer, and a guy with a suit that was too big; with no go-ahead, no backup, nobody who knew what they were doing or even where they were; without an idea what the fuck they were doing there or why, for that was what it was like, police work [204].

Oster introduces Neuman as a star detective, with his partner Bobby Redfield, in *Sweet Justice*; their departmental nicknames are Redford and Newman because they "were known for handling the nuts that were toughest to crack" (33). Superficially, Redfield is the lothario and Neuman the seasoned veteran of the standard police story. As the novel develops, however,

Redfield is revealed to be a psychologically deranged killer and Neuman a slovenly middle-aged man who, as events unfold, becomes increasingly unkempt and engrossed in his own thoughts about police work and his own domestic situation.

From early on Oster displays an acute sense of language. In *Sweet Justice* he has Jake Neuman refer to George Orwell's classic essay "Politics and the English Language:"

> I read Orwell's essay in college, ... I had a nose rubbed in it by an English teacher. I knew a lot of big words, and I used to sprinkle them in my essays. My teacher once made me copy out Orwell's essay. Along the way I memorized bits and pieces... In the kind of work Sergeant Redfield and I do, we see a lot of ugliness. To call it like we see it all the time is monotonous and tiring. So sometimes we use big words — what do they call them? — Euphemisms. It keeps us sane. Orwell said that insincerity was the greatest enemy of clean language. But we're not insincere; we're just overworked. We see rat shit, as you didn't quite put it, like your brother every day. Sometimes we call it rat shit and sometimes we call it an individual engaged in the commission of a felony, because sometimes it's hard to face up to the fact, at the end of a long day, that you spend so much of your time up to your asshole in rat shit [63].

Indeed, as the books proceed, Oster becomes increasingly absorbed in language — more absorbed in linguistic pyrotechnics than in examining police work or police character. Thus he includes long passages of near stream of consciousness from his heroes, he incrementally repeats phrases, like the "police work is" maxims cited above, he uses dream sequences and renderings of drunken consciousness, and there are lists of things for the sake of lists of things. Perhaps as a result of this his American publisher cancelled his contract in 1992 (Jerry Oster's homepage, *www.geocities.com/SoHo/Lofts*), and since that time his works have come from his German publisher, Rowohlt Verlag.

Dave Pedneau

Dave Pedneau wrote a series of cop abbreviation books, beginning with *A.P.B. All Points Bulletin* (1987) and ending with *B&E Breaking and Entering*, published posthumously in 1991. All of them trace police work in a relatively small West Virginia town, all of them feature Whit Pyncheon, the district attorney's investigator, and they also deal with cops, good ones and bad ones. The first novel, for example, centers on the murders of the wives of local cops; the actions of a brutal, racist detective play a significant role in *D.O.A. Dead on Arrival* (1988); and all of the books portray police officers. Pedneau, however, chose to place his hero and his lover outside the department and gave them professions with the responsibility of judging the actions of police officers: Pyncheon works for the D.A. and, as is noted in the first novel, investigates police misconduct (his work brought him in contact with "an incessant cycle of ... zealous or ignorant and, too often, zealously ignorant police officers" [*D.O.A.* 35]). However, he is no zealot himself, and in *A.P.B.*, while he witnesses a cop picking up free food at a restaurant he responds with a saddened comment, not a citation:

> He just accepted a gratuity. A small one, but still a gratuity. It's inbred in cops. Preachers are the same way. For some reason they think society owes them a free ride. It amazes me [83].

His companion, Annie Tyson-Tyree, a crime reporter for the local newspaper, embodies more zeal and in *D.O.A.* risks her job to find and expose the truth.

From the beginning of the first book Pedneau presents both sides of the police character. *A.P.B.* begins with Gill Dickerson patrolling the roads of Raven County. He cringes when the novice dispatcher does not follow proper radio procedure, and as he patrols the upper-middle-class section of the city the narrator comments that the "inhabitants slept, secure in the knowledge that guys like Gil kept them safe" (3). The narrator also gives Gil old-fashioned domestic values—"He and his wife worked. They were frugal. They sacrificed to own a house nicer than their level of income should permit" (4). Then Pedneau counterpoints Dickerson with Deputy Hank Posich, brutal to his bovine wife, "whose breath reeked of decayed teeth" (17), and who had been the object of Pyncheon's investigations into police misconduct. At the scene of the first murder, tension between Posich and Pyncheon explodes. In *D.O.A.* Pedneau contrasts Sheriff Early with detective Cal Burton:

> The detective lieutenant was a short, slight man, his round head topped by wispy strings of dark hair.... He was small of stature, often small of mind, but you didn't cross him, not if you worked for him [17].

Except that there is no such rank as lieutenant in the town's police force—it is one he has made up and conferred upon himself. And he gets some of his demeanor from television: "He'd been questioning 'perps'—Cal had liked that name since he had heard it on *Hill Street Blues*" (16). Burton likes procedural shortcuts:

> There wasn't a damned thing wrong with shortcuts, not when you were dealing with vermin. After all, nobody advises a cockroach or a rat about its rights before zapping them. You just get rid of them [19].

Pedneau brings all of Burton's malfeasance to a head in an episode where his incompetence causes an innocent man to be killed by a posse of law enforcement officers.

While Whit Pyncheon is not a cop, Pedneau has him think about himself as one. Thus in *D.O.A.* He muses on living in a small town:

> The bane of small-town living. Whit detested the familiarity. Big-city cops could maintain a healthy emotional distance between themselves and their victims. Not so in a place like Milbrook. The dead inevitably became friends and relatives to those he knew, and the case became "personal." It meant cops attended victims' funerals for reasons not just professional [69].

In fact, from the first book Pyncheon is ready to give it all up. At forty he can retire with a pension and move. He is divorced, irritable, irascible, and, as Pedneau points out in *D.O.A.*, suffers from seasonal depression. He also has a smart mouth, licensed by his boss the D.A. In the novels Pyncheon and the cops talk a bit about evidence collection but don't do much of it. In *A.P.B.*, for example, there is some talk about trace evidence, but no one collects any. And "Fingerprints were mostly TV stuff. Whit remembered only two cases that had been solved with prints" (*A.P.B.* 71). While investigators call in a "forensic hypnotechnician" who gets the name of the killer from the wounded bag boy (*A.P.B.* 248), mostly what happens in Pedneau's books is that Pyncheon travels about and talks to people.

Ed Naha

Writer of science fiction and of the novelizations of the Robocop films, Ed Naha (D.B. Drumm) wrote four books about Lieutenant Kevin Broskey of Bay City, California, beginning with *The Con Game* (1986). Naha presents snapshot backgrounds for a couple of kinds of cops in his books. There is Chief Medega: "Medega was a street-smart cop, one of the best. Born and raised in crime-ridden East L.A., he had become a cop in his early twenties. It seemed like a good way to stay out of jail" (*Razzle-Dazzle* 41). There's Goldstein, the honest, hard working, smart forensics cop who is killed in *Razzle-Dazzle*, and an ever faithful, long-suffering woman cop, Sergeant Andrea Fine. McGlory, the alcoholic cop,

> was a tenacious little man. He came back from Korea with a Purple Heart, became a cop, watched his wife die, and had two kids get pan fried in Vietnam. Still he stayed on the force. He got the job done and then some. Broskey would trust him with his life [*On the Edge* 73].

And then Naha introduces a bunch of rookies, naïve, disconnected, incompetent, more absorbed with their appearance and raffish image than with police work: "Broskey stared at the younger cops, cursing the day 'Miami Vice' ever hit the tube" (On the Edge 4).

Broskey, obviously, carries a lot more weight — in years, in intelligence, and in the vicissitudes of life, Southern California life. Having grown up in New Jersey

Broskey lurched from job to job, dream to dream, refusing to pay attention to his teaching certificate. Eventually Broskey drifted west and wound up attending the Los Angeles Police Academy. It was something to do, and his degree in psychology didn't hurt his chance for promotion [*On the Edge* 26].

Having tried social work

I figured everything was nuts. Not just people. Our values. The way we deal with life on every single level was out of whack....

I came out here and became a cop. It seemed like a simpler way to deal with the world. There were victims and there were perps. The victims were innocent. The perps were guilty. I got pretty good at the game. It was like putting together a puzzle. Most of the time, all the pieces were there, you just had to rearrange them. Or if there were a couple of pieces missing, go out and find them [*On the Edge* 47].

In *On the Edge* Naha notes that "All he knew was that he couldn't be anything but a cop. He was pretty much a washout as a contempo human being" (68). Broskey is a minimalist, living (eventually with two dogs) in a rundown rental property offensive to his gentrified yuppie neighbors. His clothes are rumpled and he drives an old Subaru. More importantly, Naha makes him a wiseguy, mixing his speech with ironic verbal affronts especially when dealing with powerful or with stupid people. In character Broskey seems more like a hard-boiled private eye than a cop. Naha, however, makes him a cop by connecting him with justice and with times past:

There's an honest policeman in Bay City. A cop named Broskey who tends to stick up for ordinary people.... I trust the man. He's a regular fellow. He's a real cop, like cops used to be when I was a kid. He even has a bad haircut [*Razzle-Dazzle* 91].

Archer Mayor

In 1988 Archer Mayor began his Joe Gunther novels with *Open Season*. While in the later books Gunther has become head of the Vermont Bureau of Investigation, the earlier, formative novels take place in Brattleboro, Vermont—not quite a small town but then again not quite a big city. In *The Skeleton's Knee* (1993), Mayor, in fact, makes the small town–big city comparison when Joe Gunther goes to Chicago in pursuit of facts for one of his cases:

What I came away with ... was an appreciation of the work load these people wrestled with. Never before had I seen such piles of case files, distributed among so many desks, being worked on by so many exhausted-looking people. Nor had I ever seen so many phones used simultaneously. By the time I was ushered over the chief's threshold, I was eternally grateful to be the small-town cop I was—despite the laughter and familiar corridor high jinks that I'd witnessed, the supposed allure of the "big time" just wasn't there [*Skeleton's Knee* 132].

The "big time," however, isn't different, Gunther realizes, it's just bigger: "It was like having my own provincial policeman's experience expanded and multiplied a hundredfold" (*The Skeleton's Knee* 131).

Brattleboro, though, is hardly a Dogpatch. Its police department has a chief and detectives and patrol officers. The department includes one detective, J.P. Tyler, who has forensic training; indeed, *Open Season* contains one of the best pre–DNA descriptions of blood and semen identification in cop fiction — done for the police at the University of West Haven — and *The Skeleton's Knee* turns on tracing the origin of an artificial human joint. Mayor makes a point of describing the seedy and uncomfortable police headquarters — capricious heating, cramped offices, no storage, etc. — but this presents only a scaled down version of virtually every other police station described in cop novels. Of course the people Gunther encounters as a police officer differ from urban types — Mayor gives readers native Vermonters, country folk, aging hippies, and some professionals, like Gail, Gunther's woman friend. The difference in his books, for Mayor, lies in the character of his police hero, Lieutenant Joe Gunther. Gunther is middle aged, a native Vermonter, a veteran of the Korean War. As Mayor tells visitors to his website,

> Joe Gunther grew to become the archetypal, old-fashioned, local cop — compassionate, observant, doggedly persistent. As prone to error as anyone, he is slow to judge, willing to admit his faults, and tends to follow his instincts, which more often than not stand him in good stead [www.archermayor.com].

Detailed in *Open Season*, Gunther's history lays out Mayor's view of the ideal police officer. After fighting in Korea Gunther stayed in California, attended Berkeley, and became a fellow traveler of the Beat generation but "it still hadn't settled my mind one bit" (32). To find meaning in a life that had become "rootless, frustrated, and alienated" (32), Gunther returned home and became a cop:

> It mimicked some of the more pleasant aspects of military life — that combination of specialness and fraternity — and it replaced the muddiness of my life with the welcomed rigidity of rank, paperwork, and assigned tasks. It also meant carrying a gun — the ultimate symbol of the simple answer to a complex world — and it gave me a chance, every once in a while, to do something "right," which by that time in my life was becoming an elusive quality. Korea and California had fouled the clear moral waters of my upbringing and had left me nostalgic for the innocent idealism of my younger years [33].

Over the years as a police officer, however, being a cop changed Gunther's view of what being a cop meant:

I was a Lawman — the armed instrument of Might and Right. Not that Murphy instilled that simple-minded notion in my brain. That was my own doing, and I was quickly disabused. The younger, and probably wiser Murphy showed me that most bad guys were usually regular guys with a screw loose — barring a few exceptions. But even while I was reluctantly conceding that the world was more gray than black and white, its complexities and contradictions stopped bothering me so much. The gun lost its appeal as I began to rely more on my instincts than on its authority [33].

Along with suspense, Mayor makes real attempts to show areas of police work that are more gray than black. In *Open Season* Gunther must work with a partner about to psychologically fly apart and he doesn't know quite what to do: "it's easier for cops to let a fellow cop slide, pretending he's just eccentric, than to offer to help. And on the flip side, it's normal for that cop to think he can deal with it himself— that if he asks for help, or shows he needs it, everyone'll think he's a weenie. So everyone loses" (209). The most difficult problem Mayor tackles is in *The Fruit of the Poisonous Tree* (1994), a book that refers both to the legal meaning of the term — illegal means taint all evidence subsequently gathered and developed from that source — and the spreading malignancy of rape on the victim, on women, on the police department, and on Gunther himself.

Cops in the Eighties

While fewer cop shows premiered on American television in the 1980s than in the 1970s, television continued to use the police drama as a staple of evening viewing. In the eighties thirty new cop shows appeared — including *B.A.D. Cats* (1980), *Police Squad* (1982), *Hawaii Heat* (1984), *Hunter* (1984), *The Last Precinct* (1986), *Sledge Hammer* (1986), *21 Jump Street* (1987), and *The Street* (1988). Women cops starred in *Cagney and Lacy* (1982), and John Ball's novel was made into a series, *In the Heat of the Night*, in 1988. *Miami Vice* (1984) stressed the thriller elements inherent in cop stories while *Hill Street Blues* (1981) took up the realism of Wambaugh's television series of the seventies, *Police Story*. More popular than any of these, the foundation of reality TV, *COPS*, first appeared in 1989. In terms of popularity, cop films of the 1980s made a greater impact than those of the previous decade — there were more blockbuster films. Cop films of the eighties began with the realism of *Fort Apache the Bronx* (1981) but moved firmly into the realm of adventure and even fantasy with *Beverly Hills Cop* (1984), *Robocop* (1987), *Lethal Weapon* (1987), and (based on Roderick Thorp's *Nothing Lasts Forever* [1979]), *Die Hard* (1988), each of which spawned sequels that stressed individual versus corporate action. Sylvester Stallone took time out from the

Rocky films to make a cop film, *Cobra* (1986), current police technology (in the shape of helicopters) came in with *Blue Thunder* (1984), and at the end of the decade Jamie Lee Curtis played a woman cop in *Blue Steel* (1990). The 1980s, too, saw burlesques of the cop film with the series of *Police Academy* films (1984, 1985, 1986, 1987, 1988, and 1989) and *The Naked Gun* (1988), ironically co-starring O.J. Simpson as a police detective.

Before the 1980s the police novel was a minor, and somewhat maligned, stepchild in the field of crime fiction. Few years saw more than two new writers taking up the form: in 1960 both Elizabeth Linington and Lillian O'Donnell started writing cop books, in 1970 Wambaugh and Hillerman began writing about police officers, and 1974 was a banner year with new cop books by James Mills, K.C. Constantine, and Lawrence Sanders. Indeed, in his pioneering work, *The Police Procedural* (1982), George N. Dove attempts to define the form by covering almost as many foreign writers (thirteen) as he does American police writers (fourteen). Starting in the mid–1980s, however, things got very different. In 1984 seven new police writers' works appeared — Thomas Adcock's *Precinct Nineteen*, William Bayer's *Switch*, William J. Caunitz's *One Police Plaza*, Bob Leuci's *Doyle's Disciples*, David L. Lindsey's *Heat from Another Sun*, Joseph McNamara's *The First Directive*, and Lee Martin's *Too Sane a Murder*. Only a couple of years in the eighties and nineties saw fewer than three new writers a year, and 1988 was a very good year for cop novels with sixteen writers trying out the waters: Paul Bishop, Charles Brandt, Anthony Bruno, John K. Dugan, Jack Early, William Heffernan, Eugene Izzi, Bill Kent, Jack Logan, Archer Mayor, Thomas Nogouchi, Ridley Pearson, and John Westermann. A more thorough bibliographical hunt than mine might turn up more. Clearly in the 1980s and 1990s the police novel became a major form of crime fiction, giving private eyes and amateur detectives a robust run for their money. In the 1980s police novels became saleable commodities. Crime fiction rarely appears on the best seller lists and cop books almost never, but in 1975 Wambaugh's *Choirboys*, made it to the *Publishers Weekly* best-seller list (it was number five for the year). In 1981, moreover, three police writers made it to the *Publishers Weekly* best-seller list: Martin Cruz Smith with his novel contrasting Soviet and New York cops, *Gorky Park* (number five for the year); Lawrence Sanders with *The Third Deadly Sin* (number eight for the year), and Wambaugh with *The Glitter Dome* (number nine for the year) (caderbooks.com).

Crime probably had something to do with the increasing popularity of the form. Public concerns about crime waves recur through the nineteenth and twentieth centuries. From the editorial outcries in family story papers in the 1800s to the concerns of muckraking journalists at the turn of the twentieth century, American readers have been told that they were living in times of unprecedented crime. In 1980 they actually were: Department of Justice statistics show that the homicide rate in the United States hit a high of 10.7 homicides per 100,000 (www.ojp.usdoj.gov/bjs). Although the 1960s and 1970s had their own monsters, those of the eighties seemed more frightening. In 1980, the bodies in his crawlspace and the photograph of John Wayne Gacy dressed as a clown appalled the public. In 1981 Wayne Williams went on trial for murdering children in Atlanta. The Green River Killer made Seattle the serial killing capital of the nation — an achievement even noted in guidebooks to the city. And the decade of the eighties closed with the Night Stalker trial in California.

On top of these current atrocities, the public's absorption with crime was encouraged by the publication of Ann Rule's book on Ted Bundy, *The Stranger Beside Me* (1980), and the newfound popularity of the true crime book. In a piece in *Publishers Weekly* Tom Weyr notes that the new popularity of true crime books began with Truman Capote's *In Cold Blood* (1965) and especially with Norman Mailer's *The Executioner's Song* (1979),

> but it did not explode as a publishing phenomena until the mid–80s. Hardcover books profited from the take-off, yet it was the mass markets that supplied the fuel and turned the genre into a category. True crime books walked out of stores at such a pace that chains and specialty stores began to feature true crime sections [38].

Rosemary Herbert in her *Publishers Weekly* piece on true crime books cites Neil Nyren's view that the watershed for true crime was the publication of *In Cold Blood*, Tommy Thompson's *Money* (1976), and Joe McGinnis' *Fatal Vision* (1983). The balloon of interest in true crime narratives ties in with the police novel in several ways. First, it solidified the police novel's convention of citing true crimes during the course of the narrative; occasionally used by earlier cop writers, in the eighties cop writers with regularity cite true crimes as an adjunct to portraying police reality. In *A.P.B.*, for example, Pedneau mentions Ted Bundy three times and Wayne Williams and Albert DeSalvo once each; in her first book Patricia Cornwell alludes to Richard Speck, Ted Bundy, the Green Valley Strangler, John Wayne Gacy, Chapman (John Lennon's murderer), Wayne Williams, and John Hinckley, Jr. Indeed, the brief mention of historical crimes may stand behind the creation of a small group of historical or reportorial novel cop books in the 1990s — books like Thomas Cook's *Streets of Fire* (1991), John P. Cooke's *Torsos* (1993), Barbara D'Amato's *Good Cop, Bad Cop* (1998), and maybe Marshall Frank's *Beyond the Call* (2000) — that present fictionalized accounts of real police work. There is at least one writer who crossed over from true crime to writing cop books: with *Floater* (1986) and *Smugglers Notch* (1989) Joseph

Koenig moved from writing true crime articles for *Front Page Detective* magazine into the world of the cop novel. Finally, in her *Publishers Weekly* article Rosemary Herbert notes that

> All agree that the crossover of readers of mystery fiction into the true crime area is insignificant, since as Applebaum put it, "readers who like their details filtered through fiction are often after a more genteel depiction of crime" [33].

As many cop writers moved away from the conventions of the detective/mystery story in the 1970s and began to include increasingly graphic realism in their books, they also edged closer to true crime fiction and the demands of its readership than to traditional mystery fiction. Indeed, at the end of Pocket's paperback edition of Robert Sims Reid's *Big Sky Blues* (1988) one finds a page listing the publisher's "Finest Mystery-Suspense Novels" followed by a page soliciting readers to buy books about "The Shocking and Bizarre Crimes of Our Times."

Riding along with the influence of true crime books on the police novel, the backgrounds of the writers changed. While before the 1980s a few police officers had written cop novels — Kantor, Uhnak, Wambaugh, and Barnes — the 1980s and 1990s saw a mass migration of ex-cops into the field. With William Caunitz, Ed Dee, John Delamer, Michael Grant, Bill Kelly, Bob Leuci, Dan Mahoney, and with John Westermann commuting in from Long Island, it almost seemed that the NYPD ran its own writers' group. In the eighties and nineties cops from across the country took to the computer and wrote novels: Paul Bishop (Los Angeles PD), Robin Burcell (San Francisco PD), Lowen Clausen (Seattle PD), O'Neil DeNoux (New Orleans PD), Marshall Frank (Metro-Dade PD), Hugh Holton, Dennis Banahan, and Charles Shafer (Chicago PD), Terry Marlow (Dallas PD), Anne Wingate aka Lee Martin (Fort Worth PD), Joseph McNamara (San Jose PD), Jack Mullen (San Diego PD), Robert Sims Reid (Rozette, Montana, PD), and Enes Smith (Portland PD). Although each of them brings something different to the police novel, what they have in common is carrying with them a greater sense of credibility and authenticity to the form, of nudging it a bit away from fiction and a bit toward the actuality of the true crime book. For authenticity, reporters may be the second best bet after cops, particularly in the 1980s when the number and size of urban newspapers dwindled. Starting with Thomas Adcock, the 1980s and 1990s demonstrated to a number of former reporters that they could make more and perhaps say more in cop novels than at their day jobs. Thus the two decades saw cop books from reporters Michael Connelly, Robert Coram, James Grady, William Heffernan, Stephen Hunter, Jeannine Kaddow, Jerry Oster, Dave Pedneau, and John Sandford, among others. One of the things both ex-cops and ex-reporters brought to the cop novel was freedom from the conventions of the mystery novel. Whereas in the earlier periods many of the police writers had either written or would go on to write regular detective/mystery novels, the writers of the eighties and nineties began their work without apprenticeship or attachment to the conventions of the mystery story.

Along with the new crop of writers came new views of a bunch of American cities. Locale certainly plays a part in the cop novel, but except for the differences between big city and small town and the geographical markers writers include for verisimilitude, big cities in cop books tend to be similar — business districts, slums, suburbs. Over the decades most cop books take place in New York, with L.A. coming in a distant second. While the writers of the seventies began to use new settings — Burns and Hillerman for instance — the real explosion of locale didn't begin until the 1980s. Cop writers are all over the map: Charles Brandt in Wilmington, Delaware; W.E.B. Griffith in Philadelphia; James Grady in Baltimore; Warren Adler in D.C.; Bill Kent in Atlantic City; Archer Mayor, Theodore Wessner, and William Koenig in New England; Richard Forrest in Middlebury, Connecticut; Koenig and John Katzenbach in Florida; Dave Pedneau in West Virginia; Jack Logan in Detroit; Jerome Izzi in Chicago; John Sanford in Minneapolis; David Lindsey and Lee Martin in Houston and Fort Worth; Gary Paulson in Denver; Ridley Pearson in Seattle; and on the West Coast, T. Jefferson Parker and Joseph McNamara. Granted, each of these writers includes snatches of local history and landscape and some even note regional variations of police tactics (Grady, for instance, in *Just a Shot Away* notes the use of helicopters by the Baltimore police), history, and cop slang. Nonetheless, cop writers of the 1980s present a uniform picture of the personal and organizational challenges and dilemmas confronting police officers and police departments.

One of the liabilities of the police novel of the 1950s and 1960s is that police procedures did not change much during that period: interviews, stake outs, records searches, informants, the lab boys with cameras and powder. The revolution in forensic science was another factor that changed the cop books of the eighties and nineties. In some respects the books of the eighties took up some cultural lag in that some of the significant advances in forensic sciences took place in the 1970s — the FBI began profiling at its Behavioral Sciences Unit in 1972, established the automated fingerprint database (AFIS) in 1977, and super glue fuming for fingerprints was discovered in Japan in the same year. None of these entered police books until the 1980s, but in the 1980s they became staples of the police novel. Profiling especially, both pro and con, became one of the significant themes in the books of the period. On top of these advances, the real blockbusters appeared in the 1980s.

In the 1980s at Wayne Williams' trial in Atlanta fiber evidence made a big splash, and in 1985 the FBI went on-line with VICAP database of violent criminals. But most of these new forensic tools paled in comparison to DNA. DNA became the shibboleth of forensic science and police work after DNA profiling was used to identify Colin Pitchfork as the killer of two English girls in 1986 and after it was introduced in American courts in the Florida case against Tommy Lee Andrews in 1987 (*www.forensicdna.com*). Writers now had new and technically interesting procedures to use as incidental details or around which to build plots and character. Add to this that in 1984 Tom Clancy's *The Hunt for Red October* created an appetite for the techno-thriller, books that combine details of machines and organizations with the conventions of the adventure story. Indeed, one of the first signs of a new direction of the police novel came when Thomas Nogouchi, former chief medical examiner of Los Angeles County, wrote the novel *Unnatural Causes* (1988) with Arthur Lyons. The forensic police book became a significant addition to the field in the late 1980s and 1990s with Patricia Cornwell, Jeffrey Deaver, Ken Goddard, Leonard Goldberg, Ridley Pearson, and others organizing police work around forensic science and remaking the police hero.

Unlike the influence of the techno-thriller, the other phenomenon in the crime fiction world of the 1980s had little direct impact on the cop novel. Starting with Scott Turow's *Presumed Innocent* (1987), lawyers like Turow and John Grisham began to take up a lot of shelf space in the mystery fiction area. Books written by lawyers, like *Presumed Innocent*, in general do not focus on cops as heroes or even villains or antiheroes. One of the few exceptions is Charles Brandt's *The Right to Remain Silent* (1988), a novel that uses a police hero to contrast pre- and post–*Miranda* police work and ends with a cop meting out justice not available from the courts, a relatively common theme in the mid-1980s found in William Caunitz's *Suspects* (1986), Dallas Barnes *Deadly Justice* (1987), John Katzenbach's *The Traveller* (1987), Richard Forrest's *Lark* (1986), and Joseph Koenig's *Floater* (1986).

In the 1920s and 1930s the vision of the police force put forth by American crime writers was that of the machine or the disciplined army led by educated and intelligent men. In the 1950s the vision changed to that of middle-class men fighting crime with the aid of hard work and routine. In the last part of the twentieth century, however, writers began to emphasize heroes who possessed vocation and special, unique attributes. First touched on by Wambaugh in the *Blue Knight* ("I could explain to my imaginary jurist but never to a real one about that instinct — the stage in this business when, like an animal, you can *feel* you've got one, and it can't be explained. You *feel* the truth, and you know" [12]), writers of the 1980s (and then 1990s) set the theme of instinct against statute law, mechanical procedure, and scientific investigation. Thus these examples:

> His understanding of crime and criminals was instinctive. He had no idea where it came from, and if this did not make him a kind of artist, then he did not know what art was [Daley *Wall of Brass* 38].

> There comes a time when all information must be set aside; there comes a time when passion and instinct take over [Pearson, *No Witness* 2].

> Like most good cops, Kennedy had lived so long on adrenaline and a kind of careless adolescent joy in the game, trading on his wits, his street sense, his inborn skywalker's balance, that he never noticed the erosion of his contemplative side. Few cops care to indulge in self-examination, partly because it's a hindrance to the work; it clouds the instinct, slows the reactions in a subtle way that frequently proves fatal [Stroud *Close Pursuit* 133].

> But aside from those kinds of changes, the reports were the same and Bosch decided that homicide investigation was largely the same now as back then. Of course there had been incredible technological advances in the past thirty-five years but he believed there were some things that were always the same and would always remain the same. The leg work, the art of interviewing and listening, knowing when to trust an instinct or a hunch. Those were the things that didn't change, that couldn't [Connelly, *The Last Coyote* 30].

Writers of the eighties couple the theme of instinct with that of the street. The term "street cop" becomes the highest praise a hero can achieve. Thus, for example, Christopher Newman has his Joe Dante labeled "the most highly decorated street cop, from the biggest police force in the free world" (*Killer* 201). The whole notion of the street cop ramifies in a number of different ways. First of all, it stands alongside of or behind the concept of instinct: working on the street builds up the knowledge and experience upon which instinct is based. Then some writers use the term to define the police lifestyle. Thus John Westermann in *Exit Wounds*:

> Living with a street cop is like living with a psychotic. They eat strange, they sleep strange; they're never home. Normal women don't last with cops, and cops are crazy anyway when it comes to falling for somebody [148–49].

Then, too, the theme of the street cop comes up against the theme of the law. A number of writers note the fact that the cop on the beat, in the choices he or she makes, enacts and represents the law and justice more immediately than do the prosecutors and the courts. In spite of minor outbursts of brutality and perhaps a bit of corruption, even Bob Leuci holds that "Cops that do things that maybe they shouldn't are, most times, the best street cops around" (*Doyle's Disciples* 192). Work on the street also forms part of the bond between cops, the brotherhood, the minority. Thus Robert

Daley in his 1981 *Year of the Dragon* comments about street cops that "They would respond to and respect only street cops like themselves" (78). This, of course, means that they do not respond to bureaucrats, and the street cop theme becomes part of the antibureaucratic theme of the last decades:

> What they didn't understand was that veteran street detectives hated change. They saw every new wrinkle in the system as the fuzzy meanderings of down-town punks who were more politicians than policemen. They saw each gim-mick eroding their authority, putting criminals and street slime on an equal footing, giving aid and comfort to the enemy [*Dream Street* 20–21].

In the 1980s the new twist to the theme of blind and belligerent bureau-cracy comes in the form of the impact of internal affairs. Novels of the 1980s include police corruption as one of their major themes — individual and cor-porate corruption preoccupy Bob Leuci and Joseph McNamara and also can be found, for example, in Caunitz' *Suspects*, Pedneau's *A.P.B.*, Bill Kent's *Under the Boardwalk* (1988), Tom Lewis' *Rooftops* (1982), Roderick Thorp's *Rainbow Drive* (1986), and Jerry Oster's *Sweet Justice*. Organizationally, root-ing out corruption falls to the officers in the internal affairs office of the cop shop. Very few novels, like Leuci's *Captain Butterfly*, portray IAD cops in a sympathetic light. In a number of cases they are seen as typical bureaucrats. Unlike other cops, Adcock notes in *Devil's Heaven*, "IAD types usually have enough seniority to be home by a decent hour" (28). In *Blue Mirage* when Joseph McNamara's hero visits New York he finds an internal affairs under-cover officer to be lazy and corrupt. Kelly and LeMoult link them with politi-cians:

> Less reassuring was his awareness that the police department had become a hon-eycombed network of spies and informers. Self-seeking little men with no scru-ples and great ambitions were exploiting the bond of brotherhood that had once been every cop's solemn watchword. Open communication between policemen had become a matter of who could be trusted. Who was on the hook to Inter-nal Affairs? Who was wearing a wire? [*Death Spiral* 61].

Jerome Izzi has the same take about the Chicago police: "Past the dreaded Office of Professional Standards, the Chicago answer to Internal Affairs, the ambitious headhunters who wanted to be commissioners someday and climbed their way up over the fallen bodies of their brothers" (*Bad Guys* 63). Stephen Solomita sums up the impact of internal affairs cops in *Force of Nature*:

> "Internal Affairs are the cops that put other cops in jail" he responded. "When they decide to run through a precinct, nobody's immune. They find one cop who's on the take and use him as a wedge to batter the whole force. Or they take a thief or a dealer and have him offer bribes to arresting officers. That's when cops stop caring about the people they're supposed to protect. When they

get frightened, they always react by trying to avoid contact with the public as much as possible. They expect to be set up by the headhunters and they don't trust anyone" [102–3].

While there are exceptions, cop books of the 1980s view institutional-ized corruption as a thing of the past. James Grady in *Razor Game*, for instance, notes the widespread corruption in the Baltimore police depart-ment in the 1970s but portrays it as history, not current events. A decade and more after they happened, however, the Knapp Commission's investi-gations and findings reverberate through cop novels in the 1980s. New York cop writers Caunitz, Kelly, and, in the nineties, Ed Dee and Dan Mahoney especially comment on Knapp, its impact on cops and its impact on crime. Cops, they hold, become paranoid and overly cautious and crooks, especially those connected with drugs, know this and act on it.

Opposed to the ills brought about by politicians' attempts to solve tra-ditional police corruption, novels of the eighties stress the virtues of the individual, especially the individual leading a small group of officers. Thus both Philbin in his Precinct Siberia novels and Jack Logan in his Detroit PD series start with officers upon whom the system has given up: "The 14th Precinct of the Detroit Police Department had a long reputation as a dump-ing ground for incompetents, insubordinates and misfits" (*Detroit PD: Run Jack, Run* 6) and proceed to show how police work and a dedicated leader can convert bad cops into good ones. To counter the effects of politics and bureaucracy, some writers institutionalize insubordination — they show detec-tives intent on solving a case who avoid the big bosses, turn off their beep-ers, and don't return phone calls until they have succeeded. Some writers note that their heroes have become free agents because of their records for breaking tough cases. Some have heroes with powerful rabbis who allow them free rein. And some, like Heffernan, create special units that are exempt from departmental control. In each case, writers of the eighties demonstrate the virtues of the individual both in solving crimes and in rooting out cor-rupt cops who have entrenched themselves in the system.

Along with the theme of the street cop and the attention given to anti-corruption measures in the novels of the period, nostalgia plays a major role in the cop novels of the eighties. A lot of this has to do with veterans' views of new kinds of cops. In *Devlin* (1992) Roderick Thorp's narrator reflects a perhaps too-typical response to the reality of diversity on the force:

But as a result, as all cops knew, the department was burdened with hundreds of women too small and light for the frequent hand-to-hand combat with quarreling spouses and belligerent drunks the job required. The revised liter-acy requirements were so low that many new patrolmen couldn't write a report, and more than a few sergeants couldn't read them. Some officers were disobeying orders because they considered them racially motivated, and others were wearing shields solely to prey on dope dealers, because they were dope dealers themselves — as they had been before joining the force. One story the department wanted hushed up had to do with the longtime officer's resignation the day his partner's belt fell down around her ankles in the middle of a hot pursuit [50–51].

In *Captain Butterfly* one of Leuci's characters reflects on the same issues, focusing on standards:

> Listen. Way back when, in the ol' days, ya know what I mean, back when Christ was a cowboy, in the ol' jaaaab we had standards, and they were high. Nowadays, man, you can be a midget. A midget with three collars, or an eighty-five pound broad what smokes dope on her swing and lets the boys go by, and ya can still get on the fuckin' jaaaab. The jaaaab's gone to shit. And there it is, there ain't no more, that's the fuckin' story [37].

In *Suspects* Caunitz emphasizes the loss of military discipline:

> It's not like the old days, Anthony, when a desk officer told a cop to shit, and the cop asked how much would you like, sir. The new breed is young, most have never been in the service, and only a few of them have heard terms like "military discipline" and "military courtesy" [186].

Kelly and LeMoult make the difference one of different kinds of backgrounds:

> Tommy was one of the new breed of cops, guys who saw the job as a science rather than a vocation. In Vince's day, becoming a cop had been a safe, secure job where young men without a lot of education or connections could buy a piece of a decent life for themselves and their families. Now cops were criminologists, legal scholars. They earned degrees qualifying them to do what old-timers had been doing by the seat of their pants for years.... Nobody learned the job from books. You had to be there [*Death Spiral* 17–18].

In *Dream Street* the authors extend the baleful influence of formal education to the entire police establishment:

> The main problem with the department today, he thought. More and more, things were being run by inexperienced kids who were great at taking tests but didn't know the first thing about what was happening on the streets [11].

Making police work a profession and not a job has its impact. It affects the way cops dress: "Time was, all plainclothes cops shopped at Robert Hall, which made them easy marks; nowadays, they dressed like record producers, or gigolos" (*Sweet Justice* 39). It affects, too, their attitude toward work:

> The two detectives in their nice uptown suits were the irritating type. They had smirks on their faces, the kind worn by an unfortunate new generation of cop: New York's suburban occupation force.... They consider their union dues

well spent on an army of lobbyists that keeps the legislators in Albany from including them in a law that says if you draw your paycheck in the City of New York you ought to live there. The president of this union lives so far out on Long Island he should be a lighthouse keeper [*Devil's Heaven* 78].

And then the new protections of civil liberties present something else for cops to complain about:

"The young guys ain't so bad," said Rocco. "It's the rules. You see that cartoon in the FOP magazine? The cop's got a blindfold over his eyes, a piece of tape across his mouth, big puffs of cotton in his ears. His gun is chained to his hol-ster, and his hands and feet are tied together. On the bottom it says 'Now do your job.' Hah? What are these young guys supposed to do?" [*The Right to Remain Silent* 35].

In *Black Sand* one of Caunitz's characters puts a more graphic spin on what the law has done to police work: "We used to beat the shit out of prisoners. Now we're getting them blow jobs.... That's the result of all that goddamn human interaction bullshit they teach at the Academy" (236).

While some of the books of the eighties reflect cops as misogynists, a number also reflect new emphasis on female cop heroes. This is the case with female writers like Dunlap and Paul, who write about female cops. But a number of male writers invent female protagonists — thus Leuci's Marjorie Buttera, Bishop's Fey Croaker, and Warren Adler's Fiona Fitzgerald. With female protagonists writers bring in repeated examples of the antagonism women face and overcome just to become successful cops. Many of the writ-ers (Jack Early's [Sandra Scoppettone] *Donato and Daughter* serves as per-haps the best example) stress the unique role played by the combination of ability and ambition in the makeup of female cops. They are often the first to achieve their present position —first woman detective, first woman detec-tive sergeant, etc. And, in one way or another, these women acknowledge the role that affirmative action has played in making them cops — sometimes they are defensive about it and sometimes they simply accept it as a fact and move on with their work. Many of the women want to be more than just cops — they want to be chief of detectives, or chief, or commissioner. And some writers in fact suggest that they could do a better job of running a police department than is done by the male incumbents. While some writers pre-sent antagonism and hostility faced by female officers, in most cases the women who appear in the cop novels of the eighties have enlightened bosses, team leaders or teams who value their ability and depend upon them as they do other members of the department. Claiming their roles in many ways defines the female cop heroes of the eighties, leaving for writers of the next decade the wider and more diverse examination of women who become cops. This is the case as well with the rarer introduction of lesbian detectives: Sue

Burke in Bayer's *Mirror Maze*, Maggie Higgins in Caunitz's *Suspects*, Meagan Connell in Sandford's *Night Prey*, and Sharon Levy in Heffernan's *Tarnished Blue*. Katherine V. Forrest introduced LAPD detective Kate Delafield in *Amateur City* (1984), the first cop novel with a lesbian hero, and Forrest would inspire a number of lesbian police writers in the next decade. In the eighties lesbian cops are largely incidental characters who suffer abuse from male cops but respond in kind. While Adcock sympathetically introduces a gay cop as a subsidiary character in *Devil's Heaven*, the cop novels of the eighties give witness to widespread homophobia. Gay cops appear far less frequently than lesbian officers, and then mostly as secondary characters in non-cop crime novels like Robert B. Parker's PI books and Jonathan Kellerman's Alex Delaware novels, which center on a psychologist. Unlike the lesbian police officers, the few gay cops to appear in the books of the eighties suffer more from the ostracism of other cops. In Kellerman's *When the Bough Breaks* (1985), for instance, the narrator comments on this:

> Some of Milo's initial altruism, his reaching out to help me, was a little more understandable, too. He knew what it was like to be alone. A gay cop was a person in limbo. You could never be one of the gang back at the station, no matter how well you did your job. And the homosexual community was bound to be suspicious of someone who looked, acted like and *was* a cop [30].

African American cops appear with regularity, sometimes as supervisors and sometimes as members of the team but rarely as heroes — Buck White in Koenig's *Floater* is a singular example of the black protagonist. Logan, in *Detroit PD: Run Jack, Run* connects African American cops with change in public policy:

> The Detroit PD wasn't integrated to any significant degree until the 1970s, and that had been only after the terrible riots that seared the city to its soul in the summer of 1967.
> After that long, hot summer the Kerner Commission, known formally as the National Advisory Commission on Civil Disorders, issued a report telling police across the country that it was not possible to keep order in the black areas with police forces that amounted to white armies of occupation [24].

Tom Lewis' *Rooftops* and Wambaugh's *Lines and Shadows* (1984) — and far more blandly Doug Allyn's *The Cheerio Killings* (1989) — bring up the issue of Hispanic cops. Lewis' hero, Daniel Rodridguez, makes one of the infrequent observations of the period about the way cops treat minorities:

> He had been watching scenes like this [rudeness] between white cops and brown-skinned people since he was a kid. Becoming a cop himself had changed almost nothing [*Rooftops* 27].

In the 1990s, after Rodney King, writers paid more attention to the issue of minority cops and the relationships between cops and minority civilians. In the 1980s it remained a minor issue.

In the 1980s cop writers increasingly turn to the serial killer to provide organization and purpose for their novels. The eighties and nineties, of course, did not invent the serial killer plot — it pops up occasionally throughout most of the decades — McBain's *Cop Hater* (1956), for instance, is a serial killer book. It's just that a lot more writers wrote them. In the eighties serial killer specialists emerge: Bayer, Sanford, Heffernan, and Pearson largely devote themselves to writing about serial crimes. A lot of other writers used them in one or more of their books: there's Tom Lewis' *Rooftops* (1981); Warren Adler's *American Quartet* (1981); James Grady's *Razor Game* (1985); Jerry Oster's *Sweet Justice* (1985); Richard Forrest's *Lark* (1986); Joseph Koenig's *Floater* (1986); Thomas Boyle's *Only the Dead Know Brooklyn* (1986); John Katzenbach's *The Traveller* (1988); Robert Tine's *Midnight City* (1987); Kelly and LeMoult's *Street Dance* (1987); Gary Paulson's *Night Rituals* (1989); Jack Early's *Donato and Daughter* (1988); Wamabugh's *The Blooding* (1989); Pedneau's *A.P.B.* (1989); and Richard Fliegal's *The Organ Grinder's Monkey* (1989). Part of the impetus for the multiplication of serial killers lies in the linkage of the cop novel with the true crime book. Part lies in the fact that a serial killer cop book (Sanders' *The Third Deadly Sin*) was one of the first cop books to make it to the best-seller lists. Part, too, lies in the increasing popularity of and occasional debate about profiling and the FBI's Behavioral Sciences unit — what catches criminals, knowing their psychological makeup or good old-fashioned police work? But part of the popularity of serial killer stories also has to do with the fact that they make things more interesting and a bit easier for the writer. For one, as I've noted above, because crimes happen more than once, writers have the opportunity to highlight a variety of police procedures and to show the effects of stress on their characters. Many serial killer books bring back the old-fashioned master criminal antagonist, the superintelligent deviant; this provides the opportunity for writers to split the narrative between the actions of the detectives and the actions and thoughts of the criminal. Here writers can crank up suspense, showing a murderer in the act of committing crimes, dabble in pop psychology through glimpses into the criminal's thoughts, and practice traditional detective story trickery by hiding the antagonist's identity until the end of the novel for the conventional surprise.

The stress and dysfunctional behavior attached to police work receive greater attention from the cop writers of the 1980s. One prominent sign of this lies in Pearson making his secondary character Daphne Matthews a police psychologist. While Matthews' principal role connects her with Lou

Boldt, the primary hero, Pearson includes asides about her job dealing with cops' problems — post-traumatic stress, marital problems, etc. Plenty of writers note the traditional theme of the shell — cops' need to separate themselves from the degradation and horror with which the job sometimes brings them in contact. In the eighties, however, this becomes magnified in characters like Bayer's Janek, Heffernan's Devlin, and Pearson's Boldt, who must cope both with the pressures of solving serial crimes and with the understanding that human beings are capable of such atrocities. Highlighted especially in Jance's books and in Adcock's *Devil's Heaven*, alcoholism receives new attention in the 1980s, and a number of writers mention departmental efforts to help cops deal with addiction problems. Westermann's *High Crimes* and Grady's *Razor Game* both portray heroes who routinely use drugs (marijuana and cocaine respectively). As with the cops of previous periods, divorce and marital dysfunction is the rule. Indeed, impotence is connected with the profession — characters in both Caunitz's *Suspects* and Kelly and Le Moult's *Killing Moon* suffer bouts of impotence. Writers of the period bring in characters who are violence-prone and characters who are terrified by violence, and portray police departments' measures to cope with these kinds characters — from assignments to the "rubber gun" or "bow-and-arrow" brigade to transfers to precincts where their weaknesses will not be noticed. The latter usually involves transferring racist cops to all-white precincts.

While writers of the 1980s acknowledge the psychological weight carried by police officers and the personal problems it generates, at the same time they offer excitement as a part of, even a compensatory part of, police work. A number of writers use the metaphor of the hunt to explain it. Thus Westermann says in *High Crimes* that

> Tree feels a purpose to his life, a sense of camaraderie, the thrill of the hunt. Hemingway was right, he thinks: Once you've hunted men, animals just don't make it [209].

In *Odessa Beach* Bob Leuci uses the idea of the game and describes the experience with doper's slang:

> He drove from the garage feeling an excitement rising in his stomach. Then that familiar, complicated emotion, the joy of the game and the dread of losing. To Delaney and Alex, it was a sport, even to himself he'd never been able to explain this rush [147].

James Grady, too, moves from game to sport:

> Then there's the sport. You're an egoist. You went into police work as the ultimate challenge, handicapping yourself with a creaky, blundering bureaucracy to pursue your quest for justice and revel in the chase. You've been in Homicide, the ultimate games, for three years [*Razor Game* 10].

Pearson uses the metaphor of the race in *Probable Cause*:

> It was a strange, inexplicable feeling for James Dewitt, an intense fear mixed with the exhilaration of the challenge before him. He had been thrown into a race in which other people lost with their lives if he didn't win [43].

And in *Angel Maker* Pearson notes that not only chasing criminals but finding evidence is an emotional experience:

> With this the only plasma bank in the city and a policeman's knowledge that something connected the four runaways, Boldt experienced the electricity of anticipation. He didn't believe much in 'sixth sense' phenomena, but there was no denying the quick beating of his heart and the internal sense that there was evidence to be uncovered here [63].

That so many characters thrive on excitement stands as one of the signs that the cop novel has broadened out from its beginnings in the mystery/detective story. Simply put, a lot of the cop novels of the eighties are thrillers. Indeed, what has happened is that the character and function of the police officer affords material for a variety of crime novel subgenres. Writers like Dunlap and Martin write cop novels that unfold much in the same way that traditional cozy detective stories unfold. Some writers, like Faye Kellerman, edge closer to the romance, a movement that will become full-fledged in the 1990s when Nora Roberts takes to the cop book. Some writers, like Philbin and Newman, continue the McBain pattern of slice-of-life portrayal of a group of cops. They are all bound together by the character of the police officer as hero. Thus the eighties experienced a vigorous interest in police heroes, even after intense public scrutiny in the 1960s and 1970s had laid bare entrenched systematic and personal flaws of American police departments and police officers, and after part of a generation of America's youth had grown up with contempt for cops and suspicion about what they do.

-five-

The 1990s

There are a lot more cop writers and cop books in the nineties. Of course the cop writers of the last decade were hardly sitting on their hands; writers like Pearson, Bishop, Sandford, Forrest, and a bunch of others actually hit their stride in the nineties. But more new writers took to using cop heroes in their books than ever before. If one term can characterize the cop books of the decade, it is diversity. First, to be sure, this means racial diversity. Finally African American officers become heroes of cop books, along with a sprinkling of heroes of other racial backgrounds — Asians and Native Americans. The female cops depicted are different from those of the previous decade and writers, while still concerned with affirmative action, develop a wider variety of characteristics in their female heroes. Police heroes extend from the traditional forms of crime fiction — the cozy and the thriller — into other literary subsets. Writers use police characters in lesbian fiction, romances, and science fiction. Benefiting from a profession that allows retirement in one's forties, more cops and ex-cops brought their experience into novels during the nineties. And while the traditional cop issues remained — corruption, brutality, stress, vocation, law, etc., in the nineties everybody needed an expert, and forensic science played a large role in all of crime fiction in the nineties. Cop books were no exception. Finally, one of the most telling phenomena of the decade was that established hard-boiled private investigator writers like Robert B. Parker and to a greater extent Robert Crais left the wisecracking, independent hero and shifted their attention to cops.

Forensic Writers

As the cop novel developed in the 1970s and 1980s, forensics played only a minor role in the books of most writers. While they acknowledge the need for methodical, scientific searching and analysis as well as specialized knowledge, forensic specialists in most books are either anonymous functionaries (the fingerprint crew, the crime lab worker) or enter briefly to provide the bits of arcane information the cops need. Thus autopsy scenes, while grisly and purposely shocking, feature cameo appearances of either grumpy and overworked coroners who condescend to inform the observing cops about what's what, or avuncular, enthusiastic ones who launch into lectures and explanations. In the late 1980s Ridley Pearson devised ways to both focus on the actions and character of the police officer and on specialized scientific investigation by making the cop and the scientist working partners in solving difficult cases, if not equal. His example and the popular success of Patricia Cornwell, along with the increasing public familiarity and interest in new forensic tools, ushered in another offshoot of the mystery novel, the forensic mystery. Sometimes they're cop books and sometimes they're not.

Ken Goddard

Kenneth Goddard is one of the first writers to focus on forensics and to bring expertise to the field. He was a deputy sheriff/criminalist with the Riverside County and San Bernardino County Sheriff's Departments; he set up a Scientific Investigation Bureau for the Huntington Beach Police Department and went on to establish the first full-service crime lab for national and international wildlife law enforcement in Ashland, Oregon (*http://hometown.aol.com/kengoddard/bio.htm*).

In his first novel, *Balefire* (1983), Goddard goes wide-screen, showing how the whole Huntington Beach Police Department copes with Middle Eastern terrorists and their plan to ruin the public's trust in the cops and make a horrific statement at the Los Angeles Olympics. Here Goddard presents the Huntington Beach force from top to bottom as brave and resourceful. Among the large cast of characters he includes crime lab boss Brian Sheffield, his Asian American assistant and lover Meiko, and the department's computer jock, Jeremy Raines. The forensic people are good at their jobs — even the main villain recognizes this: "The forensic lab group had demonstrated a dogged persistence, and had been rewarded with an unfortunate number of leads that were rapidly beginning to cross-link" (188). And Raines' technological acumen leads to the big break in the book. Nonetheless, in *Balefire* Goddard focuses on cops, particularly on Detective Sergeant Walter Anderson, whose strengths lie in conventional cop virtues:

Anderson was one of the new generation of officers in a police department that had grown rapidly from a handful of deputies who casually patrolled a beach town to a modern, two-hundred-and-fifty man police force that used modern law enforcement methods and equipment to maintain order in a city bulging with new developments and people. Relatively young for his investigator's stripes, aggressive, cool-headed, well-educated, protective of his men, Anderson had only one hang-up. He hated to work overtime [42].

After *Balefire* Goddard gravitated to the Feds. *The Alchemist* (1997) features DEA special agents, and even though he quit to be a criminalist in Fairfax County, Virginia, *Digger* (1991) is about an ex–CIA agent. *Prey* (1992), *Wildfire* (1994), and *Double Blind* (1998) feature former San Diego police homicide investigator Henry Lightstone, who becomes a federal wildlife agent. *First Evidence* (1999) and *Outer Perimeter* (2001) introduce crime scene investigator Detective-Sergeant Colin Cellars of the Oregon State Police.

In the books Goddard takes forensics seriously. In his *Twilight Zone* or *X Files* book, *First Evidence*, for example, he begins by renovating the old cop novel convention of including documents: Goddard starts readers off with a sixty-item, four-page "Collected Evidence List" (CASE NUMBER: OSP-09-00-6666) and a crime scene diagram. There's a speech on crime scene investigation (" It is virtually impossible for a suspect, a victim, and a crime scene to come into contact with each other ... without the exchange of physical evidence taking place" [59]). And there are the gadgets. Cellars lugs around case upon case of equipment, including night vision optics, a digital camera, and a laptop computer. In line with the *Twilight Zone* premise of the novel, Goddard even invents a TOD (time of death) device, and the Malcolm Byzor Model 7 Crime Scene Scanner that analyzes scenes by itself.

Thomas Nogouchi and Arthur Lyons

In the same year that Ridley Pearson published his first cop/forensic novel, Thomas Nogouchi, Chief Medical Examiner of Los Angeles County, teamed up with PI writer Arthur Lyons to publish *Unnatural Causes* (1988), followed by *Physical Evidence* in 1990. At the start of the 1990s Nogouchi and Lyons shift away from the police officer as crime solver and hero to the expert as hero. *Unnatural Causes* is a paean to forensic scientists. In fact Nogouchi and Lyons split the dedication of the book between Eric Nogouchi and "fellow members of the American Academy of Forensic Sciences." The writers detail the kind of graduate training one needs to be a medical examiner, include an autopsy scene longer and more detailed than those conventional in cop novels since the 1970s, explain the workings of a scanning electron microscope, show the hero doing battles for budget with bureaucrats, and predict that "as the technology advances, the applications of science are going to be limitless" (228). The hero, Dr. Eric Parker, medical examiner, is handsome, brave, devoted. In *Unnatural Causes* the cops are brutish ("He was a beefy, thick-necked man with a red face and a bluing drinker's nose, like a bruised fist" [16]), or slow. While Nogouchi and Lyons justify Parker acting as hero both by citing the statutory description of the medical examiner's duties and by inventing for Parker the concept of the "psychological autopsy" as an excuse for going out to interview witnesses, nonetheless they make him conscious that he is "usurping the police function" (119). But what the heck. For Nogouchi and Lyons, the cops don't have the tools or the talent.

And so developed a small class of medical examiner mysteries. In the late 1980s Don (D.J.) Donaldson, Ph.D. introduced Medical Examiner Andy Broussard in *Cajun Nights* (1988). In the 1990s Leonard S. Goldberg's Dr. Joanna Blalock appears for the first time in *Deadly Medicine* (1992), followed by another M.D. writer, Bill Pomidor, whose Dr. Calista Marley, deputy coroner in Cleveland, first appears in *Murder by Prescription* (1995). Louise Hendrickson's Amy Prescott is a crime lab physician and her father a coroner in a series beginning with *With Deadly Intent* (1993).

After the coroners, a variety of other experts enter what now had become the forensic mystery genre. Susan Dunlap creates a forensic pathologist for her first Kiernan O'Shaughnessy book, *Pious Deception* (1989). Noreen Ayers follows with Smokey Brandon, criminalist, first seen in *A World the Color of Salt* (1992). Elizabeth Gunn's Trudy Hanson is another criminalist. Camile Minichino, Ph.D., makes physicist Gloria Lamerino a hero in *The Hydrogen Murder* (1996). A chemist is the detective in Kaye Davis' books about her lesbian hero, Maris Middleton, starting with *Devil's Leg Crossing* (1997). Back in the 1980s Aaron Elkins, anthropology professor, invents Gideon Oliver, forensic anthropologist. Sharyn McCrumb in 1984 brings Elizabeth MacPherson, another forensic anthropologist, into her *Sick of Shadows*. Later, in the 1990s, Kathy Reichs, Ph.D., forensic anthropologist for the Office of the Chief Medical Examiner, State of North Carolina, and for the Laboratoire des Sciences Judiciaires et de Médecine Légale for the province of Quebec, makes her Dr. Temperance Brennan a forensic anthropologist in her *Deja Dead* (1997). Beverly Connor's Lindsay Chamberlain (*A Rumor of Bones* [1996]) is yet another forensic anthropologist. Techies come in with Susan Holtzer's computer consultant Anneke Haagen in *Something to Kill For* (1994), the department's computer consultant in Barbara D'Amato's *Killer.app* (1996), and Jeffrey Deaver's hacker Will Gilette in *The Blue Nowhere* (2001). Following up on a specialty introduced in *Gorky Park*, Iris Johansen in *The Face of Deception* (1998) brings in Eve Duncan, forensic sculptor. In his one non-espionage book, *Terminal Event* (1999), James Thayer introduces an investigator from the NTSB looking into an airline crash. And because crime inevitably raises the issue of why people do bad things, forensic psychologists and psychiatrists get involved with police work. This goes back to the 1980s with Jonathan Kellerman's books, and in the 1990s Sarah Lovett (Sarah Poland) creates *Dangerous Attachments* (1995) around Dr. Sylvia Strange; Anna Salter, Ph.D., expert in child sexual abuse, builds *Shiny Water* (1997) around Dr. Michael Stone; and James Patterson comes up with a cop who's also a psychologist with his Alex Cross in *Along Came a Spider*. But the most prominent, influential, and successful forensic writer is Patricia Cornwell.

Patricia Cornwell

In her first Kay Scarpetta book, *Post-Mortem*, Cornwell latches onto some of the conventional elements developed in the cop novels of the 1980s. First of all, it, like Cornwell's others, is a serial killer book. And like other serial killer books, *Post-Mortem* displays more than a passing interest in true crime—in it Cornwell alludes to the usual lineup: Speck, Bundy, the Green Valley Strangler, Gacy, Chapman, Williams, and Hinckley. Cornwell, too, takes advantage of the technological advances in forensic science made in the last decades. There is the fascination with new machines, and Cornwell is adept at describing them. Thus, for instance, in *Post-Mortem* she employs figurative language to describe the laser Scarpetta and crew use to examine the first body in the book:

> On a nearby surgical cart was the blue power unit, smaller than a microwave oven, with a row of bright green lights across the front. It was suspended in the pitch darkness of the X-ray room like a satellite in empty space, a spiral cord running from it to a pencil-sized wand filled with seawater [18].

In the same book Cornwell includes a raft of material about computers (including a Neanderthal method of computer fingerprint comparison), VICAP (the FBI's violent criminal database), and profiling. Indeed, profiling is one of Cornwell's continuing interests; Scarpetta declares in *Post-Mortem* that "Profilers are academicians, thinkers, analysts. Sometimes I think they are magicians" (73). *All That Remains* (1993) jumps on the DNA bandwagon along with many cop writers of the 1980s and 1990s. Finally, Cornwell joins in the chorus of writers who take up the issue of women in law enforcement and in positions of authority. But she's no cop writer.

Granted, Cornwell does include a police officer as a necessary but clearly subordinate character in her books. Cornwell introduces Sergeant Pete Marino in *Post-Mortem*, and one of the points of the novel resides in the mutual transformations Scarpetta and Marino undergo. Scarpetta begins their first encounter with the observation that "I wasn't sure if he didn't like women, or if he just didn't like me" (2). Cornwell thus plays the misogynist card early in the novel, only to overturn it later. But it's not just the appearance of prejudice that Cornwell uses. She employs Marino's cop experience, especially his background as a New York City cop before joining the Richmond force, as both a contrast and a complement to Medical Examiner Scarpetta's scrupulously scientific approach to crime problems. Then, too, there's class. Marino, with his non-standard speech and lower-class tastes, serves as a contrast to Scarpetta's yuppie accoutrements — the truck versus the Mercedes — as well as her flexibility. One of the themes of *Post-Mortem* is the growth of mutual respect, understanding, and friendship between the street cop with rough edges and the knowledgeable and skilled medical examiner.

Even though Marino is a continuing character in Cornwell's books, his role diminishes. True enough, he becomes Scarpetta's sidekick, but as the novels proceed he becomes increasingly subservient and even pathetic. Additionally, Cornwell tends to give police work over to the Feds — a sure sign of apostasy since almost universally cops in cop novels view the FBI (the Feebs) with suspicion and contempt. As the books proceed, Cornwell continuously uses forensic facts as the resolution to the central crime problem — from the obscure disease in *Post-Mortem* to the limitation of routine DNA analysis in *The Last Precinct* (2000) — and she carries on a running debate about profiling. But her books focus on character points distant from police work. Thus Cornwell consistently concentrates on drawing Scarpetta as both hero and victim, persecuted and hounded by evil people and evil forces. Her villains become larger, more malignant, smarter, and even international — evil geniuses beyond the capacities of a mere police force. And with the development of niece Lucy's character, Cornwell takes up issues of sexuality as a significant concern in her novels. And so Cornwell departs from the characters and conventions of the cop novel into something approaching the late-nineteenth-century sensation novel. Be that as it may, lots of people read her and her popularity has much to do with the popularity of the forensic novel in the 1990s.

Elizabeth Gunn

There are writers in the 1990s who manage to maintain the cop hero and still devote attention to forensics as a major interest in their books. Elizabeth Gunn is one of them. Gunn's series of books about Rutherford, Minnesota cop Jake Himes, beginning with *Triple Play* (1997), are about both conventional police procedure and forensics. *Five Card Stud* (2000), for example, contains substantial passages about chain of custody, scanning fingerprints and fingerprint databases, as well as the STR method of DNA analysis, material about blood splatter evidence, and ballistics. Gunn manages to maintain the police hero in a variety of ways. There is the first person narration of detective Jake Hines, who has to both conduct the investigation and understand the evidence found at multiple sites. He also has to deal with a variety of forensic personnel, from the idiosyncratic local coroner to the overworked state lab boss, whose passion is blood splatters. And Gunn also uses cohabitation: Hines' live-in partner, Trudy Hanson, is a technician for the Minnesota Bureau of Criminal Apprehension. As in Goldberg and Holtzer, the lover's job gives the police officer both shop talk with his lover and entry into the world of technical expertise, in Gunn's case the lab where Hanson works and where the evidence from his case is analyzed and evaluated.

Jeffrey Deaver

Jeffrey Deaver's Lincoln Rhyme books (*The Bone Collector* [1997], *The Coffin Dancer* [1998], *The Empty Chair* [2000], *The Stone Monkey* [2002]) and his *The Blue Nowhere* (2001) are forensic cop tours de force. Lincoln Rhyme, though now a quadriplegic, was the head of the NYPD crime lab and serves as a consultant. About forensics he's a polymath — he developed databases of all of Manhattan's soils, wrote a textbook (*The Scenes of the Crime*) and knows all there is to know about collecting and analyzing every kind of evidence — hair and fiber, tool marks, fingerprints, explosives, blood splatters, etc.. Throughout his books Deaver seeds in bits of the history of forensic science. Lincoln Rhyme often cites Locard's exchange principle — the one about the inevitability of trace evidence — and he enlightens his cop listeners with minihistory lessons. For instance,

> The word [criminalist] had actually been around for years, first applied in the United States to the legendary Paul Leland Kirk, who ran the UC Berkeley School of criminology [Bone 58].

and

> A technician working in a U.S. Army forensic lab in Japan had used Super Glue to fix a broken camera and found to his amazement that the fumes from the adhesive raised latent fingerprints better than most chemicals [*Bone* 67].

Then there are the machines. Deaver fills Rhyme's Manhattan apartment with scientific gadgets:

> The combined rooms were now a messy space filled ... with density gradient tubes, computers, compound microscopes, comparison 'scopes, a gas chroma-

tograph/mass spectrometer, a PoliLight alternative light source, fuming frames for raising friction ridge prints. A very expensive scanning electron microscope hooked to an energy dispersive X-ray unit sat prominently in the corner [*Coffin* 36].

The tour de force part comes in the fact that Deaver designed *The Bone Collector* and *The Coffin Dancer* as serial killer books so that his characters could use different forensic techniques at a number of different kinds of crime scenes.

While Deaver does devote a great deal of attention to exploring and elaborating on forensics, he also pays attention to cops and cop issues. Lincoln Rhyme, after all, was part of the NYPD and in the books acts as a consultant. Indeed, because of his disability he can do little else than consult and advise. In all of the books Deaver brings in an assortment of minimally developed cop characters who hang around Rhyme's apartment during the course of the investigation. In the books Deaver displays some interest in cop issues; in *The Bone Collector*, for instance, he slides in the conventional cop lament about crooks and lawyers:

> They sue us for everything. There's a rapist suing us now 'cause he got shot in the leg coming at an officer with a knife. His lawyer's got this theory he's calling the "least deadly alternative." Instead of shooting, we're supposed to taze them or use Mace. Or ask them politely, I don't know [107].

Most of his police interest, however, comes in through the character of Amelia Sachs. Sachs in the first novel is a novice foot patrol officer chosen by the forensic consultant, Rhyme, to be his apprentice as well as his arms and legs. While a good deal of what Sachs does in the books is forensic related, Deaver nonetheless uses her occupation to define her. She is an action hero — a crack shot and fiendishly good driver, and Deaver employs these qualities to make his thriller endings work. Notably, in characterizing Sachs he brings in conventional police background: Sachs' father was a cop and her former boyfriend was a corrupt police officer.

Minorities

Before the 1990s cop novels treated women and African Americans as the principal minorities. Female writers began to enter the field in some numbers in the 1980s. Their heroes uniformly possess talent, ambition, and more sensitivity than their male colleagues. In the nineties writers were able to expand the variety of characteristics of their female heroes. Equally important, for the first time African American writers began to write about black heroes, heroes that had hitherto been portrayed only by white writers and who typically placed African American cops in supporting roles in their books. Indeed, diversity is one of the key concepts in the cop books of the 1990s with new groups — Asians, gays and lesbians — becoming heroes of cop books for the first time.

Women

Julie Smith

In 1990, with *New Orleans Morning*, Julie Smith introduced her cop "Skip" Langdon and her city. During the decade she wrote seven more books about her policewoman: *The Axeman's Jazz* (1991), *Jazz Funeral* (1993), *New Orleans Beat* (1994), *House of Blues* (1995), *Kindness of Strangers* (1996), *Crescent City Kill* (1997), and *82 Desire* (1998).

If one goes to the cop house for technical advice — Smith acknowledges Captain Linda Buczek of the NOPD — there's an inclination to treat the cops pretty well. Smith portrays New Orleans cops as a good lot. In *The Axeman's Jazz*, for instance, the serial killer task force consists of officers Smith describes as "veterans," "solid," and "whizzes." The hero's superiors are friendly and supportive. And, of course, Langdon, as one of them, is a good cop, too.

Smith begins her description of Langdon on her website this way:

> She's possibly the most striking looking cop in New Orleans — six feet tall, tumbling brown curly hair, green eyes, and overweight. And she has one of the most curious backgrounds: former debutante and Carnival queen, Tulane flunkout, boozer, doper, all around screw-up, and daughter of one of the City's most prominent doctors. She just never felt at home in the Garden District with all those little bird-like women and heavy curtains, pushy parents who used her for their social advantage, and the mass of Southern manners and mores she was expected to know without being taught [www.juliesmithauthor.com].

Smith makes her hero stand out first by her size; almost uniformly, earlier female cop heroes fit more conventional notions of beauty. A drawback in conventional society, in police work Langdon's size liberates her:

> But police work was something she could do. She was big and she was physically adept; maybe in this atmosphere her size and strength gave her the confidence to use the brains that were really what made her good [*Axeman* 19].

Along with size, Smith confronts Langdon with typical women's problems. She makes her hero deal with the problem of what to wear to appear professional, a problem exacerbated by New Orleans weather that makes panty hose a unique variety of torture. And then there's the Southern thing about women. Langdon's family, their social position and aspirations, and the hero's rejection of them become a recurring motif in the books.

If she can escape some of the expectations of the Southern woman, she cannot escape from Southern manners and mores. Thus, for instance, in *The Axeman's Jazz* Langdon feels their pull on her:

> What did you say to a small-town woman whose daughter had been murdered after less than two months in the big city?
>
> If you were Southern, you said you wished there was something you could say, and please let you know if there was anything you could do.... You had to say that, when all the while what you really wanted was for her to do something for you. Tell you everything [12].

It's all about tradition: "But that wasn't the usual thing in the South. You did things because things had always been done that way and because someone else wanted you to" (*Axeman* 17).

Smith also centers Langdon on relationships. Langdon stays on the force and was promoted to homicide because of the friendship of Lieutenant Joe Cappello — "she still thought of him as a friend. A warm friend" (*Axeman* 14). Indeed Smith uses love as her hero's salvation. Thus at the end of *The Axeman's Jazz*, disgusted with humanity, Langdon finds the answer in love:

> The answer came to her almost as quickly as the question. Yes, burn it. Burn it with passion. With love. If it's human beings who disgust you, get as close as you can to one of them. Let the slime pour out of you as your head fills, your body fills, with life and hope. And starting over. And love [352].

Kim Wozencraft

Kim Wozencraft, the book bio relates, is a "former narcotics officer." In *Rush* (1990) she depicts a far different kind of experience and a far different kind of hero than those created by other female police writers. In *Rush*, Kristen Cates of the Beaumont, Texas, Police Department narrates her own experience as a police officer and her descent into the world of duplicity, addiction, and corruption. Wozencraft provides the usual obstacles faced by female cops of her era. The guys in charge don't want female officers, and if they have them want to keep them out of real police work: "Sergeant Quill was using his authority to keep the bane of the office, his only female detective, tracing stolen hubcaps and writing suicide reports" (41). Assigned to work undercover in narcotics, the hypocrisy of her job comes home to Cates:

> We bought their dope and wrote our reports, paying attention to times and dates and physical descriptions, omitting the details that might make them seem human to a jury [121].

She feels degraded and sullied: "Always, after soliciting confessions, I felt the need of a long hot shower" (44). It, however, is not simply this; illegal acts are the accepted practice and the routine expected by her boss. "I knew, in each case, every trial, even as I was saying 'so help me God,' that I was about to get up on that stand and lie like a thief in the name of the law. Because that was how it worked" (229). Added to this, both Cates and her partner, then lover, then husband, become seriously addicted to drugs as a consequence of their roles as undercover cops, a fact that their corrupt chief is aware of but indifferent to. At the end of *Rush* everything falls apart. The FBI arrests Cates' corrupt chief, who ultimately goes free, but Cates and her husband, both seriously addicted to cocaine, end up in federal prison: "Now, it is all with me. *Past contemptible actions.* I should sleep" (339).

Molly Hite

In 1992 Cornell English professor Molly Hite published *Breach of Immunity.* In it she combines a McBain-like imaginary city (metropolitan Hinton), serious issues (homosexual rape, AIDS, confidentiality of medical tests, homophobia, feminism), and a significant dose of comedy associated with her main characters. Hite collects much of the comedy around the chief of the Hinton detective squad, the massive, donut-inhaling, politically incorrect Lieutenant Anna Blessing:

> Scilla didn't want to think about Anna Blessing in a skirt with appropriate legwear. It was bad enough dealing with the question of where she got her uniform trousers. Most of the precinct agreed that she had a tailor somewhere, some visaless immigrant hoarding bolts of blue serge.... Almost six feet tall, Anna had been gaining weight steadily.... The Hinton Metropolitan Police Department required a yearly physical examination, but nobody had yet suggested to Lieutenant Blessing that obesity might be grounds for early retirement. Given the tendency of upper-echelon officers to spread into their desk jobs and the recent success of affirmative action suits involving public servants, it wasn't likely that Anna would be the test case for a fat purge, but in the precinct there were periodic attempts to guess her weight, with the median guess well above 300 pounds [29].

Lieutenant Blessing, however, serves as more than a caricature. She is one smart cop and a monument to the heroic persistence of women in police work:

> Some time ago she had worked out that these gross joshings had to be a legacy of Anna's early days on the force, when everybody put up with the sole big girl among the uniformed patrols.... Anna had been good at acting the part, too, and you could only guess at the work she had to put into making the transition from cop's widow and mother of two girls to just plain cop. That was the fifties, after all, when uniformed police were presumed not only to be men but to be unreflective parodies of Hollywood masculinity. In the middle of all of the bluff and testosterone, Anna had maneuvered from her clerical position as precinct manager into the traffic division, and from there into patrol training

school, where she had established a marksmanship record that stood unbroken for six years. Four years on the beat and she took the detective's exam. Establishing another record [32].

Blessing represents for the readers a statement of history as well as a commentary about equal rights and affirmative action, but to herself she is just a cop. The job is more important than reflection or personal voyages of discovery. Indeed, Hite makes Blessing violently opposed to the television show *Cagney and Lacy* because "it showed women cops as complicated human beings with rich inner lives" (106).

Hite counterpoints Anna Blessing with detective Priscilla Carmody, another daughter of a cop family. One is slim and the other is fat; one eats health food and the other snorts donuts; one is attuned to the nuances of political correctness and the other offends sensibilities of all underrepresented groups. Carmody, a karate expert, proudly thinks of herself as looking "small but mean," while Blessing seemingly does not think of herself at all. Hite makes Carmody the active feminist. Indeed, she stretches a role reversal across the entire novel by partnering the dominant Carmody with the recessive, tentative, awestruck Mike Annunzio. Scilla plays the active, traditional cop role. She has authority and Mike doesn't. Thus after even the physicians at the hospital acknowledge the unspoken authority of the police, Mike muses that

> he didn't feel part of that authority. Even the custodians of our mortality acquiesce to the armed might of the legal system. That was the appeal of the police force to most recruits, certainly to Anna, certainly to Scilla, but to him? [115].

Carmody is active and Annunzio passive: "She loved violence. It made her a better cop than he was, and sometimes it scared the hell out of him" (129). The male/female role reversal in *Breach of Immunity* culminates when Carmody unsnarls herself from her father's interference and saves Annunzio, the man in distress, at the end of the novel.

In *Breach of Immunity* Hite presents an aggressively feminist cop, sometimes bemused by the figure of another woman cop who is her foremother. She treats both Blessing and Carmody with sympathy and ironic humor, while at the same time presenting readers with serious issues about a variety of personal and societal roles. Hite incidentally tosses off one of the most prescient observations about cops and cop novels:

> "Superwomen don't wear tops... You like that for a title? For one of those hard-boiled cop novels. What do you think?"
> "Shows how much you read," said Scilla loftily. "Cops aren't hard-boiled. Only amateurs are hard-boiled. Private dicks in their little sleazy offices" [156].

Noreen Gilpatrick

Noreen Gilpatrick's *Fatal Design* (1993) centers on the investigation of murdered owners of a design firm by Seattle-area detective Kate MacLean (a popular first name for women cops, used by Forrest, King, and Burcell). At the cop house, though, they call her Mother MacLean. And they do so with cause. Thus Gilpatrick goes to some pains to show MacLean's maternal side in her reaching out to those in distress:

> Instinctively, Kate reached across the table and squeezed the sweatshirt-covered arm, just so the girl could feel some human contact. Sam lounged back in the chair, watching her, his face devoid of expression, his eyes in neutral. Kate knew damned well what he was thinking. Mother MacLean. Earth Mother to the world [*Fatal* 15].

Later in the novel, Sam, MacLean's partner, makes it clear that he both understands and appreciates this aspect of her character:

> It's everything about you. It's the warm look in your eyes, it's the instinctive way your face reflects sympathy and understanding, it's the sincerity you project.... It's the way you carry yourself, the way you listen, the half-smile of interest even when you're people watching [*Fatal* 154].

The important thing, however, is that MacLean has channeled her sympathetic nature into being a cop. Gilpartick creates for her a history of having begun her career as a juvenile officer, with daily exposure to squalor and the futility of trying to make a difference. This experience lead to a breakdown and her resignation from the San Francisco force. In Seattle, working homicide, "if I couldn't prevent the killings from happening, then maybe there'd be satisfaction in bringing the killers to justice" (39).

Gilpatrick also focuses on the issue of partners. MacLean's partner is a wise older cop—at first she thinks of him as being as comfortable as an old dog. She projects critical attitudes on him, as in the passage cited above. In an episode at a pool parlor MacLean muses on male/female partner relationships:

> It was one of the problems a female cop faced. A male partner often tended to act like a brother/husband/father. Sam was semi-okay in the role. He treated her like an equal. Mostly. And when he disapproved of something she did he kept it to himself. Mostly. She wouldn't call him her best friend, like some of the teams were. But still she would call him a friend. Sometimes. Well, occasionally. Still, it was working out okay. Mostly [101].

At the end of *Fatal Design*, however, MacLean recognizes that mostly is pretty good and she casts her lot with her faithful old friend and partner.

Carol O'Connell

Carol O'Connell's hero kicks ass. Introduced in *Mallory's Oracle* (1994), and appearing in four subsequent books (*The Man Who Cast Two Shadows* [1995]; *Killing Critics* [1996]; *Stone Angel* [1997]; and *Shell Game* [1999]), Kathy Mallory breaks stereotypes. First of all, when O'Connell introduces Mallory she gives her ninja qualities:

> Her gun cleared the holster with speed enough to fool the eye into thinking it had simply appeared in her right hand. Gun raised, she pushed open the door. All the light came from one of the back rooms. Silently, she made her way down the hall to the back office. A cat would have made more noise with its footfalls [*Oracle* 175].

Mallory has no compunction about beating people up. She is a hardcase, bristling whenever anyone uses her first name. She lives a sparse, rigidly ordered life. But O'Connell gives her more than courage and combat skills. Mallory is a computer whiz. In fact, she is a hacker with no qualms about invading privacy or breaking the law. She scares all of the other cops in the special crimes unit. For O'Connell, however, Mallory is all about background.

Mallory was a guttersnipe. Abandoned on the streets of New York, as a young child she learned how to survive. She is found and adopted by Lou and Helen Markowitz. O'Connell develops Markowitz as a legendary NYPD detective, wise and overwhelmingly successful. Bringing the feral Kathy Mallory into their home, the Markowitzes provide for her affection and the benefits of middle-class life, and from Lou Mallory gets the ambition to be a cop as well as a foot in the department's door. In the first novel Mallory's single-minded intense ferocity is directed toward finding the serial killer who murdered Markowitz, her adopted father. In densely written prose, O'Connell shows that these things aren't enough. Mallory occasionally needs the help of others, and she needs to learn about proper police procedure, her chief role in the department up to that point being that of the department's computer genius. But none of this makes Mallory less hard or less self-sufficient.

Barbara D'Amato

Barbara D'Amato is part of the Chicago cop writers' conspiracy, maybe even one of its leaders. Hugh Holton acknowledges her influence on him, and D'Amato names co-conspirators Holton and Mark Zubro in the opening material of *Help Me Please* (1999). In addition to that book, D'Amato's cop books include *Killer.app* (1996), *Good Cop Bad Cop* (1998), and *Authorized Personnel Only* (2000).

Forensics, history, domestic problems and police work form the template for D'Amato's cop books. With regard to the former, two of her books turn on computer stuff. In *Killer.app* bad guys take over the Chicago PD's communications system and hack into assorted other networks, and *Help Me Please* turns on an evil hackers' group called Bandwith. In *Killer.app* D'Amato broadens the need for widespread forensic expertise by noting the need for lab techs to have continuing education — one of them "just spent two weeks at a forensic botany seminar at the Institute of Organismic Botany" (115). In *Help Me Please* the hero, Deputy Chief of Detectives Polly Kelly, highlights the need for cops to know lots of things:

> Nowadays, it's not just a matter of searching fingerprints through AFIS, the Automated Fingerprint Identification System. The whole job is techy. From your first hour in the academy, you're taught DNA, AFIS, how to use NCIC, the National Crime Information Center, what accelerants are in arson cases, taggants in explosives. You might as well be in science class. Detectives have to know more than patrol cops, naturally, and the detective's exam is heavy in tech questions.
>
> In my job, I have to be a jack of all trades — chemistry, physics, pathology, computer science, you name it [74].

While D'Amato's books often have much to do with forensics, she consistently makes the experts subordinate to the cops whom they serve. The techies figure things out and make brief reports and D'Amato's cops stay on center stage.

D'Amato's books also display an awareness of the way history impinges on the police. The tradition of police work in families reflects this — Polly Kelly is a cop's daughter and reflects on his experience: "My dad had been a cop, back in the days when cops were paid a pittance" (*Help Me* 13). *Good Cop, Bad Cop* covers two generations of a Chicago cop family. But the novel covers more than family history. D'Amato gives readers a brief lesson on the chaos of the 1960s:

> In the mid–1960s, Chicago, like most large cities in the United States, was seeing more street violence, and the police were becoming more and more nervous. There was anti-war rioting and civil rights rioting — first, sporadic sorties and small local battles. Harlem, in New York City, in 1964. Then, in 1965, the suburb of Watts in Los Angeles, which went up like dry grass, leaving fifty million dollars worth of property damage, thirty-five hundred people arrested, nine hundred injured and thirty five dead. The long, hot, violent summers of the sixties had begun [77–78].

This general background ushers in an account of race riots in Chicago and the "police riot" at the Democratic National Convention. Then also *Good Cop, Bad Cop* turns on the December 4, 1969, police raid on Chicago's Black Panthers.

Featuring female heroes Suze Figuroa and Polly Kelly, D'Amato makes a few passing references to the difficulties female cops face: "We've got about twenty-five percent women in the CPD now, but except for a separate locker room, not much has changed" (*Killer* 17). Even though D'Amato notes that women have achieved much in the Chicago force, she uses Suze Figuroa to indicate that it is still a brotherhood. Thus after spending time in a cop bar where the topic of lighting farts arises:

> Sometimes Suze got a little depressed at these after-hours bar sessions. She was part of the team, they liked her, all but Aldo.... But still she knew that they would talk differently when she left. They would talk easier. They'd throw around comments about women and sex and generally engage in their male-bonding crap.
> Sometimes it really pissed her off. She didn't want to be one of the boys, exactly. But she sure as hell wanted to be one of the guys [*Good Cop* 153].

Unlike the boys, Figuroa has family responsibilities and concerns. Divorced, she and her son live with her sister and her family. At the other end of the age spectrum, Kelly's worries center on her mentally unstable mother who lives with her because she cannot afford a nursing home.

Ken Gross

Not all great female cop characters are created by female authors. After a foray into true crime writing with *One Tough Cop: The Bo Dietl Story* (1988), Ken Gross moved toward cop fiction with *Rough Justice* (1991), *Hell Bent* (1993), *Full Blown Rage* (1995), and *The Talk Show Defense* (1997). With his Lieutenant Maggie VanZandt, Gross avoids one of the things real cops complain about regarding fictional cops — titles. Sergeants and especially lieutenants are administrators, and mostly that's what Gross makes VanZandt. At the start of *Full Blown Rage* Gross both establishes her as an administrator and nods to the complexity of crime in a precinct by having Sam Rosen, VanZandt's Jewish, African American sergeant, read the last day's crimes for the lieutenant to assign to detectives. In *Full Blown Rage*, along with VanZandt's personal worries about the death of her best friend, she, of necessity, must concern herself with things like reading DD5s, filing reports, compiling statistics, and her departmental budget. There is so much of the supervisor in her that when she is mistakenly put in a chokehold by a beat cop, she admires that he had the presence of mind to kick her purse out of the way.

Mildly unkempt and struggling with premenstrual bloating when *Full*

Blown Rage begins, VanZandt's principal reasons for being a cop lie in her notions about order. Thus responding to a rising tide of anarchy, Gross puts into the novel passages explaining her motivations. First he tells readers that

> She had developed the cop's brittle belief in social accountability. A strict, authoritarian voice was always there whispering that people determined their own destiny. This was founded on the rock-hard belief that said that if a person went through life in a cautious, righteous way, that person could expect an auspicious fate, given a certain fickle variable [62].

And ten pages later he extends the notion of accountability to VanZandt's individual motivations as a cop:

> she believed in a higher obligation, a need to straighten out the official record. Someone had to keep the books for society. Attention had to be paid. She did not believe in anarchy. Murder should be answered [73].

Lynn Hightower

Lynn S. Hightower introduced Cincinnati detective Sonora Blair in *Flashpoint* (1995), and continued with her in *Eyeshot* (1996), *No Good Deed* (1998), and *The Debt Collector* (2000). Hightower includes some of the conventional laments about prejudice against women in and outside of the department: of civilians Blair says that "Once in a while when I worked patrol, I'd answer a call, say a prowler call, and people would ask why they sent a little thing like me" (*Flash* 117). Hightower also makes Blair comment on adjustments women need to make to be effective cops, adjustments that have to do with the way women relate to others. Thus Hightower includes the observation "that women smile no matter what.... You're a cop. Don't smile when people are giving you grief" (*Flash* 168). Before D'Amato's Suze Figuroa feels the same thing, Hightower's Blair feels, and resents, the fact that women are accepted professionally as cops but are barred from the "brotherhood." Thus in *Flashpoint* Blair notes that "I'm one of the boys at work. After work, no, I get left out a lot" (117), and in *Eyeshot* an off-color remark brings about the observation that "She really hated it when she remembered she wasn't one of the boys" (*Eye* 124).

Hightower pays liberal attention to Blair's domestic life. A widow with two demanding children, she has to cope with rides to friends' houses, teenage indifference to hygiene, and childcare. Indeed, in *Eyeshot* Blair has to take her daughter along with her on a Sunday investigation that takes her and her partner out of state. In an even-handed manner, Hightower also makes domestic issues part of the character of Blair's partner, Sam, whose daughter suffers from leukemia. They cover for each other's necessary absences from the job. Living in and wanting to live in two worlds has a

price. In the first book, Blair has an ulcer, and in *Eyeshot* she even expresses
reticence about switching roles from professional to domestic:

> Sonora was dawdling in the parking lot, not sure she was ready to leave Sam,
> not sure she was ready to launch into the mom-thing. She got into the Blazer,
> put the key in the ignition so she could roll down the window and talk [29].

As a cop, Blair has rebellious qualities. It's there in small things. In *Eye-shot* she insists on violating the department's dress code by wearing sneak-ers. And in the same novel she smashes open the dispenser in the women's
room and scatters tampons around so as to keep the men from further mess-ing up the temporary unisex facility. It's there, too, in some larger qualities.
In *Eyeshot*, for example, Blair handcuffs an interfering fellow cop to a pipe
in the john. Blair's attitude comes across in the tone of her comments about
herself as well as in her badinage with her partner, Sam. She is occasionally
sarcastic and almost consistently ironic, attitudes that can go well with both
police work and parenting — as long as there's dedication and courage, too.
And this Blair shows in abundance, especially when she confronts crime and
criminals.

Jannine Kadow

Jannine Kadow's one cop novel, *Blue Justice* (1998), depends on male
cops, veteran detective Ed Gavin and his rookie partner Jon Strega. Kadow
puts in the requisite cop themes — the brotherhood, cop talk, brutality, etc.
She puts *Blue Justice* firmly in the cop genre by citing her predecessors:

> There was a plastic shelving unit filled with paperback books. Gavin picked
> up the powerful magnifying glass. McBain, Daley, McDonald, all the big names
> in police and detective fiction [114].

While Kadow makes Gavin and Strega the cop heroes of *Blue Justice*,
the book also concentrates on a woman officer, Maria Alvarez:

> Maria graduated at the top of her class at the academy. Beat the pants off every
> other candidate in target practice. She set a record: highest target scores in the
> history of the academy. She's fearless too, like her father....
>
> She's got guts and she's ambitious. Maria Alvarez isn't afraid of anything or
> anybody. Last I heard, she was gunning for the buy-and-bust team. The minute
> she lands a high-profile assignment like buy-and-bust, she'll sail up through
> the ranks. Maria didn't go to college like you, but she's smart. Maybe not book
> smart, but she's smart [45–46]

Except that the first scene of the novel shows Maria Alvarez trying to
commit suicide. And as *Blue Justice* proceeds, Kadow shows her as a cocaine
addict and then worse. She stalks and harasses rookie detective Strega after

he has rebuffed her. And she is also the serial killer who has been killing NYPD cops and making it look like suicide. Vampire that she may be, Kadow lays the blame for Maria's acts on the continuing sexual abuse she suffers at the hands of her father, the fire-and-brimstone police commissioner.

Asians

Nan Hamillton

In the late 1970s E.V. Cunninghan (Howard Fast) introduced a Japanese American police officer, Detective Sergeant Masao Masuto of the Beverly Hills Police Department, in *The Case of the One Penny Orange* (1977). Masuto, in addition to being a cop, lives in a traditional Japanese house and studies with a Zen Master. Several years later Nan Hamilton in *Killer's Rights* (1984) brought knowledge of the history of the detective story as well as the possibilities of introducing ethnically diverse detectives into the genre. She was, after all, John Ball's wife. A couple of times in the short novel Hamilton points to the few Asian precursors in American crime literature. First, one of the medical examiners insists on calling her Japanese American cop, Sam Ohara, "Charlie Chan":

> "Always sooner he wants," Abrams grumbled. "Tomorrow's the soonest you'll get, Charlie Chan."
>   Ohara punched him lightly on the shoulder. "I'll settle for that. And by the way, try to get it right, Bob. Charlie Chan wasn't Japanese. Try Mr. Moto" [22].

Later in the book Hamilton works in a critical reference to Cunningham's Japanese cop:

> As he sat down to his lonely meal, however, he recalled a book someone had given him about a fictional Japanese detective whose efforts were aided, or soothed as the case might be, by frequent dips in a steaming hot *ofuro*, while his beautiful Japanese wife, elegantly kimonoed, waited nearby with fragrant tea and fluffy white towels. Only in books, he reflected wryly [30].

Hamilton's hero is a bit more real than that. Nevertheless the racial element is very important to Hamilton. She brings in most of the well-known popular culture accoutrements associated with the Japanese: kimonos, dolls, sushi, loss of face, hara-kiri, aikido, gardening, and the World War II internment camps. Hamilton even brings in Japanese racism in connection with Ohara's new African American partner:

> Being new was bad enough without being caught up in the old black-Japanese antipathy. Many of the older Japanese felt about blacks the way a lot of whites thought about Orientals. In Japan, the unfortunate children fathered by black

soldiers during the occupation were still outcasts in normal society, with no future, no hope. Even in America some of the Issei held on to their prejudice [19].

And she connects Ohara's occupation with his ethnic background. The reason he became a cop, Ohara tells his partner, is because of being in the internment camps:

"How did you come to join the force?" he asked at last.
    I thought about it a lot as a kid. The stories about Manzanar [an internment camp] got to me. Maybe I wanted to prove something; I don't know.... Anyway, I sure didn't want any part of the nursery business. I had to work too hard helping my dad. Then 'Nam came along. When I got back I entered the police academy. Nothing else fitted [25].

Aside from the motive Hamilton makes aikido part of her hero's mental routine in investigating the murders in the book—"Each exhaled breath took with it patterned thought and awareness of time, until his body felt light and his mind was clear" (51).

Toni Ihara and Ralph Warner

In the same year that Hamilton published her book about Officer Ohara of the LAPD, Toni Ihara and Ralph Warner came out with *Murder on the Air* (1984), introducing Berkeley police officer Sara Tamura. The book begins with the hero having just seen the film of *The Thin Man* and maintains an undercurrent of updated Nick and Nora with Tamura and her lieutenant, James Rivers, throughout the narrative. But it's not just the relationship that's key, it's the detection, too: "Indeed, looking back, it was Myrna Loy and William Powell who planted the seed which, after an odd turn or two, had resulted in her current job as—dum, da, dum, dum—Berkeley, California police officer, Badge #1642" (5).

Along with the mystery and attached environmental issues, Ihara and Warner present several problems: Tamura's race, her feminism, the growing affection between Tamura and Rivers, and the somewhat quirky nature of Berkeley and its cops. Early in *Murder on the Air* the writers bring in racial prejudice: Tamura's landlord, for instance, "believed that Chinese should wash clothes, the Jews take care of money, and the Japanese tend gardens" (6). Indeed, Tamura finds that she needs not only to struggle against racism but against her own upbringing. Thus,

Her impatience with Rivers ... clashed with her cultural heritage, which taught the wisdom of getting along with even the most difficult people [8].

And

Growing up Japanese-American meant growing up polite. It was difficult for her to be even a little anti-social without feeling vaguely uncomfortable [53].

These ambivalent feelings apply especially to Tamura's police work. She acknowledges that her being a member of the force is a result of affirmative action and a politically correct municipality. Like other fictional female cops, Tamura knows her own competence and capacity to contribute to the squad and is quick to perceive, especially with Rivers, the lack of equal treatment. If Berkeley is punctilious about its political correctness, it is also weird, and like the city itself, Warner and Ihara concede that Berkeley's cops are a bit strange: "Carl Burnett was unique, even on a force known widely as a haven for bizarre characters" (20). In fact, one of the character points they make about Tamura is that it's a bit strange, given her experience at and in Berkeley, for her to be a cop in the first place:

> I came to Berkeley as a freshman philosophy major in 1967, when I was six-teen. I showed up at every anti-war demonstration, churned out peace posters by the thousands at Guerrilla Graphics, and really believed the revolution would bring a better, more just world. For a while, it seemed like my career was get-ting hauled out of campus buildings by men with crash helmets and tear gas guns. After I graduated, I drifted through graduate school and several jobs for almost ten years. Then I found myself wearing the uniform I had despised. Most of the time I think working in Violent Crimes is as righteous a job as any. No one likes murderers. But guilty? Sure. Sometimes I get the feeling I've sold out [129–130].

Leslie Glass

Leslie Glass began with the relative rarity of Asian police officers in fiction and did several things. First she chose Chinese as opposed to Japanese, in itself an unusual move. Then she made her police hero a woman, doubling the minority status. Thus her series of Time novels (*Burning Time* [1993]; *Hanging Time* [1995]; *Loving Time* [1996]; *Judging Time* [1998]; *Stealing Time* [1999]; and *Tracking Time* [2000]) feature NYPD officer April Woo. Adding to the ethnic mix, Glass throws in Hispanic Mike Sanchez as a love interest.

Glass devotes parts of the novels to April's observations about Chinese culture in America — contrasts of the way different ethnic groups serve and eat food, the differences in body hair and smell among ethnic groups, etc. On the job, Woo muses on the inevitability of racial prejudice and the impact it has on police work:

> The race issue made her uneasy. Sure, it was always there, and it always com-plicated everything.... And color probably made the most difference of all. Color made people nervous, made them jump one way or another, changed

the way they acted or didn't act. Color raised the stakes on the possibility of political repercussions. It guaranteed deeply emotional and often dangerous responses that were camouflaged or not depending on the parties involved. And anybody who said only the facts mattered was dreaming [*Judging* 44].

In the books Woo confronts varieties of prejudice in her personal life. Not the least significant of these comes from her family:

> But Sai and Ja Fa Woo didn't stop at disliking blacks. April's parents didn't like anybody — not whites, not Hispanics, not Pakistanis or Native Americans or Koreans. Chinese were the best people to them. That was it. Nobody else counted [*Judging* 45].

Glass located the center of this kind of prejudice in Woo's dragon mother, who both disdains her daughter's choice of profession and lies in wait for her with admonitions about finding a nice Chinese doctor to marry and raise children with.

The most important facet of culture conflict that Glass explores in the April Woo books is that between the traditional behavior of Chinese women and the demands of police work. In *Judging Time* Woo recalls her rookie year and the efforts of Sergeant Zapora to make her into a real cop. He gave her practical lessons in assertiveness:

> And every day he took her downstairs. He made her stand in front of the stupid, filthy mirror and made her growl like a dog, made her raise her voice saying, "Hey you, there on the stairs, stop. Hey you in the red jacket, stop. Hey you stop" over and over until she could say stop loud enough to command attention [26].

In *Burning Time* Woo recognizes the difference between herself and a demanding and successful female sergeant:

> She [Sergeant Joyce] could swing her hips and not look stupid, make a joke back when someone flirted with her. She was decisive and powerful. Sergeant Joyce would never get stuck lowering her eyes like some caricature of the demure Oriental [76].

As Woo advances through the police ranks, becoming a sergeant herself by *Judging Time*, the conflict between the demands of leadership and culturally derived reticence become yet another quandary for her. Then, too, the same pull exists in the relationship between partners, especially when romantically involved like Woo and Sanchez. In *Judging Time* Woo is increasingly sensitive to and conscious of not being made into a gofer by the guy partner.

Glass highlights her hero's unobtrusive meticulousness as one of the keys to her success as a detective. By bringing in the continuing character of psychiatrist Jason Frank, Glass is also able to call attention to the psychological insights of both Frank and her hero. Then, too, Woo has what can only be classed as instinct:

> Right away April started having a bad feeling about this. But that was not unusual. Every time she went to a scene her skin tingled, almost as if she developed a whole new layer of antennae around her body to take in as much information as possible. Sometimes, no matter how much evidence was collected by the Crime Scene Unit, or how many witnesses or suspects told their false stories about what happened, it was April's first impressions that led her through the maze to the true story [*Judging* 24].

Native Americans

James Doss

Engineer James Doss introduced Ute police officer Charlie Moon as an ancillary character in *The Shaman Sings* (1994). As his books progress, however, Moon plays an increasingly larger role. *The Shaman Sings* centers on the effort of an ex–Chicago cop, Scott Parris — now chief of the Granite Creek, Colorado police force — to find the killer of a graduate student from the local university. On the police side, Parris deals with an inept and trigger-happy patrolman and a mystery that turns on a forensic puzzle. Largely Parris reacts rather than acts, and much of the investigation in *The Shaman Sings* is done by his love interest, reporter Anne Foster. Doss touches very briefly on Parris's background and drops a hint or two about depression, but what makes him unusual is not his police work but his premonitions — Parris has bad feelings and bad dreams before bad things happen. This links him with the old Ute woman, Daisy Perika, the shaman in the titles of Doss's books. She, too, has visions, premonitions, and deals with emanations and animations from the spirit world of Ute mythology.

In his subsequent books Doss makes Sergeant Charlie Moon of the Ute tribal police a much more significant character. But he does not present him as one of Hillerman's introspective and mystical characters. In part this comes from his companionship with Parris, whom he introduces as his partner. Doss writes in buddy banter between Moon and Parris in the books beginning with *The Shaman Laughs* (1995). Doss uses the epithets "the big Ute" and "the policeman" to establish Moon's character. He makes a point, then, that Moon is a cop — a good one, of course:

> Police Chief Roy Severo always said that Charlie Moon might take his own good time to figure things out, but that in the long run, he generally got the job done. The Utes were proud of their big policeman's remarkable ability to make sense of actions that, on the surface, seemed to have no meaning [*Laughs* 14].

As proud as his tribe may be of him, Doss gives Moon few overt Native American characteristics. Indeed, his aged shaman aunt fears that he may be thinking about taking up golf, the ultimate Anglo pastime. Some of Moon's traits come from the stereotypes of the Western, like his laconic nature and the trick played on the racist dude FBI agent in *The Shaman Laughs*. In terms of police work, Doss gives little explanation in the early books about why Moon is a cop. And, as in Hillerman, Native American tribal police operate under severe limitations — serious crimes on reservations are the jurisdiction of the FBI. For Doss it's the extrasensory stuff (Moon, like Doss's other major characters, has premonitory dreams) that links Moon to Native American roots, but at the same time the mysticism removes him from the conventions of and the world of the cop novel.

Aimee and David Thurlo

Partners in producing romance novels and mysteries, Aimee and David Thurlo put a twist on the Native American police story by introducing a woman as the hero in a series of books beginning with *Blackening Song* (1995). Former FBI agent Ella Cha is an officer in the Navajo tribal police force in New Mexico. Ella Cha is a full-service police officer. As a detective she collects evidence, interviews sulky and hostile suspects, chases bad guys, and even helps to disinter a body when no one else is around to help with the spade work. As a member of a police force she helps out on riot duty, works long hours, does (although sometimes reluctantly) what her boss tells her to do, and spends time doing paperwork. The Thurlos make her the spokeswoman for cop clichés, like "'It's time to get to that twenty-four/twenty-four rule,' Ella continued. 'The two most important things in an investigation are the last twenty-four hours in the victim's life and whatever we find within twenty-four hours...'" (*Bad Medicine* 24). They also emphasize her dedication to her job. This, however, does not come without giving up a vision of domestic happiness. Thus in *Bad Medicine*:

> "I've heard a lot about you, Ella, and how dedicated you are to your job."
> "It's my first and best love," Ella admitted. It was at that moment that she realized what she was mourning. Wilson was building a future, while her whole life had been dedicated to safe-guarding the present so that others could see their futures unfold. She knew she was doing precisely what she was meant to do, yet she envied her friend his happiness and peace [313].

While Cha faces little institutionalized discrimination in her department, nonetheless the Thurlos sometimes call attention to her role as a female cop. Thus

> She glanced at Blalock, hoping he'd have the gentlemanly urge to spare her having to step into the bristly tangle. She wasn't about to mention she was allergic to tumbleweeds. It wasn't something a male cop would do. He'd razz her for being a wimp [*Bad Medicine* 78].

And

> Ella struggled to keep herself from shaking. She wouldn't come apart in front of the men. If they could handle it, so could she [*Bad Medicine* 235].

More prominent, though, are the personal and professional difficulties Cha faces in straddling the Navajo world and the Anglo world: "Among the *Dineh*, some saw her as too modern, a product more of the Anglo culture than her own. Although there had been a time when she would have taken that as a compliment, Ella didn't feel that way anymore" (*Bad Medicine* 40). Her alienation from her own people comes in large measure from her training and dedication to her profession: "Ella was a woman in male-dominated law-enforcement. It didn't help either that Ella had spent years off the rez in the FBI, and lost the trust of many she once knew" (*Bad Medicine* 33).

The Thurlos, like others who write about Native American cops, make much of tribal myths and mysticism. In the Ella Cha books they include plenty of talk about "skinwalkers," and Cha's brother is a respected shaman. Native American mysticism also has something to do with Cha's success as a cop. Here, with the FBI background, the writers have it both ways. First readers learn that Cha's success depends on her Anglo training:

> Some said she had supernatural powers, a legacy handed down through her family. But that was only because they didn't understand how a cop developed special instincts, or how well-honed her training had made her subconscious observations. At times such things could spell the difference between life and death [*Bad Medicine* 14].

But the Thurlos also link Cha's talents to Native American mysticism:

> "But your intuitions are more than that, and you know it," he said, and then raised his hands to stem her protests. "The problem with you is that you're too proud for your own good. You don't want to think that your intuitions are part of a gift, a special magic that you alone possess. You'd much rather think that's it's simply an intellectual process going on in your subconscious because you're smart, and highly trained in law enforcement" [*Bad Medicine* 52].

Robert Walker

Robert W. Walker (Geoffrey Caine) hopped on the Cornwell bandwagon with his Instinct books (starting with *Killer Instinct* in 1992) about Jessica Coran, an FBI medical examiner. In 1997 he moved over to Hillerman and added a Native American cop to his repertoire with his Edge books:

Cutting Edge (1997), *Double Edge* (1998), and *Cold Edge* (2001). The Edge books also acknowledge Ridley Pearson's Boldt/Matthews partnership by introducing Dr. Meredyth Singer, the Houston PD's in-house shrink, as the hero's confidant, partner, assistant, and maybe love interest.

Lucas Stonecoat, a Texas Cherokee, is the hero of Walker's Edge books. In them Walker provides Native American pictographs and explanatory captions as chapter headings. Stonecoat makes trips back to the reservation, and Walker makes short excursions into Native American religion. But Stonecoat is not a reservation cop like Hillerman's. Walker makes this clear in *Double Edge* when Stonecoat notes that "I was a cop, once, on the reservation. A man could starve. It's not glamorous, not like in a Tony Hillerman novel" (123). Instead Walker invents a past of urban police work for Stonecoat, first for the Dallas department and then for the Houston force. He, however, does not benefit from quotas. Instead, after leaving Dallas on medical disability, the authorities in Houston make him start as a cadet at the police academy. Walker makes much of Stonecoat's injury, giving him bad dreams about the police shoot-out and leaving him no recourse but to take refuge in a combination of peyote and LSD to rid himself of the pain. Walker draws Stonecoat as a dark and dangerous character, between worlds. Indeed, in *Double Edge* and *Cold Edge* he becomes connected with Roundpoint, a power in what amounts to the Indian Mafia. In Houston Stonecoat comes to be in charge of cold cases, but, as in the case of so many minority cops, the bosses also assign him to any case involving Indians: "Maybe I do, maybe I don't, but either way ... the assumption on their part is racially motivated. Pisses me off" (*Cold*, 23).

Walker gives Stonecoat a combination of skills and attitudes conventionally attached to Native Americans—"His Cherokee blood rising, he wanted to hunt down Freeleng and murder him tonight in retaliation for this" (*Cold* 137)—and the accoutrements of modern police work. Along with shrink Dr. Meredyth Singer, her assistant Randy the computer whiz is a continuing character in the novels. Beyond this forensic stuff, Stonecoat gets help from the occult: in *Double Edge* he brings in FBI agent and psychic Dr. Kim Faith Desinor who uses telepathy to connect with victims.

African Americans

Eleanor Taylor Bland

Eleanor Taylor Bland's Marti MacAlister books (*Dead Time* [1992]; *Slow Burn* [1993]; *Gone Quiet* [1994]; *Done Wrong* [1995]; *Keep Still* [1996]; *See No Evil* [1997]; *Tell No Tales* [1998]; *Scream in Silence* [1999]; and *Whis-*

pers in the Dark [2001]) focus on an African American woman police officer working in small-town Illinois. While Bland's hero is African American, she focuses the books more on domestic matters than on exclusively racial issues. Lincoln Prairie, Illinois has an integrated police force where family responsibilities and casual antifeminism present as much of a problem as racial prejudice. Thus in *Keep Still* one of MacAlister's chronic problems is missing her daughter's softball games because of the demands of her job. MacAlister has a supportive Polish American partner and she understands that the attitudes of many white folks come from ignorance rather than prejudice:

> The tall, slender, dark-haired officer stepped outside, leaving the door ajar. She gave Marti a blue-eyed stare. "It was like this when we got here. I've never seen anything like it. You'll have to explain it to me."
> Marti caught the implications. She was black, like the Hamiltons and most of the people inside. She wasn't offended—she didn't think Jensen had much social contact with African Americans [*Gone Quiet* 15].

MacAlister is the widow of a cop and a former Chicago cop herself, and Bland works in a number of cop novel conventions besides police in the family. Thus in *Gone Quiet* there's the bungling bureaucracy theme: halfway through the investigation the regular lieutenants are not there—one is sick and another at a conference—and an inexperienced but ambitious lieutenant comes in and almost ruins the investigation. Bland also nods at the growing interest in forensics by mentioning forensic entomology in *Keep Still*. Nonetheless, Bland focuses on the small town. One of the gratifications of small-town living for her police officer lies in the nature of its police work:

> In Chicago, I was always working a case someone else had been called out on and somebody was closing a case I had opened. Seeing them through from start to finish is a luxury I never expected here [*Keep Still* 44].

Small towns magnify the virtues and vices of communities, and communities, like families, are about protection and support. Thus Bland centers her books on MacAlister protecting and supporting children and families: *Dead Time, Keep Still,* and *See No Evil,* for instance, all focus on children. In *Gone Quiet* MacAlister's boss, Lieutenant Dirkowitz, makes the connection between police work and communities clear:

> I'm recommending you [for a commendation] because this is what policing is all about. Going into the community, treating its members with respect, exercising discretion and common sense. This is what we're paid to do, and frankly, if you receive recognition for this it'll send a message to the rest of the department [317].

Hugh Holton (1)

Hugh Holton is the only African American man to write fiction about cops in the 1990s. He presents his hero, Larry Cole, as an examplar. Cole is among Chicago's finest as a cop and reaps rewards for his abilities, ascending through the ranks both because he is a good cop and because he has the confidence of his colleagues. All of this, Holton tells readers, is based on hard work and education. And the reward for Cole's efforts is working in a mostly harmonious and genially integrated police community. But more on Holton and Larry Cole below.

Cassie West

In *Surprise* (1994), *Killing Kin* (2000), and *Killer Riches* (2001), Cassie West has it both ways. She has a hero who is both a D.C. cop and who can act like an amateur or private detective. It's because officer Leigh Ann Warren is never on duty in the books: in the first she's on vacation, in the second she's on leave because of a bum knee, and in the third she's retired. This spotty attendance permits West to have her hero mull over what it means to be a cop and whether to go back to the job.

What Leigh Ann Warren discovers is that whether she returns to duty or not, police work has affected the ways she behaves and continues to exert a strong pull on her. The behavior part comes in both the ways the hero notices her surroundings and in some automatic reactions — when, for instance, Warren is startled in *Sunrise*, she automatically reaches for where her baton would be were she in uniform. The commitment to police work, to be sure, is more complicated. On one hand West creates a pre-novel history for Warren: while finishing law school the hero fell in love with an undercover cop who was then killed in the line of duty. So one of Warren's motives in becoming a cop is in homage to her dead lover. And then West supplies the conventional, altruistic motivations to her hero. Warren tells her foster mother both that she "wanted to make a difference," and that she "wanted to help people." In *Sunrise*, however, none of these may be enough. Recuperating from a gunshot wound incurred in a justified but tragic shooting, Warren worked out her trauma by becoming a violent cop. Recoiling from this, she almost decides to quit until her purpose and self-confidence come back when she returns to her girlhood home and becomes centered once more with family and friends in a tiny African American community in North Carolina.

Paula Woods

Paula Woods' detective Charlotte Justice appears in *Inner City Blues* (1999) and *Stormy Weather* (2001). Woods devotes the first few pages of *Inner City Blues* to an occasionally hip-hop introduction of Justice and to profiling the racial issues of the Los Angeles Police Department. In her own words, then, there is the hero:

> Twelve years, eleven months, and fifteen days into living out my *Top Cop* fantasies — *Christie Love* with a better hairdo — my Nubian brothers down on Florence and Normandie had to go and pitch a serious bitch and mess up my cha-cha. Since May of '79, when I stood in the graduating class at the Police Academy, I had survived my years with the LAPD with little more than a few bruises, a shoulder prone to dislocation, and a couple of badly torn fingernails.
>
> Survived the early years in patrol cars with partners whose every joke began "There was a white man, a Mexican, and a nigg ... black man..." Survived my first assignment as a gang detective in Southwest, where I learned more about LA homeboys in the first three months than I had in three years of graduate study in criminology. And let me not forget the edu-mo-cation I got when I went over to South Bureau Homicide... [11].

The initial incident in *Inner City Blues* puts Justice back into uniform on riot duty. This provides Woods with the opportunity to present both pugnaciously racist cops and to comment on the dilemma of non-Anglo cops in the department:

> Although Chief Gates had proclaimed after the Rodney King beating that the LAPD saw no other color except blue, every black or brown-complexioned cop knew otherwise. It was part of their job, so went the thinking of some of our paler brothers in blue, to provide a running commentary on the race of every suspect we ran in....
>
> ...Women and minority officers knew that to protest the casual racism and sexism of our co-workers singled us out as difficult, opening the door to an even more rigorous dose of fun and games at our expense. If you complained to the Internal Affairs Department, it would automatically trigger an investigation and no one would work with you [16–17].

Justice observes and comments on racism, and throughout *Inner City Blues* endures sexist remarks and fends off the unwanted attentions of her sergeant without making an official complaint. And yet Justice stays on the job. Why? Woods makes a brief reference to the power of organizing and organizations: Justice is a member of "The Georgia Robinson Association... You know, the black female law-enforcement group. Named after the first black woman cop in the LAPD" (200). Part of it resides in the name Woods chooses for her hero and her compassion and efforts in behalf of victims' families. Part of it comes from intellectual satisfaction:

Imposing order on a crime scene, sifting through the evidence and statements to discover the hard kernel of truth, had become as natural to me as breathing and, over the years, just about as essential. It gave me a deep sense of satisfaction when I broke a case and made a bust, then calmly presented the long and sometimes intricate trail of evidence in court that helped put another criminal behind bars and gave the victims' families a sense of closure [37].

Later in the novel Justice calls policing "a mission…, a calling, a life if not of joy then a certain dry-eyed satisfaction that I could protect other families" (67). There is this, along with something else. Woods, like Katherine V. Forrest, possesses an acute interest in the history of the Los Angeles Police Department. She inserts paragraphs about Chiefs Parker and Gates and the evolution and devolution of the LAPD. And yet in spite of the past and present, Wood's Charlotte Justice both finds personal satisfaction in doing a job made more difficult by history, and comes to possess the traditional cop belief that the police force is not an organization but a family.

White Guys Writing About Black Guys

Robert Coram

Robert Coram, who is not African American, began writing books about the DEA. With *Running Dead* (1993) he switched to the Atlanta Police Department and kilt-wearing Scottish American detective Jeremiah Buie, who solves murders and thwarts an Arab plot to undermine the U.S. and Israel. Among the cops on Buie's team is an outrageously politically incorrect homicide detective who reveals that Atlanta police slang for African Americans is "Willies," in the same vein as the term "Jordans" used by the Hartford cops in Pearson's *Chain of Evidence*. In *Atlanta Heat* (1997) and *Dead South* (1999) Coram introduced an African American cop hero, C.R. Payne. Payne takes off from Major Vernon Worthy, Jeremiah Buie's friend in *Running Dead*. In Worthy, Coram presents a portrait of ability, drive, and discipline:

Those guys from Princeton had never heard of Morehouse College. They thought it was a toy school in Atlanta where blacks went just so they could say they had been to college.
  But he studied long into the nights, and in every class was graduated in the top one percent of students. To realize that with perseverance and application he could achieve more that white guys — to realize that not only was he intellectually as good, but in fact was intellectually superior to many white guys — was the greatest awakening of his life [196].

Coran extends this in C.R. Payne. He makes Henry Louis Gates Payne's hero:

You see something strange about a black cop in Atlanta who idolizes a Harvard egghead? Well, His Skipness says there are thirty-five million black people out there, which means there are thirty-five million ways to be black. I don't like these ideological bullies like Louis Farrakhan or Elijah Mohammad who say, "This is what you got to do if you are black." And all this back-to-Africa stuff and Afrocentric movement doesn't work in the real world. Who wants to go back to the Sudan and use goat piss for cologne? I'm for air-conditioning and tailored suits. I'm for what works in the real world. I'm for what Skip Gates represents [*Dead South* 5–6].

About police work, Coram makes some of the same points he had made in his earlier books, the chief of which is that homicide is the pinnacle of achievement in the department: "A homicide cop is the closest thing to Superman on the face of the planet" (*Dead South* 82). Payne attaches some of his success as a detective to his experience as an African American: "I have a gift. Maybe it is because so much interviewing is based on the involuntary eye movements of the person being interviewed and, as I said, we black people have a lot of experience at reading the eyes of white people" (*Dead South* 51). In *Dead South*, however, Coram plunges his hero into the intricacies of forensic detection. Payne tosses around terms like NLP (neuro-linguistic programming) and MSE (multiple select elimination). He also has the use of the army's state-of-the-art crime lab where they have machines for the "electrostatic lifting of evidence" (255) and a RUVIS machine (reflected ultraviolet light imaging system) (257). Underlying all of this Coram endues his hero with purpose:

> I see my job as biblical. I search out and bring to justice those angry and rancid souls who kill their fellow human beings. To take a life, to decide when a child, a mother a father, a friend, or even a stranger, should depart this mortal coil is to assume the role of God.
> God frowns on that.
> He won't get personally involved in balancing the scales, but He does provide guidance to his foot soldiers.
> I am one of God's foot soldiers [56–57].

James Patterson

James Patterson has written a series of serial killer thrillers with nursery rhyme titles featuring Washington, D.C., police detective Alex Cross, starting in 1992 with *Along Came a Spider*. In them Patterson makes a gesture toward the forensic book by making his hero a Ph.D. psychologist, a career that didn't work out in private practice:

> Jezzie asked about my early days as a psychologist in Washington. "It was mostly a bad mistake," I told her, without getting into how angry it made me,

still made me. "A whole lot of people didn't want any part of a black shrink. Too many black people couldn't afford one. There are no liberals on the psychiatrist's couch" [*Along Came* 113].

And so Cross becomes a cop. But the psychology stuff comes in handy in that Patterson builds the first book, along with *Cat and Mouse* (1997), around a *Silence of the Lambs*–type combat between Cross and Gary Soneji, a crazed criminal genius.

From the first, Cross is already a super cop; he's deputy chief of detectives ("the number-six or -seven person in the Washington Police Department" [*Along Came* 13]) and then divisional chief. As *Along Came a Spider* begins, Cross is head of the Special Investigator Team "made up of eight black officers supposedly slated for better things in the department" (*Along Came* 15). As Mayor Monroe puts it in *Along Came a Spider*,

> The main idea is to make sure that the strongest black men and women in the Metro police force rise to the top, as they should. Not just the ass kissers, Alex. That hasn't always happened in the past [*Along Came* 51].

But it's not just ability that Patterson puts into his cop hero. There's also the physical presence. Thus when speaking about himself and his partner, Cross says

> Sampson and I are both physical. We work out at the gym attached to St. Anthony's.... Together, we weigh about five hundred pounds. We can intimidate, if we want to. Sometimes it's necessary in our line of work. I'm only six three. John is six nine and growing [*Along Came* 15].

But Cross and Sampson have their softer side, too: they both regularly volunteer at one of the District's largest soup kitchens. Like Warren Adler, Patterson pays attention to the political tentacles unique to the Washington, D.C., force—the bosses and the mayor are forever interfering with Cross's cases. In particular they interfere with Cross's drive to call attention to African American crime and crime victims:

> A bizarre statistic was creating havoc with my stomach and central nervous system. There were now more than a hundred unsolved murders of young, inner-city women committed in just the past three years. No one had called for a major investigation. No one in power seemed to care about dead black and Hispanic girls [*Cat and Mouse* 11].

Patterson devotes passing attention to his hero as an African American man. Inclined to use celebrity similes (a character in *Along Came a Spider* looks like Harrison Ford), Patterson tells readers that "Even with all the wear and tear, Cross still looked good, impressive, a little like Muhammad Ali in his prime" (*Cat and Mouse* 16). And consistent with the beautiful people motif, Cross's love interest in *Cat and Mouse* looks like Whitney Houston

(89). In terms of background, Patterson goes for the bootstrap theory: as a youth Cross was taken in and raised by an English teacher, Nana, who remains a permanent member of his household once he's an adult. Indeed, in one of his exchanges with the mayor in *Along Came a Spider*, Cross notes that people with ability do not need affirmative action. Repeatedly Patterson makes the point that Cross is devoted to his children, devoted practically and emotionally, but especially in providing them with educations. Unlike some middle-class blacks, Cross lives in the city and devotes his energies to helping the poor and defenseless. Patterson occasionally adds touches of racism, such as the cross burning in *Along Came a Spider*, but in the main Cross's relationships with professionals from across the law enforcement community — FBI, Secret Service, etc.— seem devoid of racial awareness. There are a couple of occasions in the books when Patterson inserts bits of supposedly African American adages into Cross' language: "Cats are like Baptists... You know they raise hell, but you can't ever catch them at it" (*Cat and Mouse* 49).

Just as Patterson touches Cross's character with bits of a certain kind of African American experience, he also touches it with bits of police experience — brief inserts of passages that begin "In police work...." He also pays attention in each of the books to the stress that police work puts on family and relationships — threats to Cross's children shimmer in the background of many of the books. In the main, however, the chief ingredients in Patterson's hero come from thriller tradition. Alex Cross does whatever his conscience and circumstances drive him to do. In spite of being part of an organization, Cross invariably acts on his own; sometimes this is against the wishes of his bosses, and sometimes he simply acts like a free agent. The books are peripatetic; Cross (and sometimes Sampson) go wheeling from place to place, state to state, at a moment's notice — almost always without seeking permission or even putting in for travel vouchers. In *Along Came a Spider* Cross, albeit facetiously, brings up not the cop but the archetypal hero metaphor to describe his motivations: "That isn't how we do things at King Arthur's Round Table. I can't give up on this case" (398).

John Lescroart

John Lescroart mostly writes about lawyers, often featuring Dismis Hardy, a cop turned lawyer. Hardy makes a guest appearance in *A Certain Justice* (1995), but Lieutenant Abe Glitsky of San Francisco Homicide is the central character. Glitsky is, in his own words, half black and half white. And he's Jewish to boot. *A Certain Justice* presents San Francisco racked by racial rioting caused by the carjack killing of a white man and then the lynching of an African American. Lescroart draws a large-scale picture to document the polarization and politicization these events cause in the city. He introduces a mayor looking for a scapegoat, lawyers in the D.A.'s office confused about whom to charge and with what, a U.S. Senator, a militant African American politician, sinister FBI agents, the police chief and a young man wrongly accused of a hate crime. But most importantly he brings in cops doing their job. And chief among them is Abe Glitsky.

Lescroart uses Glitsky to make points about the racial politics of the police department. Here he takes on promotion exams and racial bias:

> He was referring to the test the city gave and which Glitsky had taken a year ago to determine eligibility for promotion to lieutenant. While the candidates had waited for months Locke had invited Glitsky up to his office and said he was going to use his pull to get him bumped to lieutenant even if he failed the test. He had gone on to explain that "people of color" were discriminated against by the testing process, that Glitsky was a good cop and deserved the promotion even if his grades didn't measure up.
>
> Glitsky had felt insulted by the assumption that he wouldn't pass (he got a ninety-seven, second highest among the candidates) [58].

Later in the novel Lescroart interrupts the action to insert an interview between Glitsky and a member of the city's Board of Supervisors:

> "You tell me about your department and I'll tell you what it needs."
> Glitsky ran it down — twelve inspectors, all male, of which four were African-American, two he thought were probably Spanish-surname.
> "You really ought to know that kind of thing for sure," Wrightson said. "It's in your best interest." Then "What about women?"
> "No. We don't have any women."
> "Oriental?"
> "No."
> "Gay?"
> "Doubt it, don't really know. Does this stuff matter?"
> "Native American?"
> "I didn't realize we had an appreciable percentage of the city and county that was Native American."
> Wrightson gave a conspiratorial grimace. "You're going to be in good shape. You'll need at least five new inspectors."
> Glitsky sat forward. "Mr. Wrightson, we don't need more inspectors. We need more support."
> "Yeah, but you won't get support, Lieutenant. What you need is to get closer to compliance" [350–51].

While Lescroart portrays Glitsky as black, he also repeatedly makes the point that his race does not define him. Thus, "I don't think about my color all the time, about where we're going as a people ... it's more everybody, the world..." (221). Glitsky defines himself by his family — his memories of his wife, recently dead from ovarian cancer, his three sons, and his father—but mostly by his role as a cop: "he was still mostly a street cop in his heart—a protector of victims, a collector of evidence" (59). Indeed, among all of the politicians and lawyers, Glitsky alone advocates the impartial and objective consideration of evidence and observance of the law: "the whole issue [was] ... due process and ... once you started screwing with that you compromised the whole idea of keeping the law, which was his passion and his job" (160). Thus Lescroart shows Glitsky and his squad carefully and patiently doing the routine work of collecting evidence. With Glitsky and one of the other African American members of his squad, Ridley Banks, Lescroart brings in the separateness of cops from issues of race and thereby advocates the often-heard maxim that among cops there is no black or white, only blue.

Lesbians and Gays

Katherine V. Forrest

Katherine V. Forrest is the pioneer lesbian cop writer. Eight of her novels (*Amateur City* [1984]; *Murder at the Nightwood Bar* [1987]; *The Beverly Malibu* [1989]; *Murder by Tradition* [1991]; *Flashpoints* [1994]; *Liberty Square* [1996]; *Apparition Alley* [1997]; and *Sleeping Bones* [1999]) center on Detective Kate Delafield of the Los Angeles Police Department. In Forrest's created history for her hero, Delafield came to the LAPD after serving in Vietnam in the marines:

> Growing up she had been taller and stronger, more aggressive than the other girls; in look and manner, hopelessly unfeminine by their standards. Among similarly uniformed women in the Marine Corps, she had been resented for her unusual physical strength and command presence. She had been the woman reluctantly singled out in her division of the Los Angeles Police Department for one advancement after another as LAPD, in stubborn fighting retreat, gradually succumbed to increasing pressures for change [*Amateur City* 25].

In later novels Forrest makes clear the exact nature of the LAPD retreat on obeying the laws on equal employment and affirmative action:

> She had heard all the stories during the tumultuous and disastrous years when Daryl Gates was chief of police, about Men Against Women, and the West L.A. Division was the last place where any woman officer wanted to be because of the officers who had bonded together in the overt and covert opposition to women [*Apparition Alley* 61–62].

While Delafield acknowledges that her job and her advancements came about because of outside pressure on the department, she also demonstrates devotion to the precision demanded by police work: "A Kate Delafield investigation was solid, meticulous, documented, a logical tapestry of fact — no sloppiness, no loose ends, no nasty surprises to ambush a district attorney" (*Amateur City* 9). Indeed, in *Amateur City* Forrest bases her hero's calling to police work as being rooted in the need for order and precision, both in this passage and in the invented history of Delafield dropping out of law school in order to help stamp out police incompetence and sheer stupidity and bring well wrought cases to trial. This is even more evident by the time of *Apparition Alley*, where Forrest connects O.J. to a departmental history of sloppiness: "The rank incompetence of the LAPD lab had been common knowledge long before the Simpson trial had exposed it to public pillory" (53).

Forrest's books span some of the most chaotic and tumultuous years in the history of the Los Angeles Police Department. This is especially true with regard to lesbians and gays. In 1984 with *Amateur City* Forrest depicts an unwritten "don't ask, don't tell" policy toward gays and lesbians. Thus Delafield tells her new lover in *Amateur City*:

> I've never pretended to be a heterosexual. But I've never made any announce-
> ments either, and never will. Why give anyone a weapon? And it is a weapon.
> I'll give you one possible scenario: Avowed lesbian denies accusation of mak-
> ing sexual advances to female prisoner [180].

In the 1990s, however, things changed: "police officers had come out of the closet in the five years since three lesbians and one gay man had so memorably followed Sergeant Mitchell Grobeson onto center stage at 1991's gay pride festival" (63). From beginning to end, however, the problematic and difficult position of gays and lesbians in the police force does not, for Forrest, extinguish the reality of solidarity among cops. In *Amateur City* Delafield's male partner is crude and racist. Nonetheless, she admits that he can be a good cop and she feels his sympathy after she has had a shattering personal experience. And it's not just Taylor:

> Some of the men Kate worked with, with who she had never and would never
> discuss her private life, had shown similar concern over the past months.
> Through her coating of numbness she had felt their reaching out to her in a
> common humanity — awkward expressions of caring from men who had seen
> every kind of grisly horror and had layered themselves with deep protective
> coats of cynicism [63].

By the time of *Apparition Alley* Forrest both repeats this theme and gives it a metaphor to replace the conventional "brotherhood":

> She was lifted onto a stretcher. Carried downstairs, blue uniforms and sym-
> pathetic faces all around her, lining the entire path, some of them calling
> encouragement. Outside, the dark, cold street had become brilliant with flash-

ing light bars on black-and-whites, and was filled as far as she could see with blue uniforms. My God, my whole family's here, she thought, tears leaking from her eyes. My whole police family is here [5].

Linda Silva

Ex-cop Linda Kay Silva (www.risingtidepress.com) has written six novels about Delta "Storm" Stevens (*Taken by Storm* [1991]; *Storm Shelter* [1993]; *Weathering the Storm* [1994]; *Storm Front* [1995]; *Tropical Storm* [1997]; and *Storm Rising* [2000]). In the dedication to *Tropical Storm* Silva cites Katherine V. Forrest: "Katherine V.— for your quiet wisdom and path forging ways." She centers her novels on a group of women, mainly on Delta and Connie, who are both cops ("Connie and Delta, Delta and Connie; the two were as inseparable as butter and toast, and when it came to solving hard-to-crack crimes, they had no equal" [*Tropical* 6]), Megan, an ex-hooker who is redeemed by Delta and becomes her lover, and a couple of other women. A lot of the books' attention is upon Silva's depiction of the relationship between these women. Nonetheless, she makes being a police officer part of their makeup as well. Silva focuses the virtues of police character on Delta. Being a cop serves as a demonstration of competence: "What I am ... is a cop, a highly trained professional capable of taking care of herself and those around me" (*Tropical* 56). Silva also uses being a cop as a metaphor for courage:

> I go up against the unknown every day of my life. I run down dark alleys after people who would love to see me dead. I've been trapped in burning buildings, not knowing whether or not I would ever get out alive. Handling the unknown is what I get paid to do. It's my job [*Tropical* 60].

Police work, moreover, also combines courage and responsibility. It means taking care or and caring for the helpless and dispossessed.

Kate Allen

In *Tell Me What You Like* (1993) Kate Allen alludes to the fact that lesbian mystery stories exist as a category of fiction, and she makes a number of references to Katherine V. Forrest's lesbian police officer Kate Delafield. Allen's hero, Alison Kaine, like Delafield, is a lesbian. She's not a detective, but a patrol officer, and she works in Denver, not California. For most of *Tell Me What You Like* Kaine is on vacation and, consequently, fills the role of amateur or private investigator instead of a police officer. Indeed, in the small part of the action when she is in uniform the hero is relatively inept. While the focus of the plot of *Tell Me What You Like* is on the murder of lesbians, the substance of the book deals with Kaine's relationships with other women and her fascination with sadomasochistic sex. Insofar as the novel deals with police concerns, Allen briefly mentions Detective Jorgenson's well-known homophobia, and that part of the impetus for Kaine's private investigations in the novel rests on her realization that people in the lesbian community will reveal facts to her that they would withhold from straight police officers. Indeed, in *Tell Me What You Like* Allen lets readers assume that prejudice rules the Denver Police Department only to undercut this at the end of the book. Thus when Kaine's sergeant calls her into the station to explain her extracurricular investigations he upsets her expectations:

> "Yes," she said, and almost blurted out the fact that she'd found a new lover, just on the chance that it would startle him enough to save her from the lecture — and she hoped that was all it was going to be — that he was going to deliver. But he was no Jorgenson. He would just lift a polite eyebrow to inquire why she was telling him her personal life [178].

He also notes matter of factly that Kaine is not the only lesbian in the Denver Police Department.

Laurie King

In *A Grave Talent* (1993) Laurie King introduces San Francisco police detective Kate Martinelli. King also uses Martinelli in *With Child* (1996), and *To Play the Fool* (1995). In the first novel King initially emphasizes Martinelli's position as a female cop. She recognizes, with some irony, that she is a beneficiary of affirmative action hiring brought about by the police department's dread of complaints from "minority" groups:

> It amused her to think that she counted as a minority, advanced prematurely (but only to a degree) due to unexpected vacancies and one of those periodic departmental rumblings of concern over Image, Minorities, and the dread Women's Movement [12].

Working the crime scene of a murdered child in *A Grave Talent*, Martinelli's impulse is to try to touch and somehow soothe the victim. And although she assumes greater authority and independence as the novel progesses, in *A Grave Talent* Martinelli plays a supporting role to the lead detective, Alonzo Hawkin.

In her construction of *A Grave Talent* King makes the point that a police officer's private life is irrelevant and has no connection to his or her performance on the job. By giving Martinelli's partner an androgynous name she masks the hero's sexuality for the first half of the novel. Even when Hawkin concludes that Martinelli is a lesbian — he is a detective after all — he makes it clear that private lives have no bearing on how one performs as a cop. At the same time, however, Martinelli recognizes the opprobrium attached to lesbians and especially lesbian cops:

> I can't take the risk. I'm a cop, Lee. A woman cop. If we came out how long do you suppose it'd be before the papers managed to let slip the juicy tidbit that Officer K.C. Martinelli is one of the leather brigade? How long before the looks and remarks start, before I start drawing the real hard-core shit jobs, before I'm on call and someone refuses to deal with me because I'm the lez in the department and I might have AIDS? How long before some mama flips out when I try to ask her daughter some questions about the bastard that's raped her. Because mama doesn't want that dyke cop feeling up her daughter? [243].

At the end of the novel, however, in part because of the wounding of her life partner, Martinelli comes out of the closet and takes on a new role in the department. Hawkin tells her that

> There is, after all, a certain amount of renown attached to a female police officer who forces her superiors to give her an extended leave in order to nurse her wounded lover, lesbian variety, and who furthermore makes noises that the departmental insurance policy should be made to include what might be termed unofficial spouses [334].

And Martinelli laughingly accepts that "now I'm the department's representative to the chains-and-leather dyke brigade" (334), with the acknowledgement of "only in San Francisco."

Penny Micklebury

Katherine V. Forrest is listed as the editor on the publication information page of Penny Micklebury's *Keeping Secrets* (1994). Micklebury, an African American reporter for newspapers and television in Washington, D.C., writes about Lieutenant Gianna Maglione of the Hate Crimes Unit of the Washington, D.C., Police Department. In *Keeping Secrets* she follows the parallel investigations of Maglione and her African American newspaper reporter lover, Mimi Patterson, into a series of murders of gay and lesbian victims. Micklebury begins by pointing out that moving the department to target hate crimes was due exclusively to Maglione's efforts:

> She relived the year of persuading and arguing and arm-twisting required to convince the bureaucracy of the need for a special unit within the Department to investigate only those crimes committed against persons or groups based on their race, color, or sexual preference [5].

Hate crimes make her angry, and that anger drives both Maglione and her squad. She chooses her sergeant, "not only because he was her friend, or even because he was a good cop, but because his anger complimented hers and between the two of them they got things done" (25). But it's not just anger, with Maglione it's focus:

> a change overtook her that startled Mimi until she realized that it was the Lieu-tenant Maglione persona: the utter stillness, the intensity of her gaze, the low, controlled tones of her voice [89].

In addition to her dedication to the cause of investigating hate crimes, Micklebury portrays Maglione as a proletarian cop. The daughter of a cop killed in the line of duty,

> She spoke to every cop and ambulance attendant she passed, and lifted a hand in greeting to those out of speaking range. She always did that. Acknowledg-ing the existence of colleagues was a seemingly small thing, but one often ignored by officers of her rank once they'd made it to the top. But she'd always been different. She didn't kowtow to top brass and she didn't shit on the under-lings. She treated everybody the same and for that reason everybody liked her [7].

This extends to her openness in the creation of her squad where sexuality, religion, and politics are discussed openly. Ironically, Maglione herself can-not be open about her sexuality:

> I wouldn't have this job if the entire police department knew about me. Ironic and stupid as it is, there wouldn't be a Hate Crimes Unit if the people on the City Council who had to approve the money knew I was a lesbian [93].

While Micklebury makes points about staying in or coming out of the closet with Maglione and Patterson, she also focuses on their dedication to their respective professions and the price they have had to pay for their absolute absorption in their jobs — until the end of the novel when both realize their importance to one another.

Mark Zubro

While a number of writers introduce lesbian police officers, few police writers acknowledge the presence of gays on the force. In several of his Spencer novels Robert B. Parker uses a gay cop as a minor character, there's Jonathan Kellerman's Milo, Thomas Adcock's *Devil's Heaven* (1995) intro-duces a gay cop playing a minor role, and a gay police officer plays a role in R.J. Hamilton's *Who Framed Lorenzo Garcia?* (1995). Mark Zubro, however, stands as the only example of a writer to focus on a gay cop with his series of books about Chicago detective Paul Turner: *Sorry Now?* (1992); *Political Poison* (1993); *Another Dead Teenager* (1995); *The Truth Can Get You Killed* (1997); *Drop Dead* (2000); and *Sex and Murder.com* (2001).

In *Sorry Now?* Zubro depicts Turner as an average, middle-class man who works as a cop and who happens to be gay. Widowed, Turner raises his two sons in a close-knit neighborhood. Both neighbors and his sons try to fix him up with men they believe would be compatible. Zubro, however, makes the point that like other hardworking middle-class parents, Turner has little time and often little energy to date:

> Turner felt: If it happened, fine. He'd dated some nice guys over the years, but none seriously for a long while. He wouldn't go out of his way, but he wouldn't reject somebody interesting out of hand. He had two boys to rear and a hectic job. Enough for anyone [62].

In *Sorry Now?* Turner comes into contact with a homophobic evangelist politician on one hand and militant gay groups on the other, one side harping on sin and the other using guerilla tactics to force society to acknowledge gays and gay rights. Turner defines himself as a cop, explaining occasionally to militant and hostile gays that some of the difficulties they have with the police are self-inflicted.

Zubro depicts almost no homophobia in the Chicago Police Department. Turner's partner accepts and respects him, as does his boss:

> The commander, a tall black man, sat on the corner of Fenwick's desk nearest the coffee machine. Turner liked the guy. He spent a lot of time boosting the egos of men and women who usually met only the dregs of society at their worst. Cops face burnout, discouragement at the monumentality of their task, and awareness of the futility of their jobs. They can't eradicate crime and stupidity, but spend eight hours every day trying to do just that. The commander worked as many hours as the detectives, kept out of their way, and respected their professionalism [80].

Here Zubro acknowledges the stress of the job. He also recognizes the hostility and its attendant isolation cops feel. While he does not emphasize the brotherhood theme so present in police novels, he does show the department's care for its own as a complement to his hero's care for his family.

Real Cops

In the 1990s more police officers or ex-police officers published cop books than ever before. They come from all over the country — from Seattle to New York to Miami to Dallas. Most of them write about detectives, but along with the detectives come a beat cop and an auto-theft squad. Dan Mahoney is a traditional cop bar storyteller, and his thrillers look back to Caunitz's in the eighties. Terry Marlow looks back to McBain, and Marshall Frank intended his book as an exposé. There are reverberations of the Knapp Commission in a few of the cops' books. But some of the new cop writers try out different kinds of plots, from the Gothic to the romance.

Michael Grant

Post-traumatic stress characterizes retired NYPD cop Michael Grant's *Line of Duty* (1991). Like other ex-cop writers Grant details the stress caused by the job and the times, but he also shows, decades after the front-page stories, the lasting impact of the NYPD response to the findings of the Knapp Commission.

Grant includes all of the conventional police motifs. His characters harden themselves to the ugly facts they encounter in their work:

> over the twenty-three years he'd been on the force, he'd sunk deeper and deeper into the cesspool of crime and violence. Day after day he'd seen people steal, cheat, and kill ... and he'd become numbed to it; he'd lost his capacity to be shocked, to be indignant at the subhuman behavior around him. Worse, he'd come to expect it. To shield himself from these daily horrors, he'd carefully erected a shell, and it was effective — too effective, because it also isolated him from Eileen and Kathy [his wife and daughter] [183].

This leaves Grant's characters with the closing and closed society of cops:

> cops retreated and stayed among their own kind.... To his dismay, a rookie soon found he had little in common with his old friends. It was hard to relate to someone who complained about having a hard day at the office when that same day you'd found a decaying body at the bottom of an air shaft. And so cops socialized together, and in the process became more and more isolated from the rest of society [138].

Grant's cops, moreover, work in a department under siege. They confront an enemy more well armed than they are: "Many of these gangs were better equipped than some NATO countries. They were certainly better equipped than the New York City Police Department, which only recently had begun to arm narc assault teams with automatic weapons" (83). They see the Supreme Count's protections of individual's rights as directed against the police and not the criminal. And they comment on the way things used to be:

> "Damn, how did they ever catch anyone in the old days?"
> "It was easy.... They didn't have computers to drown them in useless information."
> "Yeah, and they had investigative tools not available to us," Rose said.
> "Like what?"...
> Rose smiled slyly. "They could beat the shit out of a suspect until he told them what they wanted to know" [117].

Grant chooses to emphasize some of the mundane shoddiness of life in the NYPD. This extends from police stations:

> The atmosphere in a police department facility can be depressing enough in
> the daytime, but at night, without the distraction of ringing telephones, click-
> ing typewriters, and constant chatter, the shabbiness of the surroundings is even
> more glaring. The ubiquitous bile-green paint, broken window shades, and
> cheap metal furniture did nothing to alleviate the sense of squalor [248].

to the beaten up cars the city provides, to the inefficiency of the police com-
munication system:

> Because of the great number of radio transmissions bouncing around the city's
> air, it was not unusual to pick up telephone conversations, taxi dispatchers,
> and an occasional police broadcast from Ohio, but not the transmission of
> your partner down the street [327].

Along with these bits of realism, of deconstructing the image of the police
as efficient and even heroic, Grant, atypically, admits that police work, especially detective work, requires no special attributes: "Give me a break! Being
a detective is nothing more than common sense, intelligence, and reasonable powers of observation" (*Line of Duty* 118).

Line of Duty, as well as Grant's next book, *Officer Down* (1993), is about
drugs and bad cops. He uses drug lords, drug money, and their power to
corrupt police officers as the basis for both books. In this there are reverberations from the Knapp Commission and its aftermath. Grant refers to
the Knapp-inspired edict forbidding patrol officers from making drug arrests.
He notes the complexities caused by opening up the police department to
public scrutiny: "In the past Tiny had indeed filed complaints. He'd learned
it was a sure way to jam up a cop, and it was ridiculously easy. All he had
to do was to walk into any police station in the city" (*Officer Down* 4). And
he concentrates on internal affairs. Here Grant directly connects his characters' feelings about impeaching their fellow officers with the Knapp Commission by specifically mentioning the names of the cops involved in Knapp
testimony:

> To a policeman, the lowest scum of the earth is a cop who gives evidence
> against brother officers. Names like Phillips, Leuci, and Winter were all spo-
> ken with bitterness in station-house locker rooms [*Officer Down* 191].

Although he makes tough street-wise cops the heroes of *In the Line of
Duty* and *Officer Down*, Grant nevertheless portrays Alex Rose in the first
novel as an honorable and heroic IAD cop. And in both of these novels
Grant bases his plotting on the small group of cops who conduct secret inves-
tigations into the actions of criminal cops. *Officer Down*, however, moves to
the edge of the cop novel in that it takes not only the NYPD but also the
FBI and the DEA to defeat the conspiracy of evil. And in his next book,
Retribution (1995), Grant moves out of the cop book and into the world of

the thriller with an ex–SWAT team hero coping with a crazed ex–Special Forces killer.

Terry Marlow

Dallas cop Terry Marlow wrote *Target Blue* (1991) and *Dallas Police* (1993). With *Target Blue* Marlow brings the McBain formula into the 1990s. In the novel he presents multiple plot threads involving the activities of Mexican American, Jamaican, and biker drug gangs. He also includes an internal affairs investigation of a corrupted female officer and the rigors of a woman officer working undercover in a nudie bar. As McBain unifies his pieces of plot with his focus on the personnel of the 87th Precinct, Marlow brings his plots together by focusing on one unit of the Dallas police force. Uniquely, he does not choose one of the "elite" units conventionally used in cop novels — homicide, crimes against person, internal affairs, etc. Marlow makes heroes out of the auto theft unit of the Dallas PD, the "Junkyard Dogs," a proletarian group led by Sergeant "Wild Bill" Clark and consisting of "Boots" Hamaker, "Smoky" Tunnell, "Nacho" Hernandez, "Wheels" Winger, and "Crash" Kopeck. When Marlow introduces the group they are all "scratching their butts and cutting up" (8). With them Marlow emphasizes efficiency, dedication, and good-natured camaraderie. Indeed, one of the most prominent themes of *Target Blue* resides in the brotherhood of cops. Marlow illustrates this most emphatically in an episode in which Jamaican drug pushers ambush two patrol officers; the Jamaicans cannot understand why one of the officers died trying to pull the other officer to safety.

Countering the heroic and hard-working cops, Marlow brings in a new regulation-bound lieutenant whose doctrinaire approach to police duties impedes real police work. He also provides a running battle between the chief of police and the city manager. Vexed issues between the chief and the politicians all come down to money, but in their confrontations other issues connect to finances — the public perception of police efficiency, the calculation of accurate crime statistics versus fudged ones, and the specter of a police union and collective bargaining. Marlow presents Chief Knecht as the model leader. Knecht both serves as an advocate for his officers and stands as one of the few enlightened top-level bosses in cop books. He notes, to himself, "with pride that there were ladies in his command staff, three captains and a deputy chief. Blacks and Hispanics, too. They had come a long way" (248). At the end of *Target Blue* Knecht orders that semiautomatic pistols be issued to all Dallas cops as well as body armor, but he also concludes that "Sharp minds and strong hearts keep cops alive" (249).

Enes Smith

In the early 1990s Madras, Oregon, police chief Enes Smith wrote two novels, *Fatal Flowers* (1992) and *Dear Departed* (1994). They are both serial killer books in which Smith subjugates the character and the role of the police officer to the disturbing psychology of the killers and the panic and near panic the killers' actions impose upon the characters. Splitting the narrative between killer with his victim and cops with pinches of had-I-but-known thrown in, in *Fatal Flowers* Smith brings in a variety of heroic cops whose human side he notes. The principal hero, Patrick Meredith, is an ex–Seattle cop, partially disabled while saving lives at a robbery. Now working for the Feds, Meredith chases around the country worrying about serial killers and about his adopted son. Smith also introduces an aging backwoods Oregonian sheriff, competent, politically savvy, but openly frightened for his constituents when learning of a killer in their region. Then there is the dedicated and observant Phoenix cop with whom the investigation begins:

> Patterson was fifty, and it didn't bother him as much as he thought it would. His middle-age paunch didn't really bother him either. He had decided last year that he wasn't going to grow any taller than 5'6"'. His hair was gray, and that didn't cause him much grief. In fact, he had come to terms with just about everything in his life except his receding hairline [26].

In *Dear Departed* Smith chooses a different thriller formula, the one that joins victim, hunter, and hunted in one character. That character is Natalie Collins, a Portland cop. A second-generation cop, Smith makes Collins a Jamie Lee Curtis look-alike: "You ever see her in *Blue Steel* or *True Lies*?" (43). Before the hunting and chasing begins in *Dear Departed*, Smith introduces a conventional cast of cop characters. There are the members of Collins' homicide squad, from her grizzled mentor to the rookie; there are sinister and pig-headed internal affairs cops; and there is a chief, "a strong one, a chief whose leadership had brought an end to years of turmoil and lack of direction" (40). Most importantly, Collins defines herself as a cop:

> I'm a cop, a homicide detective, and a damned good one. Oh, there are plenty of officers who look better in uniform than I do. Loads of them can give better speeches to the City Club or the Rotarians. And a lot of them have more experience than I do. But if you have a loved one killed, hurt or missing, and you want to find the person responsible or want to find out who's lying — if you want to find out who fucked with your life — I'm as good as anyone [37].

But then, with much of the department against her, she goes off with a mysterious stranger to fight dark forces on her own.

Dan Mahoney

Dan Mahoney moved from telling stories in cop bars to telling them in print in 1993 with *Detective First Grade*, followed by *The Edge of the City* (1995); *Hyde* (1997); *Once In Never Out* (1998); *Black and White* (1999); *The Two Chinatowns* (2001); and *Gibraltar* (2002). Mahoney likes terrorist and serial killer plots — *Hyde* and *Black and White* are serial killer books and most of the others bring in terrorists of one stripe or another, Irish terrorists in *Once In Never Out*, Peruvian terrorists in *Detective First Grade*, and other Latin American terrorists in *The Edge of the City*. Mahoney and his characters like to travel. While all of the books have New York roots, they also feature out-of-town excursions — to Ireland, to Singapore, to Toronto. Part of this is exotic, thriller stuff, part is clash-of-culture cop novel stuff, and part reads like it may be tax write-off travel. Mahoney's characters have a large dose of action hero about them, but they are rooted in the NYPD.

Brian McKenna is Mahoney's major continuing character, featured in all of the novels until *Two Chinatowns*, where Cisco Sanchez replaces him. McKenna is a cowboy, a loose cannon, a thorn in the side of the bureaucrats, but he's also a scourge of evil. He likes action, a fact that Mahoney underlines when he introduces him in the first novel:

> McKenna was bored and began feeling sorry for himself again. Seven-One Detective Squad. Certainly not very glamorous, the main mission being keeping the Hasidic Jews and the Blacks from killing each other or burning each other out.... Not much to smile about. And nobody to blame except myself for this current state of affairs. Myself and those jerks in the FBI. They don't appreciate anybody doing the "right thing" when it conflicts with their plans [*First Grade* 1].

Mahoney centers McKenna on action, jumping out of cars, chasing villains, engaging in shootouts. He's a predator: "Although McKenna and this man had never seen each other before, they recognized each other. The hunter was about to become the hunted. They both knew their roles and began formulating their plans. The game had begun" (*First Grade* 6).

Mahoney also adds details that make McKenna a cop. Of course there's the battle with bureaucracy about doing the right thing instead of the correct thing. On the personal level, in the first novel McKenna's future wife hates his job and wants him to quit, and Mahoney also explains that his hero has had a brush with alcoholism, the occupational disease of cops:

> Ray Burdette and Brian McKenna had first met years ago, when things had been different in the police department. Then drinking was tolerated much more than it was now. The officers routinely pulled drunken stunts both on and off duty that would certainly have gotten them fired today; though there was a limit, you didn't get fired for drinking. You recovered [*First Grade* 47].

The most prominent, defining element in McKenna's character, however, lies in the issues of law and justice. Mahoney is one of the first writers to highlight the fact that cops have rights, especially the right to counsel in departmental hearings. When it comes to criminals, however, Mahoney's characters have problems. They are rooted in the conventional complaint about the courts:

> Conviction of a guilty person who chose to fight a charge had become improbable if the police officer played strictly by the United States Supreme Court's rules, and impossible under the even more restrictive rules of evidence prescribed by the New York State Court of Appeals. McKenna reasoned that if a person committed a crime, if the police went to the trouble of investigating it and were able to arrest the person who committed the crime, and if the state went through the expense of prosecuting the person, then this accused person should not be acquitted by the New York State Court of Appeals [*First Grade* 113].

In order to make the courts work Mahoney has McKenna admit that he lies to make arrests and get convictions, a motif in cop books going back to Wambaugh. In the clash-of-cultures books, McKenna comes in contact with cops from Iceland, Ireland, and Singapore, each of whom displays a different kind of police work and different system of justice. As with lying, McKenna views his role as manipulating the system so as to achieve justice. The most prominent example of this occurs in *Black and White*, where the detectives manipulate jurisdictions to ensure that the criminals will be tried in a place where the death penalty exists in statutes. There are some cases, however, in which the cops can achieve swift justice. Thus plots like that of *Detective First Grade* end with shootouts in which the bad guys receive swift and permanent justice in a hail of bullets. The justification for all of this comes from McKenna's belief, expressed in *Once In Never Out* that "We work for God" (102).

Ed Dee

When he retired from the NYPD Ed Dee took himself to Arizona and earned an MFA at Arizona State. He did the Sun Devils proud. In 1994 Dee published *14 Peck Slip*, followed by *Bronx Angel* (1995), *Little Boy Blue* (1997), and *Nightbird* (1999). Of all police writers, Dee is the most literary, reflected in the fact that the *New York Times* chose *14 Peck Slip* as a Notable Book of the Year.

Dee includes most of the conventional cop themes in his books, touching politics and bureaucracy, the blue brotherhood, corruption, brutality, boredom and alcoholism, etc. The theme that comes in most often, however, is nostalgia. There's nostalgia about old personnel policies and the way cops used to be:

> When we first came on the job, we had cops fifty and sixty years old working in uniform, around the clock. Guys with military service and 'boo coo' experience. Taught you how to analyze a situation with common sense. Treat people with respect [*Nightbird* 163].

> The job should never have lowered the standards.... We got criminals, junkies, on the job. People can't read, women can't do one push-up [*Bronx Angel* 253].

And there's nostalgia about police stations — what they used to look like and what they used to mean:

> The One Thirteen, a two story modern tan brick structure, lacked the character of the old station houses. It could just as easily been a board of ed payroll office or the borough sanitation HQ. A large banner stretched across the front entrance said "Welcome" [*Little Boy Blue* 37].

> What I missed most from the old station houses was the raised desk. The sacred desk, high in the air, protected by an ornate brass rail you approached only when absolutely necessary ... it wasn't about fear, it was about respect. Now the desk is at eye level, anyone and everyone running behind it. Mass confusion. Gregory says that now the station house is like a campus at some pinko liberal arts school [*Bronx Angel* 92].

Nostalgia, to be sure, belongs in books narrated by a decidedly middle-aged cop and focusing on his life and that of his partner, Joe Gregory.

"The Great" Gregory is a larger-than-life glad-handing dypsomaniacal bullshit artist. A second generation Irish cop, Gregory seemingly knows everyone on the force and knows how to work the game of accumulating and using favors. In *Bronx Angel* he campaigns for and is elected president of the Emerald Society, the Irish cops' benevolent association. In fraternal and political matters Gregory displays a cavalier swashbuckling nature. In police matters, more often than not, he screws up. When first on the job he smacked himself in the testicles with his own nightstick while chasing a criminal. In *14 Peck Slip* Dee invents for him several other embarrassing episodes. One is a well-publicized discovery of Jimmy Hoffa's body that turns out to be dog bones, and another is a day-long stakeout of a mob meeting that takes place somewhere else. But Gregory's boldness and panache don't always lead him to disaster. They sometimes lead to the right action and the right person. For that, however, Gregory needs Anthony Ryan.

Dee's hero and the narrator of the novels is Anthony Ryan. In *14 Peck Slip* Ryan describes his background:

> My father drove the Broadway bus to Dyckman Street until he took his city pension and barmaid girlfriend to West Palm Beach. My mother, the only child

of Italian-speaking parents, was a high school English teacher who died never understanding the Irish or why I became a cop. I went to high school having read Hemingway and Fitzgerald; earned an MA in American lit. in night school, pushed by her firm, warm hand. But I was also the son of my father. I'd kept a pint of Jameson and a yellowed copy of Spillane's *I the Jury* behind the water heater in the basement [9].

Rather than Spillane's brand of heroism or justice, police work for Ryan includes compassion and duty and wonder:

Joe Gregory says that being a cop in this city is like having a front row seat to the greatest show on earth. At times like this I wondered if I could really give up my seat [18].

Having almost put in his twenty years by the time of the first novel, Ryan is decidedly middle aged. He has faced alcoholism and the nest left empty by his children. But he does have Joe Gregory and he has Leigh, his wife. In fact these two occupy almost equal parts in Ryan's thoughts. With Leigh it's the brief times Ryan actually shares with her at home, but on the job her judgments also provide a recurring way for him to explain people and events:

My wife says only cops and psychos stare shamelessly at people [*14 Peck Slip* 23].

My wife says two guys from New York will keep bumping into each other even if they're walking across an empty football field [*14 Peck Slip* 42].

In his partnership with Joe Gregory, Ryan supplies the details. On the job Ryan does the paperwork and looks at details too mundane or bothersome for Gregory to recognize — details of fact and especially details that lead to a compassionate view of victims. Indeed, Dee's books all have something to do with families, either Ryan's family, which appears regularly throughout the series, or Gregory's family, which stands at the center of *14 Peck Slip* and *Little Boy Blue*.

Hugh Holton (2)

Police lieutenant Hugh Holton learned the trade and then hung out with the Chicago mob of crime writers, a group that includes cop writers Barbara D'Amato and Paul Zubro. Before his death in 2002 he published nine novels: *Presumed Dead* (1994); *Windy City* (1995); *Chicago Blues* (1996); *Violent Crimes* (1997); *Red Lightning* (1998); *The Left Hand of God* (1999); *The Time of the Assassins* (2000); *The Devil's Shadow* (2001); and *Criminal Element* (2002).

Holton draws a few sleazebag cops. In *Criminal Element* there's Detective Joe Donegan and in *Windy City* there's Dick Shelby:

No one had ever accused Dick Shelby of being a good detective. Many barely saw him as adequate. He lacked instinct and was totally inept at conducting investigations. Some detectives were born with instinct and most acquired it after years of fieldwork; every detective had to work on the ability to conduct thorough investigations. Shelby lacked both, yet managed to survive and even prosper in a highly competitive field. The reason? Dick Shelby was a ruthless bastard [21].

Significantly, Holton leaves Shelby's name out of the cast of characters included before the start of *Windy City*. Most of his cops he draws as paragons. There's Lieutenant Cosmo "Blackie" Silvestri:

Blackie lived life to the fullest. He loved good food, a few beers now and then, and those funny little twisted black cigars he was always smoking. He had only two passions in life: his family and catching crooks [*Left Hand* 22].

Then there's Sergeant Manfred Wolfgang "Manny" Sherlock:

Manny Sherlock stepped up beside Blackie. The sergeant was six foot four, but not as lean as he had once been. His years in the Detective Division had given him not only bulk but greater confidence. In Blackie's estimation he was destined to do great things on the Chicago Police Department [*Windy City* 19].

Like these two, all of Holton's major cop characters are the best of the breed. Detective Judy Daniels is "the Mistress of Disguise and High Priestess of Mayhem;" Chief Govich in *Windy City* is "one of the smartest, toughest cops around" (33). Good as all of these cops are, none of them is a match for Larry Cole.

Cole is the best of the best:

I'm really proud of what you've made of yourself. Every place I go people talk about Deputy Chief Larry Cole. About you and some of the cases you've broken. That guy Zalkin a few years back. And then bagging Tuxedo Tony DeLisa, not to mention the changes you put the dear departed Rabbit Arcadio through. Some people say you're gonna be the next black superintendent of police [*Windy City* 13].

Cole doesn't make commissioner, but becomes chief of detectives in the later books. Holton makes Cole a punctilious investigator, contrasting the work of his team to the sloppiness and myopia of other cops. The members of his team, Silvestri, Sherlock, and Daniels, all are absolutely devoted to him, as is the group of detective story writers that assists him after *Windy City*. Cole is brave. He's disciplined. He's devoted to his son. And to show how good a cop he is, Holton invents larger-than-life opponents, villains with money and power, sometimes otherworldly power.

Jack Mullen

Jack Mullen put in his twenty years with the San Diego PD. In 1995 he published *In the Line of Duty*, the first of his two Vincent Dowling novels—the second one being *Behind the Shield* (1996). In both books Mullen includes scenes of cops sitting around, mostly in cop bars, telling and retelling stories of past exploits and experiences. These tales recount zany episodes in cops' lives, but they also center on learning about police and how to be a cop. In the novels Mullen makes this one of the underlying themes. He puts in bits of cop lingo: In *Behind the Shield* readers learn that the acronym AVA-NHI means "asshole-versus-asshole, no humans involved" (42). More importantly, he makes his hero, Vincent Dowling, a repository of police wisdom. This ranges from tips on technique (keep separate notebooks for each case so lawyers can't snoop into your old cases), to background and advice about the Miranda warning (suspects have the right not only to remain silent but also have the right to talk to the cops), to views on the current state of police forces: "I have a male patrol cop who wants to wear an earring and I have a lady cop who says I can't make her wear a brassiere to work" (*Behind the Shield* 27). He also includes views on evidence. Forensics don't often work:

> For every time some English chief constable on PBS showed off a dirt sample from Birminghamshire that nailed the killer, Dowling had scores of cases with nothing. He could count on two hands the number of murders that had been made on prints. Positive makes could be made on firearms—sometimes. But normally it was just slugging it out; talking to people and people and people. (*Behind the Shield* 146)

And the favorite device of serial killer novelists is mostly for the birds: "The answer is on the street. Not in some computer. Not in some goddamn FBI profile that Administration has been trying to sic on me. It's on the street" (*Behind the Shield* 97). The answer lies with cops totally dedicated and committed to the job:

> Being a cop was more than an occupation, and being a homicide detective was more than just another assignment. Dowling was convinced it was a calling, a passion, and the only people who really understood were his team and a few of the others. It was seductive. Almost divine [*Behind the Shield* 21].

For Mullen, the trouble with the passion for police work lies in its potential to destroy relationships outside the force. That's a lot of what his two novels are about. Dowling is not just a cop. He's a husband and a father. And he derives pleasure from baking: Mullen shows him whipping up complex pastries and even dreaming of someday opening a bakery. But the passion for being a cop more than gets in the way. Dowling has to confront his complicity in his wife's suicide in *In the Line of Duty*. He suffers a near break-down and is transferred from homicide to the rubber gun squad shuffling papers. By the end of the book, however, he redeems himself both with his teenaged children and as a cop. Thus the "duty" of the title ramifies in two directions. In *Behind the Shield* Dowling's family problems continue. His son has run off to Las Vegas for a hasty wedding and his teenaged daughter comes home pregnant. But Dowling copes with both in a humane manner and at the same time performs his duty as a cop.

Lowen Clausen

Lowen Clausen of the Seattle Police Department centers his novel *First Avenue* (2000) on Officer Sam Wright and on Katherine Murphy, both beat cops. Clausen presents gray and dispirited cops. Murphy is new to the force but is overcome with weariness:

> More than anything, Katherine was tired of being the woman in the squad. She was tired of them watching her, waiting for her to show fear or weakness or humanness. She was tired of them expecting her to be like them and reject-ing her if she was — these men who treated her as an experiment they knew would fail [24–25].

Sam Wright is the only person on the force to show her any kindness. Yet he, too, has little enthusiasm for the job. Near the beginning of the novel Wright muses on being a cop back in the chaotic 1970s:

> The divisions were not as clear anymore. There were no lines of men in blue — there were only men then — and angry crowds in paisley. And it was a good thing. None of them, neither side, could have stood it much longer. Still he realized that he missed the feeling that came with it — a feeling that he was somehow special [19].

But he finds nothing special about bring a cop now. Wright finds that he has lost all of his involvement and compassion:

> You investigate an accident on Twenty-third Avenue, and when you're done you go down to Twenty-ninth and see about a family disturbance. Something about a sewing machine. Call Number 12. Call number 13. They've all become the same [73].

The department, Wright reckons, also cares mostly about statistics and little about people: "Statistics. That's all they wanted. Number of calls, con-tacts, arrests. All of it amounted to nothing. You moved ahead by writing traffic tickets, generating revenue" (205). But in the novel Wright becomes engaged with the people on his beat, first a Philipino restaurant owner, then the grandparents of a dead infant, then a young woman working in a doughnut shop, and finally a homeless man to whom he gives his extra pair of shoes. The symbolic name Wright connects to a number of things — Clausen's hero, for instance, has written a book of poems and writes them on the job, and when exposed to situations that seem as inevitable as the decay of the city Sam does the right thing, even when he knows that doing so may well be futile.

Robin Burcell

Robin Burcell, a cop since 1983, began with a romance novel featuring a police officer, *When Midnight Comes* (1995). Her second book, *Every Move She Makes* (1999) steps into the world of the thriller but carries with it strong elements of the romance. Burcell's hero, Kate Gillespie, "at thirty-six … was the first female homicide inspector SFPD ever had" (*Every Move* 6). In *Every Move She Makes* Burcell occasionally comes back to the difficulties that confront Gillespie as a cop. The guys, for instance, are tougher on her than they would be on a male:

> When I first transferred to Homicide a year ago, the guys wanted to see me fall apart at the sight of my first floater. It was the rite of passage for every new inspector, but because I was a woman, it seemed my trial went on forever. I'd become an expert in hiding my feelings, just as they'd all had to do. The male double standard. On them it was masculine. Me, I was considered cold, unfeeling [74].

Gillespie struggles with the whole issue of her feelings both when dealing with crime and when dealing with the department. She finds dealing with male authority difficult: "I was an emotional person, and hiding that particular vulnerability from those around me did not come easy, especially when being taken to task by those I respected and admired" (*Every Move* 70).

Indeed, Gillespie compares her position as a cop to that of an internal affairs cop:

> It occurred to me than that because of his position, the way he was treated by others, we were in a sense really more alike than I'd realized. Those in IA were looked upon by many officers as pariahs. Women officers were about one step below that [*Every Move* 122].

Additionally, Burcell shows Gillespie to be a smart, brave, and dedicated cop. The plot of *Every Move She Makes* relies, in part, on Gillespie's loyalty to her partner, who is falsely suspected as a criminal. In part, too, the novel deals in elements of the romance. Thus the title advertises and Burcell brings in mysterious and frightening threats to Gillespie. Finally, there is also the desirable but aloof internal affairs officer who admits his attraction to Gillespie at the end of the novel.

O'Neil DeNoux

O'Neil DeNoux, ex–homicide detective in the New Orleans Police Department, actually began writing in the late 1980s with *Grim Reaper* (1988), but in the early 1990s he began a consecutive series about his cop hero Dino LaStanza including *The Big Kiss* (1990), *Blue Orleans* (1991), and *Crescent City Kills* (1992). DeNoux is also the first of a succession of cops (including John Delamer, Dennis Banahan, Marshall Frank, and Charles Shafer) determined to turn their experiences into prose and finding only minor paperback press outlets for their works.

In his first novel of the 1990s, DeNoux presents a conventional homicide office where the officers talk about whodunits as opposed to routine cases, where they affix labels like "The Buried Gook" to notable cases, where nameless crime scene technicians do their work, where police code forms part of the background ("We've got a Signal 30"), where casual conversation is often vulgar and revolves around sex, and where gruesome sights are routine. Misogyny also rules:

> Millie was a mousy girl in her late twenties with tan hair, a pudgy figure, and thin lips. She was a Yankee, transplanted from Indiana to New Orleans as a teenager, and was the only female officer in Homicide. Although she was well liked, she had problems. The word on Millie was that she did not have the killer instinct, the drive to go for the jugular when it was offered.
> Once, during a crucial interview of a killer, Millie had tried to go for the jugular. She'd raised her voice and actually yelled at the killer as she dug into her purse for a cigarette and lighter. But when she pulled out a tampon instead of her lighter, the killer laughed [*The Big Kiss* 43–44].

DeNoux emphasizes his characters' working-class background. This comes in incidental details like the necessity for the hero to repeatedly explain the meaning of the word "gargoyle," to the principal character theme of *The Big Kiss*— the hero's relationship with the daughter of a wealthy New Orleans family. They may be working-class men, but DeNoux's cops possess intelligence. Thus he extols the background of one of his cops:

> Born in a house on Felicity Street a few blocks from the Sixth District Station, Fel grew up next to the Melpomene Projects. Yet an inquisitive mind and a natural curiosity helped him through Catholic school and the police academy [62].

He is also "the bravest man LaStanza knew" (60). Of course DeNoux's hero is no slouch either. Son of a cop father, and known for cracking big serial killer cases, he also has the virtue, as DeNoux presents him, of being Italian:

He had a gut feeling about Karen Koski, but not the usual cop's gut feeling; it was an old-country feeling, an innate Sicilian instinct of preying on weakness whenever weakness presented itself. It came naturally to someone named LaStanza. It was the weak link, he would prey on that [222].

DeNoux also presents LaStanza as following a higher law than that of the statutes. The title of *The Big Kiss* comes from the close of the book:

LaStanza inched closer and with a steady hand placed the barrel of his Magnum inside Lemoni's gaping mouth. He cocked the Magnum and slowly squeezed the trigger. In the instant before the hammer fell, Dino saw stark fear in Harry Lemoni's ugly eyes.

"Kiss this," Dino said as the hammer fell, blowing Lemoni's insane brains over the base of the magnolia tree [306].

Certainly a long way from Skip Langdon's New Orleans PD depicted by Julie Smith.

John Delamer

John Delamer retired from the NYPD in 1981; he had put in his twenty years. That means that in the middle of his career he belonged to the department when it was the subject of the Knapp Commission investigations. In his novel *The Tarnished Shield* (1996), this shows. The novel centers on what Jack Harley learns about being a cop and especially his encounter with political ambition and vigilantism. With the former, Delamer, through flashbacks, portrays the NYPD as a cold and indifferent organization. Thus when Harley comes out of the academy no one tells him what to do:

There was no formal introduction here and no welcome aboard…. Strange, he thought, no one even looked in his direction, and no one seemed to care whether he was there or not. No one except the old Sergeant who would come around later to give him a "see," check to be sure he was on his post. It would take a few years for the young patrolman to realize that for the others he did not exist, nor would he until he had proven himself on the street [15].

As he teaches himself to be a cop, Harley observes that the system runs on petty bribery and bending the rules. Nonetheless, he makes himself a good, honest even heroic cop. And in the middle of the novel Delamer shows cops working together and belonging to the cop brotherhood. Along the way Harley loses his wife because of the demands of the job, but he also acquires a rabbi. The main plot of *The Tarnished Shield* concerns the illegal machinations of a foaming-at-the-mouth special prosecutor out to get cops and obsessed with making an example out of Harley, even though he knows him to be honest. Indicted by the prosecutor's pet grand jury, Harley is arrested. The evil prosecutor hounds him out of the jobs he gets while awaiting trial, and he becomes a pariah to other cops who believe that he has become an informer to lessen his sentence and stay out of prison. At the end, however, because of evidence of the prosecutor's machinations acquired by Harley's new woman friend and a plan set in motion by Harley's rabbi and a sympathetic judge, evil is exposed and virtue rewarded. But at great cost. The ambition of the special prosecutor besmirches the whole legal system, and the entrenched minor corruption and inefficiency of the police department tarnish the badges that officers wear.

Dennis Banahan

Chicago PD's Dennis Banahan published *Threshold of Pain* in 2000. In his three and one-half pages of acknowledgments Banahan gives the nod to every partner with whom he ever worked, but, after his family, thanks

> my longtime friend and mentor, Lt. Hugh Holton, best-selling author of *Presumed Dead*, *Windy City*, *Violent Crimes* and a host of fast-paced mystery thrillers. Hugh is president of the Midwest Chapter of the Mystery Writers of America and truly the motivating force behind this book [vii].

In its plotting *Threshold of Pain* has some of the same *Twilight Zone* elements favored by Holton. Indeed, Banahan's homage to Holton extends to introducing a cameo appearance of a cop with the same name as Holton's hero, Larry Cole:

> Larry Cole was one of the few high-ranking black members of the department, and ... had earned the respect and admiration of everybody he came in contact with. Early in his career, he had earned a reputation as being one of the finest detectives in the city [92].

Threshold of Pain operates in two time zones. The first portion of the novel takes place after the Democratic National Convention in Chicago in 1968 and involves partners who are members of the department's Red Squad, the intelligence gathering group watching out for subversives. The second part jumps to 1982, after the squad has been disbanded and its members distributed back to the precincts and divisions. Bridging the time, Banahan traces the career of someone connected with communists in Cuba and the deaths of Robert Kennedy and Martin Luther King, Jr., and who goes on to become mayor of Chicago. But he also draws dedicated cops who, after even more crimes, bring him to justice.

Banahan's cops are almost uniformly good guys. Misogynists, maybe, but good-guy misogynists. Granted he does throw in a couple of alcoholic sergeants, but they serve comic purposes. The Chicago brass, like Larry Cole, are conscientious, smart, committed, and loyal to their officers. T.J., commander of the Red Squad, is "not only articulate, but cool under fire" (23).

Assistant Deputy Superintendent Charles Ramford, another high-ranking African American, is "an outstanding administrator, but first and foremost, he ...[is] a street policeman's policeman" (78). Banahan's principal characters are good cops, too. Mountainous Mike Corrigan represents the emotional connections between cops and the virtues of solid, working-class values and natures. Jefferson Parrish and Rennata McCray bring in brains, courage, and dedication. Paragons all, they have no legal means of bringing the bad guy to justice. So they use illegal ones. Corrigan's job in the 1960s was installing wiretaps, a skill he maintains even though it's illegal. The hero cops not only wiretap, they perform illegal searches, and, in the end, execute vigilante justice that their superiors conspire to cover up.

Marshall Frank

In the preface to *Beyond the Call* (2000), Marshall Frank summons up the ghost of Frank Serpico—"Like Serpico, rats don't have long careers"—and alludes to the final arrest he made as a Metro-Dade cop of "five other officers charged with the beating death of an unarmed civilian." This, also in the preface, Frank tells readers, was the impetus for writing his novel—to reveal the attitudes and acts of a small percentage of cops and to demonstrate that "Internal Affairs is a worthy and noble cause, usually staffed with the finest cops inside a police agency."

Beyond the Call follows the probationary period of officer Ira J. Harvey, "a cross between Tom Cruise and a John F. Kennedy, Jr." (47). Abandoning a career as an accountant and eventually being abandoned by his fiancee, Harvey joins the force in part because of the inspiration of his uncle, a retired cop, and in part out of a longing for excitement and duty. Assigned to the midnight watch of the most brutal precinct in the area, Harvey gets his eyes opened quickly:

> In his first twelve hours as a cop, Ira J. Harvey witnessed his first homicide scene, participated in the arrest of six gang members, one of whom spit in his face, witnessed brutality to at least three subjects, prevaricated on all six arrest reports, saw a murder victim wrongfully removed from a crime scene, helped handle traffic at a major accident and never ate a meal except for two packages of crackers from a vending machine [15–16].

The precinct to which Harvey is assigned is run by Sergeant "Rotweiller" McGirk, an anti-Semitic, racist, misogynistic, brutal good old boy. His rules for his squad are "Back-up, Suck up, and Stand-up" (21) encapsulating the sycophantic culture, code of silence, and cliché of courage infecting the coterie of bad cops. The rest of the command lies in the hands of an ineffectual lieutenant and a major intent on becoming commissioner. Although the major commandeers Harvey to write his dissertation for him, the rookie sees increasing evidence of institutionalized brutality and even murder while he attempts to do his duty as a police officer. In steps an officer from internal affairs to whom Harvey begins to unburden himself and with whom he begins an affair. Evidence mounts about current cases of excessive force, about the murder of the lone African American officer on the squad, and about the case that put Ira's Uncle Bennie in a wheelchair. At the end, Harvey and others clean house and a new commissioner attentive to what happens in the field comes into office.

Charles Shafer

Chicago cop Charles Shafer sent his *On Cabrini Green* (2000) to England to have it published. The novel centers on the machinations of a master criminal and the largely bumbling efforts of Chicago cops in their efforts to figure out what is going on and how to stop it. Shafer's hero, Sergeant Paul Kostovic, Croatian American, reflects part of the ethnic mix of Chicago. As the novel begins, Kostovic has just returned to uniform after a stint as a detective. Shafer's cops are a collection of dopes and screwups. Tommy mostly concerns himself with making passes at the women on his beat; "fat assed" Detective Debolt is a "class A fool" (19) whose speech is laden with jargon: he "got that phony stuff from watching all those cop shows on TV" (19). Joe Holloway and Volly Dickman are "two of the biggest sluffoffs on the job" (36). Indeed, one of the cops calls Shafer's hero Kostovic "the biggest screw up in the Chicago police department" (31).

Schafer's cops can't do anything right. During the commission of the first crime in *On Cabrini Green*, Kostovic gets himself locked in a store, loses his gun, and is knocked unconscious. But that's only the beginning. They know nothing about doing things by the book ("What the hell you know about the book? Unless it's a comic book" [35]), and they can't even shoot straight. Shafer places part of the blame for this on Kostovic's having been a plainclothes officer: "Lieutenant Matthews had been right on when he said Paul had been a detective so long he'd forgotten what it was to be a real cop" (33). But Kostovic's salvation is that he's "one of those damned ex-type-marines ... gotta be out front, where the action is. Damn the consequences" (45). He charges about until he teams up with a gunnery sergeant from the local marine base. Together they track down the villain — another ex-marine — and use extralegal means to punish him for his crimes.

And the Rest

Michael Connelly

Michael Connelly's Harry Bosch novels take a bit of Raymond Chandler and some James Ellroy, add some of the conventional elements of the police novel, and use as background the troubles the Los Angeles Police Department encountered in the 1990s. They are dark books, and Connelly announces this in the titles—his first two books are *Black Echo* (1992) and *Black Ice* (1993). He announces it, too, by naming his hero after Heironymous Bosch, the painter who specialized in portraying grotesque scenes of writhing souls tortured by deformed, sadistic demons. And Bosch has demons aplenty. From his experience as a tunnel rat in Vietnam "he would have extended periods of deep sleep trances into which torturous dreams invaded. This would be followed by months of insomnia, the mind reacting to terrors that awaited in sleep" (*Black Echo* 70). From his police experience he has "become desensitized to violence. He speaks in terms of violence being an accepted part of his day-to-day life, for all his life" (*Black Echo* 84).

And like James Ellroy and his obsession with his mother's murder, in *The Last Coyote* (1995) Connelly details his hero's investigation into his own disjointed past and the murder of his prostitute mother. Connelly's hero repeatedly experiences one of Chandler's darkest themes, betrayal and abandonment—Bosch is abandoned by his wife and repeatedly betrayed by his department and even, in one book, betrayed by his partner. Indeed, along with these symptoms of darkness, many of the characteristics of the traditional hard-boiled private eye reside in the character of Harry Bosch—from his minimalist life to his battles with authority.

In some ways Harry Bosch is a loose cannon, out of control or at least out of step with the LAPD: "Harry Bosch was a problem.... A good cop, a good detective... But in the long run ... outsiders did not work well inside the system. Harry Bosch was an outsider, and would always be. Not part of the LAPD Family" (*Black Echo* 85). Throughout the books Bosch is either on suspension or on probation, and when Connelly introduces him he has been flopped down from the prestigious robbery homicide squad to a precinct in the boonies commanded by an ineffectual bean counter. From the first book, where two inept internal affairs investigators (Lewis and Clark) dog his footsteps, the department is consistently suspicious of Bosch. And with some reason. *The Last Coyote* begins with Bosch on suspension for having assaulted his lieutenant. The issue here and elsewhere is that Bosch isn't quite a rebel or cowboy or loose cannon. He's a perfectionist, a perfectionist about examining crime scenes—the first novel begins with Bosch grumbling about the casual and lax approach taken by supervisors, patrol officers, and detectives to the crime scene — and a perfectionist about doing the right thing the right way. Connelly even notes in *Black Echo* that Bosch likes paperwork. Bosh's assault on his supervisor does not arise from Lieutenant Pounds' ineffectuality, but from his interfering with an interrogation Bosch was conducting. For Connelly, what makes Bosch work is not simply his impatience with incompetence or his inability to tolerate fools. Some of this comes from the perfectionism — in a number of books Connelly has Bosch open up cold cases, crimes unsolved but still on the books. Much of what makes Bosch function, however, has to do with having a sense of vocation. Connelly sets this out in *A Darkness More Than Night* (2001):

> He had come to believe that homicide detectives, a breed of cops unto themselves, called upon deep inner emotions to accept and carry out the always difficult task of their job. They were usually of two kinds, those who saw their job as a skill or a craft, and those who saw it as a mission in life....
> ...This motivation in detectives could be broken down even further as to what gave them this sense of purpose or mission. To some the job was seen as almost a game; they had some inner deficit that caused them to need to prove they were better, smarter and more cunning than their quarry. Their lives were a constant cycle of validating themselves by, in effect, invalidating the killers they sought by putting them behind bars. Others, while carrying a degree of that same deficit, also saw themselves with the additional dimension of being speakers for the dead. There was a sacred bond cast between victim and cop that formed at the crime scene and could not be severed [124].

Bosch, too, is committed to justice. It, therefore, is not coincidence that trials stand in the background of *The Concrete Blonde* (1994), *Angels Flight* (1999), and *A Darkness More Than Night*. The trials in the first two of these books are civil actions seeking damages from the LAPD for violating individuals' civil rights; in *Concrete Blonde* the issue is Bosch's shooting of a serial killer, and in *Angels Flight* the issue is false arrest of an African American suspect. While the trials hold police officers and the LAPD up to public scrutiny, none of them can uncover the truth or execute justice. For that Connelly has his hero.

Connelly's Harry Bosch works in a department that encountered a world of trouble in the 1990s, one held up to national scrutiny on issues of racism, brutality, corruption and incompetence. He brings some of this into his novels. *Trunk Music* (1997) features a corrupt cop. In *Angels Flight* Connelly notes in passing that "Civil rights cases brought about the end of the department-approved choke hold while subduing suspects — after an inordinately high number of minority deaths" (18). And that same novel ends in an antipolice riot in Los Angeles. In several books he makes passing reference to the two most famous LAPD cases of the 1990s, Rodney King and O.J.

Simpson. Connelly, to be sure, includes the theme of incompetent authority, but here he follows convention and the dictates of his hero rather than
detailing what went wrong with the LAPD in the 1990s. Indeed, unlike those
who write about the NYPD, Connelly and other West Coast cop writers
brush rather lightly over the problems that affect their police forces.

Richard Price

Richard Price's 1992 novel *Clockers* isn't quite a cop novel, it's more a
sociological one. In it Price depicts the squalid life in a housing project in
Dempsey, a fictitious New Jersey city near Manhattan. *Clockers* shifts focus
between Strike, one of the African American youths peripherally involved
with pedaling cocaine in the projects, and the cops who come into contact
with the ghetto kids. Price depicts kids who know a great deal about cops
and how to deal with them. The young cocaine peddlers, for instance, know
that cops are as anxious for quitting time as any worker and won't go out of
their way to make arrests near the end of their shifts, knowing that they will
have to stay on the job until all of the paperwork has been completed. Both
the cops and the kids know about profiling. The kids know what cops on
the prowl look like and cops on the prowl profile the people they see: "Rocco
stopped for a red light and found himself profiling three black kids sitting
on a tenement stoop" (34).

In *Clockers* Price introduces a couple of kinds of cops. First there is the
drug squad that periodically swoops down on the projects to roust the sell-
ers: "They all looked like bums, except they were healthy bums, six-foot,
two-hundred-pound white bums with lead saps and Glock Nineteens on
their hips" (10). The kids call their leader Big Chief: "Big Chief clomped
over, six foot five, reddish-gray hair, bounce lurching on the toes of his
sneakers like a playground Frankenstein, wearing his Fury T-shirt—six
wolves hanging out of a police car—growling 'Strike, Strike, Strike'" (11). A
couple of these cops, Thumper and Andre the Giant, have compassion and
concern for the ghetto kids.

But the other cops in Dempsey are different. Price's Rocco Klein is a
homicide cop. For him the job was at first fascinating:

> In the beginning the Job had seemed more of a privilege than anything else —
> getting paid to walk through walls and witness the wildest and most riveting
> details of human struggle — but after a few years you could drown in it and
> what had once made you step back in awe could begin to slide past your eyes,
> as unseen as the air you breathed [35].

Unlike the drug cops, the homicide detectives experience mostly monotony:

and tonight's biggest problem was how to look like they were actually earning their pay [33].

In Dempsey, the Homicide four-to-twelve was mainly this: drinks, staring at the oversize menu wondering what to eat, watching videos or news on TV back in the office, waiting for the phones to ring or the pagers to beep [99].

What isn't monotony is "a job that dealt with an endless parade of shitskin losers — hunting them down, befriending them in order to get their confessions, then tossing them into County" (94). And none of the cops believes they do any good: "'That kid you saved tonight. If he lives that long, if he grows up? He's gonna be a real piece of shit, Rocco.' Frog says to me, 'it's the cycle of shit and you can't do nothing about it. So take it easy and just do your job'" (103). *Clockers*, however, adds racism into the formula. In the middle of the novel a black hooker berates the cops for it:

Goddamn motherfuckin' Duck, you a motherfuckin' racist, you know that? Every time you snatch some white bitch or some white boy you come on like you they goddamn relative. You always like chew 'em out, sayin' how they wastin' they lives an' shit, but you grab a nigger an' it's like, it's like ... ho shit, more garbage. You just like, fuck with us, you know, call us names, smack us around, make insults, take away the dope. But you never get upset. It's like niggers are niggers, they're supposed to be doin' this shit, they can't help it. So you a motherfuckin' racist, Duck [193].

By the middle of the novel, too, Rocco recognizes that his job makes him part of an army of occupation.

Robert Crais

At the turn of the century Robert Crais moved from writing hard-boiled books about private eye Elvis Cole and his deadly ex-cop associate to writing police books. The first, *Demolition Angel* (2000), centers on detective Carol Starkey and the intricacies of bomb squad work. The second, *Hostage* (2001), deals with hostage negotiation and features ex–LAPD hostage negotiator and now chief of the Bristo Camino police Jeff Talley. Although both books confront problems of large scope (a professional bomber in *Demolition Angel* and criminals ranging from the petty to representatives of organized crime in *Hostage*), both are haunted by past events in their careers: Starkey survives but relives the accidental explosion that killed her partner/lover and Talley replays a failed hostage negotiation that resulted in the death of a child. Starkey, now assigned as a detective, goes from therapist to therapist — furtively so the department will not find out — drinks off and on the job and rebuffs the concern for her emotional well-being and compassion of her colleagues and superiors. Talley solves the problem of on-the-job stress by leaving L.A. and becoming chief of a small department in a relatively crime-free suburb. On the job both heroes are meticulous workers — Starkey works bombs and research with focused precision, and Talley in the L.A. flashbacks works within a framework designed to save lives. In both cases, too, failure means disaster and death. Here Crais carries over the fundamental moral emphasis of his private eye books. *Demolition Angel* and *Hostage* articulate basic tenets about courage and responsibility — thus both are about "when the going gets tough the tough get going" and "getting back up on the horse." In *Hostage*, therefore, the burned out negotiator finds that he can do what needs to be done, and in *Demolition Angel* Starkey thwarts the bomber and disarms the penultimate bomb. In both cases Crais's heroes redeem themselves by saving others and saving ones they love. What Crais therefore does is to transfer the essence of his private eye hero to the cop book, where heroes protect and serve against a background made credible by allusion to actual events and by the writer's research. In this regard it's worth noting that in *Demolition Angel* Crais acknowledges the help of eight law enforcement officers, including Det. Paul Bishop, LAPD, who wrote fiction about LAPD cops a decade before Crais tried his hand at it.

Cops in the Nineties

Cable changed things. In the 1990s one could watch new network television cop shows as well as reruns of the cop shows of yesteryear, shows from *Adam 12* to *Columbo*. The years 1992 and 1993 were the most prolific years for new cop shows from the networks during the decade. In 1992 CBS premiered *Bodies of Evidence, Diagnosis Murder, Picket Fences*, and *Raven*; ABC aired *Arresting Behavior, Human Target*, and *The Commish*; and NBC brought out *Mann and the Machine*. The next year saw even more new cop shows on TV (nine of them) including two most influential series, NBC's *Homicide: Life on the Streets*, and ABC's *NYPD Blue*. Interest in new forensic techniques led in 1996 to NBC's *Profiler* and in 2000 to *CSI, Crime Scene Investigators* (CBS). Chuck Norris mingled the cop show with the karate flick with his series *Walker, Texas Ranger* beginning in 1993. In 1996 Don Johnson, toned down from his *Miami Vice* role (a show much maligned by cop writers), came back in *Nash Bridges*. And the Fox reality show *COPS* carried over from the 1980s into the new century.

Cable TV also meant that American audiences could view endless reruns of the big cop films of the 1980s — the *Lethal Weapon* films, the *Diehard* films, and the *Police Academy* films. In cinema the 1990s began with the taming of a violent cop in Schwarzenegger's *Kindergarten Cop* (1990) — his second cop film, with *Red Heat* coming in 1988. Serial killers, too, stand at the beginning of the nineties, first with John McNaughton's *Henry: Portrait of a Serial Killer* (1990) and then most significantly with *The Silence of the Lambs* (1991). Sylvester Stallone made two cop films in the nineties, first *Demolition Man* (1993) and then *Cop Land* in 1997. Keanu Reeves moved from the Bill and Ted movies to portraying a cop in *Speed* in 1994. And two large-scale, social comment cop books were made into films during the decade: first Spike Lee's film of Price's *Clockers* (1995) and then the film of Ellroy's *L.A. Confidential* (1997). Veterans Al Pacino and Charles Bronson appeared in cop films in 1995: Pacino and DeNero in *Heat* and Bronson in *Family of Cops. Fargo* dealt with cops in the frozen north in 1996, and Stephen Baldwin appeared in *One Tough Cop* in 1998.

Back in the 1980s readers could be relatively sure that cop novels would be built on one of two formulas: the thriller formula, with hunting and chasing, or the cozy formula, with talking and thinking. Both, of course, would have details of police work added, and much of the development of the main characters would depend on their jobs as police officers. While these conventions endured and prospered, in the 1990s one couldn't be quite as sure about the kind of formula a cop book would follow because some writers used cop heroes to tell different kinds of stories. One such form is the police historical. Using history as a basis for popular fiction is a device used in other genres, and the unraveling of historic crimes and portrayal of historical figures as amateur detectives both play significant roles in the history of the mystery novel. There are, for instance, all of the Jack the Ripper books, and recreated historical figures from Aristotle to Jane Austen sort out the innocent from the guilty. In the1980s the cop chronicles of Griffith and Ellroy appeared, giving fictionalized pictures of the histories of the Philadelphia and Los Angeles police departments. From the eighties onward there are one-shot historical cop novels: books that set police heroes in actual historical events and contexts as observers and as participants. Thus, in the late 1980s, Thomas H. Cook's *Streets of Fire* (1989) uses Sergeant Ben Wellman of the Birmingham, Alabama Police Department as both an observer and a reluctant and confused actor in the events preceding Martin Luther King, Jr.'s, civil rights demonstrations that took place in that city. John Peyton Cooke bases *Torsos* (1993) on actual unsolved serial killings that occurred in Cleveland in the 1930s and introduces one historical personage in Eliot Ness, who worked in Cleveland after his Chicago days. In *Good Cop, Bad Cop* Barbara D'Amato uses the December 4, 1969, Chicago raid on the Black Panthers as the fulcrum for action and character development. In the chronicling vein, in the 1990s Loren Estleman's *Motown* (1991) and *Stress* (1996), from his Detroit series, both involve cops working in that city in, respectively, 1967 and 1973. Ellroy, of course, continues to use Los Angeles cops of the

1950s as the background for his L.A. noir novels. In each case, but especially in *Streets of Fire*, the cop and the cop's point of view provide new ways of viewing historical events and people.

At the other extreme of time, the science fiction cop novel also appears in the late 1980s. J.D. Robb's (Nora Roberts) Lieutenant Eve Dallas romances are set in the future, as is Greg Bear's *Queen of Angels* (1990), and Robert Tine's *Midnight City* (1987). Bear's novel features Inspector Mary Choy in Los Angeles of 2047, and Tine's novel follows Officer Jake Sullivan's efforts to find a serial killer in a late-twenty-first-century New York where the cops use satellites and hovering vehicles to combat epidemic crime and corruption. And then some cop books use the supernatural in a manner similar to the televised *X Files*, an updated version of the older television series *The Twilight Zone*. In one of his novels Ken Goddard combines futuristic forensic technology with visiting aliens. Hugh Holton brings vampires and shape shifters into his books about the Chicago police. In the 1990s, too, the cop romance novel emerged. The connection was implicit from as early as Dorothy Uhnak's Christie Opara books, and romance issues stand in the background of Lillian O'Donnell's books as well as those of several other women. Indeed, cop Robin Burcell's first novel was a romance. With her Eve Dallas novels, one of the decade's powerhouse romance writers, Nora Roberts, turned to a police officer as a principal character in books that merge cop themes and conventions with those of the romance. The same is true with the cop books of Tami Hoag. Part of the significance of the emergence of these alternate forms of the cop book lies in the acceptance (by writers at least) of the police officer and what he or she does as something interesting and appealing to a wide variety of readers — not just traditional mystery readers.

By the 1990s the McBain formula of multiple cases solved by multiple characters is almost as dead as the Nehru jacket: Terry Marlow is the lone follower of the McBain pattern in the 1990s. In the nineties, whether the flavor of the cop books is conventional cop house, or historical, or romantic, or futuristic, with respect to solving the crime and catching the criminal, most of the plotting is based either on the character- and conversation-based cozy or the hunt-and-chase action-based thriller. But, as in the 1980s, the introduction of the serial killer affects the ways in which writers articulate their cozy or thriller plots. Partly this comes from the publicity surrounding the apprehension and trials of real serial killers. Recitation of Bundy, Gacy, Son of Sam, Green River, Zodiac, Boston Strangler, and Wayne Williams becomes a conventional feature found in lots of cop books. During the eighties a class of serial murder specialists emerged in the world of cop fiction. Heffernan, Bayer, Sandford, and Pearson all devote themselves to cop heroes and serial killers. These writers, of course, continued to publish into the nineties. Indeed, most of Pearson's and most of Sandford's *Prey* books (twelve of them) appear during the decade. But some other things made the nineties the decade of the serial killer book. One of the most powerful was the publication of Harris' The *Silence of the Lambs* in 1988 and the release of the film based on the novel in 1991. The other factor was Patricia Cornwell. Cornwell is the only writer connected to the cop novel in the 1990s whose books make it as year's best-sellers; three of them did, *Cause of Death* (1995), *Unnatural Exposure* (1997), and *Point of Origin* (1998) (Cader-books.com). A lot of writers followed in Cornwell's footsteps. James Patterson, who became a best-selling writer in the nineties, uses the serial killer as the basis of his Alex Cross books. Dan Mahoney, too, often uses serial killers. And many, many more cop writers in the decade began their careers as cop writers with serial killer books: Enes Smith with *Fatal Flowers* in 1992; Leslie Glass with *Burning Time* in 1993; Penny Micklebury with *Keeping Secrets* and Carol O'Connell with *Mallory's Oracle* in 1994; Hugh Holton with *Windy City* and Lynn Hightower with *Flashpoint* in 1995; Jack Mullen with *Behind the Shield* in 1996; bestseller Arthur Hailey tried out the cop novel with *Detective* in 1997; Jannine Kadow with *Blue Justice* and Robert Walker with his new cop hero with *Double Edge* in 1998.

Clearly, publishers were looking for serial killer books and for writers, especially new writers, who could add at least a little something new to the marketable pattern. These books provided a popular formula, an opportunity to use different locales as background, and a chance to try to put a new wrinkle in the formula by introducing different kinds of cop heroes — particularly women and minorities. Then, too, the serial killer book gave writers like Jeffrey Deaver, Cornwell, and Pearson a chance to strut their forensic stuff. Finally serial killer books gave cop and forensic writers (including FBI writers and even a few writers who feature amateurs and private eyes) a new slant on one of the interests implicit in the detective novel from its birth in the 1920s — psychology. Hence the popularity of psychologists and profiles in these kinds of books. What they uncover lies outside of the conventional set of motivations native to the detective novel — gain, jealousy, etc. During the 1980s and 1990s there was something of a scramble to find new motives for serial killers — these range from professional killers to organ harvesters to vengeance seekers to vampires. Usually, however, what the cops uncover is massively deranged individuals who wreak vengeance on their cruel or evil or absent parents by killing innocents. That a lot of writers attribute the cause of serial rampages to dysfunctional families corresponds to trends in pop psychology, but it also serves as contrast to the theme of the police family that lies under most of the cop novels of the period. The seeming arbitrariness of serial crimes, too, separates them from the orderly world of the classical detective story. Indeed, that serial killers choose innocents as victims — almost always seemingly randomly chosen women and children — connects them both to an ancient and fundamental evil but also makes them ideal antagonists for the thriller in which the hero's task involves battling something larger than one person and not simply solving one crime but affirming something about humanity through his or her actions. In practical terms, too, for thriller writers it's easier to plot a novel based on episodes than articulating a more complicated plot.

Some things don't change. Veteran, middle-aged, smart, tough men continue as the heroes of the cop books of the 1990s. The nineties saw plenty of old-fashioned conventional, rough around the edges, lone-wolf male cops serving as the focus of cop books. Mark Olden, for instance, has Fear Meagher of the NYPD in *Fear's Justice* (1996), and James Neal Harvey has NYPD Lieutenant Ben Tolliver in *By Reason of Insanity* (1990). Many of the most prominent writers depend on male heroes — Ridley Pearson, Ed Dee, Dan Mahoney, Michael Connelly, James Doss, James Patterson, etc. In the main, however, their heroes are nineties kind of guys, more sensitive and compassionate and sometimes even more introspective than most earlier fictional cops. Notably, Arthur Hailey in his *Detective* (1998) makes his hero an ex-priest. Unlike the parade of ruined relationships found in earlier cop books, nineties characters like Pearson's Lou Boldt and Dee's Anthony Ryan have real wives and real family relationships. Jack Mullen's books use the hero's failed role as husband and his growth as a single father as a significant character point. And Mullen's Vince Dowling is even an expert amateur baker. Some nineties characters are more open about their demons — Connelly's Harry Bosch for instance. And Jeffrey Deaver adds in a dimension of personal suffering with his quadriplegic hero's battles with despair. In some cases, too, heroes of the nineties need to be more knowledgeable than earlier heroes: the rise of interest in forensics during the decade requires some writers to make their heroes know more than previous cop heroes for whom "street smarts" were enough. Thus heroes like Lou Boldt know a lot, and Deaver's Lincoln Rime knows everything.

The Job is still more than a job for the heroes of the 1990s. A compound of enthusiasm for science and duty drives forensic characters. In some cases, like Cornwell and Burcell, motivation lies in a combination of passion for the job and a need for self-preservation. A passionate belief in finding justice for victims, seen best in Pearson's Lou Boldt, continues in the 1990s. There are still some vigilante cops driven by the incompetence of the criminal justice system. Thus cops become murderers in Banahan's *Threshold of Pain*, and in Mahoney's *Black and White* the cops manipulate the system to enforce their own views on capital punishment. Connected with this, some cops quite literally take upon themselves the role of God's agents, and they make this clear to the readers. Thus Coram's hero says "I am one of God's foot soldiers" (*Dead South* 57) and one of Dan Mahoney's cops in *Once In Never Out* explains that "We work for God" (102).

Not all real cops, though, worked for God in the 1990s. The Mollen Commission of 1993 considered why a group of NYPD cops had been arrested for protecting and assisting drug dealers. In 1997 NYPD cops went on trial for beating and sodomizing Abner Luioma. NYPD cops fired forty-one shots killing unarmed Amadou Diallo in 1999. In the nineties thirteen Miami cops were arrested for brutality and excessive force; and in the late nineties investigations into LAPD's anti-gang unit and Rampart Division led to the arrest of a crowd of cops for corruption and excessive and illegal force resulting in the specter of thousands of criminal convictions being overturned. Corruption and brutality remain significant subjects in the cop novels of the 1990s. While most cop novels steer away from the kind of things reported in the news, it became almost a prerequisite of the form for writers to have their characters make reference to cops on the take or brutal cops. Some of these acknowledgements take the form of minihistory lessons. Barbara D'Amato does Chicago in *Help Me, Please*:

> My dad had been a cop, back in the days when cops were paid a pittance. Mayor Daley—Daley the First, that was, not our present one—said that you didn't need to pay cops much because they could always steal. Things have changed. Cops are paid a decent living wage now, though it's not princely. And in my opinion, there's a lot less stealing [13].

Shortly before all of the bad things about his department hit the evening news, LAPD cop Paul Bishop presented a comparative view of corruption, West Coast versus East Coast, in *Sand Against the Tide* (1990): "East Coast departments have had the huge in-house corruption, but out here it has always been on a much smaller scale" (174). And in his 1995 *Pigtown*, NYPD's William Caunitz's character gives a brief overview of the wrong fix for the problems with the Big Apple's police force:

> Serpico blew the whistle on corruption. And the Knapp Commission dealt the death blow to "good money." The Job stopped enforcing antigambling laws, so no more payoffs. They closed down all the other things that brought in the clean money. And *then* the Palace Guard, pretending to stamp out corruption, prohibited uniform cops and precinct squad detectives from enforcing the narcotics laws. That opened the floodgates [310].

Some writers make general observations about corruption, like the one in Pearson's *The First Victim* (1999):

Corruption swept through police departments and other government agencies like the flu, passed one person to the next, indiscriminate of rank, race, or gender. Like any contagious disease, when its proportions became epidemic within the given population, measures were taken to eradicate or at least reduce its influence; a few scapegoats were found and hung out to dry while the others went more deeply underground [39].

Finally, a group of writers make police corruption the major focus of their books. This happens most frequently with books by ex-cops. James Delamer, Lowen Clausen, Ed Dee, and John Westerman's books of the nineties all center plots on corruption in individuals and the system. In every case the writers of the 1990s suggest that corruption was and ever will be part of police departments, they blame its persistence on poor management, and hold that their heroes and most other cops view corruption and brutality with distaste—but also with grudging tolerance.

While there are exceptions, like Marshall Frank's exposé of systematic police brutality in *Beyond the Call* (2000) and Paula Woods' attention to the same topic in *Inner City Blues* (2000), books of the 1990s pay less attention to the use of illegal force than the books of the previous decades. Indeed, police apologists see the brutality issue as overblown and emphasize that bringing it up is the last resort of scoundrels; thus in Leslie Glass's *Burning Time* (1993) there was "No one was even near him, and already he was complaining about police brutality" (76). Michael Connelly, on the other hand, reports in several of his books that the LAPD has finally outlawed the chokehold: thus in *Angels Flight* (1999) we learn that "Civil rights cases brought about the end of the department-approved choke hold while subduing suspects—after an inordinately high number of minority deaths" (18). While a number of writers mention brutality in their works, they almost always set it in the past and use brutality as a means of differentiating current cops and practices from past cops and practices. In *Line of Duty* Michael Grant introduces the contrast of past and present in the tongue-and-cheek interchange in the squad room quoted above:

> "Damn, how did they ever catch anyone in the old days?"
>
> "It was easy," Shannon answered. "They didn't have computers to drown them in useless information."
>
> "Yeah, and they had investigative tools not available to us," Rose said.
>
> "Like what?" Velez asked.
>
> Rose smiled slyly. "They could beat the shit out of a suspect until he told them what they wanted to know" [117].

Dan Mahoney puts it in a more specific and serious context in *Black and White* (1999) when his cops bring up the topic of brutality:

It seemed there was one [scandal] every few years to be suffered through by bosses, cops, and detectives who had nothing to do with the incident that had provoked the public outrage.

"The stun gun."

The early eighties scandal, McKenna knew. The 106th Precinct in Queens. Questioning a drug dealer while using a stun gun to refresh his memory. Heads had rolled from the top on down and every cop on the Job was given a black eye [26].

Linked with the issue of brutality is that of cops acting outside the law as vigilantes. In the 1990s, with the exception of Dennis Banahan's *Threshold of Pain* (2000), the cop books that treat the subject come from writers who began their careers in the last decade. Thus Bob Leuci in *The Snitch* (1997), Barbara Paul in *You Have the Right to Remain Silent* (1992), Joseph McNamara in *Code 211* (1996), and Paul Bishop in *Sand Against the Tide* (1990) all deal in one way or another with vigilantes.

One of the things demonstrated by the cop books of the 1990s is the growing success of affirmative action. While women heroes appear in books of the previous decades, in the nineties they are more numerous, and writers feel the freedom to develop facets of women beyond their struggles for acceptance in a formerly all-male institution. To be sure writers in the nineties continue to write about antifemale prejudice in police departments, but the new women heroes also demonstrate a wider variety of characteristics than found in earlier female cops — from the family orientation found in Eleanor Taylor Bland, Lynn Hightower, and Barbara D'Amato's books, to the compassion of Noreen Gilpatrick's Mother MacLean, to the isolation and hardness of O'Connell's Mallory. Women writers of the 1990s go beyond their characters' struggles to demonstrate to their supervisors and their male colleagues their competence as cops as well as to maintain their identity as women and explore a variety of other relationships made more complicated by their job. Thus there are the tensions between partners who are also lovers (as in Leslie Glass, Kim Wozencraft, Molly Hite, and Noreen Gilpatrick), tensions between partners not on the job (as in all writers who portray lesbian heroes), tensions between mothers and daughters (as in Leslie Glass and Aimee and David Thurlo), and tensions between daughters and fathers (as in Francine Mathews' novels where Merry Folger's boss is also her father).

While there are few African American male heroes developed in the nineties (and other than Hugh Holton's hero, three of the four black heroes were created by white writers), African American cops appear in most of the books of the period. Michael Connelly's Harry Bosch has two black partners over the course of the novels, and the lead detective in Eugene Izzi's *A Matter of Honor* depends on his black partner, Ellis Turner. African American partners also play key roles in Kenneth Abel's *Blue Wall* (1996) and Joseph McNamara's *Code 211* (1996). In terms of heroes, more African American women appear in the nineties than African American men, all of them in the works of three African American women writers, Bland, West, and Woods. Although they present some of the unique qualities of African American families, these writers, like other women writers, show domestic pressures affecting their heroes. While Paula Woods depicts entrenched racism in the LAPD, the other African American writers — Holton, Bland, and West — show their heroes working in relatively successfully integrated police departments. The same is true with Mark Zubrow's portrait of a gay cop in a relatively tolerant Chicago Police Department. But lesbian heroes don't see it the same way. One of the phenomena of the nineties is the use of the cop hero in lesbian fiction — sometimes as a means of exploring non-cop issues and sometimes, as in Katherine V. Forrest, as a means of discussing both sexuality and police issues. While Laurie King shows the San Francisco department as tolerant of Kate Martinelli's sexual orientation, the issue in King and in most other books that portray lesbian cops is the stress caused by keeping one's sexual orientation a secret and the possible repercussions of coming out of the closet: it's there in Katherine Forrest's and Penny Micklebury's books. Writers like Kate Allen and Linda Kay Silva, whose heroes live out of the closet, concentrate more on the hero's private personal relationships than they do on police themes. In all, these new kinds of heroes — women, African Americans, gays and lesbians, and Native Americans — demonstrate the power of the "brotherhood" theme developed in the police novel over the past half century. While each brings something new to police work, all of these new heroes come to believe in and to need what Katherine V. Forrest has her hero term "the police family."

Sure, there was Wambaugh, Uhnak, Barnes, and then Caunitz, Leuci, Westermann and Bishop, but before the 1990s not many cops or ex-cops wrote cop novels. The nineties saw a squad of cops taking to the word processor and trying to parlay their positions and experiences into novels. Dennis Banahan, Robin Burcell, Ed Dee, John Delamer , O'Neil DeNoux, Marshall Frank, Michael Grant, Hugh Holton, Dan Mahoney, Terry Marlow, Jack Mullen, Robert Reid, Charles Shafer, and Enes Smith all started to write cop books during the period. In the way of writers, of course, each felt that he or she had unique experience and credentials as well as something to say and the skill to say it. Some of them got beyond one book and some did not. The influx of cop and ex-cop writers had something to do with publishers recognizing the viability of the subgenre and looking for cop books to add to their lists. Some of this no doubt had to do with the raised educational level of police officers in the U.S. and the fact that one of the things police officers have always done is to tell stories. Partly, too, the phenomenon of cops writing has something to do with the professionalizing of mystery writing. Some of this came in the form of packaging, with cop writers like Smith and DeNoux setting up how-to programs at schools or on the Internet. Some of it had to do with the vitality of writers' groups, like the one in Chicago from which Hugh Holton emerged. As with most things, the influx of cop writers had mixed results when it came to success.

Just as cop books of the 1970s and 1980s brood over the Supreme Court's *Miranda* decision, two contemporary events color the attitudes of cops in cop books of the 1990s. The first is the trial of O.J. Simpson. O.J. allusions and discussions appear in the books of the nineties with the same frequency that *Miranda* allusions come up in books of the previous decades. And that is frequently: Wambaugh in *Floaters*, Izzi in *A Matter of Honor*, and Connelly in *Trunk Music* each cite O.J. six times during the course of their narratives. Cornwell mentions O.J., so do Mahoney, Dee, Jance, Patterson, Kudow, Walker and Abel. Some of the allusions have to do with O.J.'s guilt. Thus in Wambaugh's *Floaters* Simpson's name works its way into cop slang as a synonym for murder: "Somebody did an O.J. on a babe. Wear fishing boots. They say there's enough blood to overfeed every vampire in Romania" (134). Many of the O.J. references connect with cops' traditional feelings about lawyers and the deficiencies of the jury system, especially when trials involve scientific evidence. In Mahoney's *Hyde*, for instance, the cops see their situation as parallel to the O.J. case:

> First we'd have to have a jury smart enough to understand the basic science lesson you propose to give them. Defense lawyers hate smart jurors in a case where there's going to be scientific evidence presented and they try to get a jury too dumb to understand the evidence. They succeed all the time [155].

Michael Connelly adds the impact that Detective Mark Furhman of the Simpson case has had on the public perceptions of the police:

> Bosch knew that was usually more than enough to win a conviction. He had worked cases in which convictions were won with less evidence. But that was before O.J. Simpson, before juries looked at police in Los Angeles with suspicious and judging eyes [*Angel's Flight* 230].

The largest impact of the Simpson case on what goes on in cop books, however, is in the area of police procedure. Because one of the crucial points in the trial was the issue of tainted evidence, the handling of evidence, particularly the "chain of custody" of evidence becomes a point virtually all cop writers of the 1990s stress. In *Blue Justice* Jannine Kadow makes another, less noticed but equally important, police procedural point about the O.J. case, a point about women's safety: "Ever since the Simpson case, we're under pressure to take reports of domestic disputes more seriously than we might have in the past" (221).

Allusions to Rodney King and his videotaped beating by police also appear with some frequency in the cop books of the 1990s. Unlike the Simpson references that are made in cop books set across the country, it is mostly California writers — Paul Bishop, Michael Connelly, Katherine V. Forrest, and Paula Woods — who bring in Rodney King references. Thus, in *Tequila Mockingbird* (1997) Paul Bishop notes about the LAPD that "The department still had not recovered from the bloodletting and scandals that came to a head with the Rodney King case and the Days of Rage riots in 1992" (62). Katherine V. Forrest displays an official response that has a chilling effect on all police officers and police work:

> In these days of continuing damage control post Rodney King, post O.J. Simpson, the embattled LAPD was particularly sensitive to complaints against its officers and Internal Affairs investigated even the most frivolous allegation. Some people were using the complaint process as a weapon of revenge against law enforcement. The record of an investigation in an officer's file, even if he or she was cleared, meant some trace of the mud would remain [*Apparition Alley* 18].

And Michael Connelly, in *Trunk Music*, reflects the most cynical lesson learned from the whole Rodney King affair: "Check for cameras. Rodney King Rule Number One, don't get caught on tape" (180).

Because of the discoveries of forensic science and the use of computerized databases in the last decade, writers of the 1990s had new procedures, plot devices, and characters become available to them. As seen already, the nineties saw the introduction of expert investigators representing disciplines from anthropology to zoology, and a class of police books emerged based on following the accumulation of scientific data. Mirroring the emerging popularity of the techno-thriller — created with Tom Clancy's early novels — cop writers use readers' fascination with machines as the basis for at least parts of their books. Pearson's *No Witness* (1994), for example, makes the workings of ATMs an integral part of the novel's hunt-and-chase excitement. Additionally one can find very few cop books that do not mention the FBI's databases of fingerprints and violent offenders. And in the nineties DNA testing moves from being an unusual and expensive investigatory tool to being routine, so routine that Patricia Cornwell and a couple of other writers depend on readers' knowledge of DNA to pull off their surprise endings: see, for example, Cornwell's *All That Remains* (1993).

Among the procedures available to cop writers in the 1990s is profiling, a technique begun by the FBI in the 1970s and one that became the subject of civil rights litigation in the 1990s. Using psychological profiles in cop books occurs as early as Sanders' *The First Deadly Sin* (1972). Profiling, in the 1990s, received a boost from Cornwell's use of it in her novels. While over the course of her books Cornwell's views change, in *Post-Mortem* (1990) she has Scarpetta remark that "Profilers are academicians, thinkers, analysts. Sometimes I think they are magicians" (73). Some writers include one-shot shrinks to do the profiling. Significantly, John Sandford and William Caunitz (in *Exceptional Clearance*) introduce nuns who serve as profilers. A number of writers of the 1990s, moreover, make profilers part of their continuing casts of characters: Daphne Matthews, for instance, in Pearson, Jason Frank in Leslie Glass, and Meredyth Singer in Robert Walker. Attitudes toward profiling, however, vary. Dan Mahoney in *Once In, Never Out* (1998) introduces a profiler called the Master of Murder. The guy's a whiz:

> Along the way I'm frequently able to determine the killer's race, approximate age, education, socioeconomic background, sexual preference, probable occupation among a precise range of choices, certain factors he experienced in childhood that helped contribute to making him the fiend he is, what kind of car he's likely to drive, his personal hygiene habits or lack thereof, whether he's single or involved in a stable relationship, whether he's been in the military, and many other personality traits [172–73].

Whether for purposes of plot or for the sake of argument, a number of writers use profiling as a straw man. Thus in David Lindsey's *Mercy* (1990) there's a feminist argument against the practice:

> And you've continued to add to that data base over the years by interviewing other killers. All male. So the behavioral model used to analyze all sexual homicides is based on male psychology. All your analysts at Quantico are male. So what happens when your analysts get a case they really can't fit within the framework of the behavioral model you've established? [373].

In more practical terms, a number of writers argue that profiles offer little practical help in catching criminals. Knowing that the killer had a really bad childhood isn't much help in tracking him or her down. Thus, cop Jack Mullen's hero in *Behind the Badge* (1996) says:

> The answer is on the street. Not in some computer. Not in some goddamn FBI profile that Administration has been trying to sic on me. It's on the street [97].

And a number of writers second this view when they cite the history of serial killer Son of Sam, who was arrested because an alert cop wrote down license plate numbers.

-six-

Afterthoughts

American crime novels have portrayed police officers now for well over one hundred years. In the beginning, writers dealt with cops as little as possible. In the late nineteenth century, the well-to-do hired private detectives to solve or cover up their problems, and the books they read reassured them that well-bred people acted that way. Cops were for "those people." "Those people" meant everybody else, and they weren't supposed to be reading about crime anyway: it was uncouth and it was supposed to corrupt them. In reality, reading about real cops in the 1800s would have probably angered, rather than corrupted, readers. It certainly outraged muckraking journalists. The police forces of the time were adjuncts of the spoils system in government, and jobs were handed out as favors or bought. The Lexow Commission and other turn-of-the-century official investigations documented the wholesale corruption of a number of big-city police departments, and the chief police tactic of the time was the selective employment of intimidation and force. The first time crime novels dealt with the police in any significant numbers was during the 1930s. A few of the genteel writers of the time took up the ideas of police reformers and used the metaphor of a mechanized army to describe the role of the police force, with the brilliant, organized, educated general at the top using science, and the well-trained, strong, obedient foot soldier at the bottom. Hard-boiled writers didn't buy that social theory and pictured cops as regular men doing their job.

After World War II the generals disappeared, and writers focused on

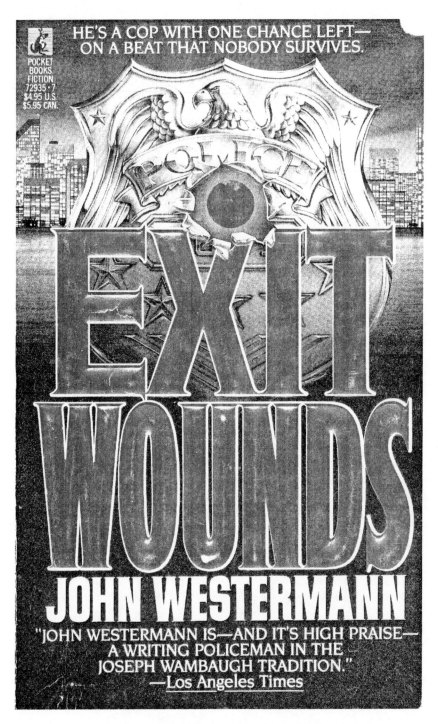

HE'S A COP WITH ONE CHANCE LEFT—
ON A BEAT THAT NOBODY SURVIVES.

POCKET
BOOKS
FICTION
72935 · 7
$4.95 U.S.
$5.95 CAN.

EXIT WOUNDS

JOHN WESTERMANN

"JOHN WESTERMANN IS—AND IT'S HIGH PRAISE—
A WRITING POLICEMAN IN THE
JOSEPH WAMBAUGH TRADITION."
—Los Angeles Times

Cover of *Exit Wounds*. Pocket, 1991.

middle-class cop heroes who worked together and, with the help of routine and records, struggled to keep the cities safe — New York and Los Angeles mostly. In the late 1960s and early 1970s this fell apart. Writers shifted their focus to the job-related problems cops encountered: alcoholism, burn-out, divorce, and depression. Shocking scenes — of autopsies, of victims with postmortem secretions, of mutilated putrefying corpses — became a convention and one of the means of demonstrating the sordid aspect of real police work. Writers also depicted how departments and individual cops dealt with mandates to bring women and minorities into the ranks, as well as the new strictures to protect civil rights placed on police behavior by the courts. Writers of the 1970s acknowledged, too, the age-old problems linked with police work — graft, corruption, and sloth. Rather than being led by brilliant, educated generals, bosses became impediments to effective police work. While the team continued to be important, writers from the 1970s onward insisted that their heroes possessed special attributes — "cop eyes," and instinct. With women cops the special attribute was sympathy for victims, a quality that male heroes of the 1990s began to demonstrate as well. Starting in the 1980s a great deal of attention shifted to cops versus serial killers, changing the structure of a lot of cop books and contributing the facilities of fiction to the contemporary interest in true crime. And finally cop writers discovered the potential of the new forensics that could be used as a complement to or a replacement for police procedures that writers had used for half a century.

While cop books had their beginnings at mid-century, they were very much a phenomenon of the 1980s and 1990s. As they developed, cop books came to include a number of popular genres, and by the end of the 1900s they could be classical detective stories, hard-boiled stories, pseudodocumentaries, romances, thrillers, science fiction tales, or all of the above. In each case, however, writers focused on the police officer as hero and included a set of conventional themes that went back to the 1950s, including brotherhood, the psychological shell, family traditions, politics, cops versus civilians, cops versus bosses, cops versus the media, paperwork, shabby stations and equipment, overwork, temptations on the job, use of force, inconvenience of the law, and past versus present.

While they attempt to portray the unique reality encountered by police officers, cop books, or almost all of them, leave things out or present apologies for them. The cop novel began to come of age during the late 1960s and early 1970s. These were not auspicious times for police forces or police officers in the United States. Television news showed cops dragging students from campus buildings. Urban guerillas shot at and bombed prowl cars, and National Guard troops patrolled burned-out sections of major American cities. Media coverage of the 1968 Democratic National Convention presented a melee of swinging nightsticks and tear gas in the "police riot." Black militants posed for photographs with weapons. "Pig" became the accepted counterculture term for cops. And, lead by New York, many cities in the country experienced budget crises that resulted in reduced spending on police and cops' responding with job actions typified by outbreaks of "blue flu." Very little of this comes into the cop fiction of the period.

More understandably, perhaps, while they often chronicle unspeakable acts, cop books rarely show their characters thinking seriously about the metaphysics or ontology of crime. Cops, the writers contend, are neither philosophers nor even sociologists. A few writers, however, do include brief and summary judgments on why people do bad things to others. Most often, however, these writers stress the failure of sociology, social work, psychology, or psychiatry to come to grips with explaining monstrous acts and behavior. In *Heaven's Prisoners* James Lee Burke's hero considers the question of what causes criminal behavior: "What produced them? Defective genes, growing up in a shithole, bad toilet training? Even after fourteen years with the New Orleans Police Department, I never had an adequate answer" (27). Steven Solomita in *Force of Nature* reflects on psychiatry's failure and society's consequent moral cowardice:

> The criminal psychopath is beyond the reach of modern medicine and responds only to drug therapy, which ... renders the person dead-in-life, as if the government had decided to take a mental life because it didn't have the guts to take a physical life [93].

Thomas Harris, who introduced the most deviant character of the 1980s, takes an ironic view of the subject:

> At least two scholarly journals explained that his unhappy childhood was the reason he killed women in his basement for their skins. The words *crazy* and *evil* do not appear in either article [*Silence of the Lambs* 357].

Most cop books that touch on the subject find that the only appropriate way to explain deviant behavior is not to explain it, but to label it as evil. Thus Kay Scarpetta in Cornwell's *Post Mortem* says "There are some people who are evil... Like dogs.... Some dogs bite people for no reason. There's something wrong with them. They're bad and will always be bad" (39). On the manner in which cops deal with the large issues of good and evil, Robert Daley perhaps gives the most accurate description:

> In fairness to cops, most of what they encountered ... was so atypical of human behavior that it could not be explained, and it was therefore not possible to understand it. Evil, by its nature, was incomprehensible. Having discovered this generations ago, cops had long since quit asking the type of question that outsiders always posed first [*Year of the Dragon* 82].

Indeed, in a large measure what defines cops in cop books does not lie in their personal views of good and evil, but their role as public servants, and the ways in which they and their society define the nature of that service.

All of this, however, does not mean that cop books do not touch upon questions of good and evil. It's just not what their characters worry much about; they worry about catching criminals, not explaining them. Writers, though, glance at facets of good and evil in other ways. First of all, the prominent and continuing argument about the utility of profiling serves in some ways as a surrogate debate on the nature of evil. As presented in cop novels of the 1980s and 1990s, profiling represents behavioral scientists' explanations of the causes of criminal acts and predictions of future patterns of behavior. Profiling rests upon the assumption that people do bad things because bad things happened to them. It is the way in which psychiatrists most often enter cop books — along with the FBI's Behavioral Science Unit. It is also most often the way in which writers show cops truncating questions about good and evil and turning their focus to the practical difficulties of finding and arresting very bad people. Thus the following outburst in William Heffernan's *Scarred*:

> So who'd they ever fucking collar, except in the fucking movies? Sure, they put together great profiles that tell you what you're looking for. Maybe. They provide the best lab work you can get.
>
> But I don't know squat about these serial killers. Almost nobody does. Most get caught from blind-ass luck and time. That's just the way it is [40].

In addition to the arguments about defining evil implicit in the presentation and use of profiles in cop books, the possibility exists for readers to form their own views on evil based on witnessing it in action. Thus the numerous split-focus serial killer books, in which the narrative switches back and forth from the actions of the killer to the reactions of the cops, in particular present material upon which readers can form judgements about the nature of evil. By giving direct, sometimes first person, accounts of the criminal's obsessions and compulsions, lust and sadism, twisted emotions and bizarre logic, these kinds of cop books provide basic materials readers can use in forming their own opinions about the nature and origins of evil. Whether readers ever do is problematic, because the main emphasis of most cop books is in the creation of suspense; because of this the principal definition of evil mainly lies in the book's demonstration that it is defeated by good.

In addition to largely overlooking certain parts of cop reality in the 1960s and 1970s, cop writers highlight resistance to change as one of the defining characteristics of the police world. Tom Lewis finds it rooted in the system:

Rodriguez looked around the squad room. He saw a bunch of generally decent, competent men; mostly Irish, some Jews, a few blacks. But they were all lifers in a nineteenth-century bureaucracy that had been outrun by the city's criminals [*Rooftops* 59].

Complaints about additional paperwork, about new management, about the law and the courts, and about tactical and strategic innovations — in fact about modern, systematic police work — stand as one of the regular features of cop books from the beginning. Kelly and LeMoult find the cause for resistance to change in the cops themselves:

What they didn't understand was that veteran street detectives hated change. They saw every new wrinkle in the system as the fuzzy meanderings of downtown punks who were more politicians than policemen. They saw each gimmick eroding their authority, putting criminals and street slime on an equal footing, giving aid and comfort to the enemy [*Dream Street* 20–21].

Attempts to change American policing, however, have been the hallmark of public policy in the last half of the twentieth century. Significantly, cop books from the beginning of the century both present the cops' resistance to change and argue on their behalf. Take the detective novels of the 1930s. From pieces in popular magazines at the turn of the century to the published findings of the Wickersham Commission in the 1930s, it is clear that significant public sentiment and then public policy opposed and then forbade beating up suspects as a police procedure. Yet a number of writers acknowledge the continuing practice of the third degree and, in fact, justify its existence by explaining brutality as a technique appropriate for lowerclass suspects who can understand nothing else. Indeed, as police novels continue they display, justify, and rationalize resistance to various changes in public policy. In the 1970s complaints about the Supreme Court's *Miranda* decision are legion in cop books. Writers describe without opprobrium a variety of ways their heroes skirt laws regarding search and seizure and privacy. In the 1970s, for the first time, writers make a point of saying that cops lie and need to lie in order to evade the altruistic decisions handed down by the courts and bring about what they know to be justice. As Wambaugh puts it in *The Choirboys*:

It was absurdly easy for any high school graduate with a year's police experience to skirt the most sophisticated and intricate edict arrived at by nine aging men who could never guard against the fact that restrictive rules of law simply produced facile liars among policemen [155].

In the 1970s, with a few notable exceptions, cop writers show no interest in or express overt hostility to the innovations that fall under the rubric of community policing. William Camp in *Night Beat* (1968), for example, goes after civilian review boards:

It's the Civilian Review Board.... Some people call it a Police Review Board, except that there aren't any policemen on it. It's made up of a bunch of old men who don't know their ass from a hole in the ground when it comes to police work, but who are empowered by our Board of Supervisors to pass judgment on any deputy that anybody has a complaint against. And you're guilty until proven innocent....

...I'll tell you the truth, the CRB's the worst goddamn thing that ever happened to this department. Look around you when you get to the station. Maybe you won't be able to see it, you being new and all, but the guys are scared — they're afraid of their own shadows. That's what happens when you set up a CRB: it makes boys out of men [77].

In the 1970s one of Roderick Thorpe's cops in *Rainbow Drive* looks at the effect that community policing has on the community:

You see, for years here in San Diego we the police have tried to integrate ourselves into the community. We have had classes in conflict resolution and all that liberal shit. In my opinion, it's the reason the San Diego Police Department has suddenly developed the highest death rate in the country [326].

And in *Twice Dead* cop Paul Bishop explains that

Despite the public push toward the concept of community policing, what goes on within the police culture is kept as secret and separate as possible from outsiders [90].

Bishop locates the reason for cops' resistance to change in the closed, minority culture of cops. The themes of professionalism and nostalgia support the resistance to change as well. From the 1970s onward cop novels increasingly show their heroes as specialists, specialists who are too often hindered by bosses, the media, and irrelevant rules and laws. Because of their unique experience they simply know better how to do their job than the politicians or the public. Not only are these heroes specialists, they are heroes endowed with the extraordinary gifts necessary to fight crime. On top of this, from the 1960s onward cop characters draw disparaging comparisons of the present with the past. Things, it seems, always used to be better. In particular, cop books often display a longing for return to a time when discipline and respect characterized the way in which both the public and the cops viewed police departments and police officers.

The single area of social policy to find eventual acceptance in cop novels comes in the form of obeying and then accepting law and policy with regard to minorities. From the 1970s onward cop books chronicle the rise of women and minorities in their fictitious police departments. African American cops gradually, almost unobtrusively, become routine members of every police squad — usually without reference to legal actions or quota hiring or racially biased promotion exams. Women as cops present a different picture. Virtually every book of the 1970s connects the presence of female heroes with governmental pressure and the reality or suspicion of tokenism. And to exempt themselves from these unwelcome external pressures, until the late 1980s women in cop books expressly distance themselves from the women's movement and feminism, emphasizing, instead, their own individual merit. Significantly, women and minority cops in fiction quickly take on universal cop attributes — they wish to belong, and the old terms "brotherhood" and "fraternity" simply morph into the new term "family."

In many ways the role of the cop depends on society's perception of and definition of the origins and nature of criminals. Almost all cop novels portray the police as society's bulwark against chaos. The definition of chaos, however, changes. In 1950 MacKinlay Kantor used the metaphors of wild animals and zookeepers to describe the role of the police: "Still tigers walked lashing their tails along the upper sectors ... there were more tigers than the law allowed, and not enough zoo-keepers to hold them mute and unravening" (139). And the animal motif continues into the 1980s with Nat Hentoff: "more and more, the streets are full of vicious dogs and rats and jackals. The human part of them, it doesn't function. It never did" (*Blues for Charlie Darwin* 177); and into the 1990s with Kenneth Abel:

> "It's [Manhattan] all animals out there, Dave. You got your hunters and your hunted. Trials of life. The whole place is just a fuckin' watering hole, we get to watch all the pigs come for a drink. They should build a wall around it, charge admission."
>
> "They did," Moser said. He nodded at Stoll's uniform. "It's blue" [*Blue Wall* 25].

Added to the animal metaphors to explain the purpose and function of the police, some writers, notably Californians Elizabeth Linington, Joseph Wambaugh, Paul Bishop, and William Camp, bring in the fall of empires as a background to their characters' experience. Here's Bishop in *Citadel Run*:

> It's history. Everything goes in cycles. The Greek empire fell, the Roman and British empires followed suit. What makes you think the American empire will be any different? Every day another wrong suddenly becomes acceptable behavior. Felonies become misdemeanors, misdemeanors become infractions, and infractions disappear into the great morass. Vice laws are always the first to go. Once a society's morals are corrupted they're hanging over the abyss by fingertips only [243].

From zookeepers controlling wild animals and centurions in a failing empire struggling to keep the barbarians at bay, the metaphors that writers have their cops apply to their job descend to those of garbage and garbage collectors:

His father had told him once that cops are the true garbage collectors of society, that cops see, consume, and store the million instances of ugliness that everyone else wants to put out of their lives…. "We see it," Wade had said; "the rest just get it from the papers" [T. Jefferson Parker, *Laguna Heat* 57].

"They think we're garbagemen with guns. We ought to belong to the sanitation union."
The police were supposed to clean up — read kill — the shits who were making life difficult. The rest of the time, the cops took it in the neck. It was always bitch, bitch, bitch about the abridgement of civil rights, excessive use of force, brutality, corruption, high salaries, and even higher crime rate [Robert Tine, *Midnight City* 20].

Me and Tree don't think of this as a career…. This is like driving a garbage truck, a garbage truck without a floor. You toss in the garbage … you drive away. And voila! [John Westermann, *High Crimes* 14].

So why do people in these books want to be cops in the first place? In mid-century novels there is never any question about why men became police officers: it was a job to be had, kept, and done well. And that motivation extends, slightly altered, into the 1990s when Westermann's heroes "succumbed to the police recruiter on campus when it looked like the only offer of gainful employment they were likely to receive" (*High Crimes* 16). On top of this comes the prevalent theme of sons and then daughters following in their fathers' footsteps. In an overwhelming number of books, police work is a family tradition. Police work, for a small number of later heroes, also means order. Thus Archer Mayor's hero says about police work that

It mimicked some of the more pleasant aspects of military life — the combination of specialness and fraternity — and it replaced the muddiness of my life with the welcomed rigidity of rank, paperwork, and assigned tasks. It also meant carrying a gun — the ultimate symbol of the simple answer in a complex world — and it gave me a chance, every once in a while, to do something "right," which by that time in my life was becoming an elusive quantity [*Open Season* 33].

In *Streets of Fire* Thomas Cook gives much the same reasoning:

The badge, his job, had served to hold him in place, guide him through the world's confusions with a reliable set of duties and obligations. He had thought it had only provided him with a living, but slowly, as the night wore on, he realized that it had also provided him with a reason to live, and that without it, he would have to improvise a certain part of his life until he could work out a new set of guidelines, hammer out a wholly different badge [259].

Finding the articulation of this kind of rationale, however, is rare. Most cop heroes join up for a different reason. A number of writers make excitement the motivation for becoming a cop. Thus in *The Onion Field* Wambaugh defines the lure as a love of change: "It was busy and exciting in the way that is unique to police experience — the unpredictable lurked. Ian Campbell believed that what most policemen shared was an abhorrence of the predictable, a distaste for the foreseeable experiences of working life" (9). Fellow cop Joseph McNamara uses the same justification:

> The feeling something was about to happen, mingled with challenge and the slightest tinge of danger. People intrigues. Adventure. Usually it was boring crap, gritty sludge, or pure gore, but, she conceded, coping with the unknown lures us to police work and keeps us hooked [*Code 211* 88].

These cop characters share the same aversion to "clerking in a store" that helps to define the cowboy hero. Often writers extend the attraction of police work from simple desire for excitement to addiction to that excitement as if it were a drug. Bob Leuci in *Odessa Beach* observes that "even to himself he'd never been able to explain this rush" (147). In *Trunk Music* Michael Connelly talks about Harry Bosch feeling "jazzed" when he can once again do police work. And Paul Bishop explicitly connects police work with drugs: "The seconds before stepping into the deep end of an investigation were as deadly an addiction as any needle"(*Tequila Mockingbird* 32). Underlying many cop writers is the idea of vocation. Thus, Daley, who is inclined to parallels between cops and priests, fields this explanation: "To be a cop is to be on the barricades.... The adrenaline rushes to your head. Your blood boils. And you're helping people all the time. It's a — it's a holy calling" (*Hands of a Stranger* 36). And Connelly uses the same concept when he differentiates Bosch from one of his partners:

> He never seemed to understand that the homicide squad wasn't a job. It was a mission. As surely as murder was an art for some who committed it, homicide investigation was an art for those on the mission. And it chose you, you didn't choose it [*Concrete Blonde* 43].

Given the way that writers portray their worlds, though, cops almost have to have a mission to stay on the job.

But they do. And people, some of them cops, write books about what police officers are like and what they encounter because of what they do. Granted, many social forces are at work here, but cop books play a particular role in the ebb and flow of contemporary fiction, popular and otherwise. Part of this role has to do with their place in detective and crime fiction. In this respect, their origins in the middle of the twentieth century mean something. After World War II detective fiction was looking for and ready for a new kind of hero. Raymond Chandler died in 1959 and Dashiell Hammett in 1961, both written out before they died. Ross MacDonald tried to remake the hard-boiled story starting in the late 1950s, but the best-selling writer of the immediate post-war period, Mickey Spillane, based his success on celebrating vulgarity, soft core pornography, and graphic violence. Hard-boiled fiction lapsed until Robert B. Parker revived it in the 1970s. On the classical detective story side of the genre, the writers of the 1930s still continued to publish and find an audience, Erle Stanley Gardner into the 1960s and Ellery Queen and Rex Stout (along with John Dickson Carr and Agatha Christie) into the 1970s. Explicitly, however, some of the new writers tired of producing what Hillary Waugh called "private-eye-cute-young-couple novels" and sought out a hero more suited to postwar reality. And they chose the policeman. They chose cop heroes at the same time that American television networks chose police dramas as one of the staples of evening programming, and there followed a reciprocal relationship between television writers and novel writers. From the 1980s onward there was also the same kind of reciprocal relationship between cop books and true crime narratives. Ann Rule in the 1980s and then Robert Ressler (with *Whoever Fights Monsters* and *I Have Lived in the Monster*) in the 1990s generated new interest in portraying and in catching serial killers. And reporters David Simon with *Homicide: A Year on the Killing Streets* (1991), Mitch Gelman with *Crime Scene* (1992), and Robert Blau with *The Cop Shop* (1993) brought new interest in the experiences of real police officers. Then, too, the fall of the Soviet Union in the 1980s sent thriller writers looking for a new hero who could replace the secret agent, and many of them found this hero on the police force.

Layered over or under the influences of trends in crime fiction publishing, reading, and writing, the conscious drive to depict the police as a distinct subculture or minority stands behind much of the cop writing from the 1960s onward. Overwhelmingly, cop books refer to police culture as a brotherhood or fraternity or family. A number of writers take this a step further and specifically use the minority label to define cops. Wambaugh uses the term, and so does John Westermann:

> I've noticed that a great many cops feel persecuted — like a minority group member might [*Exit Wounds* 148].

And so does Robert Daley:

> The principal brotherhood to which Powers belonged was the New York Police Department, but by extension this included all other police departments as well. Possibly because cops constituted the most despised minority on earth [*Year of the Dragon* 272].

The desire to establish and explain the police as a distinct group is a common element in cop books. It motivates not only the attention writers pay to explaining police procedures, but also, and more importantly, it stands behind the repeated illustrations and examinations of how emphatically cops feel removed from and persecuted by the rest of society. Frequently writers stress the fact that cops exist as a separate group because no one else can understand the danger and stress unique to the job — parallel to soldiers who cannot share the emotions and experiences of combat with those who have never been in combat. On top of this, a number of books argue that society's attitudes toward the police and what they do drive cops further and further into their own closed society. Paul Bishop expresses this notion in *Citadel Run*:

> The assholes hate us because it's our job to keep them on a leash or beat 'em back into their cages. The liberals hate us because having us around is an admission that their views on life are invalid. Average Joe Citizen thinks we're a pain in the ass because the only time he has contact with us is when he's the victim of a crime and holds us responsible for not doing our job, or when we hit him in his wallet by writing him a ticket when we should have been out stopping criminals who victimized him [217].

Part of the point of the ubiquitous emphasis on the separateness of cop culture comes in the form of demonstrations of the hardships and dysfunction with which it burdens individuals. Thus, in *Little Boy Blue*, Ed Dee, one of the most thoughtful of cop writers, has one of his characters explain that

> Movies and books focus on the wrong things when dramatizing a cop's world. They make it look like all wild chases and smoking guns. But the true dangers of this life are quieter, more insidious. The rates of divorce, alcoholism, and suicide among cops speak for themselves [76–77].

And so one of the principal purposes of cop books from the 1970s onward was to emphasize the virtues and (to a lesser extent) explain the vices of police officers as a separate, persecuted, and reviled minority whose actions are praiseworthy, important, and heroic.

Understandably, this is one of the motivations of cops and ex-cops who turn to writing about their experiences. In cop books, one of the features of police culture consists of congregating in cop bars and complaining about the job and telling war stories. Significantly, storytelling in a cop bar served as the beginning of Dan Mahoney's career as a cop writer. Along these lines, it goes without saying that writers write first for themselves, then for those closest to them, and finally for a larger audience that they hope or trust will possesses the same taste and enthusiasm for their subject matter. Cops, then, first write books for themselves and for their colleagues. A demonstration of this can be found by looking at the dedications of a number of cop books. One would expect writers to dedicate their books to parents, spouses or lovers, children, or friends, and a number of cop writers do just that. But a significant number of ex-cop writers dedicate their books to their colleagues on the job. Dallas Barnes is a particular case in point. He dedicates most of his books to cops:

> Dedicated to those men who paid the ultimate price in their efforts to protect and serve [*"See the Woman"*].

> This book is dedicated to the men who shared with me the responsibility of investigating the ultimate crime ... murder. We did it because we cared, not because we were paid [*Deadly Justice*].

> Dedicated to those few men who pursue a fading hope ... justice [*Yesterday Is Dead*].

Wambaugh mentions cops in the dedication to *The Choirboys*, Mahoney dedicates his books to heroic NYPD cops, Robin Burcell memorializes a slain officer, Jack Mullen sends his books off to cops in San Diego, Terry Marlow chooses the Dallas department, and the San Jose police get the same gift from Joseph McNamara. Writing for other cops, then, plays a role in what cop writers do. From Anthony Abbott's *About the Murder of Geraldine Foster* to Robert Pike's *Reardon*, civilian writers, too, dedicate their books to individual police officers and their departments. But the front matter in cop books suggests another, perhaps just as revealing fact about the nature of cop fiction. In the acknowledgements that a number of civilian cop writers include in the front of their books, one finds lists of various length acknowledging the help and cooperation of police departments and specific, named police officers. Along with acknowledging research assistance from the cops, a number of writers note in their autobiographical bits that their interest in and enthusiasm for cop-related matters began or was encouraged by hanging around with cops. Lillian O'Donnell and Noreen Ayres, for example, started researching cops by spending a tour in a prowl car. Having first-hand experience with cops provided Leslie Glass with more than raw material for her books; it gave her a mission:

> As she hung out with police, heard their gripes, went out on calls, and witnessed the difficulties they faced every day, her concern for their welfare became a civic duty for Glass. As a Trustee of the New York City Police Foundation, she works to improve the quality of life, training and safety for police officers as well as serving on the Crime Stoppers Award Committee [Aprilwoo.com].

The ride-along program, along with the cooperation of departments and police officers with inquisitive writers and would-be writers, were both parts of the movement toward community policing. Ironically, but understandably, this aspect of community policing did not result in new ways of policing or new attitudes of the police toward the public. It resulted in an attempt to create new attitudes on the part of the public toward the police in books that encouraged sympathy for cops as a persecuted and maligned minority, explained and rationalized their individual failures, attached their corporate blunders to bureaucrats and politicians, and upheld traditional police attitudes. So the emergence of the cop book in the 1980s and 1990s depended, in part, on the self-promotion of police departments which produced writers who protected and served cops' views of themselves.

After a century and a half of experience with professional police forces in the United States, during which time the police were alternately ignored and maligned, perhaps it was finally time for the public to listen to what the cops had to say.

Bibliography

Abbott, Anthony. *About the Murder of a Man Afraid of Women.* New York: Farrar Rinehart, 1937.

_____. *About the Murder of Geraldine Foster.* New York: Covici Friede, 1930.

_____. *About the Murder of the Circus Queen.* New York: Covici Friede, 1932.

Abel, Kenneth. *Blue Wall.* New York: Dell, 1997.

Adcock, Thomas. *Dark Maze.* New York: Pocket, 1991.

_____. *Devil's Heaven.* New York: Pocket Books, 1995.

_____. *Drown All Dogs.* New York: Pocket, 1994.

_____. *Grief Street.* New York: Pocket, 1998.

_____. *Precinct 19.* New York: Doubleday, 1984.

_____. *Sea of Green.* New York: Mysterious Press, 1989.

_____. *Thrown Away Child.* New York: Pocket, 1996.

Adler, Warren. *American Quartet.* New York: Arbor House, 1981.

_____. *Senator Love.* New York: Zebra, 1992.

Allen, Kate. *Tell Me What You Like.* Norwich, VT: New Victoria, 1993.

Allyn, Doug. *The Cheerio Killings.* New York: St. Martin's, 1989.

Ayres, Noreen. *Carcass Trade.* New York: Avon, 1995.

_____. *A World the Color of Salt.* New York: Morrow, 1992.

Bagby, George. *Bird Walking Weather.* New York: Doubleday, 1939.

_____. *Blood will Tell.* New York: Bantam, 1954.

_____. *Murder at the Piano.* New York: Covici Friede, 1935.

_____. *Ring Around a Murder.* New York: Covici Friede, 1936.

Ball, John. *Cop Cade.* New York: Doubleday, 1978.

_____. *In the Heat of the Night.* New York: Carroll & Graff, 1992.

_____. *Police Chief.* New York: Doubleday, 1977.

_____, ed. *The Mystery Story.* San Diego: University of California Extension, 1976.

Banahan, Dennis. *Threshold of Pain*. Danbury, CT: Rutledge Books, 2000.

Barnes, Dallas. *Badge of Honor*. New York: Signet, 1974.

_____. *Deadly Justice*. New York: Pocket, 1987.

_____. *"See the Woman."* New York: Signet, 1973.

_____. *Yesterday Is Dead*. New York: Signet, 1976.

Bayer, William. *Mirror Maze*. New York: Jove, 1995.

_____. *Switch*. New York: Signet, 1985.

_____. *Wallflower*. New York: Jove, 1992.

Bear, Greg. *Queen of Angels*. New York: Warner, 1990.

Bellem, Robert Leslie. *Blue Murder*. Miami Beach, FL: Macmillan, 1987.

Bishop, Paul. *Citadel Run*. New York: Doherty, 1989.

_____. *Chalk Whispers*. New York: Pocket, 2001.

_____. *Sand Against the Tide*. New York: TOR, 1990.

_____. *Tequila Mockingbird*. New York: Scribners, 1997.

_____. *Twice Dead*. New York: Avon, 1996.

Bland, Eleanor Taylor. *Gone Quiet*. New York: Signet, 1995.

_____. *Keep Still*. New York: St. Martin's, 1996.

Blau, Robert. *The Cop Shop: True Crime on the Streets of Chicago*. Reading, MA: Addison-Wesley, 1993.

Board, Sherri L. *Angels of Anguish*. Irvine. CA: Crime Zone, 1999.

Bonansinga, Jay. *The Sleep Police*. New York: Signet, 2001.

Boyle, Thomas. *Only the Dead Know Brooklyn*. Long Preston, North Yorkshire: Magna, 1986.

_____. *Post-Mortem Effects*. New York: Penguin, 1988.

Brandt, Charles. *The Right to Remain Silent*. New York: St Martin's, 1988.

Bruno, Anthony. *Bad Guys*. New York: Putnam, 1988.

Burcell, Robin. *Every Move She Makes*. New York: Harper, 1999.

Burke, James Lee. *Heaven's Prisoners*. New York: Pocket, 1989.

Burns, Rex. *The Alvarez Journal*. New York: Harper & Row, 1975.

_____. *Ground Cover*. New York: Penguin, 1987.

_____. *Strip Search*. New York: Viking, 1984.

_____. "Elements of the Police Procedural Novel," *The Writer*. May, 1977: 14–17.

Burns, William J. *The Crevice*. New York: Watt, 1915.

Buxton, Frank, and Bill Owen. *Radio's Golden Age*. New York: Easton Valley Press, 1966.

Camp, William. *Night Beat*. New York: Grosset and Dunlap, 1968.

Campbell, Robert. *Bone-Yards*. New York: Pocket, 1993.

Cain, Paul. "Parlor Trick," in *The Arbor House Treasury of Detective and Mystery Stories from the Great Pulps*. Bill Pronzini, ed. New York: Arbor House, 1983.

Caunitz, William J. *Black Sand*. New York: Bantam, 1990.

_____. *Cleopatra Gold*. New York: Berkley, 1994.

_____. *Exceptional Clearance*. New York: Bantam, 1992.

_____. *One Police Plaza*. New York: Crown, 1984.

_____. *Pigtown*. New York: Pinnacle, 1996.

_____. *Suspects*. New York: Bantam, 1987.

_____, and Christopher Newman. *Chains of Command*. New York: Onyx, 1999.

Chandler, Raymond. *The Big Sleep.* New York: Ballantine, 1971.

_____. *Farewell, My Lovely.* New York: Pocket: 1943.

_____. *Killer in the Rain.* New York: Ballantine, 1972.

_____. *Pickup on Noon Street.* New York: Ballantine, 1972.

_____. *The Simple Art of Murder.* New York: Ballantine, 1972.

_____. *Trouble Is My Business.* New York: Ballantine, 1972.

Charyn, Jerome. *Blue Eyes.* New York: Mysterious Press, 1993.

Clausen, Lowen. *First Avenue.* New York: Onyx, 2000.

Cole, George, and Christopher Smith. *Criminal Justice in America.* New York: Wadsworth, 2002.

Comstock, Anthony. *Traps for the Young.* Robert Bremmer, ed. Cambridge, MA: Harvard University Press, 1967.

Connelly, Michael. *Angels Flight.* Boston: Little Brown, 1999.

_____. *The Black Echo.* New York: St. Martin's, 1993.

_____. *The Black Ice.* Boston: Little Brown, 1993.

_____. *The Concrete Blonde.* Boston: Little Brown, 1994.

_____. *A Darkness More than Night.* Boston: Little Brown, 2001.

_____. *The Last Coyote.* New York: St. Martin's, 1996.

_____. *Trunk Music.* New York: St. Martin's, 1998.

Connor, Beverly. *A Rumor of Bones.* Nashville, TN: Cumberland House, 1996.

Constantine, K.C. *The Rockland Railroad Murders.* New York: Saturday Review Press, 1972.

_____. *Upon Some Midnights Clear.* New York: Penguin, 1987.

Cook, Thomas H. *Streets of Fire.* New York: Warner, 1991.

Cooke, John Peyton. *Torsos.* New York: Mysterious Press, 1995.

Coram, Robert. *Dead South.* New York: Signet, 1999.

_____. *Running Dead.* New York: Signet, 1993.

Cornwell, Patricia. *All That Remains.* New York: Avon, 1993.

_____. *The Body Farm.* New York: Scribners, 1994.

_____. *From Potter's Field.* New York: Berkley, 1996.

_____. *The Last Precinct.* New York: Putnam's, 2000.

_____. *Post-Mortem.* New York: Avon, 1991.

Coughlin, William J. *The Stalking Man.* New York: St. Martin's, 1998.

Craig, Jonathan. *The Case of the Beautiful Body.* New York: Belmont, 1973.

_____. *Dead Darling.* New York: Belmont, 1973.

Crais, Robert. *Demolition Angel.* New York: Doubleday, 2000.

_____. *Hostage.* New York: Doubleday, 2001.

Crawford, Nelson A. *The Ethics of Journalism.* New York: Knopf, 1924.

Cunningham, E. V. *The Case of the One-Penny Orange.* New York: Holt, Rinehart, 1977.

_____. *The Case of the Poisoned Eclairs.* New York: Holt, Rinehart and Winston, 1979.

_____. *Phyllis.* London: Pan, 1962.

Daley, Robert. *Cop Killer.* New York: Ballantine, 1978.

_____. *A Faint Cold Fear.* New York: Warner, 1992.

_____. *Hands of a Stranger.* New York: Signet, 1986.

_____. *Man with a Gun.* New York: Pocket, 1988.

_____. *The Prince of the City.* New York: Berkley, 1981.

_____. *Tainted Evidence.* New York: Warner, 1994.

_____. *Wall of Brass.* New York: Warner, 1995.

_____. *Year of the Dragon.* New York: Signet, 1982.

Daly, Carroll John. "Three Gun Terry," in *The Black Mask Boys.* William F. Nolan, ed. New York: Morrow, 1985.

D'Amato, Barbara. *Authorized Personnel Only.* New York: Doherty, 2000.

_____. *Good Cop, Bad Cop.* New York: Doherty, 1999.

_____. *Help Me Please.* New York: Forge, 2001.

_____. *KILLER.app.* New York: Doherty, 1996.

Davis, Kaye. *Devil's Leg Crossing.* Tallahassee, FL: Naiad, 1997.

Davis, Richard Harding. "The Frame-Up," in *The American Rivals of Sherlock Holmes.* Hugh Greene, ed. New York: Penguin, 1976.

Deaver, Jeffrey. *The Blue Nowhere.* New York: Pocket, 2002.

_____. *The Bone Collector.* New York: Viking, 1997.

_____. *The Coffin Dancer.* New York: Pocket, 1999.

_____. *The Empty Chair.* New York: Simon & Schuster, 2000.

_____. *The Stone Monkey.* New York: Simon & Schuster, 2002.

Dee, Ed. *Bronx Angel.* New York: Warner, 1996.

_____. *14 Peck Slip.* New York: Warner, 1995.

_____. *Little Boy Blue.* New York: Warner, 1998.

_____. *Nightbird.* New York: Warner, 2000.

Delamer, John. *The Tarnished Shield.* Santa Barbara: Fithian, 1996.

DeNoux, O'Neil. *The Big Kiss.* New York: Zebra, 1990.

Disney, Doris Miles. *Appointment at Nine.* New York: Doubleday, 1947.

_____. *Compound for Death.* New York: Doubleday, 1943.

Donaldson, Don (D. J.) *Cajun Nights.* New York: St. Martin's, 1988.

Doss, James D. *Shaman Laughs.* New York: St. Martin's, 1995.

_____. *Shaman Sings.* New York: Avon, 1995.

Dove, George N. *The Police Procedural.* Bowling Green, OH: The Popular Press, 1982.

Dunlap, Susan. *As a Favor.* New York: Dell, 1991.

_____. *Diamond in the Buff.* New York: St. Martin's, 1990.

_____. *Karma.* New York: Dell, 1991.

_____. *Pious Deception.* New York: Villard, 1989.

Early, Jack. *Donato and Daughter.* New York: Onyx, 1989.

Ellroy, James. *The Big Nowhere.* New York: Mysterious Press, 1988.

_____. *Fallen Angels.* New York: Grove, 1993.

_____. *LA Confidential.* New York: Mysterious Press, 1990.

_____. *Murder and Mayhem.* New York: NAL 1992.

_____. *White Jazz.* New York: Knopf, 1992.

Estleman, Loren. *Stress.* New York: Mysterious Press, 1997.

Forrest, Katherine V. *Amateur City.* Tallahasseee, FL: Naiad, 1994.

_____. *Apparition Alley.* New York: Berkley, 2000.

Forrest, Richard. *Lark.* New York, Signet, 1986.

Fliegal, Richard. *The Organ Grinder's Monkey.* New York: Pocket, 1989.

_____. *Semi-Private Doom.* New York: Pocket, 1991.

Flynt, Josiah, and Francis Walton. *Powers That Prey.* New York: McClure, 1900.

Frank, Marshall. *Beyond the Call.* San Jose: toExcell, 2000.

Friedman, Lawrence M. *Crime and Punishment in America.* New York: Basic Books, 1993.

Gaitano, Nick. *Mr. X.* New York: Simon & Schuster, 1995.

Gardner, Erle Stanley. *The Case of the Baited Hook.* New York: Morrow, 1940.

_____. *The Case of the Howling Dog.* New York: Morrow, 1934.

_____. *The Case of the Lucky Legs.* New York: Morrow, 1934.

_____. *The Case of the Sulky Girl.* New York: Morrow, 1933.

_____. *Murder Up My Sleeve.* New York: Morrow, 1937.

Gelman, Mitch. *Crime Scene: On the Streets with a Rookie Police Reporter.* New York: Times Books, 1992.

Gilpatrick, Noreen. *Fatal Design.* New York: Mysterious Press, 1995.

Glass, Leslie. *Burning Time.* New York: Doubleday, 1993.

_____. *Hanging Time.* New York: Bantam, 1996.

Goddard, Ken. *The Alchemist.* New York: Bantam, 1985.

_____. *Balefire.* New York: Bantam, 1983.

_____. *Digger.* New York: Bantam, 1991.

_____. *Double Blind.* New York: Forge, 1997.

_____. *First Evidence.* New York: Bantam, 2000.

_____. *Outer Perimeter.* New York: Bantam, 2001.

_____. *Prey.* New York: Tor, 1992.

_____. *Wildfire.* New York: Forge, 1994.

Goldberg, Leonard S. *Deadly Care.* New York: Onyx, 1997.

Grady, James. *Just a Shot Away.* New York: Bantam, 1987.

Grafton, Sue. *A Is for Alibi.* New York: Holt, Rinehart, 1982.

Grant. Michael. *Line of Duty.* New York: Doubleday, 1991.

_____. *Officer Down.* New York: Bantam, 1994.

_____. *Retribution.* New York: Harper, 1996.

Green, Anna Katharine. *The Leavenworth Case.* New York: Dover, 1981.

Griffin, W. E. B. *Men in Blue: Badge of Honor.* New York: Jove, 1988.

_____. *Special Operations.* New York: Jove, 1991.

Gross, Ken. *Full Blown Rage.* New York: Forge, 1995.

Gunn, Elizabeth. *Five Card Stud.* Toronto: Worldwide, 2001

_____. *Triple Play.* New York: Walker, 1997.

Hailey, Arthur. *Detective.* New York: Berkley, 1998.

Hamilton, Nan. *Killer's Rights.* New York: Walker, 1984.

Hamilton, R. J. *Who Framed Lorenzo Garcia?* Los Angeles: AlyCat Books, 1995.

Hammett, Dashiell. *Dashiell Hammett Crime Stories and Other Writings.* New York: Library of America, 2001.

_____. *The Novels of Dashiel Hammett.* New York: Knopf, 1965.

Harper, Brian. *Shudder.* New York: Signet, 1994.

Harper, Richard. *Death Raid.* New York: Dell, 1986.

Harrington, Joseph. *Blind Spot.* Philadelphia: Lippincott, 1966.

_____. *The Last Doorbell.* Philadelphia: Lippincott, 1969.

_____. *The Last Known Address.* Philadelphia: Lippincott, 1965.

Harris, Thomas. *The Silence of the Lambs.* New York: St. Martin's, 1989.

Hartsfield, Larry. *The American Response to Professional Crime, 1870–1917*. Westport, CT: Greenwood, 1985.

Hawthorne, Julian. *An American Pennman*. New York: Cassell, 1887.

_____. *Another's Crime*. New York: Cassell, 1888.

_____. *The Great Bank Robbery*. New York: Casell, 1887.

_____. *Section 558; or the Fatal Letter*. New York: Cassell, 1888.

_____. *A Tragic Mystery*. New York: Cassell, 1888.

Heffernan, William. *Blood Rose*. New York: Dutton, 1991.

_____. *Ritual*. New York: Signet, 1990.

_____. *Scarred*. New York: Signet, 1993.

_____. *Tarnished Blue*. New York: Onyx, 1995.

_____. *Unholy Order*. New York: Morrow, 2002.

_____. *Winter's Gold*. New York: Onyx, 1997.

Hendricksen, Louise. *With Deadly Intent*. New York: Zebra, 1993.

Henry, Sue. *Murder on the Iditarod Trail*. New York: Atlantic Monthly, 1991.

_____. *Termination Dust*. New York: Morrow, 1995.

Hentoff, Nat. *Blues for Charlie Darwin*. New York: Morrow, 1982.

_____. *The Man from Internal Affairs*. New York: Mysterious Press, 1986.

Herbert, Rosemary. "Publishers Agree: True Crime Does Pay." *Publishers Weekly*. June 1, 1990: 33.

Hightower, Lynn S. *Eyeshot*. New York: Harper Collins, 1996.

_____. *Flashpoint*. New York: Harper Collins, 1995.

Hillerman, Tony. *The Blessing Way*. New York: Quality Paperback Book Club, 1989.

_____. *Dance Hall of the Dead*. New York: Quality Paperback Book Club, 1989.

_____. *Skinwalkers*. New York: Harper & Row, 1987.

Himes, Chester. *All Shot Up*. New York: Thunder's Mouth, 1996.

_____. *Cotton Comes to Harlem*. New York: Vintage, 1988.

_____. *A Rage in Harlem*. New York: Vintage, 1991.

Hite, Molly. *Breach of Immunity*. New York: St. Martin's, 1992.

Hoag, Tami. *Night Sins*. New York: Bantam, 1996.

Holton, Hugh. *Chicago Blues*. New York: Forge, 1996.

_____. *Criminal Element*. New York: Forge, 2002.

_____. *The Devil's Shadow*. New York: Forge, 2001.

_____. *The Left Hand of God*. New York: Forge, 1999.

_____. *Presumed Dead*. New York: Forge, 1994.

_____. *Red Lightning*. New York: Forge, 1998.

_____. *The Time of the Assassins*. New York: Forge, 2000.

_____. *Violent Crimes*. New York: Forge, 1997.

_____. *Windy City*. New York: Forge, 1996.

Holtzer, Susan. *Something to Kill For*. New York: St. Martin's, 1994.

Hunter, Fred. *Presence of Mind*. Toronto: Worldwide, 1998.

Hunter, Stephen. *Dirty White Boys*. New York: Island, 1995.

Huston, Fran. *The Rich Get It All*. New York: Doubleday, 1973.

Izzi, Eugene. *Bad Guys*. New York: St. Martin's, 1989.

_____. *A Matter of Honor*. New York: Avon, 1998.

Jackson, Jon A. *The Blind Pig*. New York: Dell, 1978.

_____. *The Diehard*. New York: Dell, 1995.

_____. *Grootka*. Woodstock, VT.: Foul Play Press, 1990.

Jahn, Mike. *Killer on the Heights*. New York: Fawcett, 1977.

Jahn, Michael. *Night Rituals*. New York: Jove, 1984.

Jance, J. A. *Breach of Duty*. New York: Avon, 1999.

_____. *Dismissed with Prejudice*. New York: Avon, 1989.

_____. *Injustice for All*. New York: Avon, 1986.

_____. *Taking the Fifth*. New York: Avon, 1987.

_____. *Trial by Fury*. New York: Avon, 1986.

_____. *Until Proven Guilty*. New York: Avon, 1985.

_____. *Without Due Process*. New York: Avon, 1993.

Johansen, Iris. *The Face of Deception*. New York: Bantam, 1998.

Kaddow, Jeannine. *Blue Justice*. New York: Signet, 1998.

Kantor, MacKinley. *Signal Thirty-Two*. New York: Random House, 1950.

Katzenbach, John. *The Traveler*. New York: Ballantine, 1988.

Kellerman, Faye. *Ritual Bath*. New York: Arbor House, 1986.

_____. *Sacred and Profane*. New York: Arbor House, 1987.

Kellerman, Jonathan. *When the Bough Breaks*. New York: Bantam, 1994.

Kelly, Bill, and Dolph LeMoult. *Death Spiral*. New York: Signet, 1989.

_____, and _____. *Dream Street*. New York: Charter, 1989.

_____, and _____. *Killing Moon*. New York: Onyx, 1990.

_____, and _____. *Street Dance*. New York: Charter Books, 1987.

Kennealy, Jerry. *The Conductor*. New York: Signet, 1996.

_____. *The Hunted*. New York, Onyx, 1999.

Kent, Bill. *Under the Boardwalk*. New York: Pinnacle, 1990.

King, Laurie. *A Grave Talent*. New York: Bantam, 1995.

_____. *To Play the Fool*. New York: St. Martin's, 1995.

_____. *With Child*. New York: St. Martin's, 1996.

King, Rufus. *The Lesser Antilles Case*. New York: Doubleday, 1934.

_____. *Murder by the Clock*. New York: Doubleday, 1929.

_____. *Somewhere in the House*. New York: Doubleday. 1930.

Klein, Kathleen Gregory. *The Woman Detective*. Urbana, IL: University of Illinois Press, 1988.

Koenig, Joseph. *Floater*. New York: Mysterious Press, 1986.

_____. *Smugglers Notch*. New York: Ballantine, 1989.

Lescroart, John T. *A Certain Justice*. New York: Island, 1996.

Leuci, Bob. *Captain Butterfly*. New York: NAL, 1989.

_____. *Double Edge*. New York: Signet, 1993.

_____. *Doyle's Disciples*. New York: Signet, 1985.

_____. *Odessa Beach*. New York: Signet, 1986.

Leuci, Robert. *The Snitch*. New York: St. Martin's, 1998.

Lewis, Tom. *Rooftops*. New York: Signet, 1982.

Lindsey, David L. *Heat from Another Sun*. New York: Pocket, 1985.

_____. *Mercy*. New York: Bantam, 1991.

Linington, Elizabeth (Dell Shannon). *Mark of Murder*, in *Shannon's Choice*. New York: Morrow, n.d.

_____ (Dell Shannon). *Root of All Evil*, in *Shannon's Choice*. New York: Morrow, n.d.

_____ (Lesley Egan). *Scenes of Crime*. New York: Doubleday, 1976.

_____ (Dell Shannon). *Streets of Death.* New York: Bantam, 1980.

Logan, Tom. *Detroit PD: Run Jack Run.* New York: Lynx, 1988.

Lovett, Sarah. (Sarah Poland). *Dangerous Attachments.* New York: Villard, 1995.

Maas, Peter. *Serpico.* New York: Viking, 1973.

MacDonald, J. Fred. *Don't Touch that Dial: Radio Programming in American Life, 1920–1940.* Chicago: Nelson Hall, 1979.

Mahoney, Dan. *Black and White.* New York: St. Martin's, 1999.

_____. *Detective First Grade.* New York: St. Martin's, 1993.

_____. *Hyde.* New York: St. Martin's, 1997.

_____. *Once In, Never Out.* New York: St. Martin's, 1999.

Marlow, Terry. *Target Blue.* New York: Jove, 1993.

Maron, Margaret. *One Coffee With.* New York: Mysterious Press, 1995.

Martin, Lee. *Death Warmed Over.* Toronto: Worldwide, 1991.

_____. *Hacker.* Toronto: Worldwide, 1994.

_____. *Murder at the Blue Owl.* Toronto: Worldwide, 1990.

Mathews, Francine. *Death in the Off-Season.* New York: Morrow, 1994.

Mayor, Archer. *Fruits of the Poisonous Tree.* New York: Mysterious Press, 1995.

_____. *Open Season.* New York: Mysterious Press, 1994.

_____. *The Skeleton's Knee.* New York: Mysterious Press, 1994.

McBain, Ed. *Ax.* New York: Signet, 1977.

_____. *Calypso.* New York: Bantam, 1980.

_____. *Cop Hater.* New York: Signet, 1973.

_____. *Fuzz* in *Three from the 87th.* New York: Nelson Doubleday, n.d.

_____. *Hail, Hail, the Gang's All Here,* in *Three from the 87th.* New York: Nelson Doubleday, n.d.

_____. *The Heckler.* New York: Signet, 1976.

_____. *Jigsaw* in *Three from the 87th.* New York: Nelson Doubleday, n.d.

_____. *Killer's Choice.* New York: Avon, 1986.

_____. *Killer's Payoff.* New York: Signet, 1974.

_____. *Windows.* New York: Avon, 1991.

McCrumb, Sharyn. *Sick of Shadows.* New York: Ballantine, 1989.

McGraw, Lee. *Hatchett.* New York: Ballantine, 1976.

McNamara, Joseph D. *The Blue Mirage.* New York: Fawcett, 1991.

_____. *Code 211 Blue.* New York: Fawcett, 1996.

_____. *Fatal Command.* New York: Fawcett, 1987

_____. *The First Directive.* New York: Fawcett, 1988.

Mickelbury, Penny. *Keeping Secrets.* Tallahassee, FL: Naiad Press, 1994.

Mills, James. *Report to the Commissioner.* New York: Pocket, 1973.

Minichino, Camile. *The Hydrogen Murder.* New York: Bouregy, 1997.

Moore, Robin. *The French Connection.* New York: Bantam, 1970.

Mullen, Jack. *Behind the Shield.* New York: Avon, 1996.

_____. *In the Line of Duty.* New York: Avon, 1995.

Myers, Gustavus. *The History of Tammany Hall.* New York: Dover, 1971.

Naha, Ed. *On the Edge.* New York: Pocket, 1989.

_____. *Razzle-Dazzle.* New York: Pocket, 1990.

Nebel, Frederick. "Rough Justice" in *The Black Mask Boys.* William F. Nolan, ed. New York: Morrow, 1985.

Newman, Christopher. *Dead End Game.* New York: Berkley, 1994.

_____. *Hit and Run.* New York: Dell, 1997.

_____. *Killer.* New York: Dell, 1997.

_____. *Knock-Off.* New York: Fawcett, 1989.

_____. *Midtown North.* New York: Fawcett, 1991.

_____. *Midtown South.* New York: Fawcett, 1986.

_____. *Precinct Command.* New York: Fawcett, 1993.

_____. *The Sixth Precinct.* New York: Fawcett, 1987.

Nogouchi, Thomas, and Arthur Lyons. *Physical Evidence.* New York: Jove, 1990.

_____, and _____. *Unnatural Causes.* New York: Charter, 1988.

O'Connell, Carol. *Mallory's Oracle.* New York: Jove, 1995.

O'Donnell, Lillian. *The Face of Crime.* New York: Abelard Schuman, 1968.

_____. *Leisure Dying.* New York: Putnam, 1976.

_____. *No Business Being a Cop.* New York: Putnam, 1978.

_____. *The Phone Calls.* New York: Putnam, 1972.

_____. *Pushover.* New York: Fawcett, 1992.

_____. "Routines and Rules for the Police Procedural." *The Writer.* February, 1978: 17–19.

Oster, Jerry. *Club Dead.* New York: Bantam, 1990.

_____. *Fixin' to Die.* New York: Bantam, 1992.

_____. *Internal Affairs.* New York: Bantam, 1990.

_____. *Nowhere Man.* New York: Charter, 1987.

_____. *Sweet Justice.* New York: Charter, 1986.

Oursler, Charles F. *see* Anthony Abbott.

Ottolengui, Rodrigues. *A Conflict of Evidence.* New York: Putnam, 1993.

Parker, T. Jefferson. *Laguna Heat.* New York: St. Martin's, 1985.

Patterson, James. *Along Came a Spider.* New York: Warner, 1993.

_____. *Cat and Mouse.* New York: Warner, 1998.

_____. *Pop Goes the Weasel.* Boston: Little Brown, 1999.

Paul, Barbara. *Good King Sauerkraut.* New York: Scribners, 1989.

_____. *He Huffed and He Puffed.* New York: Scribners, 1989.

_____. *The Renewable Virgin.* New York: Scribners, 1984.

_____. *You Have the Right to Remain Silent.* New York: Scribner's, 1992.

Paulsen, Gary. *Night Rituals.* New York: Donald Fine, 1989.

Pearson, Ridley. *The Angel Maker.* New York: Dell, 1994.

_____. *Beyond Recognition.* New York: Hyperion, 1997.

_____. *Chain of Evidence.* New York: Hyperion, 1995.

_____. *The First Victim.* New York: Hyperion, 1999.

_____. *Middle of Nowhere.* New York: Hyperion, 2000.

_____. *No Witness.* New York: Dell, 1996.

_____. *The Pied Piper.* New York: Hyperion, 1999.

_____. *Probable Cause.* New York: St. Martin's, 1991.

_____. *Undercurrents.* New York: St. Martin's, 1989.

Pedneau, Dave. *A.P.B.* New York: Ballantine, 1987.

_____. *B&E Breaking and Entering.* New York: Ballantine, 1991.

_____. *D.O.A.* New York: Ballantine, 1988.

Penzler, Otto. *The Great Detectives.* Boston: Little Brown, 1978.

Philbin, Tom. *Cop Killer*. New York: Fawcett, 1986.

_____. *Precinct: Siberia*. New York, Fawcett, 1985.

_____. *The Rookie*. New York: Warner, 1991.

_____. *Under Cover*. New York: Fawcett, 1986.

Pike, Robert L. *Mute Witness*. New York: Doubleday, 1963.

_____. *Reardon*. New York: Doubleday, 1970.

Pinkerton, A. Frank. *Dyke Darrell, the Railroad Detective, or the Crime of the Midnight Express*. Chicago: Laird, 1886.

Pinkerton, Allan. *Claude Melnotte as a Detective*. Chicago: W. B. Kean, 1875.

_____. *The Expressman and the Detective*. New York: Arno, 1976.

Pomidor, Bill. *Murder by Prescription*. New York: Signet, 1995.

Price, Richard. *Clockers*. New York: Avon, 1993.

Pyle, A. M. *Trouble Making Toys*. New York: Signet, 1986.

Queen, Ellery. *The American Gun Mystery*. New York: Ballantine, 1976.

_____. *The French Powder Mystery*. New York: NAL, 1969

_____. *The Roman Hat Mystery*. New York: Signet, 1967.

Reichs, Kathy. *Deja Dead*. New York: Pocket, 1997.

Reid, Robert Sims. *Benediction*. New York: Bantam, 1992.

_____. *Big Sky Blues*. New York: Pocket, 1988.

_____. *Cupid*. New York: Bantam, 1991.

_____. *Red Corvette*. New York: Carroll & Graff, 1992.

_____. *Wild Animals*. New York: Carroll and Graff, 1996.

Reilly, John. ed. *Twentieth Century Crime and Mystery Writers*. New York: St. Martin's, 1985.

Reilly, Helen. *McKee of Centre Street*. New York: Popular Library, 1933.

Register, Seeley *see* Victor, Metta V.)

Ressler, Robert. *I Have Lived in the Monster*. New York: St. Martin's, 1997.

_____. *Whoever Fights Monsters*. New York: St. Martin's, 1992.

Rule, Ann. *The Stranger Beside Me*. New York: Signet, 1989.

Salter, Anna. *Shiny Water*. New York: Pocket, 1998.

Sanders, Lawrence. *The First Deadly Sin*. New York: Berkley, 1980.

_____. *The Second Deadly Sin*. New York: Berkley, 1978.

_____. *The Third Deadly Sin*. New York: Berkley, 1982.

Sandford, John. *Eyes of Prey*. New York: Putnam, 1991.

_____. *Night Prey*. New York: Berkley, 1995.

_____. *Rules of Prey*. New York: Berkley, 1990.

_____. *Shadow Prey*. New York: Berkley, 1996.

_____. *Silent Prey*. New York: Putnam, 1992.

_____. *Winter Prey*. New York: Putnam, 1993.

Shafer, Charles. *On Cabrini Green*. Birmingham, Eng: CT Publishing, 2000.

Simon, David. *Homicide: A Year on the Killing Streets*. Boston: Houghton-Mifflin, 1991.

Smith, Enes. *Dear Departed*. New York: Diamond, 1994.

_____. *Fatal Flowers*. New York: Diamond, 1992.

Smith, Julie. *The Axeman's Jazz*. New York: Ivy, 1991.

_____. *New Orleans Morning*. New York: St. Martin's, 1990.

Smith, Martin Cruz. *Gorky Park*. New York: Random House, 1981.

Solomita, Stephen. *Force of Nature*. New York: Avon, 1990.
Steffens, Lincoln. *The Shame of the Cities*. New York: Hill and Wang, 1963.
Stout, Rex. *The League of Frightened Men*. New York: Farrar and Rinehart, 1935.
_____. *Over My Dead Body*. New York: Farrar and Rinehart, 1940.
_____. *The Red Box*. New York: Farrar and Rinehart, 1937.
_____. *The Rubber Band*. New York: Farrar and Rinehart, 1936.
Stroud, Carsten. *Close Pursuit*. New York: Bantam, 1988.
Swain, Phyllis. *Find Phyllis!* New York: Leisure Books, 1979.
Thayer, James. *Terminal Event*. New York: Simon & Schuster, 1999.
Thorp, Roderick. *Devlin*. New York: Fawcett, 1992.
_____. *Nothing Lasts Forever*. New York: Norton, 1979.
_____. *Rainbow Drive*. New York: Ivy, 1986.
Thurlo, Aimee and David. *Bad Medicine*. New York: Forge, 1997.
Tine, Robert. *Midnight City*. New York: Signet, 1987.
Turow, Scott. *Presumed Innocent*. New York, Warner, 1988.
Uhnak, Dorothy. *The Bait*. New York: Simon & Schuster, 1968.
_____. *False Witness*. New York: Fawcett, 1981.
_____. *The Ledger*. New York: Pocket Books, 1972.
_____. *Policewoman*. New York: Pocket, 1967.
_____. *The Witness*. New York: Simon & Schuster, 1969.
Van Dine, S. S. *The Canary Murder Case*. New York: Fawcett, n.d.
_____. *The Greene Murder Case*. New York: Scribners, 1928.
Vicarel, JoAnn. *A Reader's Guide to The Police Procedural*. New York: G.K. Hall, 1995.
Victor, Metta V. *The Dead Letter*, with a new introduction by Michele Slung. Boston: Gregg Press, 1979.
Walker, Robert W. *Cold Edge*. New York: Jove, 2001.
_____. *Cutting Edge*. New York: Jove, 1997.
_____. *Double Edge*. New York: Jove, 1998.
_____. *Killer Instinct*. New York: Jove, 1992.
Wambaugh, Joseph. *The Blooding*. New York: Bantam, 1989.
_____. *The Blue Knight*. New York: Dell, 1973.
_____. *The Choirboys*. New York: Delacorte, 1975.
_____. *Finnegan's Week*. New York: Bantam, 1994.
_____. *Floaters*. New York: Bantam, 1997.
_____. *Lines and Shadows*. New York: Bantam, 1984.
_____. *The New Centurions*. New York: Dell, 1972.
_____. *The Onion Field*. New York: Dell, 1979.
Warner, Ralph, and Toni Ihara. *Murder on the Air*. Berkeley, CA: Nolo Press, 1984.
Waugh, Hillary. *Last Seen Wearing*. New York: Doubleday, 1952.
_____. *Sleep Long My Love*. London: Pan, 1962.
_____. *"30" Manhattan East*. New York, Belmont, 1971.
_____. *The Young Prey*. New York: Doubleday, 1969.
Webb, Jack. *The Bad Blonde*. New York: Signet, 1956.
_____. *The Broken Doll*. New York: Signet, 1955.
_____. *The Deadly Sex*. New York: Signet, 1959.
Wessner, Theodore. *The True Detective*. New York: Avon, 1988.
West, Chassie. *Sunrise*. New York: Harper, 1994.

Westermann, John. *Exit Wounds*. New York: Pocket, 1991.

_____. *High Crimes*. New York: Pocket, 1989.

_____. *The Honor Farm*. New York: Pocket, 1998.

Weyr, Tom. "Marketing America's Psychos." *Publishers Weekly*. 12 April 1993: 38.

Wilcox, Collin. *The Disappearance*. New York: Random House, 1970.

_____. *The Lonely Hunter*. New York: Random House, 1969.

_____. *Long Way Down*. New York: Jove, 1979.

_____. *Mankiller*. New York: Random House, 1980.

_____. "Writing and Selling the Police Procedural Story." *The Writer*. January, 1976: 20–22.

Woods, Paula. *Inner City Blues*. New York: One World, 1999.

Wozencraft, Kim. *Rush*. New York: Ivy, 1991.

Zubro, Mark. *Another Dead Teenager*. New York: St. Martin's, 1995.

_____. *Drop Dead*. New York: St. Martin's, 2000.

_____. *Political Poison*. New York: St. Martin's, 1993.

_____. *Sex and Murder.com*. New York: St. Martin's, 2001.

_____. *Sorry Now?* New York: St. Martin's, 1992.

_____. *The Truth Can Get You Killed*. New York: St. Martin's, 1997.

Index

291

paperbacks 55, 80
Parker, Robert B. 187, 191, 275
Parker, T. Jefferson 180, 273
Parker, William 34, 90, 220
Patterson, James 195, 221–223, 256, 257
Paul, Barbara 127–129, 186, 260
Paulson, Gary 180, 188
Pearson, Ridley 159–161, 180, 181, 182,
    188, 189, 190, 193, 216, 220, 257,
    258–259, 263, 264
Pedneau, Dave 171–173, 178, 179, 188
Penzler, Otto 55, 56
Philbin, Tom 136–139, 184, 190
Pike, Robert L. see Fish, Robert L.
Pinkerton, Allan 11–13
Poe, Edgar Allan 9, 14
Poland, Sarah see Lovett, Sarah
police: African Americans 57–58,
    71–73, 81, 97–98, 187, 216–225,
    260–261; Asian-American 209–213;
    cinema 2, 71, 77, 94, 106, 112,
    186–187, 253–254; early history 7–9,
    81; Hispanic-American 90, 93, 102,
    113, 143, 187, 211; Native American
    85–87, 213–216; radio dramas 33–35;
    television shows 2, 71, 77, 106, 112,
    170, 172, 176, 253; women 83, 88,
    93–94, 100, 115, 121–130, 143,
    151–152, 184, 186, 199–209, 260, 264,
    267
police novel conventions 38–40;
Pomidor, Bill 194
Price, Richard 251–252
private eyes, history 10–11
Professional Criminals of America 10
profiling 113, 157, 160, 161, 163, 195,
    196, 256, 263 – 264, 269

Queen, Ellery 14–17, 55, 275

Reeve, Arthur B. 14
Register, Seeley 12
Reichs, Kathy 194
Reid, Robert Sims 154–156, 179, 261
Reilly, Helen 24–25
Ressler, Robert 275
Roberts, Nora 1, 190, 255
Rule, Ann 99, 178, 275

Salter, Anna 195

Sanders, Lawrence 83, 98–101, 112, 116,
    159, 177, 188, 264
Sandford, John 162–164, 179, 187, 188,
    256, 264
Schwartzkopf, Norman 34
Scoppettone, Sandra see Early, Jack
Sehler, Raoul Stephen see Burns, Rex
sensation novels 12
serial killers 99, 112–113, 121, 156–164,
    178, 255–257
Serpico, Frank 90, 94–96, 112, 188, 247
Shafer, Charles 179, 248, 261
Shannon, Dell see Linington, Elizabeth
Silva, Linda 227, 261
Simenon, Georges 41, 76, 102
Simon, David 275
Simpson, O.J. 226, 250, 262
Smith, Enes 179, 235, 256, 261, 262
Smith, Julie 199
Smith, Martin Cruz 118, 177, 194
Solomita, Stephen 183, 268
Spillane, Mickey 41, 78, 275
Steffens, Lincoln 7, 13, 147
Stein, Aaron Marc see Bagby, George
Stout, Rex 19–20, 275
Sullivan, Mary 34
Swan, Phyllis 123
Sylvester, Richard 8

Tarbell, Ida 14
Thayer, James 195
Thompson, Tommy 178
Thorpe, Roderick 184, 271
Thurlo, Aimee and David 214–215, 260
Tine, Robert 188, 255, 273
Treat, Lawrence 35–40, 46, 55, 78
true crime books 46, 178–179
turn of the century fiction 13–14
Turow, Scott 181

Uhnak, Dorothy 73–75, 80, 81, 83, 112,
    179, 255

Valentine, Lewis 34
VanDine, S.S. 14–16
Victor, Metta V. see Register, Seeley
Vollmer, August , 23

Walker, Robert 87, 215–216, 256, 262,
    264